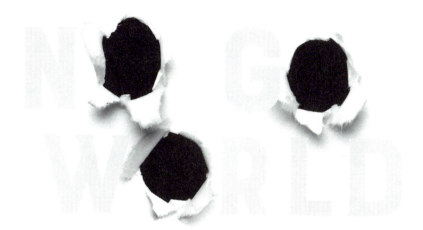

NO GO WORLD

HOW FEAR IS REDRAWING OUR MAPS AND INFECTING OUR POLITICS

RUBEN ANDERSSON

UNIVERSITY OF CALIFORNIA PRESS

University of California Press, one of the most distinguished university presses in the United States, enriches lives around the world by advancing scholarship in the humanities, social sciences, and natural sciences. Its activities are supported by the UC Press Foundation and by philanthropic contributions from individuals and institutions. For more information, visit www.ucpress.edu.

University of California Press
Oakland, California

Cataloging-in-Publication Data is on file at the Library of Congress.

ISBN 9780520294608 (cloth : alk paper)
ISBN 9780520967700 (ebook)

Manufactured in the United States of America

27 26 25 24 23 22 21 20 19
10 9 8 7 6 5 4 3 2 1

To Cristina

CONTENTS

FIGURES

MAPS

Map 1. The Psalter map, ca. 1265.

PREFACE

In London's King's Cross, deep in the vaults of the British Library, there exists another world. It is minute and perfectly round, gold-flecked and held in God's almighty grace, and it is yours for an hour if you order it by the counter. One spring day I sit in the hushed halls, looking for this world in a Kindle-sized book, turning page after crisp page stained with the nicotine of time. Manuscripts rustle behind me and a keyboard clicks in the distance, and suddenly, there it is—a thirteenth-century map, vast in its smallness; Asia on top, Jerusalem in the middle, Europe and Africa down below. The African corner hosts a menagerie of monstrous figures, headless and dog-faced, kept in a neat line of pens touching the very margins of the known world. In their opposite corner, in Asia, a wall circles the abject lands of Gog and Magog, cannibalistic races locked up until Judgment Day. Christ stands guard above it all, golden-aura'd and hands aloft, while dragons lurk below. This medieval world is navigable like a London Underground map—a perfect circle of Christian knowledge in which monsters squat at the margins, held in God's delicate grip like the page between my fingers.

A few stops down the Tube from my British Library hall lies the Cottons Centre, a corporate monolith with high-spec views across the Thames to

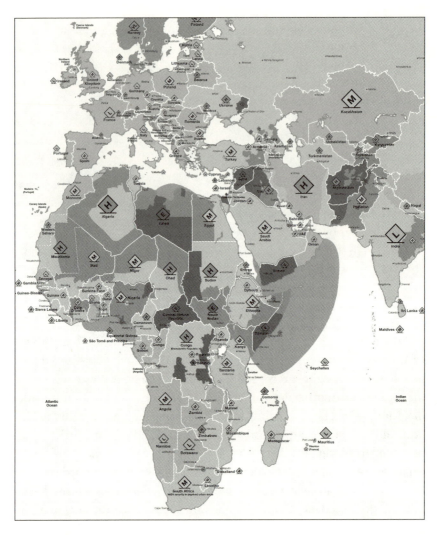

Map 2. Detail from the World Risk Map 2018, by Control Risks, the specialist risk consultancy. Color codes indicate level of security risk; labels indicate level of political risk. For full color version, see www.controlrisks.com/riskmap-2018 © Control Risks.

the City of London. There, suited risk analysts are busy building a digital map for the twenty-first century, navigable not for Christ's pious followers but for big business. Their world is not shielded by divine hands or flecked with gold; instead it is painted in shades of risk, from light green to wine-red. Unlike its medieval counterpart, the Risk Map's margins are safe and pale while its central zones are slathered with the deep reds of danger, from the Sahara to Tigris to the Hindu Kush. Zoom in and you will see the red blots bleeding outwards, encroaching on the Mediterranean and trickling toward Texas, like pools of blood gathering at a shuttered door. On the Risk Map there are no visible monsters, no Christ to contain them, and no walls or cages to keep them at bay: instead they roam wild and unseen, spreading their beastly trace as they move.

This is the story of our world of encroaching danger, of why it bleeds, and of what we may do to stop it being stained by scarlet shades of fear.

INTRODUCTION

INTO THE DANGER ZONE

Beyond the bar glittered the dark Atlantic. Beer bottles clinked in the African night breeze as expats danced to the booming tunes of a European DJ under a canopy. In the crowd of artists and hangers-on, French culture buffs and curators in expensive shawls mingled with lanky Senegalese painters and smart-shirted Western aid workers, the stalwarts on Dakar's international scene. It was May 2014 and the art biennale had come to the Senegalese capital, bringing a well-needed party to the very edge of West Africa. For out there, beyond the chatter and champagne, lurked a different reality: the vast hinterland of the Sahel and the Sahara, where in the past few years the onetime music festivals had packed up and their swirling desert blues had ceased to reverberate.

Paco Torres stood, wild-haired with beer in hand, in our awkward aid worker clique at the bar.[1] He had the same round reporter's spectacles as the last time we had met in Spain four years earlier, but his beard was shaggier, his pants baggier and stained, his voice raucous and his eyes glinting. As a stringer for two or three Spanish newspapers, he had just come back from a trip through rural Guinea, full of stories of the Ebola-quarantined villages he had sneaked into, trekking past gun-wielding police to the devastation within. "I shag a lot nowadays!" Paco told me with a laugh, his face lighting up like a child's. It was the "adventurer aura" that did it, he explained while recounting an earlier venture up the Niger River to conflict-racked northern Mali, skirting roadblocks and recalcitrant soldiers. Now Paco was mulling a trip into northern Nigeria, an area where Boko Haram had just kidnapped more than two hundred schoolgirls—and where, as one Dakar-based aid chief told me, "If your complexion is anything less than a Nigerian's, you won't really be going." All trips were at Paco's own expense and risk. "Now is the first time ever that I can afford insurance," he said, though on second thought he was not sure whether it covered his risk-filled escapades. His pay from Spanish dailies remained miserly, but at least he was now their voice from West Africa, covering disease and disaster, terror and conflict—the four horsemen of the Apocalypse—plus Senegalese wrestling shows and much else thrown in for good measure.

"I'm not a war correspondent," Paco insisted as he downed his beer. "I'm really a journalist of peace." As the DJ played away into the Dakar breeze at the biennale party, he lingered at the far edge of the canopy, his mind yet again scheming for the next trip. Unlike most of the Dakar "expats" around us—and much like one of the early colonial explorers in whose footsteps he was treading—he longed to roam the hinterland and the far-flung no go zones of our new, fearful era.

.   .   .   .   .

Look at the world today. Switch on Google Maps on your smartphone and search for Timbuktu, that onetime epitome of remoteness, and you will get car directions—three days and fourteen hours from my Oxford home via the N-6, on a route that "has tolls," "includes a ferry," and "crosses through multiple countries," as the app helpfully informs me. You can browse geo-positioned images from northern Nigeria and the Libyan desert, or get customers' restaurant recommendations for Quetta in the Pakistan-Afghanistan borderlands, a town I once crossed on my way to India (apparently, for a tandoori treat, don't go here: "Usmania at Pishin stop SUCKS. Their service is bad, prices unreasonable and food tastes horrible"). In fact, don't go to any of these places—not if you are a white Westerner, at any rate. These sites are all off limits; they are reblanked parts of the map at a time of disorderly globalization.

Hic sunt dracones. Those medieval maps may not have spelled out "Here be dragons," as we tend to think, yet they were often adorned with fantastical creatures and exotic beasts, serving as flourishes or as indicators of the limits of our knowledge.[2] Now the beasts are back.[3] Switch on the news and it soon becomes clear that deadly threats are lurking in far-fetched corners of our map, areas where the inhabitants of the rich Western world no longer dare venture. Syria and Iraq's embattled border zones, Somalia and Pakistan's tribal regions, Afghanistan's rugged terrain, and the deserted northern reaches of the sub-Saharan Sahel all harbor a litany of contemporary fears. Terror and drug running, disease and disaster, conflict and displacement: these dangers lurk on the margins of our maps, vague yet distant, seemingly at a remove until they blip by on the newscasts, temporarily bringing news of distant atrocities and random tragedies.

The signs are big and bleak. No Go. Stay away. And we do. Indeed, the first reaction for those of us sitting in well-furnished living rooms in richer nations may well be to switch the television off whenever we hear of misery in distant lands. Why should we even care? After all, Afghanistan and northern Mali are nowhere most well-off Westerners would drop by on holiday—not now, at any rate; it is easy to forget that Timbuktu was recently served by direct budget flights from Paris, while Afghanistan was once firmly on the hippie trail. In any case, our economies do not hinge on what happens in these places. They remain comfortably out of reach: remote and rarely any of our business.

This is not least the fate of the region around which this book pivots—the Sahel. For those who have even heard of it in the West, this arid southern shore of the Sahara conjures up clichéd images of chronic crisis and lawless abandon. War-torn deserts, jihadist killings, men wrapped in shawls brandishing AK-47s; trucks heaving with contraband, cocaine, and clandestine migrants; locust plagues, cracked dry soils, and starving children; Gao, Agadez, Timbuktu. Remote and shot through with dangers, the region seems the antithesis of the capital hubs of the rich world—a zone of insecurity stuck on the global margins.

This is a fallacy, as *No Go World* will show. In fact, remote zones of insecurity are becoming central to our new world disorder, in which they serve as a convenient stage for geopolitical battles; for struggles over illicit cross-border flows; and for media-fueled propaganda wars, as seen from the Afghan-Pakistan borderlands to the Sahara Desert. Yet rather than acknowledging this, Western states, and international organizations funded and supported by them, have come to organize military, border, and aid interventions in insecure zones in a dangerously myopic fashion. Through diverse forms of remote control and containment—from drones to militia middlemen, from border reinforcement to repurposed and out-sourced aid—risk-obsessed powers are in effect collaborating in the re-mapping of the world into zones of safety and danger, with the media lending a helping hand. This is a failure of imagination, opportunity, and responsibility whose consequences are already coming back to haunt the West, as chaos visits the fortified borders of Europe and terror attacks proliferate across the patchwork map of globalization.

The dangers are in some ways real enough. Terror attacks worldwide have been rising swiftly since 9/11, and in 2015, suicide bombs tore into more countries than ever before.[4] While the trend remains disputed, it is clear that armed groups now see those who were once deemed neutral to conflict—reporters, aid workers, peacekeepers, civilian visitors—as fair game. But these dangers are not necessarily new: peacekeeping, for one, was deadlier in earlier decades by some accounts, and terror attacks (however we define them) are a rather persistent historical threat too.[5] However, one aspect of this insecurity does stand out today: its distribution. Most of the victims of today's insurgent attacks are civilians, aid workers, and soldiers from poor, non-Western nations. Only a small percentage of worldwide fatalities from terrorism since 2000 has taken place in the West, while in the peak year of 2014 five countries—Afghanistan, Iraq, Nigeria, Pakistan, and Syria—together suffered almost four-fifths of such deaths.[6] This is before we count those killed by explosive weapons, which in 2017 reached a high of more than fourteen thousand civilians according to one tally, with air strikes—not homemade bombs—the reason behind the sharp increase, especially in Syria.[7] As for professionals intervening in crisis zones, more than nine out of ten aid workers killed are now national staff, and it is African peacekeepers—rather than well-equipped external forces—who increasingly man the bloodied front lines on the continent.[8] In Somalia alone, some estimates list about three thousand dead African Union peacekeepers in a non-UN operation funded by

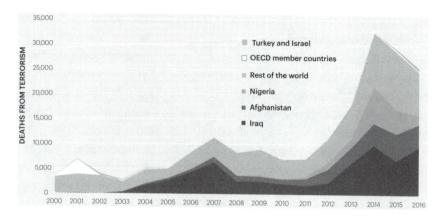

Figure 1. Deaths from terrorism, 2000–2015, are dominated by a few "hot spot" countries. (Figures for Pakistan and Syria are included under "rest of the world.") © Institute for Economics and Peace.

the United States, the European Union, and the United Nations to the tune of billions of dollars.[9]

As the money trails behind force deployments, air strikes, and aid operations indicate, it's not that powerful states have stopped caring about what happens in far-off places—rather, their focus is shifting. In military campaigns, instead of the mass peacekeeping deployments and military surges of yesteryear's Bosnia or Afghanistan, Western governments are supporting proxies and dropping bombs, as in Syria or Libya; deploying drones, as in Pakistan or Yemen; training local soldiers to do the hard graft, as in Somalia or the Sahel; or deploying select special forces as spearheads to quell transnational dangers. Security is also being outsourced to a booming private military industry with multi-billion-dollar revenues—a trend matched by the surging market for remote-controlled weapons and surveillance systems.[10] As for aid interventions, donors have in recent years leant heavily on NGOs and the UN to enter, stay, and "deliver" in distant danger zones, rather than exit them, yet these operations too are increasingly managed at one remove, through local partners and staff. In the media, a similar trend is afoot as news organizations are cutting their losses, leaving freelancers such as Paco to engage in the derring-do. Meanwhile the rich world's borders are increasingly resembling the moats of a fortress, in an ill-conceived stab at keeping the people from the wrong side of our global divides far away, in the buffer zones of the "global borderlands."[11]

This is the dark tale of *No Go World*—one of global distancing and endangerment. For a start, the relationship by remote control forged between powerful interveners and crisis-hit areas of the planet is a tragic case of failed connectivity. As new technologies are supposed to be bridging geographical divides, as global risks expand, and as the climate is heating up, peoples and governments need to be *more* connected, not less. Yet instead of deepening cooperation among the world's rich and poor, we are being torn apart. We are seeing the emergence of a global geography of fear: a parsing up of the world map in which the dirty work in distant crisis zones is left to middlemen and advanced technology while borders are reinforced and contact points severed. And this distancing should concern us deeply, whether we live in Texas or Timbuktu. Those of us in the rich, comfortable world may turn our back on global crises, yet these crises will not turn their back on us—in fact, these crises were never separable from us to begin with. For as the coming chapters will show, danger is not geographic but systemic, and it is fundamentally entangled with our fears and the response these fears engender. To move beyond the political geography of fear, we may need a different kind of road map: not the facile map of Google connectivity or the bordered-up map of security analysts and strategists, but a cartography of hope and possibility, crisscrossed by renewed connections.

.   .   .   .   .

Hello mister, let's have some tea. It was autumn 1997 and I had just arrived, as a fresh-faced nineteen-year-old, in the Pakistani frontier town of Quetta. My bones still rattled from the forty-hour journey in a garish wreck of a bus, bedecked like a circus elephant in bright reds and yellows, up the slow-grinding road from the Iranian border. Amid the shuttered shops, their fronts closed to the night, I and a Pakistani fellow traveler weaseled our way into a ramshackle hostel and caught a few hours of fitful sleep on thin mattresses until the calls to prayer rang out in the early morning hours.

Next day I walked the streets and had tea everywhere I went, a nomadic Swede on the onetime hippie trail turned celebrity of the marketplace. I scrawled my tattered Turkish notebook full with the numbers and home addresses of motorcycle mechanics and university lecturers, football players and layabouts. I let my tea glass be filled again and again, let the same questions be asked by new smiling faces, let myself be the stranger everyone wanted me to be. This was what I had desired, I thought, recalling why I had set out on my overland journey from suburban Sweden; this exhausting, exhilarating encounter; this notebook full of numbers I would never call; this, and perhaps a softer mattress.

Some two decades later, Quetta is best known for the suicide bombs tearing through that market where I once shared sweet glasses of tea with teachers and mechanics. It is a mass host to refugees and a flashpoint in between Iran, war-torn Afghanistan, and Pakistani tribal regions abuzz with the CIA's Taliban-hunting drones. I had Quetta's smiles all to myself in 1997, and so would any foreign visitors passing through today, if indeed anyone would contemplate such a prospect. The fragile bridge travelers such as myself had built with Quetta's tea drinkers before 9/11 has been torn down. In its stead another relationship has been constructed: one centered on risk and terror, on distance and fear and containment.

No Go World, then, is shot through with a sadness of sorts. As a traveler in those Quetta years, I was drawn to distant frontiers; and as I went on to train as an anthropologist in London in the next decade, I dedicated my professional life to a discipline that has historically been wedded to such far-off places. Yet now more and more of them are out of bounds, as many of my fellow anthropologists are finding out—and as I was to realize myself when I decided to study the crises besetting a different region, the sub-Saharan Sahel, in 2013.[12] With my research proposal on Mali's conflict completed, funding received, and desk eventually set up at the London School of Economics, the dilemma soon became acute. Would I actually be able to *visit* the places of most concern to me? On earlier trips to Mali, I had exchanged guitar tunes with some of Bamako's struggling musicians and researched migration trails across the Sahara; now, as conflict had visited its northern regions, going there meant exposure to multifarious dangers, setting alarm bells ringing in university offices (and in my family). Along with an array of rebel groups, the north presumably still harbored al Qaeda affiliates who threatened kidnapping and targeted attacks, much as in Quetta and its hinterland. Was it sensible to go, or

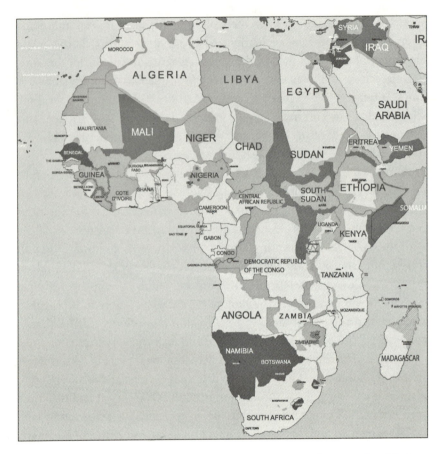

Map 3. Africa detail from the World Threat Map 2014, by Result Group, the global risk consultancy: www.result-group.com. Shading indicates risk level. © Result Group.

cowardly to stay away? Didn't locals face much larger risks? There I sat, in my London office, scheming and eyeing the news, all too aware that my risk-averse university was loath to let any researcher set foot in lands of danger. Instead of feeling like that intrepid traveler hitting the road with oil-stained trousers and dust in my hair, I prudently kept tallying the risks while "the field" receded ever further from reach.

My predicament was far from unique. Academics, journalists, humanitarians, diplomats, and even soldiers all face the problem of no go zones, although we rarely want to dwell publicly on our decisions about entering

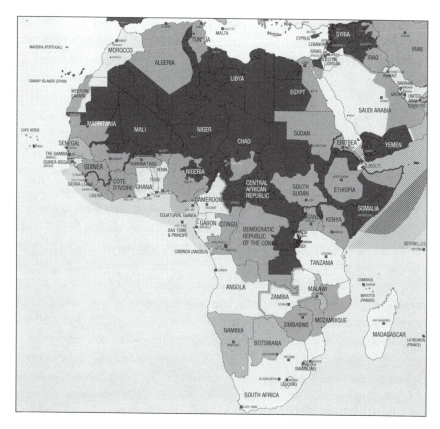

Map 4. Africa detail from the World Threat Map 2018. © Result Group.

them. Yet the dilemma can no longer be ignored as whole chunks of the contemporary world, from Mali in West Africa to Pakistan and beyond, are rife with dangers—at least if we are to trust our employers, newspapers, insurance companies, and travel advice–wielding foreign ministries. "If you follow U.S. travel warnings, *Out of Africa* is more a strategy than a summer read," quipped one radio report when looking at the State Department's no go advice for vast stretches of the continent, expanded from twelve to eighteen countries between 1996 and 2013.[13] The UK Foreign Office, meanwhile, had thirteen countries or parts of countries on its global no go list in 1997; fifteen years later, that figure was forty, again with a raft of new entries for Africa.

Western victims of terror attacks in Africa are in fact few and far between: only 15 of the 1,005 Americans killed in terrorist acts worldwide between 2004 and 2013 took place on the continent, for instance.[14] Relative to other threats—traffic accidents, crime, and illness both at home and abroad—the risk looks even smaller. As one terror expert notes, "Approximately 13,472 murders occurred in the U.S. during 2014. Yet the 24 private citizens' deaths worldwide by terrorism in 2014 got a great deal more media attention."[15] Yet quite regardless of the numbers, foreign ministries are now painting larger and larger chunks of the world in a deep, menacing red—areas that we enter, if at all, at our own risk and peril.

This risk dilemma was viscerally present for me in early 2014 as I paced up and down my kitchen floor, the irony alive in my mind—here I was, wanting to do ethnographic fieldwork on how interveners grappled with risk and danger in northern Mali, yet now I might not even be able to travel there because of these very dangers! Then I hit upon the idea that became *No Go World*. The obstacle to going there—*this* is what I must study. Instead of donning the proverbial khakis and pith helmet of my anthropological ancestors, returning heroically with my ethnographic heist, I shifted my gaze toward the distancing at work in the relationship between interveners and the intervened upon. After all, my university's risk aversion and my own dilemma over northern Mali mirrored a much broader distancing from danger among interveners of all kinds. I now set out to trace, in that relationship, the paradoxical workings of power by remote control, as former imperial masters skulked to the sidelines. In short, I had to draw a map of global risk and danger the way risk-averse interveners saw it, blanks and all.

So instead of rattling away in my bus, as I did in those Quetta days of 1997 or as Paco did when entering the theater of Mali's war, I opted for circling Mali remotely, mimicking my ethnographic tribe, the interveners, and the world they have mapped and made. I hung out among peacekeepers, aid workers, and displaced Malians working at one remove in the country's capital, Bamako, as local anger stirred among citizens fed up with the bunkered international presence. In headquarters managing faraway conflicts, from New York to Brussels to Addis Ababa, I met assorted soldiers and aid chiefs who shared a deep frustration over the receding field of intervention. I traveled along the West's reinforced borderlines from Arizona to the Mediterranean, where walls, military patrols, and surveillance systems act as magical defenses against the threats supposedly emanating from the world's danger zones. I sought out the security outfits that have made distant risk their line of business, and I met the brave and sometimes foolhardy men and women who do enter the new danger zones: aid workers, reporters, peacekeepers, migrants, and adventure seekers of Paco's kind. I also delved into colonial and pre-colonial history, whose lessons resonate with our fractious geopolitical present. Indeed, today's risk takers, much like the intrepid early colonial explorers—the Rudyard Kiplings and René Cailliés whom we will also meet in coming chapters—break through our self-imposed borders to explore the world outside, rendered exhilarating in part because of its very dangers. Out of these glimpses, we may be able to discern openings for another, more positive relationship between the global rich and poor. We may also come to see who the winners and losers are when risk and fear start framing this relationship. For the new no go zones on our world maps are not just an avoidable evil; they are also of great benefit to many powerful people and organizations, as well as to their elusive enemies.

It may seem natural that international interveners are withdrawing from danger, like pedestrians crossing the road to avoid a street fight. Yet from the perspective of powerful states, we must note how *difficult* it is to withdraw in an otherwise wired world—and how massive efforts have been expended on various levels to achieve this purpose. Distance is physical: interveners withdraw not just ordinary citizens but also key humanitarian, political, and even military staff; they build bunkers in the "field"; they develop new technologies of remote control via drones, satellites, and surveillance; and they barricade their borders to keep the threat from reaching their societies. Distance is social: they outsource risky and dirty tasks to local staff, mercenaries, or freelancers, deepening the divide between "expat" and local, intervener and intervened upon, former colonizer and colonized. Distance is conceptual: interveners promote and buy into new buzzwords and theories that, while on the surface seemingly scientific and global in their reach, in fact end up acting as metaphorical containers for those "others" affected by insecurity. Finally, distance is psychological: as "we" in the rich, safe world withdraw from danger zones, we are paradoxically tied more closely than ever to these new no go areas, which exercise a peculiar power over us and our imaginations.[16] Insurgents, knowing this, may then tap into our deepest fears as they reconnect the danger zone to our wired world with ease. A pocketknife and a webcam are now all that is needed to shake the White House or the Elysée out of their complacency.

Danger and distance, in short, are deeply intertwined—and terrorists and drug runners, state officials and soldiers, journalists and assorted visitors have all conspired to wind them ever more tightly together. Those medieval monsters have yet again come to inhabit the edges of our Google-era maps; worse, the growing fear of venturing into their domains is now steering powerful actors' quest for intervention and involvement, creating a negative spiral from which it becomes increasingly difficult to extricate ourselves.

.   .   .   .   .

Media pundits, TED talkers, and scholars have in recent years been busy at work drawing connections across the globe, and with good reason. In studies of Silk Roads old and new, the nervous system of cyberspace, the connective tissue of high finance, and the web spun by global migrations, it seems as if the fabric of the world is ever more tightly woven, its strands entwined despite the onslaughts of nationalisms new and old.[17] Yet what if we start our inquiry from the opposite end: with disconnection and rupture? What if, moreover, global distance is becoming entrenched through a most peculiar connective medium—danger itself?

The emergence of global danger zones is symptomatic of much broader political shifts. The gradual retreat of Western dominance, the rise of China, the resurgence of nationalism—at this time when the tectonic plates of geopolitics and of the world economy are creaking, danger zones are opening up as geographic rifts in the presumably smooth terrain of globalization. It follows that if we study these rifts closely enough, and if we can grasp the political and symbolic logics through which they emerge, we may find better ways to mend our fractious politics.

There are two somewhat simplified ways to understand the emergence of danger zones today. One is by examining the economies of *risk;* the other by examining the politics of *fear.* The two, as we shall see, complement each other in troubling ways.

Some sociologists would say that our world is now wired in terms of risk. Some three decades ago, their doyen, Ulrich Beck, coined the term *risk society* to describe our late modern predicament, in which technological prowess generates unforeseen risky consequences.[18] In the rich world, we tremble at the existential risks looming ahead of us: financial meltdown, climate change, terrorism, and conflict in our backyards. Against this backdrop, the contemporary political obsession with risks emanating from remote borderlands and deserts is but one expression of the anxieties haunting late capitalist society.

Yet while risk is usually seen through a negative prism, as something "bad" to be avoided, it is in fact double-edged, a source of both costs and gains. To take the most obvious example, risk (in its technical rather than existential guise) is the currency of the insurance industry; it is the magic where profits happen. It allows for setting premiums, calculating future liabilities, optimizing returns. Risk has also become a currency of sorts in international finance. In the derivatives trades at the heart of the 2008 global financial crisis, risky subprime mortgages were packaged with other financial products, traded, and speculated in until the whole system came tumbling down. Ever since the 1970s oil crisis and the revolutions in finance that followed, the global economy has thrived on risk, high-stakes gambles, and quick-fire rent seeking. In this sense, we face a fundamental contradiction in the global economy: between risk-averse citizens and politicians on the one hand, and a financial world of rampant risk taking—and even the exploitation of radical uncertainty—on the other.[19]

Risk is not just unevenly appreciated by different social groups and classes; it is also distributed helter-skelter among them, and across our world map. In her work on the global geography of capitalism, the sociologist Saskia Sassen has shown the financial world to be condensed into key locations: "global cities" such as London, Tokyo, and New York functioning as one-stop shops for speculative capital. Standing in sharp contrast to these global cities are similarly "extreme zones" for "new or sharply expanded modes of profit extraction": manufacturing hubs such as China's Shenzhen, or the land-grab and resource-cursed lands of sub-Saharan Africa.[20] Across these specialized sites in the world economy we see a transfer of risk from costly Western laborers to poorer counterparts; from blue-chip companies to subcontractors; and from mining groups to the villages or habitats they destroy. By and large, economic upswings made Western citizens comfortable with this arrangement until the credit crunch took hold. Since 2007–8, financial risk has been "socialized" and transferred back into Western societies too, with the state and its taxpayers bearing the cost of the bailouts and banking recoveries.

Where on the global map of risk do remote "danger zones" such as the Sahel-Sahara band or the Afghan-Pakistan borderlands fit? We may suggest, rather crudely, that they stand as an inverse example to the rampant risk-based markets of global cities. These zones are similarly specialized, but not in producing goods or forging out credit default swaps. Rather, they serve as sites for the manufacturing of one key "product" for contemporary world markets: insecurity or danger.[21] Seen from this viewpoint, remote zones of insecurity are no longer on the margins. Rather, they are exemplary of a "new normal" of the kind now regularly invoked by European officials amid recurrent terror threats and migration crises—a jarring state of chronic endangerment.[22]

Danger, as a bridging concept, links the economies of risk with our second concern, the politics of fear. Fear is the most base and basic of emotions: it is visceral and instinctive, and as such a source of immense political power. Trump's wild claims about Mexican rapists and terrorist-carrying caravans; the Hungarian government's proclamations of a Muslim invasion of Europe; the Italian Far Right's fear-driven portrayals of refugees and their boats—such figments and bogeymen work on a deep psychological level, as do their solutions of walls and military patrols, quite regardless of any evidence, risk based or otherwise. *Psychopolitics*, philosopher Byung-Chul Han's term for new technologies of power that burrow their way deep into the human psyche, is mobilizing fear and associated emotions (anger, shame, hatred, anxiety, indifference, and more) on a massive scale, via Big Data and the Internet as much as via traditional media. And the object to which such a politics of fear frequently attaches is the racial and geographical Other.[23]

Consider the idea of the no go zone itself. It seems straightforward; if in doubt, just don't go. If you do go, you have only yourself to blame, as the UK and US governments have repeatedly shown when they refuse to budge in response to kidnappers threatening to murder their hostages. Yet the mapping of insecurity and danger—that is, *naming* and *placing* the threat—is itself a political act. To take the most blatant example, since the 2015 Paris terror attacks, Fox News and Far Right websites have joyfully slathered urban Europe with the red paint of menace, from the French capital's banlieues to Britain's Birmingham. As I search for "no go zones" in early 2018, hits include a book by a Breitbart staffer entitled *No Go Zones: How Sharia Law Is Coming to a Neighborhood Near You* (foreword by a certain Nigel Farage of Brexit fame) and a poster issued by the Hungarian government of Viktor Orbán showing the alleged *no-go zóna* in and around London, Berlin, and Stockholm. "Alleged" because they are no such thing.[24] Little did I know that I had lived most of my life in Orbán's no go zones—in between London and Oxford, Stockholm and my hometown outside the Swedish capital, as sleepy an industrial backwater as any in well-to-do northern Europe!

These politicized no go zones of the most extreme kind should, at a minimum, unsettle any simplistic idea that the red-tinted risk maps used to depict large parts of Africa and Asia today are veracious and apolitical. They should also disabuse us of any notion that dangers near and far are somehow separate in the official imagination. Already in colonial times, Victorian cartographers and social scientists saw poor London as a "dark continent within easy walking distance of the General Post Office" while slathering the streets of "semi-criminal" classes in menacing hues of black on their city maps.[25] The color code may have changed from black to red, yet the pattern echoes down the ages as dangerous Otherness at the heart of the West is again being telescoped out to depictions of faraway danger.

As in Victorian times, assorted intellectuals are complicit in this remapping of danger. Consider Samuel Huntington and his "clash of civilizations" meme from the 1990s, or his fear peddling over the "flood" of Latino immigrants in the following decade, inspiring a generation of lower-level punditry of doom. For a more liberal perspective, consider Oxford economist Paul Collier's best-selling sketch of a biblical "Exodus" of the global poor, or his rallying calls for military intervention in the home countries of the "bottom billion." Or, for a tougher approach from a fellow Briton, take the historian Niall Ferguson, who argued amid Iraq's descent into darkness in 2004 that the absence of liberal US imperialism would herald "an anarchic new Dark Age." In their treatises and texts, such authors present muscular Western power as the bulwark against a "coming anarchy," to cite one of their journalistic fellow travelers, Robert Kaplan. As the size of their media, political, and popular audiences show, these are good times indeed for peddling rough-hewn fear with an intellectual patina and for purveying simplistic solutions to impending doom.[26]

Ours may be an "age of anger," in the words of author Pankaj Mishra, but it is also an age of fear.[27] Fear, anger, and raw power travel together in our frenzied politics, bringing among other things a phobia-ridden fear peddler into the White House in 2016. Beyond high politics, our "new normal" of high alert is also characterized by proliferating security solutions—from biosecurity to human security, from cybersecurity to climate security, all feeding on the twinned resources of risk and fear, as scholars of "securitization" have shown for some time.[28] The starting point of *No Go World*, contentious as it may be, is that this normalized state of security is itself abnormal, to the point of being pathological. Tracing this pathology across time and space will be the task of the chapters that follow.

.   .   .   .   .

Only a few pages back, I suggested that we must forge genuine connections as the solution to a world of distancing and danger. Alas, if I could only bring back those thumbed address books, those smiles over tooth-rottingly sweet tea from my backpacker days! But let us set aside such nostalgic longing for a long-lost world and roll up our sleeves: we must garner some optimism of the will and find concrete ways of confronting shared problems, one step at a time. While we may not be able to tear down the hastily erected walls between the poor, insecure territories out there and the safety of the rich world, interveners of all kinds may at least start turning the key in the door. Politically, international actors can shift some of the massive efforts behind their anxious absence toward a *positive presence,* based around opportunities rather than insecurity. In practical terms, interveners and citizens can learn from those who do not shy away—including the UN officials, freelance reporters, humanitarians, and national aid workers in Mali, Somalia, or Afghanistan whom we will meet in coming chapters. Above all, we must learn to listen to the intellectuals, activists, and ordinary inhabitants of countries in crisis: largely unrecognized by international media, they labor away at home-grown solutions and at critiques of crisis interventions thought up from afar. Through such voices, and with the help of some simple statistics, powerful politicians may also be able to reassess the shifts happening in poorer parts of the world. In sub-Saharan Africa, living standards and educational levels are *rising*, as they have been elsewhere for some time.[29] Indeed, the global migrations so feared by Western leaders and electorates are fueled by a thirst for wider horizons, not simply caused by grinding poverty or perpetual conflict. Even the seemingly intractable danger zones fretted about in the West may become vanguards of cosmopolitan interaction for a global cause—reconnecting us around shared potential rather than around fears of mounting insecurity.

We can say all this, and yet it would be criminally naive to peddle simple fixes. Rather, the problem is *systemic,* and deeply historical: how those who until very recently saw themselves at the pinnacle of progress and power are now retreating, yet pushing out; warding off danger, yet stoking it; mapping distance, yet clamoring for connections. For this reason, I offer *No Go World* not as a prescription for a simple cure but rather as a diagnosis of the interventionist ills besetting especially Western (and West-backed) power.[30]

Geopathology is a term we may borrow for this purpose. I apply this label, used for anything from quack feng shui to the study of geographical determinants of diseases, to the ways in which geography itself (or, rather, powerful interveners' understanding of it) is becoming afflicted with ascribed danger. We need to find ways of getting to grips with this pathological state besetting our interventionist "patient," and to this end we will deploy for our geopathological diagnosis one of the interveners' favorite playthings—maps.

Maps are wily things. They seem to portray certainty, they establish a gaze; yet their hold on reality is elusive and imperfect. They are a work in progress that hides their ad hoc nature. They are powerful: they define forms of intervention, and they buttress stories of the world. Our focus must be *mapping*, rather than maps: the struggle over how to draw and define what matters—and how these mappings mesh with political action, as seen when threatening arrows of Europe-bound migration help justify more border patrols, or when drones unleash their warheads on lands imprisoned by the twinned cartographies of fear and military omniscience.[31]

Imperfect mappings, somewhat like the psychoanalyst's Rorschach blots, may help us discern the complex geopathology of our interventionist patient. This is a patient, after all, who still believes himself to be mighty, if not all-powerful, and a bringer of good to *others* who are supposedly ailing. The trope of intervener-as-doctor is present whenever powerful states designate crises and how to treat them, whether via "surgical" strikes, economic "shock therapy," or gentler humanitarian or development action aimed at ridding the target country of the "infection" of terror or the "scourge" of migration (to use just a few of the idioms deployed by technocrats and politicians). For this reason, we must approach our diagnosis with care, and in discrete parts. In chapter 1, we deploy the case study method and investigate Mali's descent into danger, observing the mechanisms underlying our present geopathological condition and its most acute symptoms. In chapter 2, we deploy mapping itself to build an etiology for our patient's ills, with the aim of discerning the stubborn historical patterns lurking behind the pathological compulsions seen in the war on terror. Our third chapter, set in Somalia, deepens the analysis by mapping intervention across three dimensions—soaring into the skies, where military campaigns gain distance from the danger zone while brutalizing the relationship with inhabitants on the ground below.

If the first part of the book tells the story of the map of danger, with its quest for control and separation, the second part scrunches up the map, sullying it with the septic smears of contagion. As we visit the drone wars in global danger zones, we glimpse how danger may be *embraced* by interveners to the point where it spirals into runaway circuits of mimicry among foes. Contagion effects abound, too, at the US and EU borders visited in chapter 4, where politicians cannot help but feed red meat to the wolves slavering outside the door. If these politicians' affliction is a peculiar case of *phobophilia,* or a morbid love of fear, chapter 5 looks in the other direction—toward the power brokers and entrepreneurs in putative danger zones, who know how to satisfy every dangerous desire as they court external donors and interveners. In chapter 6, set at ground zero of global danger in Kabul, we finally follow the daredevil reporters, soldiers, and explorers into the wild world outside the protective barriers—a world where nightmare projections are made real, and where Self and Other merge under the sign of danger.

.   .   .   .   .

In mapping global danger, this book faces a few dangers of its own.[32] To some readers, it may seem to underplay real and urgent threats. Am I putting too much blame on an amorphous and fractious "West," at a time when states such as Russia and Saudi Arabia are aggressively pursuing dangerous interventions of their own, including in the very "danger zones" of concern to us here? Further, am I letting violent jihadists off the hook and dismissing fears around migration and instability as so much fantasy? That is not the intention. But whereas our public debate is replete with proposed solutions to migration "crises" new and old, and with commentaries and analyses of ISIS, al Qaeda, and their murderous ilk, we urgently need to understand the logics and politics of fear from the other side—that is, from inside the interventionist apparatus of democratic states and international organizations—with a view to redrawing the map of danger. Challenges of war and want, and of citizen anxiety and insecurity, are real and must be addressed: and the best way to do so is through partnerships, not partitions. The initiative for such a shift, needless to say, must come from those legitimate public actors, internationally and within crisis-hit nations, that may be informed by reasoned debate and by evidence of our current dangerous spiral.

To other readers, our mapping of danger may rather be seen as *overplaying* the risks and reinforcing divides. Hopeful maps and narratives of our world are after all proliferating, too, among aid groups, scientists, businesses, and civil society, or among intellectuals, activists, and politicians in countries hit by conflict. Why am I giving so much importance to stories of old-fashioned domination and doom, rather than to positive openings, alternatives, and even resistances, as anthropologists are usually wont to do? In short, because we must understand our politics of fear from the inside in order to begin the hard task of lifting its spell. To this end, *No Go World* mimics the narrative power of our global mapping of danger, the better to dispel it: like a monster-infested medieval *mappa mundi*, we may say, it seeks to ward off threats by locating them, drawing them, and so enabling a certain hold on them.[33]

In other words, and returning to our geopathological frame, making a diagnosis may at least help us acknowledge the affliction. Such self-knowledge is of the essence for any curing to take place. Not only does our interventionist patient believe he is curing someone else, but we will see how he is actively transmitting his affliction to the Other, whose illness in this way is in large part iatrogenic, or caused by the treatment. Is it delusion, then, that we are treating? We are indeed good at deluding ourselves, citizens and powerful alike, but as we will see, there is a *rational* side to endangerment that accounts for much of the longevity of the affliction. This instrumental rationality can be explained in part by reference to the risk economies of today and in part by history—especially colonial history, whose patterns of thought and action echo into our fearful present.[34]

Until a change of tack, Western states increasingly play both hostage and host to pervasive fears. Anxious citizens and politicians shudder at the thought of the great unwashed reaching our shores. Visa application offices are closed for business if you are of the wrong, "risky" profile— including, for instance, most poor people in sub-Saharan Africa, as well as refugees fleeing "our" conflicts in Afghanistan, Libya, and Iraq. Borders are sealed by radars and fences, satellites and sea sensors, patrol boats and policing networks. Embassies are bunkered up, and bureaucrats, aid workers, and officials have withdrawn from the front lines. Contact points of a positive kind are decreasing just as they are most needed.

No Go World is about the severe consequences of this highly selective distancing. For the withdrawal of "normal" relations—travel, exchange, trade—leaves the field open for darker forces. It boosts certain lines of business. It creates fiefs not just for warlords but also for anointed local middlemen: hucksters, sheriffs, and chiefs with the most modest of claims on real authority yet with a sudden hold on our purses and attentions. It kills, as people in need are left without assistance and as innocents are maimed by unaccountable militias, drone operators, or mercenary-style soldiers. It creates winners and losers—and the biggest loser of all may, in fact, be the once so mighty "West" as politicians and their voters start seeing certain Others through the lens of existential threats, while other world powers fill the vacuum it leaves behind.[35] This book is about the distance those of us in the rich Western world seek to put between ourselves and others; the buffers we build; and the dangerous effects of our highly selective shutting ourselves off from engagement. For the danger zone, as we shall see, is not as far away as we would perhaps like to imagine.

PART I THE STORY OF THE MAP

1 THE TIMBUKTU SYNDROME

> When I write from Timbuctoo, I shall detail precisely how
> I was betrayed, and nearly murdered in my sleep. . . . I have
> five sabre cuts on the crown of the head, and three on the
> left temple; all fractures, from which much bone has come
> away. One on my left cheek, which fractured the jawbone,
> and has divided the ear, forming a very unsightly wound.
> One over the right temple, and a dreadful gash on the back
> of the neck . . . &c. I am, nevertheless, as already I have
> said, doing well, and hope yet to return to England with
> much important geographical information. The map
> indeed requires much correction, and please God, I shall
> yet do much in addition to what I have already done
> towards putting it right.[1]

The Scottish explorer Alexander Gordon Laing was about to win the race for Timbuktu. It was in early May 1826 when he wrote to his father-in-law, the British consul in Tripoli, from where he had set out two years earlier on a trek across the Sahara Desert. His task was as the British colonial secretary had instructed him—to trace the course of the Niger River—yet to Laing, the race was about more than the geographical ambitions of empire. By returning alive from Timbuktu, he would claim the 10,000-franc prize given by the geographical society in Paris to the first European to set foot in the fabled city; gain glory and fame; and hopefully convince his surly father-in-law to finally let him share his new wife's bed. The sabre cuts and "dreadful gash" inflicted by Tuareg nomads in May of 1826 failed to halt Laing's onward march to Timbuktu, where he arrived a few months after penning his letter. Yet little joy awaited him in this town of supposed "golden roofs and argent streets" at the southern edge of the Sahara.[2] Murdered by his guide upon leaving Timbuktu, Laing lost out on the prize, the European glory, and his wife's warm bed back in Tripoli. News of his rumored success was confirmed only when a Frenchman, René Caillié, arrived in Timbuktu two years later disguised as an Arab on a slave canoe meandering its way up the Niger River: and it was in Caillié's sketches, as well as in his and fellow explorers' best-selling books in coming years, that Timbuktu and its remote desert environs were finally mapped out for the coming European colonizers.[3]

Almost two centuries after Laing sent his desert missive, in the slushy winter of an overcast Stockholm, a tall Swede walked into the canteen of the fortress-like armed forces headquarters with a slight swagger and an outstretched hand. To left and right, men in suit or uniform came up to greet him, asking for the latest news on his imminent departure. Lt. Col. Carl-Magnus Svensson smiled, responded, moved on, and picked up a canteen tray, spooning some mash onto a plate. As the head of Sweden's peacekeeping contingent for Timbuktu, Carl-Magnus was the military's new superstar—featured and feted in newscasts, a latter-day Caillié with an entourage to boot. *Isn't it dangerous?* the journalists would ask. *How big are the risks to our soldiers?* Carl-Magnus shrugged and responded, again and again; at the end of this glum last week of January 2015 loomed his flight to Bamako and onwards to Timbuktu, far away from the gray Stockholm skies.

Carl-Magnus had his challenge cut out for him. "The most dangerous mission in the world for UN peacekeepers"—this was how Samantha Power, then US ambassador to the United Nations, described the Mali operation the Swedes were now joining. In early January 2015, the UN undersecretary-general for peacekeeping had similarly summed up a dreadful year in Mali with these words: "No other mission in contemporary times has been so costly in terms of bloodshed." By this time, UN soldiers faced almost daily assaults by improvised explosive devices (IEDs), ambushes, and suicide attacks. Their task was peacekeeping with no peace to keep; their blue helmets were themselves prime targets.[4]

But I am getting ahead of myself. The story began, for me, as my Bamako-bound plane took off from Dakar in May of 2014. This was a clinch moment in the tense standoff in the country's north that had briefly—and erroneously—come to be glossed as a "postconflict" transition following French and UN intervention. Events that May would show how fragile the outsiders' hold was on the restive desert, which kept eluding the mapmakers and soldier-spies of the new Sahara.

·   ·   ·   ·   ·

The African continent has long been a laboratory of peacekeeping, as conflict scholars note, and by the time of my impending 2014 visit, northern Mali had become one of its most explosive experiments.[5] Here ever-metamorphosing jihadist factions mingled with Tuareg separatists and with smugglers of contraband, arms, and people. Targeting them was an equally complex constellation of security interventions, of which the UN mission, MINUSMA, was just one. French and US counterterror operations jostled with EU military training missions, a EUCAP Sahel policing initiative, and more. In echoes of the nineteenth-century race for Timbuktu, external forces were scrambling to control the desert, competing and collaborating in turns. However, our story here will not be the familiar one of grand political strategies for controlling distant crisis zones, though that is inevitably the backdrop. Instead, as we now descend on Bamako's Senou airport amid the Maytime dust of 2014, our task will be to discern from "ground zero" of intervention how external actors of all kinds are seeking to distance themselves from remote danger—with troubling implications for Mali's future and for the future of international engagement in crisis zones writ large.

Even as they squabbled over turf and goals, Mali's foreign visitors shared one thing: an "interventionist's dilemma" of ambivalent engagement and highly selective withdrawal. They *had* to venture into the desert in order to stabilize the country, quell terrorism, and crack down on smuggling routes, but the risks were too high to put large numbers of boots on the ground. The solution to this dilemma was to roll out remote controls over Mali's north—yet these often amounted to little real control, and they brought precious little prospect of recovery from war, or of a better future for the region's inhabitants. But besides these practical implications, a larger story lurks behind the fortified walls and drone-humming skies of intervention. As we shall see, the interveners' arm's-length dealings in the desert—on display in the daily struggles of peacekeepers and aid workers alike—were symptomatic of a revived Western fear of, and strategic concern with, putative global margins. Timbuktu stands as an exemplar of this "syndrome" of intervention, as we will go on to call it: an intractable state of ambivalent deployment into remote danger zones, carrying faint echoes of the age of precolonial exploration.

.   .   .   .   .

As I flew in that May morning from Dakar, the red soil and scattered concrete dice of Bamako's outskirts finally came into view. Soon the familiar heat of the Sahel hit my face as we stepped onto the landing strip of Senou airport. On the tarmac stood seven UN military planes, black-painted and brooding, lined up in waiting for the cargo and personnel making their way to Mali's war-scarred north. Inside the airport terminal, a Western woman scuttled between the police booths, overseeing Malian officers grappling with newly installed biometric equipment. Police aimed infrared pistols at us, screening for Ebola. Mali, it was amply clear after only a few minutes back on its soil, was a country under international tutelage, its security assured by UN and French soldiers and its borders controlled by Western devices and expertise. It was also a country marked by an edginess I had never experienced before, I thought as I finally found a taxi in a remote corner of the airport parking lot. As we bumped our way down empty streets toward central Bamako, I kept looking over my shoulder, as if on guard against an unlikely ambush.

The international tutelage was far from new, even if it had been growing more extreme since the start of conflict. On my last visit to Mali, in 2010–11, I had investigated Bamako's role as a transit point for migration toward the Sahara and, eventually, Europe—long the top concern of European states in the region. Spain, France, and the European Union had furnished new border posts and equipped and trained forces in Mali and nearby Mauritania, and the EU had launched a program to strengthen the administration's control of Mali's desert north. Yet the Europeans had despaired at lack of progress. The Malian military was "absolutely hopeless," one EU official had told me in despair; only some 10 percent of its underpaid and ill-equipped forces were operational, according to his estimates, and many "ghost soldiers" graced the rolls. This frank assessment was indicative of things to come, in 2012, when combating terror would rise to the top of the European agenda.[6]

I pulled down the taxi window and breathed in the hot, dusty air. Mali's capital seemed much as I had left it in 2011, despite the vicious northern war, coup d'état, and French military intervention that had followed: fume-choked streets, searing heat, children selling water sachets by the traffic lights. Subtle changes were evident as I arrived at my destination, however. At Hotel Djenne, a beautifully wonky piece of Africana and once a focal point for visiting culture vultures, my bathroom tap coughed and spat out some rust-red water. For good reason: by the second night, I was the hotel's only guest.

My trip to Mali had not been all that easy. The north was a no go zone, while the capital had "none but essential" travel advice in the United Kingdom because of the kidnap and terror threat. My university had asked me to complete a drawn-out risk assessment, fill in long forms, attend security meetings, and read up on safe procedures. The university's private security contractor had asked me to provide detailed information to be used in case I was kidnapped, and they had given me a security app through which I had to log in regularly as proof of life. My top-up kidnapping insurance mounted to £1,000 for a month—discounted, after some hard bargaining, to £750 as long as I did not leave the capital. With these rates and procedures, none but the most dedicated would even attempt a trip to Mali, at precisely the time when the country was thirsting for renewed connections.

The security risk bureaucracy might have been a hassle for academics, yet it was but a small example of the new risk-based geography of intervention rolled out for agencies working in Mali, which were multiplying by the week now that the €3.2 billion of aid promised by donors had started to trickle in following successful elections in 2013. To these newcomers, danger now divided Mali's map, splitting it along its north-south axis into a patchwork of red and green zones. Bamako, a sprawling city sometimes dubbed "the world's largest village," was becoming home to peacekeepers, EU military trainers, and European NGO workers, all of which were reluctant to send their expatriates up north. The fissure between capital and northern hinterland might have predated the conflict, yet with their arrival it was swiftly deepening.

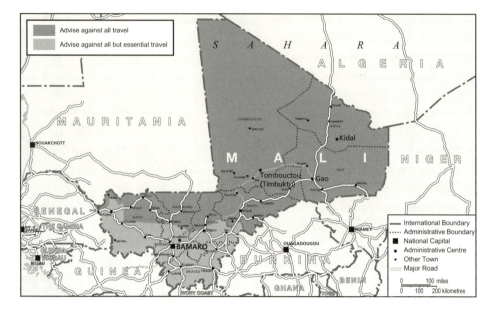

Map 5. UK Foreign and Commonwealth Office travel advice for Mali, issued in 2013, still current by 2018.

At the heart of the interveners' remapping of Mali was the United Nations, yet before we decry it too loudly, we must note that in Mali as in Somalia and Iraq before it, the world body was not for the first time being deployed to clean up the mess of others. The conflict in Mali's north was in many ways a direct consequence of NATO's military intervention in Libya. Western powers, wary of ground engagements, had launched a remote-controlled war in the country, bombing a path for rebels to oust and kill Gaddafi in 2011. As the Libyan regime imploded, and as no "boots on the ground" were deployed to secure weapons caches and bring stability, unsecured arms and Tuareg fighters formerly in Gaddafi's pay started streaming south.[7] A violent insurgency—the fourth since Mali's independence from France in 1960—soon began and was swiftly hijacked by jihadists roaming the desert.

With some justification, many Malians saw the brewing conflict as the responsibility of Western countries. As a rangy Malian military officer told me that May in his Bamako barracks: "It's NATO which went along and did all that in Libya, and it's Europe which has let all these terrorists lose."

He pointed a finger at the TV in his office, which showed the recent advances of ISIS (or Daesh) in Iraq, as his voice rose to falsetto pitch: "It's you! It's you!"

Not that the army—or indeed the administration—could absolve themselves of responsibility, as academic diagnoses of Mali's ailments have pointed out.[8] In late March 2012, a hitherto unknown, US-trained general launched a coup in Bamako, putting an end to the unpopular, corrupt, and aid-backed regime of President Amadou Toumani Touré. In the ensuing chaos, the northern rebels saw their chance. Joining forces with various jihadist groups, they had soon taken over the vast desert north and proclaimed the independence of their own state of "Azawad." After months of international reluctance to intervene, France finally launched military action in January 2013 as the jihadists advanced toward Bamako. The ground and air forces of Operation Serval swiftly pushed insurgents out of the northern towns of Timbuktu, Kidal, and Gao. Unlike NATO's air campaign in Libya, Serval was broad and put boots on the ground—yet as the French launched into military action, they were already eyeing the exit. Soon enough, African peacekeepers started arriving as part of a regional force, AFISMA, replaced by the UN mission MINUSMA that summer after French pressure at the Security Council.

In the aftermath of Gaddafi's fall, the specter of terrorism in the Sahara was finally rearing into full view. Much has been written on the deadly and absurd consequences of the "war on terror" on African soil since 9/11, and accusations of neocolonialism were soon coming thick and fast from Malian and foreign intellectuals as France launched its military action.[9] Yet we must note that Mali's descent into chaos was more complicated than simply the result of a neocolonial desire to intervene and grab the desert's resources.[10] While France initially seemed rather ambivalent about intervention, the United States was even more reluctant.[11] Their desire to combat terrorism in the Sahel was accompanied by an understanding that conflict might be localized and that large deployments might generate blowback, besides accusations of colonialism in Africa and headlines about body bags back home.

Still, for the Europeans, fears over regional instability and uncontrolled migration kept stoking the desire to intervene. Given the risks, the ideal solution was a partial presence: counterterror spearheads up north com-

Figure 2. A Senegalese UN peacekeeper patrolling in Kidal, northern Mali, July 2013. © UN/MINUSMA/2013/Marco Dormino.

bined with a multilateral UN mission doing the heavy lifting, with African and Malian forces manning the front lines.

For the UN, getting entangled with Western security objectives was a risky prospect. As it came to cohabit with counterterror, the UN peace-keeping machinery was soon to find its old norms—of impartiality, consent of parties to conflict, and nonuse of force except to defend its forces and its mandate—on ever-shakier ground. In addition, as large aid programs got under way, the lines between military and aid operations blurred even more. No bunkers, barriers, and neat divisions of responsibilities across Mali's map of danger could avoid this larger political dilemma of the interveners.

As I watched the news of conflict safely back in London in 2013–14, it was with a sense of dismay and resignation that I saw Mali transform in front of my eyes. Western donors had long treated the country as an "aid darling" and a "model democracy" for the region, yet now media pundits—security experts of uncertain extraction and expertise—started referring to it as "Africa's Afghanistan."[12] On CNN and BBC, I heard how jihadists had imposed sharia law, chopped off hands of presumed thieves, banned music, and desecrated Timbuktu's shrines. Yet even as their dismal reign came to an end in early 2013, and as French president François Hollande paid Timbuktu a visit that February to *tricoleur*-waving crowds, my unease lingered. By the time of my 2014 trip, Mali's north remained poised in a fragile truce, and those displaced still feared returning to their homes. Neither the celebrated French intervention nor the UN mission that followed it had put order back in Mali. As the events that May would show, something rather more complicated was in the making, drawing the internationals into an ever more dangerous embrace with a problem they had perhaps rather avoided altogether.

·   ·   ·   ·   ·

Like most other academics visiting Mali in its good years, I had never envisioned returning to study war.[13] On my first trip as a budding anthropologist, in 2001, I had arrived in Bamako armed with a cracked old acoustic guitar, which soon was to become the envy of the talented musicians I sought out for impromptu jams on street corners and in empty courtyards. In central Bamako's teeming cultural center, a female Michael Jackson fan with bottle-thick glasses taught me tunes on the *kora*, the ethereal West African harp made out of calabash, cow hide, and wood. She and her musician friends were gearing up to perform at the African football cup, which was soon coming to Bamako. The city's bars were jumping; Coca-Cola ads gleamed down from billboards; a democratic transition had seemingly taken hold. In the early days of the twenty-first century Mali was among the world's poorest countries, yet it also harbored hopes for its citizens and offered its bounteous hospitality—*djatigiya*—to its lucky international visitors. Wherever I went, from Bamako and Wassoulou in the steaming south to Mopti and Djenne in the central regions, endless cups of pungent Sahelian tea with newfound friends helped clear my throat of the summer dust blowing in from the Sahara. Yet I never arrived in Timbuktu; and now, in 2014, it seemed too late.

The only traveler *toubabs,* or white folk, who remained in the new Bamako were ragged adventurers of a familiar kind. The guesthouse where I finally settled, on the southern side of the Niger River, played reluctant host to rough-hewn Europeans on mad transcontinental escapes from something or other, yet the mainstay of the clientele was now those who saw Mali as their mission: young Western aid workers heading for the rooftop restaurant; African mine clearers with the UN Mine Action Service; freelance journalists, linen-clad and lanky; and African peace-keepers in uniform, squatting on the faux-tribal wooden chairs and hippie cushions of the downstairs bar, nursing bottles of Malian beer.

The sight jarred. Only a few years earlier, development workers and laidback visitors had found themselves incorporated into Mali's social fabric, taking local names as sign of affection (I, for one, held onto my conferred name Amadou Diarra for dear life). By contrast, now "Peaceland"—as one conflict scholar has called the self-contained world of international missions—had descended on Bamako like an extraterrestrial ship unloading its cargo and personnel, all according to a well-established global template.[14] And there were few honorary Diarras or Diakités among these newcomers, that much I sensed.

Monica Bermudez, a Peaceland citizen and fellow guesthouse resident, embodied Mali's divided geography of intervention in her slight figure.[15] As an administrator for MINUSMA, she was about to be sent up to Mali's north, she told me one night on the guesthouse terrace. Such trips to far-flung danger zones had been her life for the better part of two decades: she had already been through stints in the former Yugoslavia, Sudan, the Democratic Republic of Congo, typhoon-hit Philippines, and more. Arriving in Mali, she had bumped into old colleagues from Kosovo. "I'm telling my bosses I can't go north until this has healed," she said while pointing at her arm, swaddled after a moped accident. "But they keep pushing me to leave straight away." Her destination was the separatist-dominated town of Kidal in MINUSMA's "Sector North," far into the Sahara. There, soldiers and civilians lived in container-like dorms in the searing heat, in a part of Mali deemed too dangerous for Sweden's Timbuktu-bound soldiers to enter.

Monica's long experience in missions should have prepared her for the dangers, yet something unsettled her. "Now I'm starting to get afraid. I don't feel calm here," she confided one night on the terrace, lighting a cigarette. "This is the first time that I have felt vulnerable, and it's not as if it's my first mission. . . . It was different in Congo, there the mission was well established. Here they are not in control, they are not prepared. I don't feel safe." To make matters worse, her grasp of French—not to mention her knowledge of the proliferating rebel groups in the north—was tenuous at best. "CNMA, what are they called?" she asked with a laugh, referring to the main Tuareg separatist faction, the MNLA, or the National Movement for the Liberation of Azawad. Yet she knew that the UN, and northern Mali, badly needed her firm administrative hand. "I could in theory have said no to this, but it's what I signed up for, it's a peacekeeping mission."

Monica's apprehension was shared by many of the foreigners I met in the coming weeks as I skipped across town in rickety taxis and *sotrama* vans plying Bamako's heat-cracked roads. However, so far not many successful attacks against the internationals had taken place, or, as one UN officer collating data on these put it, in defiance of the security pundits: "Mali's not Afghanistan." That was sadly about to change. In late 2014, amid the escalating attacks, one high-ranking UN official despairingly asked me in New York: "There is no enemy any longer, and who is the target? We are." MINUSMA—the "Multidimensional Integrated Stabilization Mission in Mali"—had a long name that tried to hide the fact it was a peacekeeping mission with no peace to keep, hostage to elusive dangers lurking on the horizon.

As it set up shop across Mali in mid-2013, the presumably "robust," enforcement-focused peacekeeping mission had geared its operations toward these yet-to-be-realized dangers. In the northern towns of Gao, Timbuktu, and Kidal, peacekeepers and civilian UN staff lurked behind high walls, from where—or so locals complained—they all too rarely emerged to keep the people safe from attacks by either rebels, stray Islamists, or the Malian armed forces. Robust, in a word, it was not.

The geography of intervention did not just divide Bamako from the north, and northern interveners from local society; it also imposed an alien security model on "Bamako HQ" itself. There, a thousand kilometers away from Timbuktu over desert-chewed chunks of tarmac, Monica and her colleagues labored at one remove from the capital's residents. For its headquarters, MINUSMA had commandeered the five-star Hotel l'Amitié, rising like the brutal Soviet-funded colossus it was from the derelict quarters of central Bamako. For Mali's government, the very decision to locate the mission HQ in the capital was provocative, as it broadcasted the state's failure to manage its own affairs. For the UN, however, the reason behind a Bamako base was simple: insecurity in the war-scarred north—that is, precisely what it was there to prevent. Amitié was off bounds to any locals behind its cement vehicle barriers, curls of razor wire, and tanks manned by armed Blue Helmets. Its pool, long a favored haunt of the local elite, now hosted restaurants serving up crisp pizzas to Danish soldiers and American political advisers. As UN staff drove up to the gates at lunch-time in their identical white four-wheel drives, they clogged up the busy road outside, frustrating local drivers—a problem that stung all the more since local rumors insisted that the Malian government had to pay a large subsidy for housing MINUSMA in the hotel.

The divided geography of intervention was symptomatic of a deeply political problem we have already alluded to: how the UN and humanitarian agencies had become entangled with "new wars" in which old rules of engagement and neutrality no longer applied.[16] The watershed was the brutal 2003 bombing of the scantily protected UN hotel headquarters in occupied Iraq. After this, a new UN security structure had been put in place worldwide through its often rather inept and overbearing Department for Safety and Security (UNDSS). The new security technocracy sidestepped larger questions around the politics of intervention in times of counterterrorism and invasion as it provided a template for working under a besieged blue flag. The barricaded UN headquarters soon formed an international "archipelago" of intervention, scattered islands of green and safe zones that connected Kabul to Juba, Tripoli to Baghdad.[17]

The geography of "Peaceland" entailed, at its core, a separation from the host society. During luncheons with UN staff around Amitié's pool in those early summer days of 2014, I could not help but recall accounts of the Baghdad Green Zone, set in Saddam Hussein's palatial grounds after the US invasion. Inside the "Emerald City," journalist Rajiv Chandrasekaran reported, US soldiers and contractors "lay sprawled on chaise lounges in the shadows of towering palms, munching Doritos and sipping iced tea" while Iraq's postinvasion chaos unfolded outside the walls.[18] Yet while stories of peacekeepers' high life in five-star Malian hotels would eventually make their way into European newspapers, the excess on show in the US bubble of postinvasion Iraq was a world away from the Bamako cocoon:

theirs was a cut-rate green zone, an expat bubble with a shallower pool and shabbier offices.[19]

For Monica, MINUSMA's Bamako quarters certainly left much to be desired. "It's utterly subhuman!" she laughed. Beds removed, the carpeted hotel rooms had morphed into offices into which UN bureaucrats had been squeezed helter-skelter. Worse, the air-conditioning did not work. "We can either open the window and get the stench of the river in our faces, or else keep it closed and sit there frying!" To top off the misery, the building had only three half-functioning elevators, hardly any landlines, and no directory for the civilian staff; to get anything done, Monica had to walk up and down the stairs to visit bureaus in person, losing valuable time. And the food, she complained, half in jest: the indoors canteen served the skinniest chicken she had ever seen, "pure bones!" We laughed; soon she would anyhow leave it all behind. "I came here for the challenge," she told me. In her previous posting, at a sleepy UN regional office, "I wasn't happy; it was the same every day." As in Congo and Kosovo, "the field" was where Monica really wanted to be: that was where she was needed, though she would be sitting behind a fortified compound wall.

The UN was not alone in bunkering up in Bamako. If anything, their measures were lax compared with those of the French embassy a few streets away from Amitié, which by 2014 had become a green zone of its own making. Its walls were clad with antiblast, soil-filled "HESCO bastions," first employed at Afghan military installations, which jutted out onto the pavements and blocked traffic. Other international actors were also gearing their operations toward the unseen dangers. Crowds of security guards loitered outside donors' offices and embassies; NGOs situated their bases close to easy evacuation routes, or had no go zones and curfews drawn up by in-house security officers poached from the military sector, again taking their cue from Kabul. "Stay in the Radisson," one officer from the EU military training mission in Mali (EUTM) had advised me before I left for Bamako. "It's the only hotel with armed guards." The EUTM's hotel base was itself surrounded by fenced-in walkways and barriers. Still the military officers, many of them arriving fresh from Afghanistan, complained that protection was too basic compared with Kabul.

Bamako was quite untouched by the faraway northern war, yet even here the internationals had hunkered down as if in waiting for the catastrophe.

The clutches of security guards and the transport routines, the tanks and bollards and barriers, all signaled a new distance between intervener and local host—a distance that was soon to come back and haunt the internationals.

.   .   .   .   .

Mali's divided geography of intervention drew lines of separation between visitors and residents in Bamako, as well as boundaries between capital and northern hinterland. There, in the north, frontline tasks were largely left to "others." European military trainers were not allowed to venture beyond southern Mali; instead, they waved off the Malian battalions they trained as soon as they had completed their drills, with some of them sent straight back up into the remaining zones of conflict. In peacekeeping, as we will see, the most dangerous sectors were left to African soldiers. Among UN agencies and NGOs, meanwhile, operations up north were almost exclusively manned by Malian and "regional" West African workers, who moreover often labored at arm's length through subcontracted partner organizations.[20]

The reason for this intricate division of labor, international aid officials down in Bamako insisted, was the security and kidnap risk faced by white Westerners. Yet while it was true that Westerners had increasingly been kidnapped in the Sahara in the past decade, and some had been killed in captivity, national or African staff were not necessarily better off. Four Malians working for the International Committee of the Red Cross had been taken hostage in early 2014 before eventually being liberated by French forces. As in Afghanistan and Somalia before it, Mali's north was becoming a zone of uneven risks, transferred to often ill-prepared soldiers and workers.

Monica was among the exceptions, and she was primed to handle the impending dangers. Before arriving in Bamako, soldiers had drilled her in the Italian port town of Brindisi, in one of the standard security trainings now offered up by UN security. "They shout at you, they insult you, *vaffanculo, cazzo,* they beat our bus windows with their pistols," she recalled: she knew the score, having previously endured a hostage training with Irish soldiers. Now she was scheduled to face yet another one in Bamako with Senegalese peacekeepers. "They make you strip off, they take off everything!" You are trained not to look captors in the eye, she said; give them all you have and tell them the truth, even about that most precious piece of information—your nationality. "Though think of what your country means," Monica said with some apprehension, nodding at me. "Sweden means money, but [a poorer country such as hers] is just another body to them!"

As we spoke, the guesthouse kept filling up with a more carefree breed of expats. On the terrace above our veranda, twenty-something aid managers from Europe shared plates of Thai curry and hummus before heading off to the city's party street, rue Blabla, across the river; the bass beats of the sound system reverberated down to my room below through the early morning hours most nights of the week. Locals frowned and pointed at the party-seeking expats and the white UN four-wheel drives; see, here they come again! "They take our girls," said some men about UN officials, worried they could no longer compete for local women's affections. "They only come here for the money," said others. One guesthouse worker, himself displaced from central Mali, asked one night as the reggae started booming and glasses clinking on the terrace upstairs: "If you're in a country to help it, you don't go out like that at night, no, you spend all time thinking about it, right? How is this helping Malians?"

Those on the circuit did not see the Bamako bubble as a great obstacle to their operations. As in Afghanistan, Somalia, or Syria, "remote programming"—including "flash visits," teleconferencing, phone calls, and e-mails to local staff and partners—had become the norm. To aid managers, these workarounds ensured Mali's northern danger zone remained at a distance yet comfortably within reach.[21] Or so, at least, went the story before the worst possible news hit the headline that May.

.   .   .   .   .

The trouble started with a visit by the pugnacious Malian prime minister, Moussa Mara, to Kidal. Seat of the principal Tuareg rebel faction, the MNLA, Kidal had been left as their bastion after the French intervention, much to Bamako's chagrin. The French were playing a double game in the north, keeping the MNLA as allies while routing jihadist factions in the hinterland, and Mara now wanted to give this cozy arrangement a political push as he arrived in Kidal, against UN and French advice, on Saturday, May 17. His intention was to show support for patriotic state administrators, while hopefully forcing MINUSMA to take the government's side in the struggle with the rebels.

He failed. As Mara tried to make it into central parts of Kidal, armed men took officials at the town's governorate hostage. Then, as Malian forces attacked and French and UN soldiers stood by, the hostages were killed. "I have a picture of me surrounded by all of them," one of the UN's top peacekeeping officials later told me in New York, "and then ten days later they had all had their heads cut off."

The news had not yet sunk in when the protests began. On our grainy guesthouse TV, I saw angry protesters screaming into the night in downtown Bamako: rumors had it a UN vehicle had been torched. The next day aid workers were scrambling to exit the north, but no flights were leaving. Anger against perceived UN and French inaction in Kidal was mounting—as well as against Tuareg and Arab northerners, seen as partial to the separatist cause. Mali was yet again a tinderbox about to ignite; yet the events that Saturday were but the parting shot in the cruelest week Mali had seen for some time.

Have you heard the news? I was in a plush hotel in northern Bamako on the night of Wednesday, May 21, when a well-connected European researcher, affiliated with a security think tank, broke the latest developments to me. Malian forces—some of them recently trained and equipped by the European Union—had attacked the rebels in Kidal without informing the French or MINUSMA; then the MNLA had routed them. Kidal had fallen, followed by Menaka further south. "The Malian soldiers just ran away," the researcher confided; they had hidden in the UN camp while the rebels stole their EU-provided vehicles. We walked upstairs to the hotel restaurant, set on a fanned terrace brimming with soldiers and UN workers, to dine with an NGO friend of ours. What would the implications be, down here in Bamako?

At the table our mutual friend, Miranda Bennett, sat scanning her iPad for news on #Mali, a glass of wine in hand.[22] A Canadian in her thirties with years in international missions under her belt, Miranda was in her element: she had an embargoed press release ready for midnight, she coolly told us—this was the time to get some visibility for humanitarian priorities as Mali was finally back in the spotlight. After catching up on Twitter, Miranda looked out over the gathered men in uniforms, nodding hi to an old UN colleague from Chad, one of her previous stations. "I shouldn't really be here," she said, but let it be. Bamako's humanitarians tried to keep separate from the military, yet this was proving impossible; they all mingled on the same circuit, going to the same clique of high-end haunts. The researcher was nervous, too; she was not allowed to go anywhere on foot, according to new security instructions from somewhere (her embassy? Intelligence? She would not say). Instead she borrowed Miranda's driver. After she left, Miranda explained that she herself was allowed to move about in daytime only by using the NGO's own driver, and at night only with a designated taximan; she was not meant to be out around nearby rue Blabla after dark either. Still, like others she broke the rules; sometimes she felt like a naughty teenager sneaking back past the doorman at her NGO's residence too late at night.

As I left the plush hotel that Wednesday night, Bamako appeared to me in a new guise. It was as if another, hidden city emerged from under the cracked lanes, mud-stained cement houses, and tea-drinking clutches of youth that I knew so well: an uncertain city where a wrong turn might bring a mob, where my skin color was suddenly a liability. I entered the compact darkness of the lanes on foot, as always, and stood on the corner of the tarmacked thoroughfare, waiting to hail a taxi. Finally a yellow-painted car rattled past, 1,500 franc CFA to the Palais de la Culture, next to my guesthouse—I didn't say my exact destination, *Remember the university's security advice.* I was ridiculously chatty as we wound our way down an abandoned rue Blabla and past the darkened city center. *I togo? Ne togo Amadou Diarra,* I said, my name is Amadou Diarra, the name given to me by my local hosts thirteen years back, in a more innocent era. *Ah musulman?* responded the young driver. But Sweden, isn't Sweden Christian? Is Swedish similar to French? Not much, I insisted. Later I would hear how my guesthouse owner had traveled past the French embassy during the day: angry protesters had crowded around her taxi, hitting the windows, screaming *Down with France!* "But I'm Swiss!" she exclaimed. The politics of skin was no longer present only in the kidnap circuit and the "communal" conflicts up north; it had now pierced our

Bamako bubble. We crossed a bridge to southern Bamako—*Is it the right bridge?*—and arrived at my guesthouse gates. *Bonne soirée.*

The next day I awoke to a Bamako in lockdown mode. The angry crowds outside MINUSMA's walls and the French embassy's blast-protection barriers were not going away. International organizations had told their staff to stay indoors and away from the center. Bureaucrats had started peeling off the black "UN" letters from the sides of their white four-wheel drives, vainly trying to look less conspicuous. My meetings were canceled. An interviewee from the EU training mission could not see me, he explained, since they were in "alternative planning" for the foreseeable future—military officers could not leave their barricaded hotel without security escort.

The rumor mill, fed by politicians and the media, kept churning hearsay about the Malian forces' bloody humiliation. From my Bamakois friends, I heard how the French military had called the MNLA to warn of the Malian army's impending attack; or how they had flown a plane over Kidal to shut down the army's electronic equipment; or how their helicopters had dropped ammunition for the rebels. "France has no friends, only interests," said one of my confidants, citing Charles de Gaulle and echoing many Malians' deep mistrust of the former colonizers. And the UN, to most Malians, had become France's unwitting helper.

Those days, risk was encroaching on the expat Bamako bubble in an almost visceral way. As I talked by phone with the barricaded European soldiers, I realized how pathetically unprotected my UN staff–hosting guesthouse was. But at least it was inconspicuous; downtown at Amitié the blue-helmeted troops with their tanks and barricades would not be able to do much should the restive crowd begin to roil, as security-savvy UN workers were all too aware.

Most internationals including myself seemed to be wearing red-tinted glasses those days, seeing danger round every corner. As I reflected on this in later months, an academic concept came to mind: *dangerization.* In a prescient piece, criminologist Michalis Lianos and anthropologist Mary Douglas had in the year before 9/11 used this somewhat clunky neologism to describe a growing Western "tendency to perceive and analyze the world through categories of menace."[23] Their focus was on relationships between well-off and marginal groups *within* rich Western nations: as they imagined a middle-class driver speeding past a housing project because of the potential danger lurking inside, they asked whether a new "norm of distance rather than proximity" was being forged at the heart of our societies.

Their example resonates with the Far Right mappings of putative urban no go zones of the kind we encountered in the Introduction. But the speeding driver is a rather apt metaphor, too, for the wider international engagement with *global* danger, as seen in the bunkers and four-wheel drives with peeled-off UN stickers in Mali, as well as in the anxieties on show once such physical separations fail. In those hot-headed days of protest, dangerization and distance making went hand in hand. Risk aversion opened a gap between interveners and intervened-upon, as well as between foreign and local workers. The result was not the quelling of danger but rather its proliferation: dangerization gave way to endangerment. The interveners might step on the gas as much as they want, but they would never outspeed the menace hovering outside, fingers pawing at the armored car doors in the night.

Monica was among the internationals who kept the red-tinted glasses on her shelf when she went into her Amitié office during that day of fear and loathing; she even bought some fruit outside the gates, among the protesters. "They are pacific," she insisted. Her security training had been called off, the Senegalese officers being too busy with guarding the bollards at Amitié. The chaos of Bamako was but a small taster of the conflict in Kidal; yet once Monica was in the field things would look different, or so she thought. After her escape from Bamako's crowds and the MINUSMA canteen's skinny chicken, at least the soldiers guarding the Kidal camp might cook up some West African grills for her at night, as the desert stars lit over the UN fortifications and improvised explosive devices went off in the distance.

.   .   .   .   .

"Mali's biggest security risk is its own government." Mikael Lundberg ushered me toward MINUSMA's hotel entrance, where he stepped through the metal detector.[24] It beeped, detecting his weapon. The Malian security officer walked up to check him, but Mikael just pushed ahead, angrily shouting *"Arrête!"* Stop! "For Malians every day is the first day at work," he complained; impossible to teach them anything.

Mikael was a muscled package of a man, bouncy and bristling in his fatigues, with the manners of someone fresh from Afghanistan, as he and many of his colleagues indeed were. Forty-nine days left in Mali and counting, he said as we sat down in MINUSMA's shiny lobby. He was one of the early troops sent from Sweden to Bamako before Carl-Magnus and his Timbuktu-bound contingent. The sofas around us groaned with uniformed soldiers, administrators, and political advisers; the TV screens on the hotel walls showed the good works of the UN in a loop; and posters depicted blue helmets on a spectacular background of sculpted clay walls in Mali's north. Yet their solemn message of peace did not convince Mikael, who scorned not just Mali's government but also his own chiefs. MINUSMA's chain of command was faulty. The mission should have supported the French as they planned to liberate the hostages in Kidal, but this had not happened—and for that reason the French would not enter either, leading to the atrocity. "Then they made it into 'This is not MINUSMA's mandate,'" Mikael growled; as in so many instances before, blame was dissipated by bureaucracy.

MINUSMA's problems went deeper than bad chiefs, however. "It's a giant with a bloated head and clay feet," Mikael said. A huge bureaucratic base had been set up in Bamako, while the military presence up north was in the hands of inept commanders and ill-equipped soldiers. Nigeria had initially offered to send in troops but did not have enough uniforms, so was forced toward an ignominious exit. The Africans who did end up manning MINUSMA were hardly storm troopers either, bereft as they were of proper equipment even as their governments claimed the UN cash.[25]

In the UN, "everyone's supposed to be the same," Mikael said with a frustration that echoed that of many of his NATO-trained Western military colleagues.[26] In a face-saving exercise, the military commanders of MINUSMA were all Africans inherited from the previous AFISMA mission, even though some could hardly use a computer, he said. "If you want to get something done, you go to the deputies," who were all Western. "Cultural differences" was how Mikael explained the problem. "We look at them and think they are lazy, but they haven't worked so hard in their

Figure 3. A Chadian peacekeeper offers a boy a drink of water, Kidal, December 2016. © UN/MINUSMA/2016/Sylvain Leichti.

whole life! Give them two twenty-hour shifts and they don't even get it! In Africa you work less and less as you are promoted, it's the beginning of your retirement." Fuming, he left with a firm handshake to yet another crisis meeting about the chaotic north.

In Sector North around Kidal, the mission's clay feet were already wobbling. Here, low-ranking African soldiers—especially Chadians and Guineans—had been chucked in at the deep end. The mission's groaning civilian supports system failed to provide them even with fresh food and water, and salaries were being withheld because of bureaucratic glitches.[27] The troops had no armored vehicles, scant supplies, and little protection against the dangers that now stirred in the hinterland. Meanwhile, reports and rumors circulated of African peacekeepers on a bender, of prostitutes galore, of looting and attacks on civilians—and even of Chadian soldiers killing their own superiors.[28]

Carl-Magnus, as head of the Swedish contingent, was well aware of his African counterparts' dire state. "For a soldier from Burkina Faso, his sunglasses will cost more than anything else on his person," he noted. This lack of equipment was deadly: "If eight guys from Burkina travel in an open pickup and get ambushed and shot at, then all eight will die." By contrast, the Swedes were Afghanistan-hardened special forces who, like their Dutch counterparts in Gao, were equipped with armored cars, surveillance drones, and the latest weaponry. Besides the resource gap, the Swedes' task of intelligence gathering was itself much less risky than the patrolling duties of the Africans, relegated as the latter were to the dangerous northeastern regions. Intel is normally "cold, wet, boring, and monotonous," Carl-Magnus quipped, "and now it will be hot, dry, and monotonous."

One independent report would later lambast the "two-tier" mission of MINUSMA, in which European special forces came in with advanced equipment yet were assigned highly specialized tasks and enjoyed specific "caveats" for where their troops could deploy.[29] This meant the mainstay of MINUSMA frontline duties, especially accompanying convoys, fell to the Africans. "The willingness of the Chadian and Guinean governments to send their troops to some of the most exposed parts of Mali thus stands in stark contrast to the risk-aversion of their European counterparts," the report said—with severe consequences for the mission, and for the fate of the soldiers.[30]

Carl-Magnus himself had little patience with the fears of attacks drummed up in the media back home. Instead he was willing to take some risk: "We are not half as worried as any enemies would be; in firefights I think no one is capable of defeating us."

Meanwhile, the peacekeepers stuck near the front lines were frequently accused by locals of simply doing nothing, or not doing enough, or doing the wrong things altogether. UN-provided water bottles were sold on the black market in Mali's northern towns, yet while such supplies exited the camp gates, many Malians said the soldiers rarely did—something confirmed by Monica once she was up in Kidal, where she kept track on who came and went from the camp, trying to press military chiefs into action.

"The Africans among them come here with deals," said Moussa ag Assaleh, a Malian employee of a Western humanitarian NGO, elaborating on the widespread local rumors about inaction.[31] "They might pay 20 percent to their boss [for being sent on mission], so why would they take any risks? They have all come here to live, not to die." Amid such accusations, it was clear most Malians had had enough of the international presence already.

Something similar was happening in the aid world, too, and Moussa was one of the workers letting me in on this darker side to the humanitarian division of labor across Mali's map. A young Tuareg from Timbuktu, with short-cropped hair and a skinny frame, Moussa was himself displaced from conflict. His well-to-do family had fled the onward march of the jihadists in 2012, arriving in Bamako like thousands of other northerners. Yet soon enough he had set out for the north again, now as a humanitarian, working with the thousands still displaced or trying to return home. Stationed in Gao until that fateful week in May, Moussa had eventually made it out on a UN plane, he explained one day as we drove up the rutted mud road into his Bamako neighborhood. His wry smile failed to hide his frustration with the aid world that employed him and the UN mission that it depended on.

His colleagues in Gao were Malian, and his boss there was from the Ivory Coast on a renewable short-term contract; the head office managers in Bamako, meanwhile, were largely European. Like his siblings—one brother was also stationed in Mali's north, while his elder sister worked in Somalia—Moussa was among a growing professional class in the international aid world. They were the well-educated nationals shouldering the risk that the managerial "expats" in Bamako, Nairobi, Dakar, or Geneva were unwilling to face. They were also paid considerably less. "Here, normal [national] staff earn about 500 euros, regional African staff 3,500 euros, and expat staff 5,000 euros," he remarked as we reclined on the cushions of his hilltop home, doing his calculations. You could get about ten Malians for the price of one "international," as the head of UN humanitarian operations in Bamako would later confirm—and that was even before counting the expensive private insurance that covered only the latter group.[32] Moreover, "they put national staff in front, who take on all the risks," Moussa said. "Simply being with a Western organization means you may become a target." He sipped his tea and flashed that wry half-smile again. "Humanitarianism, it's a business like any other."

Ironically, that troubled week in May revealed the largest risk to national aid workers such as Moussa to be their very Malian-ness—or, more specifically, their ethnicity. By the Monday after the Kidal governorate killings, he recalled, black northerners had started attacking lighter-skinned Tuareg and Arabs in Gao. A friend at the UN gave Moussa a number to call at MINUSMA for emergencies, but the peacekeepers offered no protection; instead, they remained ensconced in their camps. Moussa went off to stay in a guesthouse, hoping to ride out the storm. "Neither MINUSMA nor Serval will protect anyone," he frowned. "They are just there for their own security."

As the Malian forces were routed that Wednesday, angry patriots hatched plans for a large protest for the next day in Gao, and Tuareg residents started fleeing the city. "We knew that the manhunt would begin," said Moussa. "Our difficulty was Thursday, to survive the day was our only goal." That morning, as even the Malian administrators took flight, "we woke up without a bank, without administration." Yet suddenly the government softened its tone against the UN. Protests were called off; on national television, a minister wheeled out in front of the cameras tried to make amends. UN flights started departing, and Moussa made it out of Gao. He felt safer in Bamako—for now. "Here you can hide in a friend's house and no one will find you," he said. For the many thousands of northerners still displaced to Mali's south and to neighboring countries, planned returns were called off. After the previous year's respite from conflict, danger was yet again pounding on the door.

The risks to aid workers in northern Mali were tied up with the UN's bunkered withdrawal. As Moussa, Miranda, and other humanitarians insisted, MINUSMA had failed to guarantee security either for locals or for aid agencies, which had to enter the danger zone "at their own risk and peril," in Moussa's words. The mixed nature of the UN mission added to the risks: as humanitarians kept complaining, it dangerously blurred the lines with the French counterterror operations. Yet simply blaming the UN for the risks was, again, a little too easy. The Malian state's administrators were themselves anything but keen to return up north after that violent May. Meanwhile, the withdrawal of senior NGO staff from the front line meant that their operations were increasingly out of sight and out of control, which brought further risks for locals and internationals alike.

As I spoke to Malian community leaders I kept hearing tales of flamboyant fraud of almost farcical levels—accusations that were often hard to prove yet that would be repeated with variations by aid workers themselves, *sotto voce* and with sardonic smiles, throughout my stay in Mali. I heard how in Gao a consortium of local notables had started monopolizing aid, with each layer of officialdom taking its share of the spoils; instead of reaching those in need, supplies were used to stock neighborhood delegates' own corner boutiques. I heard about NGO leaders up north serving as contact points for the rebels, and about big UN partners skimming off funds without oversight. I heard how in northern towns residents with well-connected relatives gamed the system by splitting their houses into separate "homes" via makeshift partitions—and so securing one aid kit per room. In an ambitious initiative for counting and assisting Mali's internally displaced people (IDPs), funded by the International Organization of Migration, those displaced seethed at the false beneficiaries gaining in their name. "We've received nothing! It's better to stop!" exclaimed one IDP leader, her finger aloft as she sat on a tattered mattress in her rented home in southern Bamako. "The humanitarian question in Mali, it's really something very bitter."[33]

While local leaders raised their voices to little avail, and workers such as Moussa just flashed a resigned smile at the pilfering, donors were also not amused. "We see cartons of Plumpy'nut [a nutritional supplement] in the market of Gao, and the supplies that are distributed just disappear!" exclaimed Patrick Barbier, the head of the EU humanitarian aid body in Mali. His round spectacles and short curls betrayed his past on the front line of French humanitarianism, and he had little patience with Western NGO managers' "self-limitation": "It's security that justifies everything." While he carried out field trips to remote regions, NGO administrators stayed behind in Bamako with its endless meetings, parties, and paper-pushing. "They eat all resources, produce reports, and create new little strategies," he said, echoing Malian complaints about the inaction of peacekeepers. "They have to justify their salaries!" And as with UN soldiers, this created a huge acceptance problem. "Who was attacked when [rebels] entered Menaka?" Patrick asked, referring to the armed groups' entry into this northern town after the Malian forces' routing in Kidal. The NGOs that had failed to build any local acceptance, he said. "It's the ones that don't have a grounding in the community that are being attacked." Not only had risk aversion in head office increased financial and program risk in operations and stirred resentment among African workers and soldiers—it had also fomented *political* risk as seen during the protests, and a higher risk of being attacked for the UN and NGOs alike.[34]

Again, we see how a "dangerized" perception of local worlds in terms of menace resulted in the endangerment of mission objectives as well as of individual aid workers, peacekeepers, and locals. The trend worried not just humanitarians with an ear to the ground but also well-placed UN insiders. As one adviser to the UN deputy secretary-general told me in New York in late 2014, "If the price to be up north is essentially that we have to hunker down in bunkers, then what's the point?" No stabilization and no policing could happen from within the fortress, he said. As for UN civilians and aid agencies, the world body's second-in-charge in Mali, David Gressly, made the same point as we met in the fortified compound of the UN Development Programme in southern Bamako. "We need to get out of this complacency," he said, referring to the comfortable remote-aid arrangement that had developed across Mali's divided geography. Gressly's task, as it had been in South Sudan before, was to press for more senior international staff to head into the north—yet this was to prove hard work as risks kept mounting. Miranda, my aid worker friend who was among the few Bamako-based internationals to regularly venture north, was all too aware of the trade-offs. A kidnap would pose a "huge problem for everyone else's work," she said, stalling operations while all NGOs took stock of the risks. Other aid operatives agreed, with one saying that "not sending internationals sends the wrong message," yet that "if an expat is kidnapped, it will sink a program, if it's a national staff [member], probably not. It's harsh to say but it's the reality."[35]

Soon after the May protests had receded came the deadly incident that aid agencies had long feared: two Malians working for Miranda's NGO, itself a humanitarian partner to a UN agency up north, were killed when their UN-branded vehicle was blown up by a remote device. A week later, a suicide bomber rammed his way into a crumbling peacekeeping camp, leaving four Chadian soldiers dead. In the coming months, attacks on peacekeepers escalated via suicide bombs, lobbed missiles, and IEDs placed on roads.

Remote-controlled operations may not have enabled effective control over the northern hinterland—that much was clear. Yet if we momentarily swap our red-tinted glasses for a cynical pair of specs, we may observe that they were at least quite "successful" in distributing the risks of operating there in a way favorable to the most powerful interveners. Unlike 1990s missions such as the UN Mission in Somalia (UNOSOM), which saw a

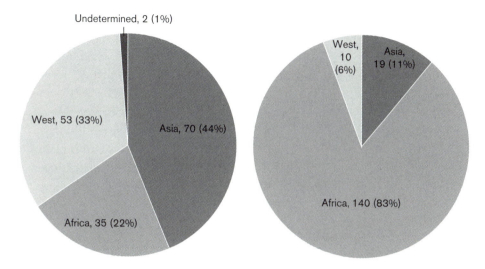

Figure 4. Fatalities in UNOSOM (1990s) and MINUSMA (2010s), by region of origin.

fairly equal division of fatalities among Asian (44 percent), African (22 percent), and Western (33 percent) troop contributors, the mission in Mali was an example not just of the much-touted "Africanization" of peacekeeping but also of Africanized fatalities. By the end of April 2018, there were 169 dead in the mission. Only 10 of them were Western (6 percent); 19 were Asian (11 percent); while 140 were African (83 percent), with 49 of them from one single country—Chad, whose soldiers had manned both the French counterterror front line and the riskiest regions covered by MINUSMA.[36]

It was amid this mounting bloodshed, in January 2015, that the UN peacekeeping chief stepped into the Security Council to deplore the violent attacks. Casualties could mount for only so long before eyebrows started being raised, including briefly by the otherwise so steadfast Chadian government. By this time it was becoming clear that the UN's blue helmets, poised between the resentment of southern Malians for their seeming inaction and renewed targeting by insurgents, had been drawn into the conflict, not as keepers of an elusive peace, but as hapless combatants and soft targets while the French drew down their forces. Instead of distancing themselves from the danger zone, they had been pulled right into it.

Back in early June 2014, Monica's time to move north had finally arrived. As she shared a break from packing and shopping supplies, she confided that, for the first time, she had sent her brother all her financial details before leaving, insurance numbers and so on, "you just never know." Monica was used to the risks, yet amid the Bamako chaos she was getting frustrated. "I have asked myself since I arrived whether this is what I should keep on doing," she said; perhaps this would be her last mission. She talked of UN colleagues with difficult family lives and broken relationships owing to life on the road, as well as of her own story of once packing her bags, ready to leave her itinerant field existence for a faraway love. It had not worked, and she would not do it again. "In future, maybe I'll set up a bar back home," she thought out loud; yet for now the field was all that mattered. In later months, as we caught up on Skype after fresh attacks via suicide bombers or lobbed missiles at the camp gates, her account carried the tagline "in my lovely Kidal."

"It will take time to learn everything," Carl-Magnus had said in his Stockholm office that winter, referring both to Swedish lack of expertise on the Sahel and to the harsh conditions up north. He was in it for the long haul, as he had been in his previous Balkan and Afghan postings, yet he feared that risk-averse politicians back home would not be. "I hope everyone will be patient and recognize that this will take time." By March 2015, he had at least found his northern joy in Camp Nobel outside Timbuktu. Photos on the military's Mali blog showed a sunburnt Carl-Magnus ringing a Norwegian-cast church bell for the faithful African and Scandinavian soldiers. As he rang that bell, he may have heard—if listening closely enough—how it echoed down the ages, to the time of the precolonial explorers and their fateful approach to the "argent streets" and hidden dangers of Timbuktu.

·   ·   ·   ·   ·

This chapter is entitled "The Timbuktu Syndrome," and as we now close our story of Mali's messy interventions it is worth dwelling on the term's two components. First, the name Timbuktu. Today's global dangers map onto those from the colonial and precolonial past, as the insurgent groups themselves knew when they invoked nineteenth-century jihads against the French colonizers as their heritage.[37] We will soon delve further into the wider historical mapping of danger, yet for now let us note how, in Western capitals, the Sahara and its ancient outpost of Timbuktu have long served as repositories of murky fears and desires. The travel writer Bruce Chatwin once wrote that there are two Timbuktus: one "a tired caravan town where the Niger bends into the Sahara," the other "altogether more fabulous, a legendary city in a never-never land." This was the "Timbuktu of the mind" that Caillié, Laing, and their forerunners transmitted back to their avid readers in the salons of Paris and London.[38] Worthy of long expeditions, fine prizes, and great sacrifices, this distant place yields its truths only slowly to the most intrepid of explorers. And no one knew this better than René Caillié, the Frenchman, as he lay disguised as a Muslim in the hold of a canoe snaking its way up the Niger River in the spring of 1828, hiding from Tuareg bandits who wanted the rich Moor's money.

Much like the colonial offices and geographical societies that once lured Caillié, Laing, and their predecessors toward the desert, the interveners of the early twenty-first century are obsessed with the dangers and rewards of the "Timbuktu of the mind." However, as France, the United States, and the UN send in the drones and as the "international community" deploys remotely into the Malian north, they would do well to recall some basic lessons from those nineteenth-century explorers. Caillié managed to enter, map, and escape from Timbuktu only after years on the road, months of learning Arabic and local customs among the nomads of the Sahel, and long tribulations with neither entourage nor comforts. By contrast, Mali's interveners of the early twenty-first century depend on middlemen for the hard graft and heavy lifting, much as did the colonizers who followed in Caillié's wake, as well as some of the well-equipped yet ultimately futile British missions that preceded him. Today's top-tier interveners distance themselves from the African forces and aid workers on the front lines. They flit between near-identical missions in the world's danger zones, with little local knowledge to anchor their efforts. They pour money into these zones with little oversight over who receives it, who distributes it, who gains and loses. The drawbridge to the international compound has been pulled up; its lines of division are increasingly traced in terms of risk and danger.

If Timbuktu resonates historically as a signifier of remoteness both desired and feared, the term *syndrome* carries more recent historical echoes. After the Vietnam war, US politicians and military figures bemoaned the "Vietnam syndrome": as the failure of mass ground offensives became evident and as US body bags kept being sent back, the political will to risk American lives in insecure regions diminished. Things have changed since then. Aerial bombardment at a safe distance, combined with intense "media management," has come to define latter-day Western military escapades.[39] After the brutal legacies in Iraq and Afghanistan, some commentators even glimpsed an Obama-era revival of the Vietnam syndrome in the "fundamental reluctance to commit American military power anywhere in the world, unless it is absolutely necessary to protect the national interests of the country."[40] Yet rather than such a rerun of the past, Mali's international missions suggest that new modes of intervention are emerging in relation to changing political and military priorities, triggering a new syndrome of sorts. Thanks to a concern with elusive transnational threats—notably migration, drugs, and terror—Mali has pulled in Western actors, and with them the UN; yet this pull has been accompanied by a deeper disengagement on the ground. The push-pull of dangerization, as powerful interveners circle the danger zone while obsessively peering into the darkness, is what I gloss here as a Timbuktu syndrome. In this syndrome, Timbuktu itself serves not just as a key site of intervention in Mali's restive north but also as a revived symbol of absolute remoteness in the Western "geography of imagination."[41] International actors obsess over controlling and monitoring the Timbuktus of the world map of intervention. As they resist fully entering these putative danger zones, they try their best to keep them at arm's length. In this way, they foist remoteness upon insecure regions, yet in the process these regions' pulling power paradoxically grows. Danger is in this way reproduced not just on the grand level of politics, where it remains a supremely useful tool for combatants and governments alike, but also in the daily toil of interveners and aid workers, as seen from the bunkers of Mali's north to the tense expat geography of Bamako.

Treating the dangerized relationship of intervention as a syndrome helps us see that simply pouring more resources into "solving the problem"—as Western donors were doing in 2018, through backing for a regional counterterror force—may in fact entrench it. On its crudest level, this intractability is at work whenever risk aversion triggers larger risks, whether financial, physical, or political. We see this in local resentment and mistrust of aid and peacekeeping operations; in the rising attacks on underequipped African soldiers; and in the mounting protests against the international presence. In early 2015, as such protests unfolded yet again in Mali, peacekeepers fired into the crowds outside the MINUSMA camp in Gao, killing three. Meanwhile insecurity kept spreading as the peace process between rebels and government faltered, eventually reaching Bamako itself. In March 2015, a masked gunman fired into a popular nightclub in the capital, leaving five dead; the following autumn, the Radisson was attacked—the very hotel one Swedish official had recommended to me because of its armed guards, who served little purpose against well-armed jihadists looking for a high-profile target. As a response, the government announced a state of emergency, which kept being extended. In March 2016 the EUTM's fenced-off hotel was next on the hit list. Meanwhile, jihadist groups were splintering into al Qaeda and ISIS-affiliated factions, which clashed with similarly fast-shifting pro-government militias in the Niger-Mali borderlands. Mali's divided map of danger was being redrawn, bringing the long-anticipated terror threat right into the expat bubble of Bamako, as well as mounting attacks on civilians in the central regions.[42]

Our story so far may seem too dismissive of the interveners' efforts, but as we have seen, many among them were acutely aware of the limitations and did their best to overcome them. Monica had been sent back to Bamako by late 2015, amid escalating violence against the UN camp in Kidal. "They attacked us in October [2014], then in November, then in January," she said over a shaky Skype line one day, matter-of-factly reeling off a list of IEDs hitting the camp. Amid a complete lack of support, she had had to manage everything inside, from the dismal water provision and the rice-and-goat diet to the task of pushing African peacekeeping chiefs to carry out more patrols. "Yes, I might be small, I might be white, I might be a woman," she said, and moreover she didn't speak French, but she got her way. "It's very hard to gain the respect of the military forces, but I did it! I never imagined I would go to the desert to mount a military camp and confront that kind of insecurity," she said, a genuine sense of joy in her voice. She had been happy in Kidal, even though she could not leave the camp. Now, back in Bamako, she moved only between office and home because of the risks, with not a single restaurant outing to interrupt the routine.

Carl-Magnus eventually returned to Stockholm, his mission over and his fame undimmed: as we spoke, he told me of his forty-plus speaking engagements since his return, in New York, in Vienna, in London. Sweden had succeeded in its goal with the deployment—securing a rotating Security Council seat, untainted by any deaths in the Sahara—and so had Carl-Magnus in his. Reflecting on his mission, he insisted that he had pushed beyond the "zero-risk" vision of his headquarters, using the strategic gap of MINUSMA to his advantage. Bending security rules, Swedish soldiers had helped defend Timbuktu against attacks, he said, showing that they were not just gadget-equipped "tourists" (as some rebels labeled the Europeans) and that they were willing to shoulder some risks. He then buzzed the Swedes' surveillance drone over a rebel hideout outside town before driving there in full armory and warning their leader, a former New York taxi driver, that there would be consequences if attacks continued. "He called me *mon colonel dude*," Carl-Magnus laughed. Yet amid limited advances of this kind, the Swedish media pounced on any small risk: at one point, they wrought prominent headlines out of the lack of food in the camp, blaming Carl-Magnus, who insisted provisions were a "zero-sum game" as the Swedes could not consume all resources meant for Timbuktu's African and Bangladeshi soldiers. "We can't shower ourselves in *gravlax* every day!" he told me, exasperated by the media's risk obsession.

Yet for all the individual efforts to overcome the divisions of Mali's map, dangerized intervention kept generating lopsided tragedies. Draped peacekeeper coffins were honored in Bamako by the Danish force commander while UN communications officers in New York churned out press releases, condemnations, tweets, and condolences. The attacks kept sending to their graves not just UN soldiers but also Malian forces and former rebels encamped in the north as part of the faltering Malian peace agreement that darker forces wanted to break at any price.

.   .   .   .   .

The Timbuktu syndrome, unlike its Vietnam counterpart, did not involve complete withdrawal. Instead, it kept alive an illusion of remote control over Mali's restive north. On the one hand, it did so by converting uncertainty and diffuse danger into risk: manageable, calculable, and knowable. On the other hand, it did so by way of an acute amnesia, as the interveners staggered along without reflecting on the wider historical and political failures that had led to Mali's descent into chaos.

The country's divided geography was in other words only a symptom of a deeper problem besetting interventions across our world map of danger; and it is onto this wider terrain that we must now tread. Back in the summer of 2014, I caught a glimpse of the bigger story in the scrum of Westerners and Malian emigrants at the exit gates of Senou airport. Ahead of me, the stenciled T-shirt stretched across the muscled back of a male passenger—presumably a private security contractor—shouted out in big bold letters: *May the last person to leave Afghanistan turn off the lights.* In its dreadful irony, the T-shirt told a larger story of how a warped mode of intervention had traveled from America's post-9/11 invasions all the way to the Sahel, where it was now wreaking fresh havoc. For the remote controls applied to fearful geographies were tested well before Mali: in Afghanistan, Iraq, and elsewhere in the "war on terror," to which we must now turn.

2 REMOTENESS REMAPPED

So Geographers in Afric-maps
With Savage-Pictures fill their Gaps

Jonathan Swift, *On Poetry*, 1733

Maps are weapons.

Dennis Wood, *"How Maps Work,"* 1992

One sweltering September afternoon many years ago, I was sitting among my Bamako neighbors on a plastic string chair, sipping sweet Sahelian tea. "Diarra! *I sigi!*" *Please sit!* I'm pretty sure one of my host's friends and helpers, Diallo from Dogon country, had cried out, rising into his customary falsetto, as I had approached him and his friends under the shade of the lone tree on our mud-packed road. I must have responded in kind, as I did during those interminable afternoons: "Please sit!" "No, you sit!" I tried and tried to choose the wooden box or the chair with missing plastic strings, but to no avail: in the battle over hospitality, the guest always loses. Amadou Diarra the *toubab* got the choice spot, and as soon as I sank into the wiry seat as best I could, the jokes about my fellow adopted Diarras would begin, especially if one of the Diarras' joking relations, the Traorés, happened to be present. Diarra, have you had your fill of bushmeat yet? Ah, Diarra, you flatulent beast! Everyone would roar with laughter, someone would shift the teapot on the coals, and another round would be served, sweeter each time.

But I digress. It was on one of those days, in 2001 after the rains and dust clouds of summer had settled and the skies above Bamako had cleared, that the news rattled out over our tea-drinking clique courtesy of Radio France Internationale: the Twin Towers had fallen.

As the heat subsided I set out ambling through central Bamako's streets, bewildered. I still remember glancing through the open doors to a French-style café, set behind market stalls bulging with imported Chinese trinkets, to see the towers fall on a TV screen, again and again, on a surreal repeat from another, distant world. As soon as we had gathered our wits, my host, a Soninké trader and small-time politician, insisted that I write a letter of condolence to New York mayor Rudolph Giuliani. After I had taken down his message on ricepaper-thin airmail, Mr. Doucouré sealed the envelope and wrote *Monsieur le Maire de New York* on it in a scrawling hand. Neighbors and friends pitied the victims in New York, among them Diallo, who also worried about what the aftermath of the attacks would bring. "Now poor people will suffer," he said, shaking his head as he fretted over impending US military action somewhere in the world.

It came, and fast. On September 14, Congress gave George W. Bush sweeping powers to use military force against the perpetrators of 9/11. Three days later, Bush's Presidential Finding authorized covert activities by the CIA to kill or capture those responsible, "effectively abrogating the existing US ban on assassinations."[1] By October, as I was back in my London lecture hall, the United States was invading Afghanistan, and the first lethal drones unleashed their Hellfire missiles. By December, the Taliban had been driven from power, and US military bases were scattering across the Afghan landscape. Soon this world of terror and dirty wars was reshaping our political maps in ways I and my fellow students and lecturers did not fully grasp in 2001, caught up as we were in the moment of invasions and protestations. In fact, I don't think most of us—scholars, politicians, media commentators, citizens from Bamako to Oxford—fully understand this shift almost two decades on.

One small slice of our world-in-the-making lingers in my mind as I look back at this heady time of war and of my own political awakening. Amid the frenzy of the 2001 invasion, we had heard that bin Laden was hiding in a place called Tora Bora, deep in the mountainous border regions of Afghanistan. To my young ears, it sounded like a joke—a name from a Donald Duck cartoon of weird foreign lands with rhyming names. Enterprising journalists, not content with just an exotic name, went whole hog on the lurid dangers by rendering the lair of bin Laden as a comic-strip fantasy of tunnels, ducts, and advanced equipment. This vision was keenly exploited by Donald Rumsfeld, the US defense secretary, who, when interviewed by NBC in early December 2001, said that "Afghanistan is not the only country that has gone underground. Any number of countries have gone underground." In one journalistic account, Tora Bora's lairs were said to reach as far underground as the World Trade Center had stood over ground, in an inversion of the world. Tora Bora, in the media's and Rumsfeld's rendering, was an abomination—an "ants' nest" of terrorists, cinematic in its villainy. In the battle of Tora Bora in December 2001, the equally cinematic denouement to the saga, US special forces moved in but found no bin Laden amid the dead bodies. They also "found no underground fortress, no hydro-electric power plant, no 2,000-room hotel, no ant farm, no iron doors, no ventilating shafts."[2] By May 2013, when the Afghan invasion had morphed into the Americans' longest war, President Obama still echoed the Tora Bora tales as he motivated his administration's drone attacks against insurgents with these words: "They take refuge in tribal regions. They hide in caves and walled compounds. They train in empty deserts and rugged mountains."[3] In remote Tora Bora and its long-tail aftermath, fantasy interplayed with fact to render up a global enemy ensconced in the world's margins and depths.

After the last chapter's visit to ground zero of intervention, it is now time to lift our gaze and take in the global cartography of danger of which the beleaguered Mali missions form a part. We will skip across the blanked-out spaces on our maps and the story they tell us about how powerful forces perceive and intervene upon world margins. And we will see how, at a time when the geopolitical earth is trembling, particular kinds of remoteness are being remapped onto distant corners of the formerly colonized world, where they mark peculiar fault lines of power.

We begin our story of the global map of danger on that day in September 2001. Bush Jr. and his reaction to the terror attacks is well-trodden terrain, yet we must revisit this moment—not to emphasize it as a divider forever stamped on political time as "9/11" but rather to see it as part of a reinvention of older tales of faraway danger. The "war on terror" in its various iterations exemplifies how external interveners have come to reinforce geographical difference at a time of supposed global connectivity, reviving imaginaries of safety and danger, of metropoles and blank spaces, inherited from colonial and precolonial eras.

Remapping the world entails remaking it. Before the dust had settled over Ground Zero, the reality makers were already at work remapping the world for their own purposes, drawing on plans for a "new American century" and full military dominance forged in neoconservative circles in the Clinton years.[4] Less than a year after the launch of GWOT (*gee-wot*, the "global war on terror") and as the White House was gearing up for the Iraq invasion, the dark prince of Bush's White House, Karl Rove, spelled this out in an infamous rant to a probing journalist, which it is worth revisiting: "We're an empire now, and when we act, we create our own reality. And while you're studying that reality—judiciously, as you will—we'll act again, creating other new realities, which you can study too, and that's how things will sort out. We're history's actors . . . and you, all of you, will be left to just study what we do."[5]

The world of endless, nebulous war that beckoned seemed, to both Rove and his detractors, to be a radical break with the past. Yet the Afghan invasion of 2001, the starting point for the story traced on these pages, was in many ways simply a reinvention of much earlier conjurings and mappings of global danger. *We're an empire now:* as the Machiavellian Rove himself indicated, in the post-9/11 years colonial and precolonial stories of the world were being repurposed, reinvented, and remapped, bringing new terrors to distant territories supposed to be harboring them.

·   ·   ·   ·   ·

In the early twenty-first century, the world is being remapped, but not without a fight. Cartographic battles pitch the brigades of connectivity against the forces of doom, danger, and disconnect. The optimists see the world as a dense web of connectivity, for good and ill. "Connectivity has replaced division as the new paradigm of global organization," says TED talker and jet-set intellectual Parag Khanna in his *Connectography* ("a must-read for the next president," says former US defense secretary Chuck Hagel on the cover, a recommendation probably gone unheeded by Trump's book club).[6] What's more, Khanna and his fellow connectographers have the smooth and shining imagery to prove it. Theirs is the world that blinks and glimmers to us on seductive maps of global flight paths, power grids, Internet connectivity, financial transactions, international mobility, and global corporate risk.[7] But if the cartographers of connectivity have the most impressive maps, the devil has the best tunes and imagery. Tora Bora trumps telecoms grids. And so unfolds a carto-battle among Panglossians and doom peddlers in which both, in a sense, come out winning, one kind of cartography feeding off the other.

In the liberal wave of optimism at the long fag-end of the Cold War, the evangelists of globalization had proclaimed not only the end of History, in Francis Fukuyama's words, but also the end of distance. Among those doing so was Thomas Friedman, the *New York Times* columnist, who on a visit to high-tech India had an epiphany of sorts: the world was now flat. "Here I was in Bangalore," he wrote in a trademark romp, "more than five hundred years after Columbus sailed over the horizon, using the rudimentary navigational technologies of his day, and returned safely to prove definitively that the world was round—and one of India's smartest engineers, trained at his country's top technical institute and backed by the most modern technologies of his day, was essentially telling me that the world was *flat*—as flat as the screen on which he can host a meeting of his whole global supply chain." If the voyage of Columbus had once inaugurated "Globalization 1.0," Friedman said, "right around the year 2000 we entered a whole new era: Globalization 3.0. Globalization 3.0 is shrinking the world from a size small to a size tiny and flattening the playing field at the same time."[8]

Friedman's blustering style has generated some well-deserved spoofs ("Yesterday's news from Uruguay is earth-flattening, and it raises questions about whether there might just be light at the end of the tunnel," reads one specimen),[9] yet he was far from alone in striving to find a language apt for a world of borderless financial trades and outsourcing chains. While he resorted to metaphors of a flat earth, cartographers of globalization have used the graphic tools of their trade to send similar messages about the great promises of connectivity. On their maps, even the remotest parts of the flattening globe are now plugging in. In a Google-financed project to bring airborne Internet to "rural and remote areas worldwide," maps track the flight path of high-altitude Wi-Fi balloons as they glide from South America across to the Pacific by way of southern Africa.[10] Inland in Africa, plans for a transcontinental highways network now trace a brightly colored route from Lagos to Algiers via the Sahara

Desert. Internet maps show undersea cables wiring African coastlines to the global information highway, and China's new "Silk Road" renders visible sea connections to the continent while linking up remotest Central Asia to a rebooted economic order.

Some connectographers may see strategic risks in who heads such projects, who benefits from them, and whether the flat earth's surface is tilted in favor of the powerful. More subtle voices worry about risks and contagion effects, often drawing on complexity theory and language borrowed from biology—the world as a nervous system, in which threats in one distant location may swiftly set nerves jangling in core regions. What the connectographers tend to agree on is that, with some political fine-tuning and innovation, the benefits of the connected world with its smooth tarmac and glimmering grids will by far outstrip the dangers.[11] Get used to this world of ceaseless motion and build "resilience" against its risks, Khanna, Friedman, and their fellow travelers suggest, or you may well find yourself or your country scattered like roadkill along the global highway.[12]

If these are the "optimists," in the other camp are the doom-mongers who draw maps of global distance, on which connectivity—when acknowledged—is depicted as a threat, even as they depend on it for their lines of business. In the advanced control rooms of security companies that I have visited over the years, interactive wall charts track risks to wealthy corporate clients, using Twitter clouds to pinpoint real-time dangers in faraway lands. In foreign ministries, border agencies, and police organizations, I have seen digital and whiteboard maps on which sharp arrowheads point outwards from the global danger zones: migrants, terror, conflict, and drugs infiltrating from the outside world. In government travel advice offices from London to Ottawa, civil servants keep removing pieces from the global jigsaw with their proliferating "advice against all travel" or "advice against all but essential travel." In the editorial offices of policy journals and news magazines, security pundits join the fray by pinpointing one "fragile state" after another before proceeding to connect the dots of global danger. Besides these sophisticated cartographers of doom, others of a cruder kind showcase their wares on the evening news, in portrayals of the Sahara or parts of Central Asia as dark red stains peopled by outsized jihadi fighters with *Mad Max* weaponry, rather than as stopovers on continent-wide infrastructure projects.

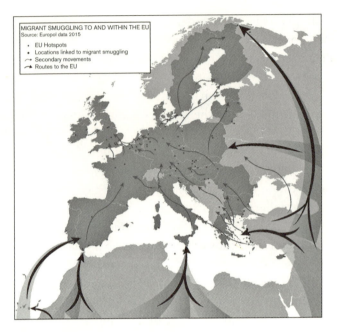

MIGRANT SMUGGLING TO AND WITHIN THE EU
Source: Europol data 2015

  · EU Hotspots
  · Locations linked to migrant smuggling
  ↝ Secondary movements
  ↝ Routes to the EU

Map 6. Map of migrant smuggling routes by Europol, the
European law enforcement agency, 2015. © Europol.

The catalyst for the doom mappers' innovation, much as for their connectographer counterparts, was the end of the Cold War and its promise of perennial US domination. As the red menace vanished, conservative voices of the Samuel Huntington kind lost no time in announcing the West's new geopolitical Others—or even its new "monsters." In an influential *Foreign Affairs* piece, the neoconservatives William Kristol and Robert Kagan used this very term as they argued, pace 1820s president John Quincy Adams, that America must "go abroad in search of monsters to destroy." The alternative, they admonished their fellow conservatives, was "to leave monsters on the loose, ravaging and pillaging to their hearts' content, as Americans stand by and watch."[13] Their exhortation to go find the monsters enlivened the neoconservative Project for a New American Century, from which the coming Bush administration drew much intellectual force.

Kristol and Kagan were not alone in conjuring up monsters. Another doom mapper with a good strategic eye was the journalist Robert Kaplan, who had similarly relished the chance to cast a pall of insecurity over the early days of the post–Cold War era. In his (in)famous piece for the *Atlantic* in 1994, "The Coming Anarchy," Kaplan set the tone for post–Cold War anxieties over the poor non-Western world and its lurking dangers. His case study of global anarchy was our old haunt, West Africa: if this was a flat earth, he admonished us in a preemptive strike at Friedman and his ilk, it was one where vectors of disease and danger spread uncontrollably:

> West Africa is becoming the symbol of worldwide demographic, environmental, and societal stress, in which criminal anarchy emerges as the real "strategic" danger. Disease, overpopulation, unprovoked crime, scarcity of resources, refugee migrations, the increasing erosion of nation-states and international borders, and the empowerment of private armies, security firms, and international drug cartels are now most tellingly demonstrated through a West African prism. . . . To remap the political earth the way it will be a few decades hence—as I intend to do in this article—I find I must begin with West Africa.[14]

Kaplan's "remapping of the political earth" caught the eye of the Clinton administration, and it was not hard to see why.[15] It unveiled a shadow world of risks to accompany the glimmering map of global connectivity, and so wedded the connectographers' promise of prosperity with hardheaded strategic purpose. It warned that while globalization might bring a borderless world of instant connection, this world was also ripe for the spread of criminal danger. Like Kristol and Kagan's monsters, it allowed for the scripting of a coherent story for US foreign policy in the post-Soviet era, as scholars have noted.[16] Criminal anarchy was now haunting "failed" and "fragile" states, the story went, and the US hegemon needed to "stabilize" these godforsaken parts of the world.[17] In these ways, Kaplan and his fellow cartographers helped shift military, political, and media focus to the wild areas lying beyond the superhighways of the globalized era. Their monstrous cartographies would prove to be the inspiration for other doom mappers who, in the post-9/11 world, would have free rein to rethink the political earth, to draw its areas of light and shadow, green and red, connection and disconnection.

·   ·   ·   ·   ·

On September 11, 2001, "The world's wild zones and safe zones collided over New York City."[18] Fear was brought to the "homeland." Yet this fear was also invigorating for right-wing forces, who saw it as stirring Americans out of the liberal consumerist slumber so despised by the likes of Kristol and Kagan. Political theorist Corey Robin paraphrased this political posture in his *Fear: The History of a Political Idea*—"Fear restored to us the clarifying knowledge that evil exists, making moral deliberate action possible." As in earlier periods of historical upheaval, fear could be mobilized as a "delightful horror," the red and orange terror alerts stirring the American beast into action. Some of history's actors, of the Rove variety, saw this as a supreme political opportunity: for the nation "to be in thrall, perpetually, to fear."[19]

Fear came to be organized in a peculiar spatial fashion, recasting our cartographic battles. While the press, politicians, and much of the public saw a wild Other pounding at the gates, bringing Third World destruction to the "capital of the world," experts were busy applying modern geographical techniques to securing the "homeland" and visualizing any spot of risk or vulnerability. Expert and populist cartographies are each other's inverse, as geographers Derek Gregory and Allan Pred note: "One conjured up wild spaces, the other safe spaces." To them, both are "failures of geographical imagination," yet that mattered little to reality makers such as Rove.[20] These cartographies—alternately popular and scientific, fear-laden and reassuring—are not mere representations of the world, Gregory and Pred remind us; rather, they "enter directly into its constitution (and destruction)." Joined up, these two models for mapping the world have proven a formidable weapon indeed.

Let us spool ahead to one example of weaponized mapping from the latest stage of the Afghan war. *It feels like the whole wide world is raining down on you,* croons country singer Toby Keith as a black-and-white map rears into view on *Fox & Friends* one day in April 2017. On it, Afghanistan's mountain regions appear as a blur of rocky terrain that suddenly dissolves into a great black patch—the impact of the largest non-nuclear weapon ever used in combat, unleashed by Trump and his forces in a hail of fire. *Brought to you courtesy of the red, white and blue,* the soundtrack intones as the camera pans to the studio sofa. "At least thirty-six ISIS fighters have lost their lives," the host says as the country voice gives way to a guitar solo.

"That's what freedom looks like, that's the red white and blue," says the female cohost before introducing their mustachioed studio visitor, Trump's friend Geraldo Rivera, who adds in joy: "My favorite thing in the sixteen years I've been here at Fox News is watching bombs drop on bad guys."[21]

More than two decades on from 9/11, it is fair to say, the connectographers are losing out to the doom-mongers, and to the nationalists and wall builders trailing in their wake. Or, more appropriately, we may say that the connectographers' once-optimistic vision of a connected earth is now being repurposed to promote danger and distance. In an age of full military and corporate mapping of distant lands, in which "the third world [is] offering up its data for first-world consumption," two kinds of cartography are coming together under the sign of global danger: connective and distanced, optimistic and doom-laden, scientific and popular.[22] This is a time when a detailed topographical aerial shot of the Afghan hillsides can be obliterated as a site of mute evil, and on country-crooning prime time to boot.

Globalization may have promised a borderless, flat world, and in some ways it has surely delivered. Yet geography is at the same time roaring back with a vengeance. The world map is creasing. Instead of a two-dimensional flat earth, our world may be better depicted as a rugged terrain of alternating connections and disconnections, of highland plateaus and rugged escarpments. Our times of vast cartographic reach for militaries and marketers is also a time when blank spaces on the map are reemerging.

·   ·   ·   ·   ·

I am not alone in being fascinated by world maps present and past: the stories they tell and those they don't. As a boy I drew my own maps of invented, faraway lands, fantasizing about their inhabitants. Reading *Lord of the Rings* and *The Hobbit,* I followed Tolkien's dotted lines from the safety of the Shire to the depths of Mordor and the lairs of dragons across deliciously jagged mountain ranges. Then, in my teenage years, before hitchhiking to Asia from my own Shire of suburban Sweden and long before embarking on anthropological fieldwork in West Africa, I would trace routes across the pages of our family atlas, lingering on the rugged folds of mountains and the red blots of exotic cities I knew I had to visit: Karakoram and Khyber; Lahore, Varanasi, and Timbuktu.

The atlases I had traced my hand across as a travel-thirsty teenager were by the 1990s already becoming outdated. In a way, they had always been fantasies in their own right—a product of centuries of cartographic labor under the shadows of empire building, nationalism, and the Cold War. Fixed territorial boundaries set decolonizing countries on a checkerboard, each with its own neat national box. On world maps, Europe stood center stage, blown out of proportion, as it has been since Mercator reshaped our vision of the world in the sixteenth century. "Maps are seductive but also dangerous," writes connectographer Khanna: "Competitive cartography is a centuries-old duel as map-makers promote nationalistic versions of reality."[23]

Cartography is power, critical geographers tell us, and one source of maps' authority and allure is their capacity to convey stories of the world. This is also, incidentally, why writers and scholars love to consult and describe them. As Robert Louis Stevenson reflected upon his own invented map of Treasure Island in the 1880s, he wrote of how "the future characters of the book began to appear there visibly among imaginary woods; and their brown faces and bright weapons peeped out upon me from unexpected quarters, as they passed to and fro, fighting, and hunting treasure, on these few square inches of a flat projection."[24] The Treasure Island map served as a conduit for the author to imagine alluring, savage, distant lands. I must have sensed this "soft power" of maps as an atlas-browsing teenager making up my own tales of future travels along the old hippie trail to Varanasi and further east. Friedman and Kaplan deployed it, too, as they "mapped the political Earth" in radically different (yet interrelated) ways, selling their scenarios to the highest bidder.

I was no doubt afflicted by a benevolent bout of Orientalism as I imagined that traveling east would somehow reshape my young life, projecting adventure outwards from the self.[25] This divide between safety and wild, distant places has a long history in the Western geography of imagination, reaching from Kaplan to Stevenson and beyond.[26] Good and evil, safety and danger, past and present have in Western thought frequently been *spatialized*, that is, mapped unevenly onto the world's terrain.[27] If we travel back in time, nowhere do we see this spatial potential at work better than in the *mappae mundi* of Europe's medieval cartographers. Indeed, scratch our contemporary world maps, and underneath, those medieval stories still peek through.

On the Hereford *mappa mundi,* a medieval thing of beauty kept in a dusky British cathedral, the Christian story unfolds across the vellum's perfect circle of the world. Europe is decentered, Jerusalem is at the bull's-eye, and the Garden of Eden awaits at the outer rim. Fantastical creatures lurk at the edges of this world: the *sciapods,* who have but one single massive foot; the dog-headed *cynocephali;* the snake-eating *troglodites,* who dwell in caves in Africa; and their fellow African *blemmyes,* warlike, headless humanoids with eyes peering out from their chests. Many of the monstrous peoples on medieval *mappae mundi* were inherited from the classical, pre-Christian era; and it often fell on another pre-Christian figure, Alexander the Great, to subdue them. On the magnificent Catalan Atlas of 1375, Alexander barricades the monstrous peoples of Gog and Magog somewhere north of the Caspian mountains in Central Asia.[28] Gog and Magog, the atlas explains, are "very diverse peoples who do not hesitate to eat all kinds of raw meat; for this is the people from which antichrist will come, and their end will be caused by fire that will fall from Heaven and confound them."[29] (Courtesy of the "red, white and blue," we may add, updating this story for the Trump era.)

If narration and fantasy make up one side of the coin of cartographic power, the other side is strategic and realist. Maps reveal the lie of the land, the better to conquer and dominate it. Military mapmakers travel side by side with devout pilgrims, taking their cue from Alexander and his mighty army.[30] Already by the thirteenth century—as the Hereford was drawn—the Carte Pisane, an early sea chart, showed Mediterranean coastlines in astonishing detail. As the military and navigation potential of such maps grew momentously, so did their power to tell stories of the world on their own, unaided by overt myth. Maps from the age of exploration no longer needed the heroism of Alexander or the reassuring circle of Christian knowledge. Instead, the art of cartography itself projected power, as European rulers and diplomats knew when they exhibited their awe-inducing wall maps to visiting potentates from abroad.[31] The hand that drew and the eye that gazed even intruded into the territory of the divine. "Give me a map; then let me see how much / Is left for me to conquer all the world," wrote Christopher Marlowe in the sixteenth-century play *Tamburlaine,* setting the tone not just for the Central Asian emperor Timur but also for the new imperialists waiting in the historical wings.[32] Scholars have noted how, in colonial discourse, sovereignty was to become intimately linked to sight, or as the poetry of eighteenth-century William Cowper had it:

> I am monarch of all I survey
> My right there is none to dispute;
> From the centre all round to the sea,
> I am lord of the fowl and the brute.[33]

The mapping and parsing of distant lands staked out sovereign claims, spheres of influence, markets. The bifurcated world of Europe and its Others drew legal lines across sands and seas, allowing colonizers and conquerors a free hand in their foreign domains.[34] Yet as the colonizers populated their maps with symbols, towns, and roads, the medieval-era fascination with, and fear of, the uncanny Other lingered. In the eighteenth century, geographers traced the word *cannibals* over the empty spaces, seeking to ward off the threat of the unknown by naming it.[35] As empires consolidated, these Others seemed to be brought under control. The nineteenth-century Imperial Federation Map of the World, prepared in time for the colonial exhibition of 1886, was a statement of power at a high tide of empire (beset, however, by fears of Russia's eastward expansion). On it, the world is accurately rendered, all British domains blushing a reddish-pink hue; and along the margins, white explorers stand guard amid tigers and bare-breasted, dark-skinned women.[36]

My ancestors are in that picture, too, peeping out from the foliage behind the Amazons, as it were. Anthropology emerged as a discipline at this time of high colonialism. Early anthropologists had sought to understand the evolution of Man by recourse to those they thought were latter-day representatives of past eras on earth, the "primitive" and "savage" tribes dwelling on empire's margins. Their work exemplified how the blank spaces on the maps were not just sites to conquer and exploit, or places where the uncanny lingered: they were also projects of knowledge. On colonial maps, the blanks yearned to be filled through expeditions, observations, drawings, and diagrams. For the colonizers, much as for the connectographers of our time, the creases and folds of the map had to be flattened, the uncanny driven out and replaced by certainty and perfect knowledge. This drive to fill in the blanks was memorably satirized by Jorge Luis Borges's story of a fictional empire:

> In that Empire, the Art of Cartography attained such Perfection that the map of a single Province occupied the entirety of a City, and the map of the Empire, the entirety of a Province. In time, those Unconscionable Maps no longer satisfied, and the Cartographers Guilds struck a Map of the Empire whose size was that of the Empire, and which coincided point for point with it. . . . In the Deserts of the West, still today, there are Tattered Ruins of that Map, inhabited by Animals and Beggars; in all the Land there is no other Relic of the Disciplines of Geography.[37]

"As much as guns and warships, maps have been the weapons of imperialism," the iconoclastic cartographer Brian Harley once said, echoing the epigraph to this chapter.[38] As Edward Said observed, "It is quite common to hear high officials in Washington and elsewhere speak of changing the map of the Middle East, as if ancient societies and myriad peoples can be shaken up like so many peanuts in a jar."[39] Yet as Harley and Said both recognized, the mapped peoples fought back against the mappers, often using the master's tools. As Britain set out to map colonial India in the Great Trigonometrical Survey of the early nineteenth century, natives pulled up the stakes marking the survey's baseline, frustrating the colonial cartographers' efforts.[40]

As in our GWOT era, the strategic and fantastical aspects of mapping—their hard and soft power—worked at times in tandem and at times at cross-purposes. Karen Lynnea Piper, author of *Cartographic Fictions*, suggests that the colonial map helped set the boundaries of modern human identity, with its residue of the uncanny lurking within. In the British Empire, by the early twentieth century aerial cameras had eliminated the native laborers from the quest to map Mother India, thus neutralizing their acts of resistance.[41] Through conquest and its cartography the sovereign was "pushing out fear from the territory," Piper writes. Yet these eliminations are never perfect. Cartographic anxieties, even paranoias, abound.[42] The blank spaces, and the lure of the unknown, keep haunting our maps. Those pushed out to the margins may return, Piper suggests, like a Freudian symptom repressed under the surface of consciousness.[43]

In short, in the "cartopolitics" of the precolonial and colonial West, the quest to know and dominate difference interacted with a lingering residue of untamable Otherness. This residue kept luring explorers and colonizers to distant lands through the double mapping of danger and desire, scientific and fantastical by turns. To see this at work, we must return to the Sahel and the Sahara, and to the cartographic layers lurking underneath the region's danger-laden present.

·   ·   ·   ·   ·

In 1879, the French government endorsed plans for a trans-Saharan railway, with the aim of connecting their patchwork colonial lands. Like today's trans-Saharan road network, this was a vastly ambitious project—and, to some, quite mad. "The railway would change the whole character of the Sahara, bringing civilization to one of the earth's last areas of wilderness," writes one of today's trans-Saharan explorers, best-selling author Michael Asher, in his *Sands of Death*. "The man who led the Trans-Saharan survey mission would go down in history as the last of the great Saharan explorers."[44]

The Frenchman Paul Flatters wanted to be that explorer, and he was well equipped for the task. He had spent years dreaming of leading an expedition to Timbuktu, following in the wake of Laing and Caillié. Like his latter-day fan Asher, Flatters was a military man. He was a speaker of Arabic, a scholar of sorts, happy on horseback and in his role as "benevolent autocrat" for the French colonial Arab Bureau in deepest Algeria. Yet things did not go according to plan as he took up the survey mission. In the spring of 1881, Flatters departed on his second survey, and once his large party had advanced well into the desert, armed Tuaregs attacked and killed Flatters and the other Frenchmen among them. The French tried to revive ideas of the railway over the ensuing years, as they kept nursing hopes of joining up their African colonies while dealing Britain, their rival in the scramble for Africa, a defeat. Yet it had never been quite clear what the *transsaharien*'s concrete purpose was: there were no great commercial gains to be had in unspooling this thread of connection deep into the fabric of the desert.[45]

The desert has time and again kept working its way into the Western geography of imagination, as mirror and projection of the self with its

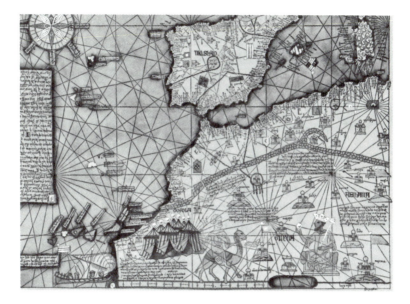

Map 7. Catalan Atlas (detail), ca. 1375.

desires and fears. "Since at least the fourteenth century, the Sahara has served the West as a canvas on which to paint its greed, fears and ambitions," writes one leading scholar of the region, Ann McDougall.[46] Here was the tale of wealth: on the Catalan Atlas, Timbuktu (referred to as *Tenbuch*) makes its first appearance on a medieval *mappa mundi*. Its desert environs are represented by a depiction of the Malian emperor Mansa Musa, with golden crown, golden scepter, and golden nugget showcasing his splendid fortunes.[47] Such dreams of the riches of the desert and its "shore" (the Sahel) spurred plans for the *transsaharien* railroad and for expensive expeditions. At the same time, the desert was haunted by stories not just of monstrous races but of ship castaways taken captive, slave traders, and the desert's supposedly cruel, cunning, and bloodthirsty inhabitants. No European could go into the desert without being disguised as a Muslim, or so the story went, a call heeded by Caillié and many of his fellow explorers.

Britain was as infatuated with the desert as the French. When the "Association for Promoting the Discovery of the Interior Parts of Africa" set up its operations in 1788 in London's Soho Square, its members soon pitched their scientific exercise to the popular cartographic imagination.

One missive of the association extolled how "the luxurious city of Timbuctoo" was attracting "the marchants [*sic*] of the most distant states of Africa" and offered up a gilded desert rife with commercial opportunities in a world of ancient empires and boundless adventure.[48] Again, popular and expert mappings of the world came together, as they have in our own "colonial present."[49]

An intrepid forebear of Laing, Caillié, and Flatters set off on a ship from Liverpool one day in the late eighteenth century. The Scotsman Mungo Park had been contracted by the association to trace the bend of the Niger River through present-day Mali and to find Timbuktu. As he eventually returned to write about his forays into the Sahel, he did his best to titillate his readers with reports of African riches. The Niger at the town of Segou, he said, was "broad as the Thames at Westminster"; the dyed cloth of the Mandingoes was "equal to the best Indian or European blue," and the natives even brewed their own beer, much like his native Scots. He at once normalized, romanticized, and stirred desire for the "interior parts of Africa." As one scholar writes, "Instead of savages, barbarians, cannibals, or people with tails, as was generally believed in Europe and Britain at the time, he found perfectly normal human beings with their own music, arts, and manufactures, and even some learning."[50]

Yet in the desert's inhabitants, the "Moors," he found something else entirely: a "nation of lunatics." Park had been taken captive in the desert, to whose trials he would eventually succumb, on his next expedition. Perhaps this colored his writings about the Moors, permeated as they are by a visceral sense of disgust and racial hatred: "I was a *stranger,* I was *unprotected,* and I was a *Christian;* each of these circumstances is sufficient to drive every spark of humanity from the heart of a Moor. . . . Cut off from all intercourse with civilized nations, they are at once the vainest and proudest, and perhaps the most bigoted, ferocious, and intolerant of all the nations on the earth—combining in their character, the blind superstition of the Negro with the savage cruelty and treachery of the Arab."[51]

In today's world, the Sahara keeps working its magic as mirage, with these earlier stories inscribed as a palimpsest upon the present. The best seller detailing Flatters's failed expedition, *Sands of Death,* was itself a small example of this reworking of old tales of adventure and woe (subtitle: "an epic tale of massacre and survival in the Sahara"). Indeed,

McDougall suggests that the ease with which the Bush administration grafted GWOT onto the Sahara "can only be understood as part of the historical process by which Islam, violence, and terror have been identified as generic to and synonymous with this desert region." The desert, she writes, was the "'the fearful void' where all Christians were sure to meet death or worse (slavery), and where veiled Muslim fanatic 'barbarians' crisscrossed the desert sands in camel caravans, leaving skeletons of women and children in their wake."[52]

·　　·　　·　　·　　·

So far, our story of the map is one of the West, its foes and its historical claims to domination. Yet if we take off our Western-centric blinkers just for a moment, we may note that blank spaces and their lure are by no means unique to this "West"—if indeed a distinction between this brittle historical construct and "the Rest" can any longer be sustained at all.

From the vantage point of the North African Maghreb, the Sahara was already in the fifteenth century portrayed as *bilād al-sība*—lands of dissidence, or of denied connections. The desert, scholars of the Sahara tell us, was itself a patchwork of civilization (*hadāra*) and threatening wilderness (*bādiya*), "inhabited by raiders and thieves," fears of whom helped relegate the *bilād al-sība* "not only beyond the realm of the polity, but of civilization *tout court*." Yet interaction across this stark divide was frequent. Even the desert "bandits" could pass across it during their lives, much as "a Saharan 'empty space' could become pasture," or a desert oasis could flourish, then turn fallow.[53] In other words, civilization and its others were constantly blending into one another. As in more recent times, a story told through idioms of separation was also one of uneven connection.

Remote areas elsewhere have similarly tangled histories, extending far beyond any one-way European deployment of modern cartographic power. Besides recognizing these histories, we must avoid falling into the trap of seeing certain parts of the world—from Timbuktu to the Hindu Kush—as part of an unchanging global periphery. The Sahara, for one, has bridged civilizations since medieval times, while being crisscrossed by connections all its own. When Mansa Musa traveled to Mecca, his lavish gifts of gold depreciated the value of the metal in Egypt, while Timbuktu stood as a thriving center of trade and learning in the midst of Saharan crossroads.[54]

Looking across our world map, we do see how histories of connection and distance are being resurrected, or reinvented, for a time of disorganized capitalism. My fellow anthropologists have delved into such remappings of the remote around the world, displacing our West-centered vision still further. Among other findings, they have brought back accounts of the riches to be had for savvy frontier entrepreneurs who find themselves straddling distant political fault lines—illustrating how remoteness may prove a tremendous resource if played right.

Consider, for a start, the borderlands of Southeast Asia's Golden Triangle. Historically a part of what anthropologists have called "Zomia"— the Asian highlands where hill tribes once escaped colonial and state rule—this remote border zone has seen the mixed glories of its opium-scented past revived through hybrid forms of state-racketeer capitalism. Here casino towns, shady trades, and special economic zones now bring together frontier entrepreneurs and an expansive Chinese state in a potent mix of licit and illicit commerce—a mix, moreover, that banks on the region's frisson of danger and its legal-political remoteness. Or, moving across our map, consider the banditry-ridden highlands of Madagascar. Designated by the government as a "red zone" of danger, this is presumably a wild land marred by cattle raids and unpoliced highway robbers. Yet if we peel away the no go stickers, we see how the red zone allows state officials and criminals to collude in trafficking rosewood, vanilla, and rare animals to international clients. Finally, consider the "deep Amazon," cast as an exotic void of uncontacted tribes. Yet here, wildcat gold mining today ties indigenous and foreign fortune hunters alike into criminal networks and global commodities markets, whose fluctuations get inscribed as scars on the landscape.[55]

As any anthropologist would tell us, we cannot assume that the ways outsiders perceive these sites—as distant and marginal—correspond with how locals think of their place in the world.[56] However, our ethnographies do reveal some shared features. From the Golden Triangle to the Amazon by way of northern Mali and Madagascar, remoteness is actively being unmade and remade by both the poor and the powerful, in interaction with capital and national capitals.

In short, and to retake our earlier cartographic point, remoteness is entangled with the power to draw and dominate the world. In fact, the verbal root of the term *remote*—the Latin *removere*, to remove—captures this political dimension. We may approach remoteness as a transitive action of *removal*: "lifting," displacing, and perhaps misplacing an inhabited area and reshaping the social space around it in ways that implicate outsiders, insiders, and various kinds of go-betweens. Such removals may serve to keep hidden shadow parts of local, national, and world economies, as when "removed" areas come to act as conduits for clandestine trades in the Malagasy highlands, the Sahara, the Amazon, or the Golden Triangle. At a time of global connectivity, those economic circuits that cannot be easily visualized on Khanna's connectography come at a premium: the cartographic blanks are places where fortunes can be made.

Besides serving economic functions, remapped remote areas may be useful symbolically and politically, including for the conjuring and control of danger and risk—taking us back to the West and its pet monsters. With the global map of remoteness and its historical layers in our pocket, we now head back to the past decades' cartographic battles across the Sahel and the Sahara, which are not for the first time proving the trial ground for Western interveners and their quest to control the global margins.

·   ·   ·   ·   ·

There was for some time, in the Cold War days, a map of Mali as one nation among others, colored in the usual insipid hues of a school atlas, its borders solid and well defined since the breakup of the postcolonial Mali Federation. On independence, its new rulers had sought to resurrect the country's resplendent past, drawing on the tales of Mansa Musa's empire—Mali as the mythical "land of gold" described by Arab explorers and fantasized about by the late-coming Europeans. This eventually attracted tourists, too: by the late 1990s, Mali was positioning itself as a safe space for escapades into the desert and to the hillside huts of Dogon country, while hosting academics studying the rich Mande culture of the south. Yet already before conflict was let loose upon Mali in 2012, Western news media had started unfolding another set of maps, showing blood-red or black streaks of an al Qaeda presence. In foreign travel advisories issued by Western governments, the north was being colored a deep red, signify-ing advice against all travel, while the rest of the country was smeared with orange, signifying advice against all but essential travel. Mali was yet again becoming a land of danger, a faraway terrain: do not tread here.

In northern Mali before the conflict, remoteness had indeed been an economic asset of the kind seen from the Malagasy banditry zones to Southeast Asia's Golden Triangle. Cigarette smuggling toward North Africa and Europe was a local lifeline, using well-worn desert tracks on which all sorts of goods, and people, traveled. Owing to crackdowns on global drug routes, a narco-corridor opened in the 2000s from coastal Guinea-Bissau and onwards into the hard-to-police desert borderlands between Mali and Algeria. As in the highlands of Southeast Asia or Madagascar, links between elements of the state and the illicit trades were strong: Algerian security forces and Malian government officials alike had created intricate networks that tapped into the lucrative streams of con-traband. The wider desert region was also "globalizing" in more positive ways, from the thriving economy of Tamanrasset in Algeria to the desert festivals and tourist trades of Timbuktu and Niger's Saharan gateway of Agadez.[57]

In the post-9/11 years, as the perceived jihadi threat started to dominate the international agenda following a string of high-profile kidnappings, the economic niche of the desert came to be seen as a "haven" for extremism, violence, and—as European fears around trans-Saharan migration grew— human smuggling. Talk of narco-jihad spread between Bamako, Paris, New York, and Washington. The Sahara, one *Air Force Magazine* article memorably said, was a "swamp" that needed to be drained.[58] Old stories of blank spaces were swiftly being reactivated.

One such story stands out. At the time when the Bush administration was invading Iraq, news surfaced of a jihadist kidnapper from Algeria— nicknamed El Para—escaping across the desert with his Western captives. The ensuing spectacular chase was well timed, as anthropologist Jeremy Keenan notes in his investigations of the Sahara's shadow world . The cin-ematic El Para saga provided one justification for the Bush administra-tion's reality makers to push the war on terror onto African soil. In May 2003, one US general summed up the stakes in this region: "We might wish to have more presence in the southern rim of the Mediterranean, where there are a certain number of countries that can be destabilized in the near future, large ungoverned areas across Africa that are clearly the new routes of narco trafficking, terrorist training and hotbeds of instability." Meanwhile, the US ambassador to Mali suggested that the country's north was essentially "a no man's land," a *terra nullius* of terror potential and real.[59]

America was actively conjuring the monsters it needed to destroy, to paraphrase our neoconservative pundits. In this Quixotic endeavor, the map of the Sahara proved particularly suited for fantasies to multiply. One anthropologist working among cross-border smugglers in remotest Mali and Algeria notes how the cartographic blankness of the Sahara has worked visually as a ready-made canvas for the depiction of multifarious dangers.[60] Today, in a world linked up through the "nonplaces" of airports, transport links, and special economic zones, the desert appears as a peculiar kind of nonplace: a haven, in the war-on-terror terminology, ripe for *certain kinds* of intervention—that is, interventions focused on threats to the West.[61]

Fantasy and strategy intermingled in the Sahara, and so did the economic and political functions of the danger zone. By 2002, counterterror funding was already being channeled to the region, generating initiatives for regional security cooperation overseen by the Americans. First via the Pan-Sahel Initiative (PSI) and then through the Trans-Saharan Counterterrorism Partnership, Washington started financing military collaboration with regional states including Algeria.[62] Like a latter-day Mansa Musa, the Pentagon had arrived with a huge pot of gold, which soon created ample opportunities for rent seeking. "Just as African governments during the Cold War could bid for U.S. financial, military and diplomatic support by depicting themselves as under siege from Marxists, so they can now do the same by claiming that their enemies are radical Islamists," wrote one commentator, while noting the biggest beneficiary—Algeria and its security apparatus, accused by Keenan of playing a double game in the desert as instigator and exporter of jihadism.[63]

We may start to discern several tangled strands of a story of dangerous difference—threads of medieval fantasies of Otherness, of colonial exploration, of post–Cold War strategic renewal, even of encounters with the Islamic othering of the "wild" Sahara. Some of these strands came to be tied together at particular moments, as when the UK prime minister David Cameron, in the midst of the French deployment in early 2013, referred to northern Mali as an "ungoverned space"—ignoring how too much state involvement, especially in the cross-border drug trade, was at the heart of the problem.[64] These strands were also woven into the emerging patchwork map of *global* danger. Officials and analysts soon started talking about the "ungoverned" Sahara-Sahel belt as part of a grander whole stretching to Africa's Horn and onwards, all the way to Afghanistan. This so-called "arc of instability" had by the early 2010s become so commonsensical a reference point that one British diplomat told me with a suppressed giggle that it had received its own moniker in the Foreign Office—the "banana of badness."[65]

The "banana theory of terrorism," as Keenan calls it, was to be about more than just the threat of terror, however, as we will see when we now return to the present, revisiting the various misfortunes befalling Mali and its once so resplendent map.

·   ·   ·   ·   ·

One day in December 2010, I stood looking out over a smog-hazed Niger River from the offices of the EU Delegation in Bamako, where I had come to interview a senior diplomat about irregular migration through the desert. By this time, things had not yet gone wholly downhill: Bamako roared with thousands of imported Chinese motorbikes, and its skyline was graced by Libyan-owned hotels. On street level, posters of Colonel Gaddafi next to the Malian president, Amadou Toumani Touré (ATT), showed who was bankrolling Mali's political class. What was missing, however, was the Western presence of earlier years, as travel advice had cut tourist numbers.

On the surface, the reason for the changed advice seemed quite simply worsening insecurity owing to jihadist (and criminal) kidnappings in Mali's north. However, there was a catch, as I heard at the EU offices that day. The travel warnings were "pure politics," according to the diplomat. Rather than being principally based on actual threats, they were meant to force Mali to cooperate in crackdowns on terrorism, drugs, and irregular migration in the desert north—Europe's top three priorities, with migration in particular a key concern. "You hit people where it hurts, and that's tourism," the diplomat said, adding: "You could go and tap-dance naked in Kidal and nothing would happen." A couple of years later, in November 2013, two French journalists were kidnapped and killed outside Kidal. By then, the political posters of downtown Bamako and the world they repre- sented were gone: Gaddafi dead following the NATO air campaign, ATT in exile after the spring 2013 coup, Mali haltingly recovering from war. The north had become what European governments had preemptively announced in 2010: a no go area of nebulous risks and dangers.

Those days in 2010, Malian tourist officials were fuming as a lifeline for the country's economy was being pulled away. Visiting the town of Djenne, whose mud mosque was once a must-see on the Malian tourist trail, I noticed an anger I had not felt on previous visits: children making faces and adults giving us blank stares where before Mali's famous hospitality would have promised warm greetings and long discussions over pungent green tea. The withdrawal of tourism had not forced Malian cooperation, as the Europeans had wished: instead it was simply ruining local liveli- hoods and stirring resentment against the meddling foreigners.

In Bamako, it was not only Malian tourism officers but also foreigners invested in the industry who were up in arms. Among them was Hervé Depardieu, the French director of a tranquil ecolodge, Kangaba, that I had visited that winter. Six years later, as Bamako was gearing up to host the French-African summit of 2017, Depardieu penned a piece for *Le Monde* arguing that the travel restrictions just scared people off. "For the past four years, we have tried to resume our normal, peaceful lives, as we always had in Mali," he wrote. "But the alarming safety instructions issues by the con- sulate and the dissuasive 'travel advisories' on the website of the Foreign Affairs Ministry seriously dent the enjoyment of our lives and our liberties." E-mails and text messages arrived randomly, imposing "advice" that employers often took as orders: "Don't leave Bamako this weekend," "Don't move around at night." Embassy officials had vested interests in issuing these severe restrictions, Depardieu said, as they received extra risk pay as a function of them. Locally, however, the consequences were "enormous," as "families and our friends hesitate to come and visit us" while expatriate workers became an ever-rarer sight—slowing, in his view, Mali's progress back to normality. Is it legal and is it "fair play" to "paint the world in three colors in this way," he asked, given that cities such as Nice and Paris had suffered terror attacks similar to Bamako's, and given that most tourist trouble involves traffic accidents and disease, not terrorism?[66]

We do not know if what happened next was related to his tirades, but the coincidence was jarring. It was June 2017, in the run-up to another clinch meeting where Emmanuel Macron, newly installed as French president, was to meet with the Sahel's Group of Five countries to build momentum for the financing of their regional counterterrorism mission. The insurgents had their chance to make an impact, and they took it. News spread over Twitter of an armed attack at a "luxury hotel" outside Bamako; soon I realized it was Kangaba. French and Malian forces moved in. Smoke billowed into the hills. Armed men had attacked the lodge, leaving five dead. At a time when Bamako had already become "an enclave set in the middle of danger, transformed into a besieged citadel," to cite *Libération*, the jihadists had chosen to target one of the few foreign holdouts who tried in his statements and in his day-to-day hotel business to normalize expatriate life in Mali.[67]

Mali, of course, is but one stark example of a wider trend. The red stain keeps spreading across the maps of travel advice, insinuating itself as far as South Africa by early 2018.[68] In country after country, kidnappings, terror attacks, or threats of such attacks have triggered mass withdrawals of tourists. In Tunisia, the United Kingdom pulled back its holidaying citizens after a spectacular beach killing, severely denting the country's postrevolution economy. In summer 2017 southern European beaches were crammed as a result of the insurance-canceling risks attached to trips not just to Tunisia but to Turkey and Egypt as well (though the situation eased the following year). In Kenya, attacks by Somalia-based al Shabaab have left parts of the Indian Ocean coastline deserted by tourists. In Mali's neighbor, Niger, the threat of jihadism and rebellion has left the guesthouses of the trans-Saharan outpost of Agadez abandoned to the desert dust, or to alternative trades. Timbuktu itself, whose economy was once dependent on tourism, was by 2017 a place where "the tourist guides have emigrated or started to drink," as one forlorn news report put it.[69] Towns and coastal hamlets that once appeared as destinations on departure boards and travel websites find themselves actively removed from the global map of connectivity.

African politicians have often warned against the issuance of blanket travel advice, arguing that curtailing tourism may in fact fuel terrorism as one economy is replaced by another.[70] Powerful governments rarely seem to consider such implications of their blanket bans, yet my focus here is another one: the performative power of the mapping of danger. For violent groups, the mass withdrawal of tourism is precisely what they seek— that is, cutting economic or social connections between the local population and foreigners, and especially "crusading" Westerners, as the foundational tracts of ISIS/Daesh make clear.[71] In other words, risk-averse governments play into the terrorists' hands with their cautionary advice, yet for these governments the map of danger remains useful for different reasons. The EU diplomat's words above may have been too dismissive of the risks: kidnappings, after all, had by 2010 already raised millions for al Qaeda in the Islamic Maghreb (AQIM). Yet his words indicate how Western states may sometimes deploy the seemingly apolitical tool of travel advice selectively, in a bid to force cooperation on key political objectives with weaker governments in Africa in particular. Moreover, his assertions reveal the "danger" of the danger zone to be a slippery signifier indeed. Instead of simply being concerned with security risks toward Western citizens, the diplomatic strategy for Mali bundled such risk with quite distinct "risks" (drugs, migration), all the while placing this bundle in a discrete geographical space.

There is a peculiar time frame to this bundling, as future probabilities of danger are projected into a rather generic spatial distance. Consider, for instance, this 2014 UK House of Commons report on North Africa and the Sahel:

> [In] Mali, an al Qaeda-ruled rump state was a reality for some months, and some of our witnesses considered that Mali's neighbors were potentially vulnerable to a similar fate. Niger and Mauritania were singled out, and Mali itself was not yet seen as being out of the danger zone. It is reasonable to assume that an Islamist statelet *somewhere in north-west Africa* would be a centre of smuggling, people trafficking and kidnapping; activities that already go on in the region ... A rump state would have the potential to disrupt or destabilize its neighbors and—although this point is speculative—launch attacks on more distant enemies.[72]

"A center for smuggling and people trafficking": one well-placed official at the UK Foreign Office later described his country's rising interest in the Sahel in terms of "turning off the tap" of migration while containing the wider risk of destabilization. The French defense minister echoed these concerns in May 2014 as his Mali-based forces were regrouping into the regional counterterror operation Barkhane. "There will be 1,000 soldiers that remain in Mali, and 3,000 in the Sahel-Sahara zone, the danger zone, the zone of all types of smuggling," he told reporters. "We will stay as long as necessary. There is no fixed date."[73] As he indicated, in an echo of our US general of the previous decade, cross-border flows—drug trafficking and especially irregular migration—were besides terrorism coming to function as key drivers of intervention; moreover, they were part and parcel of the constitution of certain areas as danger zones, taken as no-man's-lands rife with criminal activity.

The mapping of danger onto discrete, distant sites, in other words, serves potent functions for both insurgents and Western interveners, who wittingly or unwittingly collude in reinforcing the danger zone in its distance and strangeness. In this double mapping of danger, northern Mali and the wider Sahel-Sahara belt have come to play host to a potent threat cluster in the eyes of Western interveners: "removed" yet connected, distanced yet hardwired into global politics and into the febrile media circuits of late capitalism.[74]

The clustering of threats, and the redrawing of maps around them, were central to international interventions across the Sahel-Sahara belt and beyond, as I noticed in my interviews in Western ministries. One high-level French diplomat, for instance, reframed and renamed the wider geographical region in terms of danger. To him, "When we speak about Sahel it goes from Nouakchott [Mauritania's capital] to Mogadishu. For me Somalia is Sahel, it is one world." His reason for this redesignation was that the armed groups active there—from al Shabaab in Somalia to Boko Haram in Nigeria and AQIM in Mali—shared the same ideology and so the same "culture." A highly placed Swedish military officer relayed a similar regional remapping for other reasons. "We have to see Mali in the larger picture. . . . MINUSMA is part of an entirety that starts in the Gulf of Guinea and ends in Somalia," he said. However, he added a different emphasis as he drew a mental map, plotting one existing military or humanitarian intervention after another along this arc. He continued: "Which risk is it really that we are trying to handle in Mali?" As for the UK diplomat cited above, the answer was principally (though not

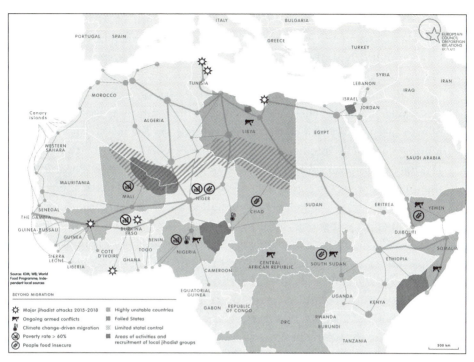

Map 8. "Migration through the Mediterranean: Mapping the EU Response," 2018, by European Council on Foreign Relations. See www.ecfr.eu. © ECFR, author: Stefano M. Torelli; map: Marco Ugolini.

exclusively) migration. Elsewhere, in one northern European foreign ministry, a map drawn on a paper whiteboard for an internal meeting showed how these multiple threats converged as they approached Europe: on it, arrows pointed outwards from Libya's conflict, representing internally displaced people, international migration, and terrorism.

Western states have in the Sahel-Sahara belt played fast and loose with their inherited cartographic power. In word and deed, they have mapped out a discrete field of intervention defined by bundled and overlapping dangers—a threat cluster—in which one kind of threat may nest within another, so generating and reinforcing a generalized sense of danger and a concomitant need to intervene.

Yet after last chapter's travails in Timbuktu, I do not need to remind anyone that the Western cartopolitics of danger was superficial. Despite the official talk of a single reality of the Sahel/Horn of Africa belt—a banana ripe with badness—practicalities and politics constantly got in the way. In Mali, UN staffers showed me map after map that spoke reassuringly of peacekeeper deployments and aid provisions. Thanks to advanced technology including surveillance drones, there was no part of the country that could not be reached and monitored, humanitarians and military officers insisted. Yet scratch the surface a little, and the mastery becomes a mirage. One UN intelligence analyst from Sweden, deployed to a tent HQ full of European spies outside Bamako airport, was painfully aware of the limits. "It's easy to come in as a Swedish soldier and look at the map and see that here is a squad, here's a battalion and then you know more or less what effect you get out of that sort of unit, but it's not quite that way over there." On the desert border with Algeria, he said (and I paraphrase), a box stating "Chad" on a UN deployment map referred to a ragged and frustrated bunch of Chadian fighters in constant peril, on endless mission on someone else's behalf. "Some of them have been here since 2013 and haven't received a salary, they haven't been allowed home. Some of them are deserting, so I don't really expect them to write a good recon report when they are out on patrol, they have worse problems to deal with." Tokens of an international presence, their fate spoke of a mission unspooling, and of African soldiers as castaways in the distant sands.

To reiterate, remapping the world entails remaking it, however imperfect this remaking turns out to be. In the desert and its imposed remoteness, prophecies were becoming self-fulfilling. A mere decade after Kaplan mapped the future political earth, his and other pundits' doom-laden cartographies were merging with reality, as the Roves of the world would contentedly observe. The map was the territory, and it was being populated by barbarians and beastly forces roaming, like the beggars of Borges's story, amid the faraway cartographic ruins of Empire.

.   .   .   .   .

Maps tell stories of the world, and with this in mind, the preceding pages have traced a metastory of a peculiar mapping of world "margins" by especially Western powers. In short, it goes something like this. There was once a European *mappa mundi* that enclosed the world in a perfect circle of piety and divine knowledge, haunted by monstrous figures roaming its peripheries. Gradually, the monsters and beasts were swept aside and replaced with place-names, mountain ranges, and rivers. As the blank spaces receded, the margins of imperial expansion were robbed of some of their allure: no longer did monsters or cannibals roam there. Yet even as the map expanded, as science advanced, the remaining cartographic blanks still held the attention of the coming colonizers. For a long time, Timbuktu lured in the explorers gathering on the desert like an early crowd of reality-show contestants looking for gold and glory in the distant sands.

At a time of chaotic capitalism and shifting geopolitics, such blank spaces are now reemerging in full political force across our maps, where they are invested with renewed fears, fantasies, and desires. On the one hand, they serve as fortune-hunting frontiers for today's disorganized (or reorganized) capitalism. For smaller-scale frontier entrepreneurs, illicit trades are booming in the blank spaces, from the banditry-hit highlands of Madagascar to the narco-trade of the Sahara and the casino and drug markets of the Golden Triangle. Meanwhile, for powerful corporations and governments, oil and gas, minerals and uranium—as in Niger's French-managed mines—certainly retain their lure. Yet in remote places that are "removed," revived, and reinvented for a time of global war, these fantasies of distant riches are being surpassed by a concern with clustered threats. These areas are not just removed from their surrounding social fabric but also deprived of one aspect of their affective power—their allure as distant lands of compelling riches. Mansa Musa, we may say, has been robbed of his golden scepter.

In the danger zones that remain after this stripping away of historical layers, the rewards of entry are no longer mainly concerned with the putative gold and glory that once led explorers such as Caillié toward Timbuktu or that motivated the mad *transsaharien*. For here, in the heart of the severed danger zone, lies the promise of converting uncontrollable global danger into manageable (countable, containable, and "killable") risk. Here, interveners may work to stem citizen anxiety about insecurity and migration well away from prying eyes and often well outside established legal boundaries.[75]

In other words, we must not get lost in the alluring story of the map, forgetting about the hardheaded *functions* of the cartography of danger.

In distancing danger zones from the legal order, today's interveners echo their early colonial predecessors, who already in the sixteenth century differentiated a European "sphere of peace and the law of nations" from the world "beyond the line," outside the legal, moral, and political norms of "civilized" society.[76] Furthermore, in the mix of political, symbolical, and legal functions of the danger zone lies another promise, too, however faint: that of continued strategic dominance. Yet much like Caillié's frustrated quest to discover Timbuktu's long-lost riches, this fantasy of global control is riddled with monsters of the interveners' own making. It generates economies of violence and rent seeking as jihadists, rebels, and regional forces use the danger zone as an asset for their own purposes. It clashes with the powerful connectography of the new globalizer, China, on a quest for economic and political expansion. And it confronts the mapmaking of the enemy, as jihadists increasingly extend the danger zone into the heart of Western capitals—undoing, in one fell swoop, the facile official mapping of dragons onto distant lands.

The story told by a divided map of danger, in sum, is fiction. Instead of being place bound, danger must be seen in a systemic light: the red zones always threaten to bleed outwards despite efforts at containment and remote control. As connectographers of the gloomier variety insist, today risks and threats spread at blinding speed through the multitude of connective channels wiring together "centers" and "margins."[77] Jihadists, of course, know this as they wield their weapons and upload gruesome snuff movies from distant quarters. Counterterror warriors know it, too, as the US Joint Special Operations Command, drone pilots, and French special forces turn such remote areas into the terrains of a global shadow war. Yet even in its blatant fictional aspects, the divided cartography of danger remains functional. By spatializing danger, Western interveners remove its systemic aspects from view, including not least their own implication in it. In so doing, they draw on the affordances offered up by the Western geography of imagination—or, more specifically, the capability to conjure dangerous yet desirable Otherness in all its historical power of narration and emotion.

The author Adam Hirsch has said that although, compared to Vietnam or the Second World War, the "forever war" on terror seems an anomaly, "It would have been quite familiar to a nineteenth-century Briton: For these are the border wars of empire, which can never be won because no empire is ever free from threats."[78] Yet for all the historical resonances, we must keep interrogating the imperial comparison. We may persist in labeling this particular form of organization of the world into hinterlands and centers of power an empire, or we may prefer, as I do, to chip away at this colossal term, bandied about by Rove and his ilk as much as by their critics.[79] We must not just decenter the presumed dominance of the West by noting other cartographies of the past and the present. We must also peer into the cracks of the imperial edifice itself, spot the tears in the map of intervention and danger, and see the map for the Borgesian mirage that it is.

Today's cartographies of risk and danger, for all their conceit in conjuring faraway monsters, are not the equivalent of the red-blushed domains of the Imperial Federation Map of the World of late nineteenth-century Britain. Their red stains, after all, denote danger rather than colonial control. These danger maps may offer up political and extralegal spaces of brutality and war, yet the broad brush and uncertain hand with which they are drawn indicate that they are symptomatic of a larger malaise. They express, in short, the cartographic paranoia of postimperial power. Returning to the times of Laing and Caillié, or even the epochs preceding their tentative advance, we may discern how the danger maps of today above all recall precolonial cartographies in which knowledge is imperfect, state authority is no longer absolute, and the uncanny stalks the global edges.

3 THE TYRANNY OF DISTANCE

All spake of him, but few had seen
Except the maimed ones or the low;
Yet rumor made him every thing—
A farmer—woodman—refugee—
The man who crossed the field but now;
A spell about his life did cling—
Who to the ground shall Mosby bring?

Herman Melville, "The Scout toward Aldie"

One early autumn day in 2007, Ryan Henry, a principal deputy undersecretary in the US Department of Defense, made his way from Washington, D.C., to Warrenton, Virginia. Driving past the Beltway, he must have known he had a delicate task ahead of him that night. US Africa Command was about to be launched, and a large gathering of African potentates— wary of American military designs on their continent—were in his audience. And so that evening, Henry began his speech on an offbeat note. "As I was driving west this afternoon," he said, "I found myself drifting back to a different time and place as we gather tonight in this area steeped in Civil War history." In Warrenton Cemetery not many yards away, he noted, the Civil War fighter Colonel John Singleton Mosby lay buried, "an innovative and daring leader of small detachments of irregular cavalry whose exploits harried Union leaders all across this area."

Nicknamed the "Gray Ghost" for his fear-inducing art of appearing and disappearing to his foes at will, Mosby was a legendary Confederate fighter, immortalized in Herman Melville's poetry. Extolling a Confederate guerrilla warrior to a gathering of African leaders did not seem to strike Henry as irksome, though Mosby's methods did—up to a point. They were "unorthodox for the time, and not without some controversy," Henry conceded, "but he met success where it counts and that is on the battlefield. And it struck me that there is an analogy here between Mosby's legacy and what we are developing with Africa Command. We intend to be as bold and daring in the implementation, experimentation and evolution of Africa Command as Mosby was during the Civil War."

Henry's conjuring up of Mosby's Confederacy, as the fighter's maverick guerrilla band was known, hinted that the Americans had learned their ill-gotten lessons from post–Cold War interventions in Africa. In the infamous "Black Hawk Down" incident of 1993, two US military helicopters had crashed over Mogadishu in a secretive special forces raid on the warlord General Haidid gone spectacularly wrong. Eighteen soldiers were killed, while hundreds of Somalis were mowed down by the Americans.[1] As footage emerged of US servicemen stripped and dragged through the streets of Mogadishu, Bill Clinton swiftly pulled out all forces. The US military were leaving Africa, tail between legs, yet now—amid quagmire in Iraq and a full-throttled global war on terror—the Americans were back again. And Henry's words indicated they had no intention of repeating their mistakes.

AFRICOM was indeed a "bold and daring" experiment, using Africa as its laboratory. Set safely at a distance from the United States' key strategic regions, it would focus on preemptive intervention and "interagency" collaborations of all kinds, from Ebola response to extremism awareness-raising. AFRICOM may at times have been presented like a cuddly development program on steroids, yet the Mosby analogy indicated none too subtly where its beating heart was—in swift military force projection and counterterrorism, sometimes dressed up in humanitarian garb.[2] It drew justification from the pan-Sahelian initiatives of the Bush administration and from neoconservative calls for a forward positioning of the American "cavalry."[3] AFRICOM was to have a light footprint and little of the flash-bang, shock-and-awe tactics of the kind seen in Iraq or Afghanistan in the early 2000s. Like Mosby's Confederacy, it would melt into the distance whenever needed. And it would be able to strike lightning-fast and in close collaboration with African forces—an irregular cavalry of the highest order.

AFRICOM would achieve this feat through low-visibility infrastructure, new technology, and an "Africanized" division of labor—three levers of effective remote control that should already ring familiar to us from Mali. Except for a base at Camp Lemonnier in Djibouti, it would have no permanent official bases or permanent troops. Instead, a vast archipelago of small, movable, and largely "invisible" bases and forward operating stations ("lily pads") in strategic areas, along with African base-sharing agreements, ensured rapid intervention; unmanned planes and drones monitored and attacked high-value targets; and African "partner" forces and fighters, together with US covert operations, dealt with the deadly front lines.[4] The pad, the drone, the African soldier: together they would help create a security environment favorable to US interests, in which threats could be preemptively attacked and contained before they blossomed. In this way, AFRICOM would allow power to be projected swiftly, obliquely, and *vertically*, from distant headquarters and airspace, yet linked up to local forces on the ground.[5]

As we revisited 9/11 and its aftermath in the last chapter, we saw how the "war on terror" helped repaint the world map with the reds and blacks of danger. However, our cartography so far remains rather two-dimensional. As we now follow American forces back onto African soil, and into the fighting grounds of Somalia, we will soar above this flat map of danger, extending it into three dimensions.

Three-dimensionality, geographers tell us, is fundamental for understanding shifting forms of power today. The "volume" of our world is saturated with high politics—from the micropollutants filling our lungs and radio waves diffusing across borders to strategic struggles over the ocean floor or airspace.[6] And warfare, as so often, leads the way in such spatial innovation. The geographer Stuart Elden has shown how the battle space of the war on terror is best conceived as aerial, atmospheric, volumetric, rather than as a flat plane. Taking his cue, and that of Henry's lightning forces, we will now consider the *vertical politics* of control, to use a term coined by another three-dimensional thinker, Eyal Weizman.[7]

AFRICOM's forays in Somalia exemplified vertical power not just in the literal sense. Rather, the Americans came to mobilize distance to Somalia via a chain of operations across different planes—drones in the sky, special forces dropped in for punctual raids, and below, African soldiers treading the battlegrounds. AFRICOM also drew on strategic mappings of the world that situated the theater on another plane from that of the interveners. Through these vertical innovations, the 1993 crunch of US boots on the ground was to give way to a distant whirring in the skies and to the rustling of papers in distant headquarters. As we shall see, this form of vertical power enables an abstract, shallow form of domination— which may turn out to be all the more brutal for that very reason.

As we expand our map into three-dimensional space, we also segue away from the Bush White House to the Obama years, getting nearer, step by step, to our danger-laden present. Yet we must start by noting the *continuities*, as much as the ruptures, between their administrations, as AFRICOM itself illustrated. Unlike earlier US mass deployments combined with "population-centric" counterinsurgency, the Americans' Africa operations were already in Bush-era 2007 envisioned as distant yet swift, invisible yet pervasive: ghostlike à la Mosby. As Obama took over the reins of a war-weary nation, he embraced this innovation. Low-scale yet pervasive kinetic operations were soon to become the norm from Afghanistan to the Horn of Africa. In this respect, the incipient AFRICOM was a reconnaissance mission for Obama's shadow wars, which by the time he left office had made him the longest-running president at war in US history.[8] Conservatives liked to berate Obama for "leading from behind," but the "forward positions" taken in Africa during his administration revealed a smarter aspect to his strategic approach: controlling from above.[9]

The vertical power exemplified by AFRICOM may seem omniscient and all-powerful: watching the enemy from afar, after all, establishes a fundamental inequality unlike that of urban battle or traditional war. Yet as we now embark on a vertical journey up the chains of command in Somalia, we must remain alert to the limitations of vertical power, just as we were to the deceptive allure of two-dimensional maps. At any rate, for all the fanciful talk about AFRICOM that night in 2007, the Mosby analogy creaked, as Henry must have known. For a start, it would not be so much a swift guerrilla force as a lumbering creature: underresourced, often ineffective, and rarely operating in sync with other parts of the US state machinery. Limitations were moreover built into its vertical schema, into its political parameters, and into the mapping of dangerous lands that underpinned it. The Gray Ghost's men had once mastered the forests within sight of the Capitol in Washington, D.C., or as Melville wrote: "The Capitol dome— hazy—sublime— / A vision breaking on a dream / So strange it was that

Mosby's men / Should dare to prowl where the Dome was seen." American soldiers were never going to be that close, for so long and so intimately, to the enemy. They remained in thrall to Africa's "tyranny of distance," as strategists liked to call it, giving our chapter its title: the continent was simply too vast to monitor and intervene upon swiftly and fully.

In his closing remarks, Henry suitably reined in his ambitions as he tried to assuage African fears over the US military footprint on the continent. AFRICOM was "a bold departure from how America usually establishes new military organizations," he said, since "historically, new commands only emerge after some crisis or disaster has occurred." By contrast, AFRICOM would "help us create the conditions so that problems do not erupt into crises and crises don't result in catastrophes. Personally, I think we can deem it a success if AFRICOM keeps American troops out of Africa for another 50 years."

No army of American boots would march over African ground; this much Henry seemed to promise. AFRICOM, as its commander put it, would help foster "African solutions to African problems," a catchphrase increasingly heard in both Western and African capitals.[10] The Pentagon hoped to have its cake and eat it—no blood spilt, yet potentially unlimited force projection from above and beyond. The terror threat could be contained from afar, the tyranny of distance circumvented. Or could it?

In Somalia, forgotten by the world, these ambitions would be put to their most severe test. But before visiting its bloodied battlegrounds, we must consider some of the intellectual justifications for vertical power, taking our cue from cartographic battles past. As with the post–Cold War watershed, the Iraq invasion and its tortuous lead-up were triggering calls for a bold remapping of US dominance worldwide—nowhere better exemplified than in the theories of a man with a keen ear in the Pentagon and a new strategic map in his pocket: Thomas P. M. Barnett.

.   .   .   .   .

Chronic lack of governance. · Chronic food problems. · Chronic problem of terrorist-network infiltration. · We went in with Marines and Special Forces and left disillusioned—a poor man's Vietnam for the 1990s. Will be hard-pressed not to return.

So did Barnett, Department of Defense visionary-in-chief, style Somalia in his influential 2003 article for *Esquire* magazine, "The Pentagon's New Map."[11] As he saw it, Somalia was one of the ne'er-do-wells of the globalized world, a ragtag mobster in a world of bankers. Somalia needed to be brought back into the global fold, fast and by force if necessary. But why should anyone care enough to do it? Barnett's map offered a simple answer: because the country was dangerously disconnected.

The chaos engulfing Somalia seemed at first glance to prove Barnett right, but its disconnection was itself tied up with US action and inaction. As Clinton had pulled out his troops in 1993, he had intransigently blamed the UN for the Americans' disastrous raid on Haidid. The withdrawal sounded the death knell of UN peacekeeping in Somalia as other, weaker troop contributors soon followed suit. The attempt to "restore hope" to a country ravaged by war and famine since the 1991 fall of dictator Siad Barre, which had begun with a large-scale US mission of that name the previous year, was swiftly coming to an end. The "poor man's Vietnam" of Barnett's bullet points was to languish, chronic and chaotic, without any intervention at all.

"The world abandoned Somalia, allowing it to create for the world whole new forms of civil chaos and human suffering," recalled Kofi Annan, former UN secretary-general, in his memoirs. As he penned his *Interventions,* Annan was still smarting from Washington's blame game in Mogadishu, but more so from the terrible consequences that followed in the Black Hawk's churning wake. For Rwanda was next, where the United States and other powerful states now refused to put troops at risk, leaving the genocide to run its gruesome course.[12] Africa, it was swiftly becoming clear, was far from a strategic priority for the Americans.

The early 1990s had been a period of hubris: of trying to do too much with the outdated tools of postwar peacekeeping across Africa, as Annan diplomatically recalled. Next, the period after the Mogadishu debacle was, especially for the United States, one of withdrawal. The sun was setting on "humanitarian intervention," if not on piecemeal military operations. Clinton's decision, following the 1998 US embassy attacks in Nairobi, to bomb a supposed arms factory in Sudan was but an itch and a scratch for his administration. At this time, telling the US military establishment they needed to go into the poor, fragile spaces they had left in panic a few years earlier was a hard sell—yet Barnett was the man who took this mission upon himself.[13]

A military geostrategist with a Harvard PhD, Barnett had spent the post–Cold War years doggedly trying to persuade US forces that they were looking in the wrong place for their future foes. The military-industrial complex had faced a huge challenge as the Soviet Union crumbled: How to justify massive military investments and avoid sharp funding cuts as existential threats receded? Barnett skipped ahead of the military, a scout reconnoitering the terrain for a latter-day Mosby. Stop searching for the "Big One"—a Soviet-style confrontation—he told the US Navy. Instead, he said, echoing Kaplan's "Coming Anarchy" essay, look toward long-ignored Third World spaces to define your future purpose.

The military ignored his overtures. So Barnett set about building his case, painstakingly and single-mindedly, through the tool favored by world powers old and new: cartography.

Barnett decided to pinpoint all US military interventions since 1990 on a world map. As he did so, he realized that if he drew a line around them, the world magically divided in two. The divider, as he saw it, was the connective tissue of globalization. All areas where the United States had stayed out militarily, he called "the functioning Core" of globalization; those where it had entered were the "non-integrating Gap." The latter were regions beset by instability: disconnected from globalization and threatening to the West for that very reason.

Barnett's groundwork was done. He had his map. What he needed next, he thought, was to mount it on a PowerPoint "killer slide"—without this graphic, there was no way he would be able to convince his busy political and military superiors during the tiny time slot allotted to advisers such as himself.

His message had started to seep in when the Twin Towers fell. Barnett had been running brainstormers on national security and globalization from the 107th floor of World Trade Center One, and he now looked on with horror as his "workplace suddenly transformed from a sleepy college campus into an armed camp."[14] But he also saw his chance. As he recalled, "Suddenly I understand the danger isn't a *who* but a *where*." He relives the moment in his book on the Pentagon's new map, in breathless italics:

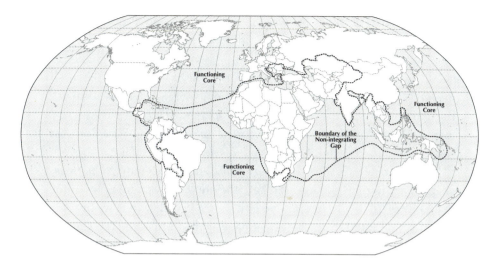

Map 9. Barnett's "Core" and "Gap," as rendered in Roberts, Secor, and Sparke (2003). © Dick Gilbreath/University of Kentucky.

Suddenly my eyes lit up ... because I know I've finally found that one slide.

Soon after, Barnett comes onto the central Pentagon payroll; and in March 2002, he finally walks into the secretary of defense's briefing room. Seizing his moment, he displays his slides and offers his Core and Gap hypothesis. "I have their attention, all right," he recounts, "but I can see them searching the slide for the answer to the 'So what?' question. Then I click my remote and that big red blob dissolves into view, encompassing all the regions they intuitively realize are now in play for the Defense Department in this global war on terrorism. I say, 'What you are looking at are the battle lines in this war. This is the expeditionary theater for the U.S. military in the twenty-first century.'"

Barnett pauses, savoring his triumph: *"Suddenly their eyes light up ... and the Pentagon has a new map."*[15]

That same year, 2002, the US National Security Strategy stated that "America is now threatened less by conquering [strong] states than we are by failing ones"—precisely the message Barnett and other pundits had been pushing.[16] As the Bush administration invaded Iraq, Barnett was poised to be one of the strategic thinkers who helped draw up the wild

new world map of the global war on terror and the intellectual justifications for it. "Let me tell you why military engagement with Saddam
Hussein's regime in Baghdad is not only necessary and inevitable, but
good," he wrote. "The real reason I support a war like this is that the resulting long-term military commitment will finally force America to deal with
the entire Gap as a strategic threat environment." The war, to him, was a
matter of principle—of facing up to the "new security paradigm that
shapes this age, namely, *Disconnectedness defines danger.*"[17]

The Gap may look a lot like the arc of instability encountered in the last
chapter, yet Barnett professed to hate the arc. He styled himself a rather
liberal Harvard intellectual, and to him the arc called forth atavistic fantasies of US oil interests pitting Americans against Muslims. The Gap was
instead defined by its absence of connection to mainstream globalization
and by its "Hobbesian" nature. There—whether "there" meant Kabul,
Zagreb, or Harare was irrelevant—life was disconnected, nasty, brutish,
and short. The Core, meanwhile, consisted of "Kantian" lands promising (if
not always delivering) "liberal peace" and long life spans. Barnett's key
message was that the United States had to intervene preemptively and
forcefully to safeguard economic globalization and global security. Yet
through his remapping of the world, he also assured non-Western "Core
powers" that they had nothing to fear. All such military operations would
take place in the Gap, where the United States could act as a Hobbesian
Leviathan instilling rightful fear among people who "still go medieval on
one another."[18]

Barnett's vision was a mishmash of the ideas bandied about by our
1990s scenario builders, from Fukuyama to Kaplan and Kagan. Like
them, he had his fame and his influence: his TED talk has been viewed a
million times (and this despite slides with one-liners such as "Most interesting challenge is sorting out Service capabilities"), and his *Esquire* article has been passed up and down the Pentagon like a bag of sweets. His
ideas are not merely quack theories, then; rather, they have helped map
the diffuse and interminable "everywhere war" against terrorism onto discrete and distant sites.[19] Unsurprisingly, he has for that reason been
depicted as a hawk and an apologist for the war on terror. His *Esquire*
piece gained notoriety—and a huge audience—partly thanks to its hard-
hitting views on Iraq.

Yet for all the martial rhetoric, all the self-serving logical jumps, and all the US exceptionalism baked into Barnett's project (the wars in Afghanistan and Iraq had been Bush's two great successes, he maintained), there was a curious mix of menace and concern in his mapping endeavors. "If disconnectedness is the real enemy," he wrote, "then the combatants we target in this war are those who promote it, enforce it, and terrorize those who seek to overcome it by reaching out to the larger world."[20] Barnett in fact wanted to *extend* connectivity rather than divide the world in two, he insisted as he took on his critics. In a spirit of American optimism, he saw a "happy ending" through preemptive intervention. The United States, accompanied by other Core states, must shrink the Gap, he said: those languishing in it could be dragged out of the depths and into the bright light of globalization.

As we have already noted, the global scenario makers of the post–Cold War moment have sometimes produced prophecies that, once they have a good ear at the White House or the Pentagon, may prove rather self-fulfilling.[21] Yet while Barnett's Gap helped justify AFRICOM and much else besides, his hopes for new connections faltered. It was true that a new US doctrine of global "integration" was taking hold amid Barnett's breakthrough, and his writings fed into this neoconservative sentiment of the time.[22] Instead of Cold War containment, the thinking went, recalcitrant and rogue states would be incorporated, by force if needed, into a US-led international order. Yet already by the later Bush years, this grand vision was blurring amid the chaos of Iraq. With Obama, it was narrowed further, then combined with a stripped-down version of Cold War containment.[23] This was, as we shall see, the moment when the "tyranny of distance"—in more than one sense—came to haunt US military expeditions, as well as other international interventions trailing in their wake.

Barnett's own map, for all his talk of integration and connection, had provided a rhetorical frame for this deepening of global distance. In trying to make intellectual sense of the "Gap" in which post–Cold War dangers emerged, Barnett thought he had simply drawn some neat lines over a flat map, creating that "killer slide" to convince the DoD to change its errant ways. Yet there was a spatial depth to his thinking, revealed by his odd mix of metaphors. The Core was not set against its usual antonym, the Periphery, as it was in Marxist "world systems theory" of the 1970s, at the opposite end of the political spectrum. Instead, it was set against the Gap. A gap connotes—among other things—a chasm or gulf, according to the thesaurus. On his map, Barnett was replacing one fantasy of global dominance with another: the world of endless military growth on the flat Cold War chessboard was yielding to a vertical projection of power. We, up here, all-seeing; they down there, in the gap or abyss, a space of political otherness from which little light emanates.

As it happens, this vertical vision of power resonated with that of Barnett's forebear, Robert Kaplan. "Imagine a cartography in three dimensions, as if in a hologram," Kaplan had written in 1994. On this "ever-mutating representation of chaos," he suggested, "shadowy tentacles" stretched out overhead, representing "the power of drug cartels, mafias and private security agencies."[24] To Kaplan as to Barnett, this vertical dimension of transnational danger had to be contained and controlled by a reinvigorated US Leviathan, operating across three dimensions.

Even as Barnett's hope for shrinking the Gap was not materializing, his map helped justify an ever-larger extension of American and Western security interests and investments of the kind that a few years later brought AFRICOM. In the war on terror, big powers could no longer ignore the world's poorest and most ill-governed regions, even as branches of the US military insisted on the misguidedness of this new ambition.[25] Instead American forces had to head down into the deep, "where the wild things are" in Barnett's words (citing my favorite childhood book, infuriatingly enough). And none were presumably any wilder than Somalia.

·   ·   ·   ·   ·

DATELINE MOGADISHU. It was nighttime in Camden, north London, when the pager buzzed at my bedside. *Ethiopian military enters Somalia*, said the news report. That December of 2006, I was working for the Reuters humanitarian news service AlertNet. My job involved sharing alerts of impending emergencies with aid groups around the world, and now it was my turn with the pager that fed big news to our team, 24/7. I pushed the report to subscribers that night, in a proto-tweet of sorts, and went back to bed. More than a decade later, Somalia has still not woken up from the nightmare unleashed by the US-backed Ethiopian invasion of 2006 to unseat the Islamic Courts Union, which had established some sense of order in war-ravaged Somalia during its short, fitful, and partial reign.

This is the time for my own confession. That message in the night in December 2006, on the eve of AFRICOM's launch, is the closest I've been to Somalia's brutal conflict. My knowledge of the country, its language and society, its globalized diaspora and its intricate clan system is as superficial as that of any of today's far-removed pundits and interveners, from TED-talking Barnett to drone operators. Unlike the aid workers and journalists who have descended into the heat of "the world's most dangerous place," to cite the title of reporter James Fergusson's book on Somalia, I have stayed well away. And unlike them, even if I did try to go, I would have little chance of securing a sightseeing tour with AMISOM, the African Union "peace operation" now fighting the ICU's illicit offspring, al Shabaab, in a never-ending war of trenches and attrition, of insurgency and counterinsurgency, the latter financed and supported by Western powers and the United Nations.

To be absolutely clear: this makes me deeply unqualified to speak about Somalia. But then, Somalia is not what I will speak about. I will rather show how scholars' and analysts' distance from war-ravaged Somalia is but a small symptom of a much larger withdrawal from this purest of danger zones. US drone operatives and Brussels bureaucrats, UN officials and international aid workers, journalists and researchers all increasingly work at a remove, or from on high, under the illusion that they know and control realities on the ground.

Somalia has come to be seen as the epitome of global danger, to the point where some of the lucky few visitors take delight in it as they live to tell the tale. As violence entrenched after 2006, reporters were filmed heading down pock-marked Mogadishu streets flashing their flak jackets and telling audiences back home just how dangerous it all was. Sometimes a nineteenth-century colonial explorer and unapologetic imperialist, Francis Burton, was wheeled out to prove that 'twas always thus. In 1856, in his book *First Footsteps in East Africa,* as he embarked at the imperial stopover of Aden on his grand Somali expedition, Burton had heaped scorn on the British colonial inhabitants who tried to talk him out of the adventure. "The rough manners, the fierce looks, and the insolent threats of the Somal—the effects of our too peaceful rule—had pre-possessed the timid colony at the 'Eye of Yemen' with an idea of extreme danger," he wrote. Still, his book went on to confirm the "savagery" of "the Somal" for the benefit of curious readers back home.[26]

In the early 2000s, even better-informed commentators could not quite resist the old lure of danger. Richard Dowden, then executive director of the UK's Royal African Society, wrote in his *Africa* that Somalia was the "exception" on the continent—a country beset by a "culture of war" and fearless fighting. Its postinvasion leader Abdillahi Yusuf, he said in words recalling Burton's, had "a face that makes a vulture look gentle." The journalist James Fergusson, for all his keen observations from Somalia's front lines, couldn't help himself when quipping that "however often the four Horsemen of the Apocalypse rode out into the world, Somalia was where they always came back to, because this was where they were stabled; this was their home."[27]

If it housed the four horsemen, everyone else except the African Union troops fighting the jihadist insurgency was declining the invitation to Hotel Somalia. The UN political mission and support services for AMISOM had for years been managed remotely from a large Nairobi base, with some officials holed up in Kenyan holiday resorts.[28] Even after their partial and belated move to Mogadishu, UN staff kept heading back to Nairobi for as many "rest and recuperation" breaks as possible. Others worked from Addis Ababa, seat of the African Union. One American disarmament expert, working remotely on Somalia from the UN offices in Addis, admitted to me that he had never visited the country—every time, a new attack happened and the trip was canceled. But there was little point going anyway, as he saw it, since his colleagues there barely stepped out of the UN/AU compound at Mogadishu airport, where all the internationals were ensconced behind walls and wire.[29] Now he was leaving Addis to work on the UN's Libya mission from a base in Tunisia. Remoteness had long since stopped being a problem for the United Nations: this was how things worked, and Somalia was just its most extreme example.

Almost everyone else stayed well clear of the Somali badlands, too—and quite understandably so, given the security risks. The stalwarts at Médecins sans Frontières had seen sixteen staff members killed. By summer 2013 they were pulling out, though not because of the attacks in themselves but because of the impunity and the acceptance of such violence against humanitarians among powerful actors on all sides, including the government holed up in Mogadishu.[30]

If aid workers' retreat was perhaps easy to understand, the international security sectors' distance from the field remained remarkable. We will soon return to the American military presence, but for now let us linger on Somalia's manifold multilateral security interventions. "Security experts" and consultants of all kinds flew in for a day or two if that, and then only to peek at Mogadishu through the smudgy panes of an AMISOM tank. The EU's military training mission for the Somalis had for years been organized remotely, in Uganda; the civilian capacity-building mission against piracy, EUCAP Nestor, was also awkwardly poised on the edge of Somalia, even after relocating its headquarters to Mogadishu in late 2015. Such was the fear that, in one anecdote, European military officers were at one point stuck in a hotel in safe Djibouti next door and were not even allowed to leave the place except on patrol "even though the largest risk is a sunstroke!" as one Scandinavian military researcher recalled.

This distancing also delimited the purpose and reach of the European naval forces' celebrated mission to quell Somali piracy, as I noted on a visit in 2016.

One August day, I get off the Tube in an unassuming part of northwestern London, and a short bus ride along sleepy suburban streets takes me to a vast fenced-off compound. Inside is the navy headquarters of Northwood, hosting antipiracy central—the EU's Operation Atalanta. Their multinational Joint Operations Centre (JOC) displays a reassuring digital map keeping track of all registered boats traversing the Gulf of Aden between the war-torn twins of Somalia and Yemen, all vessels colored according to their level of risk. Atalanta, its operatives make clear, is a success: all graphs of pirate attacks are pointing sharply down. Still, all is not back-slapping and joy. Political will is faltering for the mission; twenty-six hostages are still being held in captivity; and the pirates have melted into the distance. As an official presents Atalanta's successes, one of his slides on screen rhetorically asks, "Why are they not attacking? What are they up to instead? How can we assure they don't return?"

On land, one analyst explains, local rumors accuse Atalanta of abetting illegal foreign fishing off Somali coasts. "We need to understand fully [what happens in] fishing, the normal patterns of life," he says, sounding like an anthropologist. I interject: Is not this precisely the problem—the lack of any local presence to understand those concerns, those patterns? The head of the JOC speaks up: "This is one of our core problems, we don't really understand what's going on. . . . The power game is changing very quickly." Another officer says intelligence ashore is based on open sources and information from international organizations. But which? None are really present in Somalia, or equipped to understand the local worlds lurking beyond the "High Risk Area" of the open seas that Atalanta safeguards—that globalized highway connecting Europe to Asia via the Suez Canal.

The blank spots on land were not formally part of Atalanta's mission, yet the operatives' frustration in our 2016 meeting was symptomatic of how external actors of all kinds have approached Somalia from afar, through middlemen, through reports, and through maps of uncertain reliability. As our meeting drew to a close that day, one analyst pondered the whereabouts of the former pirates. They might be turning to other lines of business, he suggested: trafficking, weapons smuggling, and worse. And they were still holding their hostages. "It's a land-based problem, and who is going to tackle it?"

This perennial question usually received the same answer: the Americans and the AMISOM forces, which we must now visit in turn.

.   .   .   .   .

The Europeans might have been peeping down at Somalia through a Perspex glass, yet their viewpoint was positively ethnographic when compared with that of the Americans. Above Somalia, a ghostlike presence of drones and planes stole across the scorched terrains, occasionally raining down their ordnance. Up there, in the air and by way of distant control rooms, the second part of our story of vertical power unfolds, safely in US hands.

The Americans' return to Somalia coincided with the launch of AFRICOM, and with the country's descent into chaos. As the ICU crumbled in 2006, the many-headed Islamist hydra grew a new head. Al Shabaab—"the youth"—rose out of the chaos, and in 2008 Washington labeled it a terrorist organization and started targeting it from on high. In May that year, a Tomahawk missile killed al Shabaab's leader, Aden Hashi 'Ayro. As a consequence, the group labeled all Western and UN officials and organizations as legitimate targets. The result was "a dramatic shrink-age of humanitarian access" on the ground, in the words of one leading expert on Somalia's conflict, Ken Menkhaus.[31] At the same time, attempts to "stabilize" Somalia through support for its corrupt and violent Transitional Federal Government gave its internationally paid and trained forces a free hand in driving locals away from Mogadishu and then block-ing aid access to them, further adding to the humanitarian disaster.[32]

The Americans were deploying their military resources in a peculiar fashion, using Somalia as a testing ground for their vision of remote-controlled force projection. In other words, they kept working much as they had done since the backing of the Ethiopian military invasion of 2006; clandestinely, selectively, remotely. The externally inflicted chaos that was yet again to engulf Somalia was not to soil any American hands. Except for small special forces detachments and military trainers sta-tioned in the region, there was little by way of a ground presence. US power, as Henry had said at the AFRICOM launch, would not be affirmed by the marching of boots and the building of bases—rather, it would be projected via a vertical chain of remote controls. This took two comple-mentary forms. The first, much publicized kind, consisted of US airborne surveillance and assassinations.[33] The second, which the Americans shared with the Europeans and the UN, was a reliance on a rather more extreme division of military labor than the one seen in Mali, using the African forces of AMISOM to man the front lines.

Let us dwell for now on the airborne kind of remote controls. In October 2015, an investigation by the online newspaper the *Intercept* offered a small window onto the vastly expanded US presence in Africa—including above Somalia—as well as its severe limitations. "Eradicating blank spaces on maps of the 'dark continent' was an obsession of Western powers during the 19th-century Scramble for Africa," the report began, in lines familiar to us.[34] Through remote technology and lily pads, the Americans were belat-edly trying to realize that ambition, as shown by a leaked 2013 Pentagon study of the "shadow war" waged via secret drone operations in Somalia and Yemen between January 2011 and the summer of 2012. During this time, a secretive task force, headquartered at Djibouti's Camp Lemonnier, "operated from outposts in Nairobi, Kenya, and Sanaa, Yemen. The aircraft it used—manned and remotely piloted—were based out of airfields in

Djibouti, Ethiopia, and Kenya, as well as ships off the coast of East Africa."

This distanced militarism was being rolled out not just for Somalia, we should note, but also for the Sahel. The Americans were building a drone base in Agadez and conducted an annual "Flintlock" military exercise with regional forces, as well as bilateral "training" initiatives that easily led to mission creep—as seen when US special forces' shadow presence was brought into the open by the killing of four soldiers in Niger in 2017.

As for the Horn, the leaked Pentagon files showed that for all the technological advances, "the tyranny of distance" still ruled in its brutal ways. Drones and small manned planes taking off from Djibouti at the Gulf of Aden had to traverse such long distances that their usefulness for surveillance of targets was seriously curtailed, according to the internal study. This limited the intelligence available for "find, fix, finish" (FFF) operations—in essence, killing people remotely in drone attacks, as the Obama administration had been doing in Somalia and elsewhere, in an approach that the Trump administration was to scale up across African theaters in coming years.[35] Moreover, on top of the "FFF" cycle, two additional elements—"exploit and analyze," referring to the use of material gathered in interrogations and on the ground (summarized in the letter soup F3EA)—were cut short thanks to the preponderance of killing over capturing, and to the extremely limited ground presence.[36] As the *Intercept* put it, US forces were "firing blind," with little regard to what happened down below and who would have to pick up the pieces.

This may seem a far cry from the dreams of AFRICOM stated by Henry at that Virginia meeting. Not only was the new command adding to the chaos in Somalia through its actions, but it was also nowhere near as bold, swift, and effective as advertised. Still, the Americans clearly knew what they were doing. On the ground, a small and short-term ground presence of special forces, in combination with AMISOM and select US-backed warlords, ensured an "irregular cavalry" of sorts.[37] And in the skies, drones, signals intelligence, and small manned planes complemented the proxy and punctual ground presences via surveillance and violent, unpredictable forays.

The armed drone finally rears its head in our story of the global danger zone—but only as one example of a larger reorganization of intervention by means of distant, vertical power. Like Mosby's fighters, the Americans' multilevel presence in Somalia could melt away at any moment: it was the lightest of footprints upon a terrain watched from afar. Such stealth came with costs, including limits to the visual reach of the interveners. Insiders bemoaned the "soda-straw effect" of drone operations, a metaphor that acknowledges the vastly reduced understanding of the world below, seen in little round glimpses afforded by the burning eye in the sky. But the soda straw metaphor also dovetails with the mapping of vertical power of concern to us in this chapter, including Barnett's Core and Gap thesis. It frames that world in terms of stealthily suctioning out as much intelligence as possible from the ground below and then acting on it to devastating, sudden effect. Let's return to Melville's poem and its eerie link to the drone wars, as he recounts an ambush by the Gray Ghost's men:

> Out jets the flame!
> Men fall from their saddles like plums from trees;
> Horses take fright, reins tangle and bind;
> "Steady—Dismount—form—and into the wood!"
> They go, but find what scarce can please:
> Their steeds have been tied in the field behind,
> And Mosby's men are off like the wind.

"Off like the wind" was a suitable motto for the US vertical projection of deadly force. For policy makers and citizens in the United States, internationally and in Somalia itself, little insight could be gleaned concerning "black operations" and remote attacks unleashed upon a country disconnected from Barnett's mainstream of globalization.

In short, AFRICOM and associated US interventions did not help "shrink the Gap," as Barnett had hoped. Instead the Gap kept deepening as the vertical politics of intervention extended its reach. An abyss was opening in which interveners and observers were staring down, peering for signs of the natives and fighters stranded below, including the bloodied African soldiers manning the front lines: the other side to vertical war, which we will now visit from a safe distance.

·   ·   ·   ·   ·

Joseph Borg, sharp-suited and sturdy, seemed ill at ease in his Brussels offices.[38] As he picked me up in the glassed-in lobby of the European

External Action Service in late February 2016 and buzzed me up the elevator, he wondered whether I had come to hear about his earlier work on EU-UN relations out of New York. Perhaps that was simply because he found it a preferable topic to his current task—managing EU funding for African "peace operations."

"It's very complicated!" he exclaimed as he sat down behind his desk, hands raised in exasperation over the lack of information. "The big AMISOM monster," as he called it, swallowed 85 percent of the EU's African Peace Facility funds, which financed the $1,000 that each African soldier received every month for fighting in Somalia. Meanwhile, as for the UN support operation, "Last time I pulled up the amounts of money . . . just for 2015–16 . . . it [amounted] to 540 million dollars. Just transport, food, accommodation for AMISOM." He looked perplexed. "Nobody is really keeping tabs, I think."

AMISOM was a strange beast. It was manned by Ugandan, Burundian, Kenyan, and Ethiopian solders, bankrolled by the EU, and equipped (inadequately) by the UN, while it benefited from U.S. assets, training, and intelligence. In parallel to arming and paying the AU troops, big powers were also busy training Somalia's ragtag forces. Besides individual European states, this also included Washington, by way of Obama's Counterterrorism Partnerships Fund (CTPF), replicating what the Americans were doing in the Sahel through Flintlock.[39] While Congress complained about the lack of strategic direction of CTPF (and the Trump administration eventually cut it back), African Union officials I met in Addis Ababa bemoaned the wider lack of coordination between all the training and funding efforts for both Somali and African forces. "We don't know how much the US is donating to each country contributing troops," Borg admitted.

He now had a bigger accountancy headache, as Brussels had decided to bring the payment per AU soldier down by $200 a month—a large cut. "We need to see some sunset," he said. An AMISOM mission hemorrhaging money indefinitely was a no-no at a time of refugee crises and Syrian conflict, which had seen the EU launch a naval mission on the model of Atalanta in the Mediterranean. In Somalia, this meant neighboring African states manning the front lines would have to pick up the slack. As Borg and others saw it, it was in their own "strategic interest" to secure the Somali backyard.

Figure 5. A Burundian AMISOM soldier manning a position around Baidoa airstrip, central Somalia, May 2012. © AU/Stuart Price.

Before I left, I asked about the high fatality count in AMISOM; had these countries not paid already, in soldiers' lives? Though I knew Borg was quite new to his duties, his answer still shocked me.

"Is it high? I don't know."

His response was indicative of the chasm between funders and front lines, but at least some high-level officials were aware of the toll. One top French diplomat told me that AU member states "are ready to do things that we are not able to do. They are able in Somalia to accept incredible losses." At UN headquarters I heard a similar story. "Only Uganda in AMISOM has lost more than 3,000 men in Somalia," one peacekeeping chief told me. "I don't see the UN [having] the stomach to lose 3,000 men in a peacekeeping operation." (The figures are contested, and exact numbers are impossible to ascertain, in contrast with UN practice.[40])

Both officials agreed AMISOM was not a "peace" mission—this was why the UN was only supporting it, after all, rather than running it themselves—but a counterterror operation. It kept Somalia's brutal conflicts out of sight, out of mind, and with no end in sight. "Traditional" troop contributors to UN operations, including the South Asians, did not want to touch it, so the task was left to regional powers with their own strategic interests or an ax to grind.

.   .   .   .   .

At the Kenyan embassy in Addis Ababa, Colonel Minyori sank into the sofa and mumbled eagerly into my microphone as we spoke about his country's Somalia mission. Suited rather than uniformed, he styled himself a keen student of international security—he was among the Addis-stationed African officers being trained by a private UK university, and he recorded our conversation himself for an impending assignment. But he was no beginner: unlike Borg, the colonel knew what the score was.

"We are willing to pay. We pay with blood, you pay us the cash," he said. "If you provide the cash, we provide the bodies. That is the balance. But now it has reached a level where we are being asked to provide both."

The pay cut was fraying tempers. AU soldiers would now earn $500 less than their UN peacekeeping counterparts guarding the base at Mogadishu International Airport. This was not good for soldierly morale. Yet it was easy to understand the Europeans' unease about funding the mission. In those days of early 2016, it was hard to find anyone who had a good word to spare for it. Everyone in Addis seemed to agree AMISOM was stuck in a quagmire. The UN officers in charge of security cooperation with the AU said it; the attachés said it; even the AU chiefs in charge saw that things were not working out to plan, whatever the plan once had been. The UN should take over AMISOM and adjust the mandate, AU officials even suggested—clearly frustrated that the mission's fighting objectives let New York off the hook.[41]

"There is no one else who wants to really touch it," Minyori acknowledged. "You remember the issue of Black Hawk Down, UNSOM 1, UNITAF, UNSOM 2?" he continued, reeling off failed attempts to "pacify" the country in the 1990s. "The world left Somalia alone."

In 2012, Kenya—under pressure from al Shabaab attacks on its territory—had launched its first-ever foreign military operation, Linda Nchi ("protect the country"). Soon the key port of Kismayo in southern Somalia was captured and al Shabaab driven out. Ethiopia, seeing the game raised

in its backyard, entered again; by 2013 both forces were awkwardly integrated into AMISOM, sidelining the Ugandans and Burundians. But the
colonel was hardly enthusing about the mission; instead he cleared his
throat to give me his honest assessment. "The mission in Somalia, Dr.
Andersson, to my mind, seems like we stirred the hornet's nest."

While the early onslaught of the Kenyans reaped rewards, and the
AMISOM forces pressed back al Shabaab, by early 2016 things did not look
good. AU troops, taking orders from their separate national commanders,
launched their own forays and attacks. Time and again, al Shabaab staged
ambushes on this badly coordinated set of forces. In Somalia, it was al
Shabaab that played Mosby's Confederacy with the foreign militaries,
ambushing them through suicide bombs and other asymmetric fighting
tactics.

Borg's argument that Kenya and other troop contributors had their
own strategic interest in staying put, while shouldering both financial and
human costs, did not impress Minyori. "It's not our *problem,*" he said with
emphasis. "Somalia is not a regional problem. The reason why the EU is
funding it is that they want the problem to be contained in Africa" and
they don't want "large masses of Somalis knocking at the door of Europe
trying to seek refugee status." The United States had the same concern
over the diaspora, he added. "They want the problem to be in Africa, so
therefore, since the nearest tool is regional countries with security interests of their own, the best way to solve this problem is to give them the
money and to save the lives of the West and also keep the problem contained and controlled in an environment within the region. However, it is
threatening now to escalate," he warned. "If funding is not coming it will
be difficult to sustain operations, and it may reach a level where regional
states begin to say, we pull back to our borders. . . . We are not going to
submit world peace so that Europe remains safe, America remains safe."

Minyori had powerful backers for his analysis. In their political rhetoric, everyone from Obama downwards did seem to agree that Somalia's
conflict was a global problem—however, it had stubbornly been *treated* as
a regional "African" one via the politics of distanced intervention. The
boots on the ground were African, the funds in the pot were European, the
support chain was run by the UN, the drones in the sky were American.
This vertical chain of intervention, in turn, was motivated by that slippery
catchphrase "African solutions to African problems." Insofar as the phrase

indicated growing regional responsibility for conflict, and—by extension—
the end of colonial-style meddling, it was perhaps a welcome development. Indeed, the AU and African states have increasingly taken robust
action, with UN or Western backing, in crisis spots around the continent.
Yet the issue was less the principle of regional intervention itself, which
many African capitals agreed upon, than how the problem was increasingly framed and treated as "African." One AU general, echoing Colonel
Minyori on the global nature of the Somali "problem," put it simply: "We
are taking these casualties on behalf of the world."

Minyori and other high operatives I spoke to in Addis were painfully
clear about the ultimate goals of intervention and who set them. Indeed,
if terrorist groups, piracy, and unwanted migration were the three principal threats Western interveners sought to control at one remove, the AU
forces were providing, to paraphrase anthropologist Alex De Waal,
"African solutions to Western problems," at great cost and trouble.

If the costs were huge for ambushed and maimed soldiers, they were
even larger for Somali civilians left without full international support and
with the additional risk of being killed in indiscriminate AMISOM fire.[42]
As for AMISOM, for all the complaints, the blood-for-cash deal was a big
earner for regional forces in more ways than one. The EU money for
troops often bypassed national budgets—which meant unaccountable
resources could easily be accumulated while the hold of national governments on the military could potentially be weakened. As studies have
shown, after almost ten years in operation AMISOM had become a self-
perpetuating machinery of bloodletting, trench warfare, smuggling, and
large payoffs. Military chiefs had become accustomed to the funding
streams, which ranged from illegal coal trafficking down to Kenya to the
EU money paid to soldiers, from kickbacks for the benefit of being enlisted
to the propping up of shaky defense budgets. Moreover, bringing all the
soldiers back to unemployment at home was tough to contemplate. By late
2017, AMISOM had commenced a drawdown, but it was to be slow and
uncertain, depending on the state of Somalia's security forces for its full
sunset. In the meantime, the show had to go on, at everyone's expense.[43]

An endless African military operation, then, was not an African solution to African or even Western problems but a global mess-up. If this was
not the solution, then what might be?

．　　．　　．　　．　　．

Over at the African Union headquarters, once I got the eventual all-clear at the tiny reception window and entered the precinct of this Chinese-built complex, straight ahead an unsightly old mid-rise loomed into view: the offices of the Peace Support Operations Division. And up in his office, its chief, Sivuyile Bam, was trying to contain his discontent.

"So why do you want talk to me?" he asked from the other end of a vast wooden table stacked with military memorabilia, a Somalia map adorning the wall behind. Bam was a veteran—he had been at the division since 2008 and had been through all of AMISOM's ups and downs. I had talked to his staff instead of going straight to him and so had failed to respect protocol, he said. As I launched into a defense and mentioned the general I had talked to, he corrected me: "Here he is simply one of my employees, not a general. This is a *civilian* operation." As he eventually yielded and we sat down, I suspected this was not the first time he had had to correct his overseas visitors. Here, as in Somalia itself, everyone came for the bang-bang rather than for Bam and his insights into the slow political grind.

"Al Shabaab is not going to be resolved through a military-only option," he said, finally warming to the interview. "The military can only hold and create space for negotiations." The problem with negotiations, though, was that "you can't see them. Negotiating takes place behind the scenes," and there was a "tendency to see it as having no impact, but it does."

He set out the rules that the "international community"—code for the West—was largely failing to follow. "First, you don't negotiate with your friend, you negotiate with your enemy. As unpalatable as your enemy is, he is part of the solution. Second . . . you must try by all means not to have a 'winner takes all' attitude. . . . And thirdly, if possible try without preconditions." He continued: "The Somalis have to find each other, they have to start to talk to each other, and the more they talk, the less there's a specter of violence. The country has huge potential." Its people, he added, were innovative, resilient, and entrepreneurial, as the vast diaspora had shown.

Bam could have added that Somalis had their own political-legal contract for nomad life, called *xeer:* early anthropological studies saw the consensus-based discussions through which relative peace was maintained between clans and subclans as a "pastoral democracy."[44] Siad Barre's regime had eventually undermined this system by manipulating clan affiliations while extolling a society beyond such affiliation. Outsiders' interventions and the warlords' predations since the fall of the dictator had further scattered *xeer* to the winds.

Bam was adamant: security operations might look like a quick fix for international funders, but they were leading to a quagmire. "You can bring in as many troops as you want in Somalia, but if the political process is dead, that will not resolve the issue."

At least, those in the know agreed that part of the solution had to be to channel proper money to Somali authorities in a well-coordinated fashion, unlike today's piecemeal approach. One seasoned Ethiopian security expert who had helped reform his country's military—the very military that now extended its presence and funding through AMISOM—said defiantly that he would have "added all the money and given it to Somalia" instead of to the AU and its troop contributors. This would have allowed local leaders to build their own political alliances, using money and negotiations to corner the "political marketplace" of the Horn.[45] As it was now, the wrong insiders stood to benefit from the chaotic international attention showered on the country, but it was outsiders who stood to gain the most. The AU machinery was self-perpetuating, with each new funding cycle justified by the problems of the last one. Western powers and the UN preferred to look the other way and write that check as long as the problem was out of their hands, safely contained beyond their immediate horizon.

.   .   .   .   .

Post-ICU Somalia exemplifies the blinkered, remote vision also applied to the Syrias, Afghanistans, Yemens, Malis, and Libyas of today. Through the dual workings of remote military operations and al Shabaab's predations, Somalia was actively being disconnected from the outside world. Further, legal blockages on aid and remittance transfers distanced Somalia financially from external sources of assistance, including from its diaspora, at its time of greatest need. Reliance on African and Somali forces without oversight distanced powerful Western interveners from the local population, and the latter from life-saving international attention. Drone technology and punctual raids distanced US warriors from the political and human consequences of their attacks. By the time famine hit in 2011, aid organizations failed to reach those in al Shabaab–controlled areas not just because of the insurgents' wish to punish ordinary people but also because of aid officials' fear of prosecution over support or collusion with the insurgents under the US Patriot Act.[46] As in Saudi Arabia's Western-supported brutalization of Yemen a few years later, order was instituted "above," in headquarters and in the skies; chaos and horror ensued down below. The chasm of the Gap kept deepening.

So far we have treated distanced interventions in Somalia as an expression of vertical power, and it is worth drawing out some of the analytical and historical implications of this term, expanding the dimensions of our map of danger. To do so, let us first return to the Israeli intellectual and "forensic architect" Eyal Weizman, who in his haunting book about the Israeli-Palestinian conflict, *Hollow Land,* set out the notion of a "politics of verticality" under shifting conditions of occupation. Weizman shows how the conflicts and containment in Gaza are a struggle played out no longer in just two dimensions, on the surface of the earth, but in three—reaching up into the skies and even down into the subsoil. As Israeli forces withdrew from Gaza in 2006, they retained control of airspace: they could strike and monitor anything, at any moment. The 2006 evacuation and the building of the separation barrier, he writes, are "indicative of an attempt to replace one system of domination with another. If the former system of domination relied on Israeli territorial presence within Palestinian areas and the direct governing of the occupied populations, the latter seeks to control the Palestinians from beyond the envelopes of their walled-off spaces, by selectively opening and shutting the different enclosures, and by relying on the strike capacity of the Air Force over Palestinian areas."

Weizman sees in the Israeli "distanciation" from Palestine elements of a global trend that includes, in his view, the "Israelization" of US militarism. However, drawing on our story of AFRICOM's emergence and Somalia's interventions, we may rather discern how "distanced" interventions arose somewhat independently in various defense headquarters around the same time. As in US operations over Somalia since 2006, Israelis and Palestinians are now separated "vertically, occupying different spatial layers," in Weizman's words. And as in the hands-off, drones-on approach in Somalia, the withdrawal of the physical Israeli presence from Gaza has gone hand in hand with an abdication of the limited degree of responsibility for the Palestinians that previously existed. One result of this vertical reorganization, Weizman asserts, is a "radical increase in the level of violence," as seen in the targeted assassinations and military flattening campaigns besetting fenced-off Gaza on and off since 2006.[47]

We may be forgiven for thinking that the global war on terror is what has allowed vertical power to be unleashed with such brutal force—and we may be right. Yet the distancing at work in Somalia and Gaza also draws on a longer heritage, stretching back to the colonial deployment of violence from the sky. Looking down at enemy territory from above, and then proceeding to bomb it into submission, has been the dream ever since airpower was first applied to subdue the colonial natives in the early twentieth century. In 1911, Italy went to war with the Ottoman Empire over Libya, and in the following year, the world's first aerial bombs were falling over its territory. The futurist and fascist-to-be Filippo Marinetti praised the "sculpture wrought in the enemy's masses by our expert artillery" before complaining Italy had not gone far enough.[48] Even more sober generals seemed to be learning similar lessons. Among them was Giulio Douhet, the Italian proponent of strategic bombing, who wrote in his 1921 text *The Command of the Air:* "By virtue of this new weapon, the repercussions of war are no longer limited by the farthest artillery range of guns, but can be felt directly for hundreds and hundreds of miles." On the battlefield of the future, he prophesied, "All of their citizens will become combatants, since all of them will be exposed to the aerial offensives of the enemy."

Vertical domination of this kind was not limited to poor non-Western lands, even if it was initially tested in them, much as Somalia is today used as a testing ground for war by stealth. "Distance threads through the genealogy of bombing," the geographer Derek Gregory notes. In the Second World War, the mayhem unleashed on German cities appeared as blips on "grey faceless maps," while UK bomber pilots saw the fires from raids burn as "sparkling diamonds on a black satin background." In Vietnam, prefiguring today's drone wars, General Westmoreland imagined that full electronic surveillance would soon let the US military "destroy anything we locate through instant communication and the almost instantaneous application of highly lethal firepower." As Gregory notes, critics were already in the 1970s worried about distanced wars fought via robotics and machines, raising the specter that such advanced technology could be used in countering insurgency all over the world—a point we will soon revisit.[49]

The vertical technologies and tactics in Somalia had a long history on which to build, in other words. Something similar was the case, too, for the *strategies* through which they flourished. In colonial times, as we noted in the last chapter, "unbridled conflict" was frequently relegated to the margins of empire—that is, to a lawless space reminiscent of the "medieval" wilderness of Barnett's Gap.[50] In Somalia in the 2000s, the conflict scholar Menkhaus has noted that it was in America's interest for the country to remain *unstable,* since "terrorist networks, like mafias, appear to flourish where states are governed badly, rather than not at all."[51] The removal of the Islamic Courts Union in 2006, the chaos that followed, the African forces' ensuing quagmire, the lack of international scrutiny, the US targeted raids—from a cynical standpoint this was all of a piece with sending Somalia hurtling back into the Gap, where it belonged.

·   ·   ·   ·   ·

Domination generates its own dominant narratives, and it is easy to be taken in by these tales and to exaggerate the awesome power of vertical systems of containment and violence. But let us note again that, as in Mali, dominance was anything but secured. Thinking themselves omniscient and in control, remote interveners invariably falter. Their Achilles heel is a visual arrogance, as they see only the limited tactical field in front: the soda-straw target. Meanwhile, down on the ground, proxies can stake a claim to their turfs with little oversight—generating predatory economies of the kind seen among AMISOM forces in Somalia, as well as leverage for those manning the front lines, as seen in African operatives' barely veiled threats to the Western funders.

To return to our chapter title, US operations remained in thrall to the tyranny of distance in Somalia in more ways than one. To military men, distance may seem a tactical problem of how fast to monitor and strike the enemy, but the very obsession with such geographical distance masks a more fundamental *social* distancing. Staring down a soda straw, after all, makes you one-eyed—the theater of operations recedes from full view and comprehension. Noting this problem, concerned military thinkers have argued that remote-control tactics cannot be allowed to masquerade as strategy. To make their case they may wish to wheel out the example of the 1912 Libyan bombings, which stirred sympathy for the victims and anger against imperialists "as far as Malaya."[52] Or they may bring up the Somalia of the following decade, when Winston Churchill unleashed airpower on recalcitrant rebels, and may insist that what really "won it" was the ground presence. Less belligerent voices would add that if the ground presence is simply a repressive force of proxy soldiers and weapon-bearing occupiers, little will be achieved in the longer run, as the AU security chief Bam insisted. Others such as our Ethiopian military expert may argue that in a wobbly international order, illustrated by persistent fragility in countries like Somalia, Western powers must limit their reach, leaving nationals to sort out their conflicts.[53] Yet in Somalia, it was hard to separate out responsibilities in this fashion, as Colonel Minyori had indicated. Rather than the "world's most dangerous place," we may say it was the world's most *dangerized* place. Here international powers and actors—from AU officials to Kenyan colonels, from Brussels bureaucrats to the US State Department—collaborated in framing and justifying an endless military intervention by recourse to distance and danger.

Now that Mosby has had his word, it is worth also citing another historical figure who gave al Shabaab leaders their own local inspiration. In the late nineteenth century, the British colonizers had begun fighting a drawn-out insurgency by the "mad mullah," a religious leader and poet-fighter (known as the Shaheed in Somalia) who pulled in a large following and waged asymmetrical warfare with great success. "If the town is cut off from the interior, the Angel of Death soon comes to it on his errands," the insurgent warlord wrote in one of his poems, which are read even today in Somalia. Disconnection fueled the violent spiral. When, in October 2017, Mogadishu was hit by the deadliest terror attack in years, news emerged that the perpetrator driving the explosives-laden truck was a former Somali soldier whose hometown had been raided by US special forces.[54] As two "insurgent" campaigns—the remote-controlled US one and the ground-level one by al Shabaab—faced off with similar deadly tactics, the end result was a vicious cycle of perpetual violence, of danger feeding on danger: a nightmare borne of a fantasy of power.

"Disconnectedness defines danger" read Barnett's motto, yet we need to turn it on its head. Defining danger, interveners generate disconnectedness. And through this disconnect, the tyranny of distance morphs into tyranny *by* distance.

Our story of the map of danger has taken a dark turn, now that we have replaced the human scale of Mali's interventions with Somalia's vertical one. But let us not forget, as we close this chapter, those who keep *humanizing* Somalia. Among them are the unsung ordinary Somalis who keep hope and everyday life going, trading in markets and demonstrating against the violence. Among them are civilian leaders and officials inside and outside the country, whose efforts helped secure a peaceful transition of power after the 2017 presidential elections.[55] Among them are also aid workers—Somalis as well as a scattering of internationals, including Somali diasporans willing to risk it in the world outside the Mogadishu airport compound. One London-based diasporan, once employed with the UN in Mogadishu, reminisced to me one day of how she had kept visiting remote corners of the country at great danger to herself and to local helpers. She told me how she had sought every chance to shed her flak jacket for a spot of bartering and banter in Mogadishu's markets, and how she had occasionally skulked out of the UN compound to sample fragrant cardamom tea at a makeshift stall outside. Amid the vertical distancing to danger, in other words, attempts to generate horizontal connections still kept trying to flower.

However—and to get drawn back into our darkening Gap—danger itself also helped facilitate horizontal connections of a deadlier kind, as al Shabaab's fighters knew when they uploaded their recruitment videos online and posted atrocities right, left, and center. The "danger project" of al Shabaab, like that of Mali's various jihadist groups, was moreover tied up with external funding, with drug running and contraband spanning continents, and with propaganda and recruitment campaigns that as often as not started in a living room in the British Midlands or a Scandinavian suburb. Mirroring such dangerous connections from below, the United States was doing something similar from above. Raining down its Hellfire

missiles, policing and projecting force at one remove, it not only enacted
the medieval, Hobbesian Gap below but also helped tie the Somali battlefields unevenly into global economies of power, raising the stakes for
the insurgents and their global recruitment campaigns. Somalia, the
Sahel, Afghanistan, and other sites were not "disconnected" from globalization: they were very much at its core as sites of experimentation in insecurity and fear, feeding their products into global circuits.

After drawing our map of danger in three dimensions, we have now
come to the end of our cartographic journey. For as the last paragraph
suggests, attempts at distancing oneself from danger zones by means of
vertical power come up, time and again, against the systemic nature of
global danger—including its nonlinear spread beyond well-defined "theaters," as we will see in our second part of *No Go World*.

In this respect, at least, Barnett was right: interveners cannot hope to
contain the Hobbesian Gap: "There is no exit strategy," as he put it.[56] The
threat will always find its way across what he called the "seam states" to
infiltrate the Core, visiting our Kantian world with uncanny, unpredictable dangers. When Barnett dismissed his isolationist critics as wanting to
"build a big fence around this nasty neighborhood called the Gap," that
was however precisely what they were trying to do.[57] The rich world's
borders, which we will be visiting soon enough, are turning into hot
spots for struggles over contagious danger and are as a result becoming
afflicted with the interventionist ills we have so far seen at work in Mali,
Afghanistan, and Somalia. But before heading to these borderlines, we
must linger a little longer on the war on terror, reflecting on the pathologies propagated within it. We will travel up the soda straw into the military circuits where warfare is a struggle not just for vertical dominance
but also for informational space—from where it may spread, virus-like,
into domains well beyond the battlefields of the distant danger zone.

INTERLUDE

THE DRONE, THE WEB,
AND THE WORLD OF MIRRORS

On a night map of the earth, the electric glimmer of capitals and coast-lines contrasts with darkened areas inland, in the poor interior parts of Africa and Asia. Light against shadow. On versus off grid. Some war-on-terror operators talk about the off-grid world as their terrain. There, in its mountainous folds, the night air swarms with metallic *machays* (wasps), as Pakistani Pashtuns call the killer drones. Sensors alert, the wasps search the grounds with patience and care, their unblinking eyes fixed on human targets rendered in thermal infrared.[1]

Drones swarm through the hive mind of our times. The "unmanned aerial vehicles" (UAVs) or "remote-piloted aircraft" (RPAs), the Predators and Reapers of the global war on terror, keep spawning Hollywood flicks and news stories that range from fascination to horror to horrified fascination. Drone-speak has also migrated from shadow warfare into the light of day, as newspapers lap up stories of home-piloted minidrones in near crashes with airplanes or discuss the pros and cons of Amazon's Prime Air. Strategists fear terrorist weaponization of the toy drones, generating a growing market in antidrone defense systems, while others worry that the migration of drone-speak into the civilian realm normalizes the technology's military usage.[2] As I watch my son's favorite cartoon, *Paw Patrol*, I am inclined to agree as he cries out "Drone!" whenever Chase the police puppy unleashes a surveillance UAV from the back of his primary-color-blue vehicle.

Drone fetishism is all around. To some, killer drones are the principal tool of an everywhere war without end and without legality, the omen of robo-wars to come. To war-on-terror strategists, drones rather allow for targeted killings with "minimal collateral damage," or civilian deaths (usually, though, they define all more or less adult males as combatants, misrepresenting the figures). Still others hail drones' capacity to monitor distant areas for humanitarian or peacekeeping purposes, especially where soldiers or aid workers cannot tread—witness UNHCR or MINUSMA extolling their unarmed UAVs in the Sahel as they respectively monitor displaced people and jihadist movements.[3] Unarmed drones can be used for both surveillance and intimidation in a form of militarized policing of rebellion first tested by peacekeepers in the Democratic Republic of Congo, and later deployed by the Swedish forces around Timbuktu.[4] At the gates of the rich world, UAVs are also of a piece with the militarized quest to detect and intercept migrants from Mediterranean coastlines to the deserts of Arizona, where they hold out hope of an omniscient techno-border of sorts.[5]

Leaving aside the rights or wrongs of today's dronophiles and dronophobes as they debate such applications, they share a tendency to treat UAVs as things somehow magically imbued with action. In this, they are but the latest in a long line of technological dystopians and utopians, ranging from nineteenth-century Luddites to glorifiers of the "revolution in military affairs" at the turn of the millennium. Yet we must set aside any lingering technological determinism to see—as Marx would advise—the drone as part of a system of human labor, inquiring into the logics of this system as well as into its resonances beyond the battle space.

One thing should be clear from our descent so far into the global danger zones: that the windowless wasps buzzing through the "AfPak" borderlands are but part of a wider architecture of warfare. In this "shadow war," the US Joint Special Operations Command (JSOC) launches its killing sprees in cooperation with the CIA, the National Security Agency, and the US Army, who work together via drones, door-kicking, and military intelligence. Theirs is "a new kind of warfare where men and machines merge," as one much-touted journalistic profile, "Confessions of a Drone Warrior," puts it. They form a network, and they operate in a world where killings are talked about as "mowing the lawn" and drone victims as "bugsplat."[6] As one of JSOC's number renders their godlike powers: "We're the dark matter. We're the force that orders the universe but can't be seen."[7]

Ignore the boasts—the key part of the phrase is that they *can't be seen*. The danger zone serves many useful functions, as we have seen, but one of its most powerful perks is the secrecy enabled by a "no entry" sign slapped on the door.[8] Yet as we now tread onto the high-tech terrain of shadow warfare, managed from a safe distance, we find that entrance is blocked here too. In the post-9/11 years, the shadow US security state has expanded into a warren of secret offices, underground bunkers, and clandestine programs inaccessible to even the most inveterate diggers, as journalist Dana Priest and former soldier William Arkin find in their *Top Secret America*.[9] Given this secrecy, all we may hope for is to catch a brief glimpse of the logics underlying the remapping of military intervention—while divining, as we will try to do, how these innovations have come back to haunt us, citizens and observers kept in the dark about the dark universe.

THE INTIMATE DRONE

Security scholars have been sticking their hands into the wasps' nest of "late modern war" for some time now. What they find there, and what they see the drone as exemplifying, is a disturbing remaking of the legality of war and the battle space. For one, drone warfare seems to enact the very "bifurcation of the world" first announced by our cartographer *manqué*, Kaplan. To anthropologist Hugh Gusterson, drone strikes reinforce "the abject status of countries that do not have the legal right to territorial integrity" and so divide the world between those countries that may be hit by drones and those that may not.[10] Further, no "boots on the ground" means no risk of dead soldiers, and consequently no "war"—allowing the US executive to bypass Congress, as Obama did in Libya.[11] This legal loophole has implications for the space of battle and its extension. In his *Drone Theory*, Grégoire Chamayou writes that the "kill boxes" of lethal drone action dissolve old "geocentric" concepts of warfare, as armed conflict is redefined as "a mobile place attached to the person of the enemy," following him wherever he goes.[12] At the same time, drone warfare compresses the battle space into global circuits, promising both spatial and temporal dominance. "Speed has always been the advantage and the privilege of the hunter and the warrior," the French philosopher Paul Virilio has observed.[13] Now, man hunting can be world-spanning, extended in time, and without risk to the hunter.

Consider a Reaper hovering over its target for days on end in Pakistan or Afghanistan, where the CIA and the air force respectively operate their drones. As the drone's Hellfire eventually obliterates its human target, it leaves a visual trace on monitors in a satellite-linked web of military control rooms, from the Combined Air and Space Operations Center in Qatar to the Distributed Common Ground System in Langley, Virginia. At the far end of the "invisible data highway" linking up these disparate sites, in an American trailer park on an air force base, the operator scans the blurred scenes of carnage before he eventually winds up the day and commutes back home to his children.[14] When Kaplan visited one such trailer park in Nevada, where one trailer each hosted Iraq and Afghanistan, he quipped: "So much for the tyranny of geography."[15]

Banality, awe, and horror intermix in this kill chain crossing continents. I recall one bizarre episode of a British sitcom—and there is more where that came from, as we will see shortly—where the good-for-nothing heroine lazes on her bedsheets, clicking away on a laptop; she has been contracted to finish the kills somewhere out there in the meatspace, earning pocket money for her sloppy habits. In this ridiculous scene resides the horror of the kill chain. The potential for vicarious warfare without risk, combined with the voyeuristic pleasure in dominating whatever we see on screen, is both shocking and darkly titillating. If warfare is cinematic at its core, as Virilio has argued, drone warfare is surely its most lurid manifestation, as the "Predator porn" genre of blurred surveillance and kill shots online testifies.[16]

Pornography implies a peculiar kind of nearness and distance. As "Confessions of a Drone Warrior" puts it, there is a "voyeuristic intimacy" at work in how the operator follows people for days, building evidence of "pattern of life" and seeking positive identification. In his report, Kaplan notes how operators in the Nevada trailer park observe their human targets having sex on rooftops in the Afghan night or watch "a guy walk into the courtyard at night to take a crap, registered by the heat signature."[17] "Unclean" is what another observer, attuned to the voyeurism, calls UAV campaigns. Critics may compare them to "video games," yet if anything they are even more immersive than the 3D shoot-'em-ups on which many a teenage boy spends his days and nights. For the soldier-turned-assassin, drone warfare "holds all the horrors of war without any of its comforts." In ordinary war, the soldier finds solace in bravery; in a Nevada trailer park, there is no honor, and as yet no bravery medal, to be had.[18]

This idea of intimacy is oddly comforting, as it seems to humanize drone operators (many of them get post-traumatic stress disorder, was the news story a while back). Yet the geographer Derek Gregory, with his trademark touch, picks this intimacy up as an object, studies it, and finds in it a phenomenal military function. For rather than creating empathy with the victim, or with civilians in the crosshairs, the intimacy of drone campaigns allows for military camaraderie to reemerge. As one commander recalls, "You hear the AK-47 going off, the intensity of the voice on the radio calling for help. You're looking at him, 18 inches away from him, trying everything in your capability to get that person out of trouble." The war is only as far away as the screen. On it are *your* men, the ones who are in charge once a strike has been called, and who often decide to use their newfound power to escalate the aerial attacks. Gregory concludes that the network of drone warfare produces a one-sided kind of intimacy, while the time-space compression of the kill chain reinforces "the techno-cultural distinction between 'their' space and 'our' space, between the eye and the target."[19]

We are back, then, with our bifurcated world. In the shadow universe of war, the Gap and the Core, the green and red zones, are *made* to emerge in brutally stark guise across spatial and temporal dimensions dominated by the aggressor. We hold this map of danger in our palms, thumb it, see its contours from new, starker, and darker angles as we wind our way from Mali to Somalia and Afghanistan. However, we must now leave this map behind. The drone's world of light and shadows is real enough, yet it is part of our old top-down tale of the lie of the land. For the coming chapters, we need to fold this map into our pocket, raise our view, and tread into another territory. A cursory peek beyond the bifurcated map with its kill boxes, its crosshairs, its God fantasies, and its "Predator porn" reveals something more intricate at play, beyond the lopsided time-spaces of battle. Our glimpses into the shadow war will, in fact, suggest that the red and green zones of the world map are not as far apart as they seem: rather, they reflect back on each other in a darkening hall of mirrors.

MCCHRYSTAL'S MIRROR

One man who helped tear me away from my own obsession with the map of danger and distance was Stanley McChrystal, a wiry and close-cropped general of global fame. Variously know as Big Stan, the Boss, the Pope, and the "rock-star warrior," General McChrystal had a beef with military maps—but we will get to that shortly.[20]

First, though, his rock-star fame. As his epithets hinted none too subtly, McChrystal was in his every fiber the celebrity of the shadow universe, to the point where he ended up trashing his own figurative hotel when, as America's commander in Afghanistan, he attacked the Obama administration in a disastrous *Rolling Stone* interview that eventually saw him dismissed and disgraced.[21] But all that was still in the future. Like General David Petraeus, under whom he worked in Iraq after 2007, McChrystal had been dispatched to Baghdad as the occupation was descending into an utter mess. It was in quagmired Iraq where he made his name, heading up JSOC as it hunted al Qaeda in Iraq (AQI), which had emerged after the US invasion and subsequent "de-Ba'athification" of the Iraqi administration. There he forged a new JSOC out of its past as a hostage-rescue force, and out of the deep morass of Top Secret America. JSOC was swiftly turning into a "self-sustaining secret army" as it grew from 1,800 troops in 2001 to something like 25,000 a decade later.[22]

McChrystal's good luck came courtesy of the turf wars in the US administration. With the CIA's drone program well under way, Defense Secretary Donald Rumsfeld wanted to wrest control of the war on terror, and he eventually managed to do so with his executive order (EXORD) of September 16, 2003. With it, Rumsfeld created a new category of top-secret activities for "disrupting, capturing, or destroying the al Qaeda network and its supporters anywhere in the world," which—unlike the CIA's covert actions—required no congressional notification.[23] This move "hit

JSOC's Fort Bragg headquarters like a lightning bolt," Priest and Arkin write, and set the stage for its secretive entry into the heart of the global war on terror.[24] Unlike the flabby AFRICOM, McChrystal's lean and mean operation was the Gray Ghost reborn.

Now, to the map scrunched in his pocket. In his business how-to manual *Team of Teams*, published as the general picked up his career after the disgraced Afghan exit through consultancy and corporate advice, McChrystal starts by tearing up the military maps of intervention. Reflecting on his days holed up at the Balad airbase of the Joint Special Operations Task Force, he writes:

> When we first established our Task Force headquarters at Balad, we hung maps on almost every wall. Maps are sacred to a soldier. In military headquarters, maps are mounted and maintained with almost religious reverence. A well-marked map can, at a glance, reveal the current friendly and enemy situations, as well as the plan of future operations. Orders can be conveyed using a marked map and a few terse words. There are stories of Pentagon office renovations removing a wall only to find behind it another wall covered in maps dating from a previous conflict. For most of history, war was about terrain, territory held, and geographic goals, and a map was the quintessential tool for seeing the problem and creating solutions. But the maps in Balad could not depict a battlefield in which the enemy could be uploading video to an audience of millions from any house in any neighborhood, or driving a bomb around in any car on any street.[25]

So far, so predictable: we already know that the war on terror plays out in ways not captured on two-dimensional maps of global red and green zones—across cityscapes, in the air, in cyberspace. But then came McChrystal's innovation, delivered as if in a police procedural. Instead of maps, "Whiteboards began to appear in our headquarters," he continued. "Soon they were everywhere. Standing around them, markers in hand, we thought out loud, diagramming what we knew, what we suspected, and what we did not know. We covered the bright white surfaces with multicolored words and drawings, erased, and then covered again. We did not draw static geographic features; we drew mutable relationships—the connections between things rather than the things themselves."[26]

Whereas maps and screens worked as a one-way mirror, revealing the theater of operations to the invisible all-seeing viewer, the whiteboard reflected back on the soldiers as they stood in their Balad lair, marker pen in hand. On it, they saw the enemy emerge through their scrawled connections as a *network;* and gradually the JSOC warriors themselves began their own process of transforming into one. As McChrystal wrote, "We all understood that we were now part of a network; when we visualized our own force on the whiteboard, it now took the form of webs and nodes, not tiers and silos. . . . To defeat a network, we had become a network. We had become a team of teams."[27]

This was McChrystal's Law, as some of his admirers called it.[28] As everyone started working as one and delegated decision making down the chain, McChrystal reflected, "the *quality* of decisions actually went *up.*" Before, raids had numbered ten to eighteen per month, but "by 2006, under the new system, this figure skyrocketed to three hundred. With minimal increases in personnel and funding, we were running *seventeen times faster.* And these raids were more successful," with more human targets found.[29]

JSOC was becoming an "executive assassination ring," in the words of investigative journalist Seymour Hersh.[30] Security insiders agreed: one described JSOC as "Murder, Incorporated"; another, as the "most dangerous people on the face of the earth."[31] It was JSOC that Obama unleashed to kill the long-hunted Saleh Ali Saleh Nabhan in Somalia.[32] It was JSOC that killed bin Laden. It was JSOC that pursued and killed Abu Musab al-Zarqawi in the chaos of postinvasion Iraq.[33] And it was JSOC that launched a campaign of killing in that country so scientific in its brutality it would make any neoconservative armchair strategist blush. In the first months of the invasion of Afghanistan, JSOC teams killed thousands; in the first weeks in Iraq alone, they helped kill hundreds, and then the death toll only grew. By summer of 2005, as chaos mounted in Iraq, JSOC executed some three hundred raids a month. This was McChrystal's "success"—an ever-expanded roster of killings and captures. The bird's-eye map had been torn apart and replaced with his whiteboard and the connections drawn across it, forming a network structure that consciously mimicked that of the enemy.[34]

Amid this killing-machine innovation, it is easy to succumb to an alternative to the technological fetish and style McChrystal as the hero or villain of the piece. This is what the media did, after all, as they readily lapped up stories of "America's top hunter-killer," replete with descriptions of his weird jogging routines, gaunt face, and austere habits.[35] McChrystal may have been a catalyst for networked warfare, yet from another viewpoint he—like the drone technology accompanying his every step—was simply a bit player in a much larger military assemblage. Moreover, this machinery of state was far from fail-safe and all-seeing, however much insiders drummed up its omniscience and omnipotence.[36]

Instead of mythologizing "Stan the Man," then, let us focus on one key *logic* at work in these adaptive war systems—that of mirroring and mimicry illustrated by McChrystal's Law. The JSOC network mirrored the enemy, as the general-turned-consultant told his new corporate audiences when advertising the methods of Murder, Inc. in *Team of Teams*. But the mimicry went further, encompassing the killing technology on both sides. Military operators themselves have noted that armed UAVs, in withdrawing the aggressor from harm, are the mirror image of improvised explosive devices, the insurgents' weapon of choice. The armed UAV "turns against the guerrillas their own long-established principle, namely, deprive the enemy of an enemy," Chamayou notes. Invincibility cuts the costs of lethal action, and it allows for "projecting power without vulnerability," in the terminology of the US Air Force.[37] To put it differently: drones and IED attacks both seek to terrorize with minimum vulnerability for the aggressor. Suicide bombs extend this logic—when the aggressor is willing to die in the act, the enemy is similarly deprived of an enemy.

The hoped-for repercussions also mirror one another. With drone attacks, the idea is, in the words of one US Air Force major general, to "dislocate the psychology of the insurgents" and to engender a sense of "hopelessness that arises from the inevitability of death from a source they cannot fight."[38] A similar sense of terror, demoralization, and confusion was achieved by JSOC's shadow assassinations. It is also, needless to say, one of the main strategic aims of terrorist groups today. As one Afghan villager exclaims in Chamayou's *Drone Theory:* "We pray to Allah that we have American soldiers to kill." Yet, deprived of military targets, insurgents seek soft targets elsewhere. In the words of one American soldier, "Attempts to armorize our force against all potential enemy threats" shift "the 'burden of risk' from a casualty-averse military force onto the populace." This may well include civilians in the interveners' home countries, or, as Chamayou writes, "By maximizing the protection of military lives and making the inviolability of its 'safe zone' the mark of its power, a state that uses drones tends to divert reprisals toward its own population."[39]

Mimesis between invader and "native" was once a feature of the early colonial encounter, anthropologists tell us, and here it appears again, in the postcolonial twilight of the off-grid world and its shadow wars.[40] To be sure, this is far from the innocuous mirroring of the kind seen in, say, the Melanesian "cargo cults" where locals mimicked the comportment of war-time soldiers in order to magically bring forth the long-gone cargo drops from the sky. Rather, a monstrous mimicry is at work: the killing machine kept spitting out new monsters, from AQI to Daesh and beyond, each round of violence begetting the next. The search for monsters to destroy kept bringing forth new generations of them, as the "mowing of the lawn" metaphor itself suggests.

This is well known. But as we will go on to see, the hall of mirrors of the war on terror stretches further than that, into the very corporate world that McChrystal was now trying to impress in his postwarrior incarnation. We will next try to catch a glimpse of this reflection between the military and civilian realms, where networked intel was to spawn political mon-strosities of its own by way of what the Pentagon refers to as the fifth dimension of war: cyberspace.

FLYNN'S MIRROR

In August 2017, one small news item caught my eye. It was about military man Michael Flynn, Trump's onetime national security adviser, who had been fired after the Russia revelations. Now Flynn had belatedly disclosed that he had briefly held an advisory role with a Virginia-based company called SCL Group. This outfit's subsidiary, Cambridge Analytica (CA), was said to have contributed—through advanced data-mining operations—to the surprise wins of Brexit and Trump, as it allowed for ads targeted at small segments of the voting population on the basis of their psychological, social, geographical, and political profile.[41] By March 2018, the dark opera-tions of CA and their alleged usage of an academic's psychometric test to pull in the Facebook data of some fifty million unaware Americans had become big news, thanks to first-rate journalistic digging. Yet even without this full picture, the story had piqued my interest as I first drafted these pages the preceding autumn: it seemed to offer up an intriguing link between the war on terror and the political battleground of Western democracies. But more on that shortly.

Major General Flynn was a "legend of the military intelligence world," as Jeremy Scahill puts it in his *Dirty Wars,* who side by side with McChrystal was "on the knife's edge of the intelligence technology that would be at the center of the mounting, global kill/capture campaign."[42] Key to JSOC's assassination merry-go-round was intel, and Flynn was the man to purvey it—or as he put it, when writing as director of intelligence at US Central Command (CENTCOM) in 2008, "Today, intelligence *is* operations."[43] In brief, intel permeated the find, fix, finish, exploit, and analyze cycle (F3EA) we have already encountered. First, put suspected "terrorists" on a kill list, map out their network and the functions of each insurgent within it, and then decide priorities. Find them, monitor them through sensors mounted on drones, on vehicles, and even on military dogs sent to houses around Baghdad. At the same time, mine mobile phone metadata from a distance, and identify each target via their phone "signature" (often it wasn't theirs, but no matter). After "fixed" comes the "finish"—kill or capture—through the JSOC teams kicking in doors in the Iraqi night, through a drone strike, or via air power. Next, exploit and analyze anything you can get your JSOC hands on—loose pocket scraps, any electronic devices—and with these fragments build your picture of the network. And so the cycle starts again, the intricate network blooming on the whiteboard in the Balad lair.

And larger it got. With each set of kills, more names were added to the list. The lawn had to be mowed, and the grass grew back faster each time. Someone alarmed by this trend was David Kilcullen, an anthropologist-turned-strategist who had been at the core of efforts to rework counterinsurgency for the Iraq era. He had advised Petraeus and McChrystal on how to sort "reconcilables" from "irreconcilables" and on how to avoid a quagmire. However, Kilcullen lamented, the cycle of shadow killings was turning local society against the invaders, creating more "bad guys" in the process, which in turn made the whole business harder to stop.[44] Other warriors and strategists expressed their doubts, too. One Ranger, while praising McChrystal, saw the dangers of his model as it spread outwards from Iraq.

"You have an empowered executive branch that more or less has license to wage war wherever it determines it needs to, worldwide," he said. "You've got this great hammer, and, you know, why not go hammer some nails?"[45]

The killing machinery was well oiled, capturing increasing government funds while extending its reach. As suggested by the moniker Murder, Inc., it worked as a predatory corporate entity succeeding in a capitalist war market red in tooth and claw. Indeed, McChrystal himself had explicitly compared counterinsurgency with corporate competition in *Team of Teams*, as he promoted his martial methods to business executives. JSOC kept finding more nails to hammer, because that was what it knew and what it had the free hand to do in a freed-up market of kills.

In short, JSOC's operations resembled a runaway business, built upon the extralegal opportunities of GWOT as well as on the technological and networked advances of intel-driven war. With this in mind, let us now briefly suspend disbelief and leap from danger zones to green zones in order to see the corporate linkages between the two.

Shock the system, Flynn had admonished the *Rolling Stone* journalist-turned-nemesis embedded with his boss during their Afghan period, Michael Hastings.[46] This seemed an apt motto, too, for SCL, the business Flynn had briefly advised. The tools, trade, and goals of SCL, Cambridge Analytica, and their kind were clearly different from those of Murder, Inc.—yet the logics of their political campaigns, and the networked technology underlying them, show resemblances to the world of network wars that cannot be easily dismissed.

SCL and Cambridge Analytica, as media reports were finally telling us in the spring of 2018, were not any old civilian businesses in the profitable market of electioneering. Rather, they had started the trajectory toward electoral business stardom in militarism and war. The UK Foreign Office had contracted SCL to counter jihadi propaganda in Pakistan; SCL then received Pentagon contracts for psychological operations (PsyOps) in Yemen and Iran. The company spawned Cambridge Analytica, which developed psychographics and behavioral profiling for political purposes. By 2015, SCL was producing "target audience analysis" for NATO strategic communications (or PsyOps) in settings such as Afghanistan. Meanwhile, CA was about to make it big with the Brexit campaign and the presidential candidacy of Ted Cruz followed by Trump.[47]

Much ink and social media outrage has—somewhat ironically—been spent on the role of Facebook in spreading "fake news" by playing on users' emotional reactions through their algorithms. It was this emotional Big Data that CA exploited in its behavioral profiling operations. Journalistic exposés have dug into the workings of the outfit and its cast of characters, including billionaire backer Robert Mercer and Trump's now estranged sidekick Steve Bannon, who once sat on its board and allegedly guided its operations. Some voices—including, at times, Cambridge Analytica itself—argue that behavioral profiling is not as powerful as alleged. Others disagree, seeing its Orwellian potential.[48] Whatever the case, we are not concerned here with efficacy. Rather, SCL and Cambridge Analytica—which already had a global roster of shady electoral business by the time of the US presidential campaign—are of interest to us because of their dual-use methods, honed via their military heritage.

Cambridge Analytica's work for the Trump campaign constituted, according to data scholar Jonathan Albright's extensive investigations, a form of "military-grade PsyOps." Psychometric profiles of voters were built from open-source intelligence—via not just Facebook "likes" but also ad technology, machine learning, and more. This allowed for intensive targeting of specific groups with propaganda tailored to their psychological profile, with the aim—as with the NATO PsyOps campaign—of changing behavior, not simply modifying attitudes. As Albright puts it, the task was to find "people who can be *influenced enough* to actually go out and vote," as well as those who could be convinced to stay at home rather than vote for the opponent.[49]

The story is bigger than Cambridge Analytica and SCL alone, as the Trump campaign was bolstered by advanced behavior-tracking and data-mining techniques in the online shadowlands. Mapping this world, Albright renders it into a network of sites, connected around the movements of the user into what he calls a "privacy Death Star." Not shying away from his *Star Wars* metaphors, he continues: "People's personal info and activities are traveling unshielded through space and time, like an X-wing fighter that's been hit by the Death Star's superlaser." By being lured in through Facebook "like" buttons and other tools, readers can be tracked and their private lives laid bare, opening up scope for "predictive modeling" used to influence future behavior in even more intrusive ways.

The targets include not only those "naïve enough" to spread propaganda, but also those "trolled" into responding. The visible content, or "micro-propaganda" as Albright calls it, is set in a feedback loop with the invisible "weaponized, behavioral-tracking shadow tech." "The more we argue, the more personal information, context/sentiment and rich emotional data gets captured to better target the Death Star's superlaser."[50]

Flynn's link to SCL, in all its brevity, offers us a disturbing glimpse into the space where the bifurcated geography of danger disintegrates into networks, and where state power melds with its corporate counterpart. Here, to be crude about it, Murder, Inc. intersects with Propaganda, Ltd. via their overlapping business models and methodologies. Even if SCL's expertise lay in military PsyOps and influencing, rather than in counterterrorism, its Cambridge Analytica spinoff increasingly came to rely on the kind of strategies discussed in McChrystal's business manual: shallow data harvesting identifying individuals and groups; deep, invasive tracking of individuals through cyberspace and via geo-location; network analysis, building a picture of how they connect to one another; and the building of an aggressor network, the better to attack key parts of the target network.

What does this tell us? That we can all speculate quite freely on the linkages between the on- and off-grid worlds, for one, when access remains blocked and secrecy rife! But it should also tell us a few substantive things, however tentatively. First, the militarization of the global danger zones by way of a multidimensional battle space is coming back to haunt the putative safe zones of Western democracies and of the online world, which are now being militarized in turn. Second, this militarization of both faraway lands and democracies at home increasingly coheres into a global security market—as was seen, for instance, when Trump came to power and SCL obtained a lucrative US State Department contract to fight Daesh propaganda, or when McChrystal promoted his networked warfare to executives. In short, advanced "surveillance capitalism" is feeding on counterinsurgency innovations in the danger zones, which constitute a laboratory of sorts for militarized methods of wide application.[51] US liberal media and politicians like to focus all their energies on Russian meddling in the 2016 presidential election, and with good reason, but until the CA story broke in March 2018 they had spent precious little time considering how the very techniques of surveillance developed in America's wars of choice had infiltrated their own political process, with a little help from corporate power.[52]

Third and finally, this corporate-military infiltration feeds on a fundamental resource, which itself chimes with and draws sustenance from the war on terror: fear. Fear was a tool to JSOC, which promised to hit with ferocious force against anyone at any time. Fear was also at the heart of the Cambridge Analytica campaign in the United States, and allegedly in Nigeria before that, where reports suggested that it (or an offshoot) had used clips of jihadist violence to intimidate voters.[53] As one CA executive told undercover British reporters in a sting, their method was to prey on people's fears through microtargeting: "Our job is to . . . drop the bucket further down the well than anybody else, to understand what are those really deep-seated underlying fears. . . . It's no good fighting an election campaign on the facts because actually it's all about emotion." Their business was, in essence, an insurgent, covert campaign to economize fear and inject it "into the bloodstream" of the Internet, as the executive put it: a *phobonomics*, if you will, that mirrored how JSOC conducted their operations, as well as how jihadists tore apart the bifurcated map of danger whenever they brought spectacular violence to bear on the presumed safety of the "homeland."[54]

THE BLACK MIRROR

When I was little—maybe a preschooler, I can't quite remember—I used to be haunted by a nightmare whenever I had bouts of high fever. In the dream, a military tank came rumbling toward me: it was grim, big, loud, its gun turret creaking, its amphibious wheels crunching nearer, and nearer, and nearer still. I was stuck in some sort of hole in the ground, as if in a trench; but I was not a soldier, just myself—a civilian, a dreamer, a small boy—motionless with visceral fear. I twisted in my sodden sheets as the tank approached but never quite mowed me down.

I don't think many preschoolers have nightmares about tanks today. My fever dream of a tank invasion fed on the politics of the time: the clang and roar of the Cold War's military-industrial complex; TV news of wars threatened or real; my parents' history of marching against them. Air alarms were still tested regularly, should the bomb planes come flying over suburban Sweden; the basement of our apartment complex served as a bunker and as a perfectly spooky place for hide-and-seek. That world is not gone, by any means—witness Trump's nuclear threats, Pyongyang's missiles, the return of big-power confrontations over Syria. Yet today other threats tend to assail our dreams, transforming the national security fears of the era of nuclear Armageddon into something more intimate, and in some ways more horrific for that. "I can't remember exactly when I stopped dreaming of nuclear annihilation," writes one British journalist, as she reflects on the nuclear threats reemerging into world politics. "Slow environmental collapse took over from the imagining of a nuclear winter. Now I fear terror and robots more. Both on the same day sometimes."[55]

A strange mix of fear and desire attaches to technological dystopias, as illustrated by the uproar over the Cambridge Analytica story in early 2018. As some commentators have noted, and as I myself realized when I first drafted these pages in the preceding year, the tawdry tale of CA and its weaponization of Facebook data mirrors science fiction. So does, of course, drone warfare. Already in the 1950s, as the world entered its nuclear midwinter, Robert Sheckley penned the short story *Watchbird* about a future of deadly drones that ended up turning against their makers.[56] But rather than delve into Sheckley's eerie prophecies, let us cast an eye on a more recent specimen of sci-fi horror—the wildly popular Netflix series *Black Mirror*.

One episode in particular resonates with our case. In it, we visit a United Kingdom in the near future in which the country's honeybees are dying off. To solve the problem, the government has hired a visionary innovator and his Google-lookalike tech company to produce Autonomous Drone Insects—robo-bees—to pollinate flowers and crops. One day, a robo-bee goes astray. It whirrs its metallic wings into the home of a hate-stirring newspaper columnist and burrows its way into the pain center of her brain. In agony, she kills herself. It eventually dawns on police that a shadowy criminal is hacking into individual bees in order to kill, with victims chosen through a social media poll under the hashtag #DeathTo. More bees disappear from the tech company's control screens, and soon they buzz into the skulls of each one of the top-polled victims. A minister fears being the next victim, and asks for his minders to smear a rival candidate on social media so that he can be saved. Belatedly, the police realize that before the robo-bees were hacked, UK military intelligence had already repurposed them to spy on ordinary citizens, at every street corner, over every flowerbed. And then comes the twist (and my spoiler alert): the hacker, who has a beef with social media trolls, finally turns the killer bees on the #DeathTo poll voters themselves, using the military's surveillance data to pair their phones and culpable tweets to their faces. Now the swarms gather on screens in the control room, and around thousands of ordinary citizens wearing their Twitter missteps as a "signature" for the kill. The robo-bees buzz their clickety metallic buzz outside the panes of the control room itself, where one police officer had tweeted with #DeathTo to find the killer; his colleagues now stare at him as a dead man walking as the pane starts giving way. Then the bees turn up in front of a female schoolteacher's windows, whom we know from her #DeathTo tweet against the first victim. Her little pupils crane their necks to watch as the pane starts cracking and the whirring noise draws near. . . .[57]

The *Black Mirror* episode is so effective precisely because it taps into our fears of faceless, intrusive, intimate dangers. The monitored self of our age is our own worst enemy, it tells us. This is so, we may add, whether we live in the green or red zones of the world, which in *Black Mirror* fold into one another like two sides of the famous Möbius strip, united via the violence of the drone. In both worlds, our pet hates and small moves leave traces—signatures—that can be used against us by powerful forces (even if death by robo-bees is still some way off). To its credit, the robo-bee episode does not obsess about drone technology itself but rather captures our key concern in this interlude: the runaway quality to *systems* of technology, manpower, and statecraft through which surveillance, violence, and corporate greed may start spiraling out of control at a time when rich citizens live lives mediated and monitored through the "black mirror," the shiny devices tucked into pockets and poised atop beds or tables.

That mirror reflects back, too, into the off-grid world. There, a Reaper lingers over a Pakistani village. Unlike its predecessors, it does not buzz: it remains silent and unseen. Yet the villagers know it might be there. Insurgents turn off their phones to avoid "signature strikes" targeting networks of enemy mobile signals, not humans of flesh and blood. Weddings and gatherings are canceled. Neighbors inform on neighbors. Some use the drones to sort out local spats, rending the social fabric and generating more names for the kill lists. Meanwhile the persistent surveillance fattens up the "pattern of life" analysis and adds detail to the picture of the network. Sooner or later, the strike might come, a brief whizz through the sky. Few of the citizens in the drone-wielding world will see the links between the stretched battle space where these killing machines operate and the security risks the machinery may pose to vulnerable civilians including themselves, the soft targets of a global war. Even fewer will look beyond the fetishized drone technology itself to see how the invisible data-mining and networking methods tested in this laboratory have already come home to roost, firing their PsyOps death lasers into the heart of our body politic.

PART II **CONTAGION**

4 WOLVES AT THE DOOR

Lasciate ogni speranza, voi ch'entrate.
Abandon all hope, you who enter here.

Dante Alighieri, *The Inferno*, canto 3

Late one summer night in 2015 on the Italian island of Lampedusa, the word spreads: several boatfuls of people escaping Libya's horrors are on their way into port. I make my way to the harbor, and just as I arrive, the first coast guard vessel pulls into the quay's military zone. Firefighters have wheeled up a sharp spotlight that casts long shadows over those gathered there: *carabinieri* and border guards, Red Cross helpers and refugee officials, detention camp workers and our motley crowd of volunteers. On board stand coast guards dressed in biohazard suits and African migrants who clutch the railings, gazing emptily toward us. They are eased off the boat, have their trouser linings checked for scabies, and are then pushed gently ahead, toward the waiting bus. As they move, shoeless and shivering in the humid night breeze, a woman in our clique of volunteers leaps forward to wrap one of the young men in her own shawl. We follow her cue and offer them plastic cups of tea, thermal blankets, and whatever warm words we can find: "Welcome to Europe!" "You are safe now!" And off they go, one by one, into the night.

Walls carve out state borders on our world maps today, yet the mightiest barrier of all is not a fence but the Mediterranean waters off Lampedusa. The tiny island has become synonymous with Europe's migration "emergency," a near-perpetual crisis gathering force ever since the EU started closing its common external borders in the early 1990s.[1] This is where the global danger zones rub up against the green zones, and where mass deaths ensue. Scholars have for years shown how forceful border security has led to more chaos, as we will see, yet there was something more going on at Europe's borders in 2015 than the familiar cycle of short-sighted migration policy. We could sense the shift in the panicked military response, in the warship deployments and the drones circling overhead, and in the latest horrific news from the battlefields of North Africa and Syria. In the Mediterranean, European leaders and border agencies were no longer just dealing with the unremitting migration emergency; rather, they were staring into a black hole in part of their own making, trying to divine the best way out with little available light. They grappled with a bundle of fears, which confusingly mingled on the screens of their "situation rooms" and on the television news: fears of migration, of illness, of terror, of instability, of crime and conflict and coming chaos. As I stood on that Lampedusa quay, among the biohazard men and the shoeless "boat people," the borders of Europe appeared to me less like the fortress wall that activists so often denounce and more like a fluttering cordon sanitaire, hastily drawn to separate the safety of Europe from the dangers outside, the tourist beaches from rusty refugee ships, the rescue workers from potential contagion.[2]

As the second coast guard vessel entered that night on Lampedusa, the reserves of hot tea were running out. The third boat arrived and docked—a grey Guardia di Finanza hulk—carrying not just young African men but women too. A Red Cross helper with a face mask walked past in the dark, carrying a baby swaddled in a blanket.

"*Fast, fast!*"

The female volunteer goaded us on as I tilted the tea dispenser and handed out our last plastic cups to hesitant hands. The thin thermal blankets glistened and rustled as we unfolded them, mechanically, and draped them over the Africans in their still line on the quay. To the coast guards and detention camp workers, these people were but numbers in the crisis tally; to me and the volunteers I had joined, they were anonymous shoulders to wrap and hands for holding tea, their stories untold, their faces inexpressive in the surreal gloom of the spotlight.

"Thank you." A little girl of nine or so, clutching her mother's hand, jolts me back into reality as she takes the teacup: it suddenly hits me that these are *real people* who have just crossed the deadliest peacetime border in the world, and here we are, bizarrely "welcoming" them in the brief moment between the biohazard suits and the detention center, between Libya's horrors and European limbo. As the boat empties and we head away from the pier, I see coast guards handing a plastic bag full of mobile phones to officers from the EU border agency Frontex. It is a pitiful piece of evidence for their effort to track and halt the human smugglers, but it is almost all they have. For past the dark waters lurks the Libyan coastline, temptingly close yet dangerous and out of their reach. It is a world that the polite little girl and her mum could tell us all about, but now they are off, packed into the bus, driven uphill and out of sight.

It is here, among the survivors of Libya's danger zone—amid their bravery and our fear—that we will start scrambling up our neat map of danger to reveal the rampant economics, potent symbolism, and contagious realities lurking underneath its reassuring lines of separation. At the rich world's deepest and deadliest border, one kind of no go world clashes with another: that of officialdom, traced so far in our story, set against the geography of no-entry signs faced by "unwanted" migrants and refugees. In this encounter, the map's red and green zones bleed into one another, setting off contradictory responses from the leaders invested in the global geography of danger and distance. This is where hopes for containment fall short and where fears of contagion seep into political consciousness. For as the emergency response to the Mediterranean arrivals shows, Western leaders, border workers, and citizens recoil not just from the danger zone itself but also from those escaping its horrors, as if afraid of infection by an unknown virus creeping up onto those pristine Mediterranean beaches.

·   ·   ·   ·   ·

Over many years now, I have traveled along the Euro-African borders, seeing firsthand the distressing results of the EU's emergency response to unauthorized migration. I have stood below the six-meter-tall border fences surrounding Spain's enclaves of Ceuta and Melilla, the European Union's

Figure 6. The "border spectacle": Migrants straddle the fences surrounding Spain's North African enclave of Melilla, 2014. Credit: José Palazón Osma.

only outposts in Africa, as border guards explained the intricate machinery built to halt the undocumented sub-Saharan migrants who kept clambering desperately over the barbed-wired barriers. I have followed African police on the patrols they carry out on Europe's behalf in the hinterland of the Sahel, hearing about their frustrated efforts to police all border crossers over thousands of miles of desert sands despite the new gadgetry at their disposal. And I have observed the border from above, in the coordination centers set up in European capitals and coastal towns, marveling at the tenuous sense of mastery instilled by surveillance maps on which radars and patrol vessels track specks of migrant boats across the seas.

At these sites I have seen, in short, how Europe's fight against unauthorized migration has created more chaos as fatalities rise and smuggling networks grow stronger with each new punitive measure—which in turn justifies reinforcing the border security industry that helped cause the chaos in the first place.[3] "Migration is something that will never stop," one Spanish Civil Guard major told me matter-of-factly in 2011 even as he showed me the latest surveillance systems rolled out for his coastlines. His assessment rang all too true from Lampedusa's harbor, where the shoeless arrivals that night in late June 2015 were among the lucky ones. Almost four thousand people perished in the Mediterranean that year. In 2016, that figure reached five thousand, and in coming years the tally of the drowned and missing kept swelling while the risk of dying escalated dramatically owing to the EU's no-holds-barred deterrence. The Mediterranean was once a bridge between civilizations; now it is a front line crisscrossed by EU naval patrols and circled by drones, its blue waters a deep trench of bodies.[4]

At this time of resurgent nationalisms, one thing is clear: our world of uneven globalization has not led to the "borderless world" that some liberal optimists hoped for when the Berlin Wall came down, but rather to the globalization of border security itself. One consultancy estimates that global technological expenditure on border and maritime security will reach $56 billion by 2022—almost doubling over just a decade.[5] Militarized sea patrols are one example of this rampant globalization of border security, and another is the walling up of land borders. At the end of the Second World War, there were hardly any such barriers; by 2016, their number had surged to more than sixty.[6] The trend is not just Western, even if it is the West that leads by example in the fortressing department: witness the barriers built by the Saudis against Yemen and by India against Bangladesh, or the walling projects for the Tunisia-Libya and Kenya-Somalia borders. Walling and patrolling may lead to more chaos, yet the fortified border fills one important political and symbolic function: it promises to serve as a final rampart separating here from there, safety from danger, citizens from a supposed external affliction.[7]

In this chapter, we will consider two of the most remarkable sites of such rebordering today: the Italy-Libya and US-Mexico borderlands. We already have studies aplenty of violent borders and humanitarian borders, of biopolitical borders and of the border as business.[8] What I offer here, in keeping with our inquiry into the geopathology of intervention, is a complementary modality—the *infected border*. Traveling from the Mediterranean to Arizona, we shall see how methods and myths honed in global danger zones have come home to roost, and how poor and desperate border crossers have come to be inscribed with signs of affliction through high politics and advanced risk management operations. We will see how the defended borderline works almost magically on Western politics: it is deployed at once as a catalyst for the stirring of fear and for the promise of protection, while it hides in its smoke and mirrors the much larger operations to police migratory "risk" across transnational frontiers.

In our feverish politics, we easily lose sight of how infected the border itself has become—how it transmits affliction and chaos, even when it seems to protect. The fortified border, in short, lets us glimpse another side to our geopathological condition: the defense mechanisms that set in once containment gives way to the risk of contagion. If chapter 1 presented a "Timbuktu syndrome" of ambivalent desire to intervene in distant danger zones, we must here unearth a parallel syndrome—a "border security complex" (to give it a diagnosis with both economic and Freudian dimensions) whose workings are every bit as pathological as what we see in the Malis and Somalias of today.

But first, a note of nuance. In 2015, the year when the global "refugee crisis" knocked on Europe's doors, migration was about to become the most infectious political issue across the Union—a shift that complicates the argument of a vicious cycle of controls offered by myself and others over the years. After initial panic in European capitals, a blanket security response soon ensued, cost what it might in financial or human terms. This mass investment, in turn, led to some notable "successes" in containing people behind the borders. We may quarrel that this "score sheet" ignores how the problem has only been displaced elsewhere for the time being, alternately shielding the horrors from view and pushing migratory routes toward fellow EU states (with Spain the latest hot spot in 2018). But let us not get bogged down in this dismal science of deterrence by numbers, in its putative "successes" and "failures." Instead we will approach border security in an anthropological vein, with the aim of unearthing some of its symbolic dimensions and deeper operative logics. The notion of an infected border serves this task well. Besides chiming with popular anxieties over "uncontrolled" migration, it helps us elucidate the *methods* used both to stir and to quell such fears in the politics and policing of borders. And what better place for commencing this diagnostic task of ours than Lampedusa in 2015, which was swiftly turning into one of the hotbeds for Europe's rising political fever.

·   ·   ·   ·   ·

Alice Cosentino rolled her tobacco in the breezy whitewashed yard of her guesthouse and frowned as she read yet another e-mail on her phone. A room cancellation. In early 2015, hotels on Lampedusa—closer to Tunisia than to Sicily, and a handy summer escape for the well-off *milanesi* and *torinesi* of the north—started receiving such bad news. Some correspondents were subtle, like the client who had just written to Alice. It was simply a bad time now, with everything in the news about terrorism and the Strait of Sicily, the client wrote, before hinting at the migration emergency. Others were more direct. You must understand, some told Alice and other guesthouse owners, that we cannot go to a place overrun by so many *profughi* and *clandestini* (refugees and illegal migrants). Others went further, saying they would not risk Ebola or a terror attack on their holiday.

However absurd such fears seemed to most *lampedusani,* they were perhaps to be expected: Far Right Northern League politicians from the tourists' home turf had said the situation was "like a bomb ready to go off," with one regional president in Lombardy telling municipalities to refuse refugees and migrants the opportunity to settle or have their funding cut, while another in Veneto suggested migrants with scabies should give the Italian prime minister a hug.[9] Meanwhile, news reports across Europe—often citing dubious North African sources—had hinted that jihadist fighters were joining migrants on the rust buckets, groaning fishing boats, and inflatable rafts setting off from Libya. We'll come back, perhaps another time, Alice's correspondent assured her. *Scusa tanto!* "I'll just respond 'OK,'" Alice said as she lit her cigarette, a resigned smile across her lips. Then she looked around. "It's only thanks to migration that we have visitors now!" she exclaimed. Besides myself, she was hosting a medical anthropologist who was studying the various afflictions of the residents hosted by the island's reception center; an intern with an activist group; and yet another anthropologist looking at how Lampedusa's inhabitants were coping with the enormous media attention they had endured ever since becoming synonymous with Europe's migration emergency.

Yet as the cancellation notices Alice was receiving indicated, it was not simply migration that people worried about: it was disease, conflict, and terrorism too, all rolled into one single story of encroaching danger familiar to us from earlier chapters. The people shuttled off the rescue boats on

Lampedusa, Sicily, and Lesvos were simply the most tangible emissaries of the danger zone out there, its unwitting representatives. Fleeing from danger, they were sullied by it.

Borders are darkly thrilling places, not least to anthropologists, including our conspicuous little clique on Lampedusa. Our discipline has long showed how boundaries of all kinds weave their own potent magic, and nowhere is that dark magic more evident today than at the Western world's fortified boundaries. Borders define inside and outside, who or what belongs and what does not, while serving as a threshold where the strange encroaches on the familiar. They are a place for warding off perceived danger and for welcoming the benevolent stranger. They are also increasingly an irrelevance for global capital flows and commodities, whose circulation—especially when emanating from the West itself—knows few bounds. Yet in the Mediterranean, alarm ensues over the wrong kind of circulation as people of the global South step across the threshold, breaching the cordon sanitaire. They sow panic. They do not belong. They are diseased, dangerous, or just plain costly; they are described as a horde, a tide, a swarm, or an avalanche. They are people out of place—a threat to established political orders, to the health of nations.[10]

Today's attempts to keep the dangerous Other at bay have long histories on which to build.[11] In colonial times, black Africans were often treated as a source of disease and contagion, their conquered territories depicted as "a hothouse of fever and affliction" in the reports of early explorers, missionaries, and officials of empire.[12] By way of the biopolitics of modernity and colonialism, affliction and disease have time and again been linked to race, whether to enable genocide or to justify control and containment. Consider Nazi Germany, and the virulent anti-Semitism preceding it, which adapted modern germ theory to posit the Jews not just as diseased but *as* disease on the body politic.[13] In a more literal sense, fear of foreign affliction has long been tied into the drawing and control of borders.[14] This was the case in the Mediterranean during earlier "globalized" eras, and it was also the case for those who once left this region for the New World. A few days before that night on Lampedusa's quay, I had walked through Rome's emigration museum, tucked into the corner of the vast *Altare della Patria,* Italy's monument to national unity. In the humble museum halls, posters told the story of mass Italian emigrations, including the four million people who according to some estimates had left the country without papers after 1876. Among those setting out for the States—documented or not—many would perish in "death vessels," rusting and unseaworthy steamships packed way beyond capacity. Those who did arrive looked even more destitute than the Africans that night on Lampedusa. A horrified health inspector, Teodorico Rosati, reported in 1908 how "the emigrant lies down fully dressed on the bed, with his shoes on, alongside his bundles and baggage, amidst the urine and faeces of the children and the vomit of practically everyone; after a few days, all of them, one way or another, have reduced that bed to a kennel. When the trip is over, if the bed isn't replaced, and it rarely is, it is left there just as it is, filthy and infested with bugs, ready for the new passenger."

Human tonnage was how the passengers were known; large profits were made off their suffering, their bunked bodies serving to buoy the global shipping industry into its modern shape. Yet the filth on board—a by-product of the inhuman passage across the seas—was seen as the passengers' own dire fault; it stuck to them like a stigma. Those who managed to enter the United States proper faced racial slurs much like those meted out today against Mexicans and Central Americans. Others were simply sent back, deemed unfit for the New World's glories. Anyone likely to be a "public charge" was in trouble, and the passengers' afflictions were meticulously recorded in an industrial-scale sifting on Ellis Island, where "physicians marked any immigrant suspected of disease or defect with chalk."[15]

The intersection of poverty, race, and supposed affliction echoes eerily into the present, from the scabies checks of Lampedusa to the disease rhetoric of xenophobic parties and even the scrawled numbers on the hands of recent arrivals in Sicilian ports. However, there are important differences between the mass emigrations of yore and the irregular routes into today's West. Yesteryear's transatlantic travelers moved through a rapidly globalizing world in which the passport controls we know today did not yet exist.[16] The human tonnage of the twenty-first century, by contrast, sustains a multi-billion-dollar industry of smuggling rather than of legal passage. This industry has grown in direct response to the border security industry, the two feeding off each other—indeed, evidence shows that the smuggling business invariably involves strong collusion by border agents themselves.[17] Further, unlike the Sicilian farmhands of a hundred years ago, today's mobile poor and desperate are treated as an emergency, news of which spreads across the tabloids and TV networks with viral speed. In the French port of Calais in 2015, UK news channels featured rolling coverage of a few hundred Syrians, Eritreans, and Afghans trying to jump onto lorries as the tabloids riffed about a "national crisis," about risks of terrorists sneaking past, and about fear-struck truck drivers, while the UK foreign secretary fueled the panic with talk of millions of "marauding" African migrants.[18]

Imaginaries of affliction and infection have added to the moral panic across Europe. In Spain the previous autumn, a small group of West Africans arriving on the island of Gran Canaria were kept quarantined on a scorching beach for five hours as aid workers did not dare touch them for fear of Ebola; eventually they were mounted on a rubbish truck and driven away. Once the summer of 2015 hit, the fears extended even into countries with hardly any refugees at all—among them the Czech Republic, where Far Right bloggers whipped up fear of militant Syrian "hordes" and Africans bringing AIDS, lice and fleas. In Hungary, fear-mongering became official policy as the government sent out "surveys" to voters about the link between terrorism and migration while closing local rail stations because of the "infection risk" presented by refugees sleeping there overnight. In July 2015, the prime minister asked "whether what we call Europe today will continue to exist" as he fast-forwarded plans to build a border fence along the frontier with Serbia—and all this in response to some seventy thousand migrants and refugees arriving over the Balkans in the first half of the year.[19] Even as numbers of entrants into the EU by land and sea grew into a record one million by year's end, the longer trend—counted in the hundreds of thousands per year—remains small in the larger scheme, considering European countries' annual non-EU immigration rate of 2.4 million in a union of some 500 million inhabitants.[20]

We may well deploy such number crunching to disprove doomsday scenarios of a cross-border "invasion." Most irregular migrants in Europe have over time been visa overstayers, not sea arrivals, as Frontex itself has at various points made clear. Most African migrants stay within the continent: Libya itself has long been a major destination, even if this pattern has been dented following the fall of Gaddafi, as we shall see. Almost nine out of ten of the world's refugees are today hosted by developing countries, not by Western states. Claims of violent newcomers also fail to align with the evidence. One exhaustive study by the Cato Institute reports that, while more than 3.2 million refugees were admitted to the United States between 1975 and 2015, only twenty refugees had attempted or succeeded in carrying out terrorist attacks in that period. Similar studies in Europe have shown the biggest threat to be "home-grown extremists," not new-comers. And as for fears of disease, scholars have noted how health controls at the border are "both ineffective at controlling threats to public health and an inefficient allocation of resources"—not to mention how disease vectors do not neatly map onto the mobility of humans.[21]

Yet however much of this evidence we line up, it does not affect the border security complex, which involves politically exaggerating the threats and fears, and proposing more patrols, fences, and surveillance as the silver bullet. Indeed, in 2018, the EU announced plans to triple its spending on border control to almost €35 billion over 2021–29, followed by another bid by Brussels for ten thousand armed guards to patrol the borders.[22] The vicious cycle of chaos that regularly ensues justifies our treatment of border security as pathological: it is an attempt to do the same thing over and over again while each time expecting different results, to paraphrase Einstein's old definition of madness. Yet the pathology works across several layers, beyond this superficial level of ignoring evidence. To unearth some of these layers of the border security complex, we must pay a visit to that other hot-house of infected borders across the Atlantic, the United States, before returning to Libyan and Italian shores. There, the "Great Wall of Trump" is but a latecomer to the gold rush for border security, which has long stood as an example for other states and regions to follow, including in Europe.

.   .   .   .   .

In November 2015, a migrants' rights activist is driving me toward Mexico through Arizona, and around us watchtowers rise out of the dry soil like tall cacti. The highway is adorned with clutches of cameras and blocked by a vast Border Patrol checkpoint. Down at the border itself, a tall fence of rust-brown steel drives a wedge between *ambos Nogales*—"both Nogales," as the interlinked US and Mexican towns are known. In the hinterland, drones buzz over the rattlesnake-infested grounds, which is dotted by sensors whose antennae sprout like desert weeds.

"You have to watch where you step," says one middle-aged Central American man I meet at a shelter in Mexican Nogales, as he mimics a mine-clearing movement. The other migrants around us murmur and nod. Some of them are new to the route, some veterans, others deportees bent on returning home to the United States. All are caught up in the cat-and-mouse game of the border, where they are chased like prey while also playing another, complementary role: as guinea pigs in a state-of-the-art, multi-billion-dollar border control laboratory.

The current White House occupant wants to build a tall wall, yet here it stands already, sovereignty at is ugliest. Its story began in earnest in the early 1990s. While Bill Clinton praised the fall of the Berlin Wall, the first barriers were already being erected on the southwestern border. Initially, discarded military landing mats from the Gulf War were stood on end, in a sign of what was to come after 9/11, when the border was swiftly militarized under the newly created Department of Homeland Security. The principal objective of the Border Patrol, now under the DHS, became to prevent terrorists and "terrorist weapons" from entering the United States. Little did it matter that such weapons were no different in nature from the automatic guns bought, supermarket-style, within the United States itself for export to Mexico for its deadly drug wars (or for use in schoolyard killings and extremist violence within the country)—more funds kept being poured into border defense, and the barrier itself became a sideshow to the advanced new gadgetry.

In the early 2000s, as one top-ranking border operative recalled as we met, "We had to buy our own batteries for the flashlights!" Then came the radar systems, sensors, advanced barriers, and Predator drones, shorn of their missiles yet in all other respects a direct import from the war on terror. The hardware served a simple purpose: "We're gonna take all our hammers and hit all the nails out there"—a futile task, as the operative himself acknowledged.

It never "worked," but then it was never really meant to. Cheap Mexican and Central American labor remained a mainstay of the US economy, and militarized controls simply pushed these workers further into the exploitative economic underground.[23] Meanwhile the border security industry kept fattening up: the DHS was by fiscal year 2018 receiving some $44 billion annually, with almost half of the budget shared out among the US Coast Guard, Immigration and Customs Enforcement, and Customs and Border Protection, the Border Patrol's mother agency.[24]

Thrown headlong into Trump's tumultuous presidency as we are, we must not forget a simple historical observation: the border was already infected well before he laid his hands on it. It has long been an object of political-psychological fixation, or unhealthy attachment, to borrow Freudian terminology. Ever since the 1990s efforts to "hold the line," political debates on migration have fixated on the border despite the continued reliance on migrant labor inland, and despite statistical evidence suggesting that the most important consequence of border enforcement has been a much *larger* undocumented population, given the new difficulties for seasonal workers of circulating back home.[25] But again, let us not dwell on such analyses of "counterproductive" border controls. Let us rather, in an anthropological vein, keep our focus on how the border's ancient role as threshold has been resurrected at this most potent of dividing lines. At once defiled and defended, the US-Mexico border keeps serving political and symbolic purposes as a deviously constructed catalyst of fear, harboring huge potential for the emotional mobilization of voters.[26]

Two years before Trump bagged the presidency, in 2014, a stark example illustrates how the border was being infected in a near-literal sense. That October, Ebola was all over the news networks, and on CNN one medical expert extended the disease rhetoric in response to a rhetorical question: *Is Ebola the ISIS of biological agents?*

Dr. Alexander Garza, gray-suited and close-cropped, looked calmly into the camera as the news anchor asked him about his "chilling analogy." It had been derided on social media, but his answer was as straight-faced as it gets. "If you think about Ebola as an agent that spreads throughout and kills innocent people it's directly like ISIS, right, it infects people and kills people," he said. "And so the response, if we are calling this a national security issue, needs to be equivalent as if this was a form of terrorism, meaning we have to attack the problem overseas, like we do with terrorism, and like the president is doing, sending the military, but we also have to protect the homeland."[27]

Garza was no simple medical expert but a former chief medical officer and bioterrorism adviser at the DHS.[28] His focus on the borders was in other words hardly surprising, yet he was far from alone in conjuring up dangers around it and calling for more "security" as an antidote. Fox News pundits and Republican politicians argued for cutting all flights from West Africa against all medical advice. But it was the US-Mexico border, rather than airports, that was the principal scene of the coming apocalypse, much as it was to be a year later after the 2015 Paris attacks, and the year after that during the presidential campaign. "If I were a terrorist from the Islamic State," one senator told the media, "I'd go and expose myself to Ebola and come across the border and infect as many people as I could."[29] Back in July 2014, one Republican House representative and medic, Phil Gingrey, had written to the head of the Center for Disease Control and Prevention to express his concern about "reports of illegal migrants carrying deadly diseases such as swine flu, dengue fever, Ebola virus and tuberculosis."[30] No outbreaks of Ebola had ever been detected in Latin America—still, the cluster of inchoate fears just kept on spreading and mutating, virus-like, through the transmission channels of media old and new.

Democrats were not immune to the contagious language of fear. That October, US vice president Joe Biden put an academic gloss on the dangers in front of a Harvard audience. "In a globalizing world, threats as diverse as terrorism and disease cross borders at blinding speeds," he said. "The international order that we painstakingly built after World War II and defended over the past several decades is literally fraying at the seams right now," he continued, while adding that ISIS and Ebola were two of the "wolves closest to the door," symptomatic of the falling apart of this postwar order.

Biden may have been right in calling for a global response to border-crossing troubles, yet his imagery fed into the same myth of insecure borders and the disasters and diseases awaiting outside. This was the very myth invoked in Trump's presidential campaign, as he told Mexico to pay for the border wall in order to keep supposed rapists and drug dealers out of the United States; and it was the myth he would yet again invoke when claiming "Middle Easterners" and hardened criminals were among the Central Americans peacefully making their way through Mexico before the 2018 midterms.[31]

We will return to Trump's role in the border security complex, yet it is worth lingering on Biden's phrase—*wolves at the door*. The metaphor is potent: civilization at home, wilderness outside, the threshold as the place

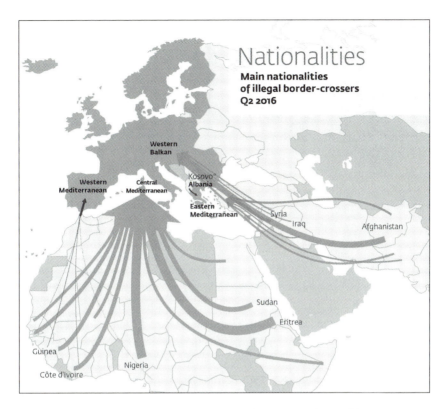

Map 10. Migratory and smuggling routes toward Europe, as depicted by Frontex. ©
Frontex.

where we must keep the wild at bay. Early anthropologists, pondering
totemism and tribal cosmology from their Paris or Oxford studies, had
seen such thresholds as potent places indeed. Borders, corridors, or margins, they theorized, were sites of intruding danger; crossing the line
might be a "rite of passage" leading to a higher status—as from boyhood to
adulthood—but it also involved association with defilement and pollution.
"A polluting person is always in the wrong," anthropologist Mary Douglas
wrote in her *Purity and Danger* in the 1960s, in words that resonate with
the tribulations of border crossers half a century later: "He has developed
some wrong condition or simply crossed some line which should not have
been crossed and this displacement unleashes danger for someone." But as
Douglas and her anthropological ancestors noted, marginality is not just

polluting: it may also unleash hidden powers, to be harnessed for good or ill, as Trump did when he called forth the world's troubles at the US-Mexico border while rallying the Republican vote. Disorder, Douglas wrote, symbolizes both danger and power, and to have been "in the margins" is to have been in contact with that danger, at the source of that power.[32]

In short, the political potency of infected borders is itself contagious, as seen in the back-and-forth between Biden and Republican fear peddlers. And this potency can be tapped into by both friend and foe—as we can observe most clearly if we shift our story back to Mediterranean shores and to the conflicts flaring up around Europe's margins.

.   .   .   .   .

In early 2015, the wildest of wolves were howling at Europe's door. In a gruesome video, unnaturally tall, black-clad, and masked men led twenty-one Egyptian Coptic Christians in orange jumpsuits to the Mediterranean shores of Libya. The captives were beheaded, and as their blood leached into the sea, the camera lingered on the red water in snuff-movie fashion. The video may have been full of fakery, with the beach descent superimposed on studio footage and the blood a cheap special effect (corn flour–based, one expert suggested), yet its message was what mattered as newscasts and social media readily spread the murderers' propaganda across the world. Through these nightmarish images, the Daesh killers cunningly staged Europe's bundled fears of mass migration, conflict, and terrorism, sullying that perfect medium—the turquoise Mediterranean waters—with the encroaching red of danger. Like latter-day black magicians, they were harnessing the power of the borders as European leaders and their security forces helplessly looked on. Beyond this red line they dared not venture, and the murderers knew it; the Europeans were fearful of the wolves lurking in the wild and apprehensive of those who dared cross this most potent of thresholds.

Soon, the wolves came across it. The Paris attackers of November 2015 (most of whom were European citizens) succeeded in their quest to cluster fears of migration and terror through what seemed a conscious performance of danger. They chose to travel back to Europe along the migrant trails, leaving traces as they went, and then conspicuously left a Syrian passport behind at the scene of the crime. Through this small token, they sullied Europe's refugees with the suspicion of terrorism, just as they had wanted—their violence succeeding beyond their wildest dreams as fear propagated through the European body politic.[33]

Daesh's spectacular murders are but one example of how Western states' border fixation opens up opportunities for exploitation by enemy groups. Hostile states have also jumped on this opportunity, as NATO's senior commander in Europe seemed to acknowledge when accusing Russia and Syria of "weaponizing" migration toward Europe (and something similar is afoot among nominal "partner" regimes, as we will soon see).[34] Yet from a domestic political perspective, the fear-gripped border remains potent as a site both of pollutions and of solutions. Through this back-and-forth among foes, the border is becoming fetish-like, to again borrow from Freud: that is, invested with powers of its own.

Other border scholars have noted this fetishistic potency, and foremost among them is political theorist Wendy Brown. In her seminal *Walled States, Waning Sovereignty,* she offers a psychoanalytical take on the fixation on fortified borders at a time of globalization. Walls, she says, respond to "psychic fantasies, anxieties, and wishes" at a time when state power and control are eroding: they reassure, they contain, and they seem to render the nation "impermeable" to impure elements from the dangerous outside.[35] To understand how the border security complex has consolidated at a time of border-breaching global flows, she deploys Freud's notion of defense hysteria. Denying and repelling an experience, she notes, is one pathological strategy for dealing with uncontainable danger to the Self.

We may well wish to query the extent to which sovereignty is waning, yet the fears conjured and combated at the rich world's borders do resonate with Brown's analysis. As it happens, so do the personal foibles of the man who is now the poster boy of our global politics of fear, Donald Trump. We may think that Trump is an expert in *deploying* fear, yet Trump himself is also fearful and phobic. In interviews on the *Howard Stern Show,* Trump has confided that he often drinks through a straw to avoid contamination. He is a self-confessed "germaphobe"; he hates shaking hands, washes his own compulsively, and allegedly avoids pressing the ground-floor button in hotel elevators because it is the most frequently touched one. But his fear is more profound than that. As his onetime ghostwriter Tony Schwartz puts it, "Fear is the hidden through-line in Trump's life—fear of weakness, of inadequacy, of failure, of criticism and of insignificance." In fact, his own phobias serve as a potent tool for pro-

Figure 7. "The Beautiful Wall," by Martin Rowson for the *Guardian*, September 2, 2016. © Guardian News & Media Ltd.

jecting fears outwards, to the electorate and onto the border. His racist tirades against Mexicans and Muslims, Schwartz suggests, "skillfully exploited the fears of supporters who felt powerless and disenfranchised by presenting himself as their angry champion, even though the policies he has since pursued are likely to make their lives worse."[36]

Yet as Trump finally stomps onto our map of danger, arms a-swinging, let us keep recalling that he remains beholden to rules written before his arrival. Schwartz argues that "Trump has made fear the dominant emotion of our times," making opposing camps retreat into their safe corners. This may be so, but in catalyzing this divide, Trump has used the emotional arsenal of fear already placed on the global map of danger, including at the US-Mexico border. In his vain prototypes for the new border wall, erected in California right next to the existing one, we may perceive how Trump has readily assumed the role of conduit—host body, if you will—for a preexisting affliction, in the process spreading it further still.

The Trump era also helps us see more clearly the wider implications of the afflictions besetting Western powers respectively at their borders and in distant danger zones. For all the panics around the walled-up US border, crossings are sharply down amid demographic and economic shifts in Mexico. Elsewhere, across Africa, Asia, and even Latin America, China is gaining economic ground vis-à-vis the United States. In the Middle East, Russia, Turkey, and Iran are newly assertive as Washington retreats. In this wider context, the "Great Wall of Trump" is more than a fantastical monument built against foreign "contagion" in an age of uneven globalization. It is also a cry for both personal and national significance in a world where the United States is losing its preeminent role. Yet out there, in the wilderness, only the wolves seem to be listening.

.   .   .   .   .

Some analysts may not take too kindly to a psychoanalysis of the border security complex and its political masters, and they may have a point. Whatever the case, we must pair such a "psycho-political" account with a more hard-headed analysis of the everyday policing of the rich world's borders. If we look at walling and policing in practice, it soon becomes clear that border professionals are quite clear-headed folks, not Freudian basket cases. Unlike Trump with his hand-washing phobias, they *must* get their hands dirty. Officials have to move beyond the cordon sanitaire and connect with forces, organizations, and politicians on the other side in order to solve anything at all—on this everyone with any experience of border policing agrees.

I saw firsthand this building of frontier zones of connection when accompanying Spanish and African border agents, and I would see it again on my 2015 visit to Arizona. In fact, on both sides of the North Atlantic, border fixation is inimical to the main objective—to deal with migratory "risk" preemptively, in collaboration with neighboring states.

One day in November 2015, in the Joint Intelligence Operations Center (JIOC) in Tucson, I found myself glancing down in awe at the advanced command terminals as the uniformed director of JIOC extolled the latest technology. "Europe is where we were some ten–fifteen years ago," he told me matter-of-factly. In the border areas traced on huge wall screens in the command room below us, the policy had long been "prevention through deterrence"— making the crossing so dangerous that people desisted. A risk-based strategy now gave a scientific guise to the whole enterprise,

channeling resources to "high-risk" areas and focusing on preemptive, layered controls before migrants reach the actual borderline.

The mapping of migratory risk, replicated in cruder form in Europe,
tears apart the geography of our global map of danger with its neat borderlines and red zones. What we see here, instead, is an operative logic
aligned with the guiding metaphor of this chapter: the control of contagion—or, more specifically, what may be called an epidemiological model
of migratory risk. The JIOC intelligence gatherers target high-risk areas
and "flows" with the aim of keeping risk levels within the right bounds
rather than separating, sealing off, and halting for good.[37] Risk-based
migration controls involves preemption in space and time—that is, as in
the drone wars, halting any infraction before it hits the Homeland. Its
map is four-dimensional, its border potentially anywhere.[38]

The rust-brown barrier of Arizona may seem like a nineteenth-century
field surgeon's bone saw next to the fine scalpels and serums of the border
epidemiologists, yet it does serve functions for both the social organization
and the *temporality* of controls. There are good policing reasons why the
present border wall is not solid but see-through, and why it does not cover
the full length of the US-Mexico border but only built-up areas. The see-
through bars allow the Border Patrol to communicate with their Mexican
colleagues while also spotting and preempting entries before they are
attempted—often violently so. The selective barrier building serves to
reroute migrants, steering them away from publicly visible crossing points
toward treacherous terrain where the border guards have the "tactical
advantage," as one leading US operational chief put it to me. This "optimi-
zation of natural obstacles" has pushed migrants into the deadly Sonoran
Desert, where drones stare down on human specks from above and thermal cameras trace their movements until helicopters and patrol vehicles
swoop down on their prey, in a procedure adapted from counterterror
operations in Afghanistan and Iraq. Here, risk is actively transferred onto
migrants, who fall into ravines, suffer snakebites, reel from heatstrokes,
and die of thirst by omission or even commission. If lucky, they may find
themselves rescued by the very Border Patrol itself, in a humanitarian-
security nexus repeated with variations at the borders of Europe.[39]

JIOC, everyone pretty much agreed, did not need more agents and
taller walls to combat migration. Its methods of exclusion and endanger-

ment were by 2015 much more sophisticated than that.[40] Yet as savvy border officials knew, the border fixation remained politically and symbolically effective on the home front, and so it was no surprise when one
Border Patrol union endorsed Trump in the 2016 presidential race.
Congress still kept pushing for more agents, though high-level border
operatives I spoke to saw this as pointless ("Keep your opinions to yourself," one top operative chief was told by his boss when raising doubts).
That November 2015, news of the Paris terror attacks again sparked calls
from US politicians for crackdowns at the border. Meanwhile, the JIOC
director conceded that "we're not typically gonna see terrorists walking
through the desert." They were well placed enough to fly in with a visa, like
the 9/11 attackers, or were homegrown like the Orlando shooter of the following year. Still, the show must go on, and the director defended the
investments as a way of cutting the billion-dollar costs of rescuing
migrants—put in peril, let us remember, by border enforcement itself.

We saw in our previous sections how, in a climate of fear, the border
emerges as an almost limitless emotional resource for a certain breed of
politicians. Idioms of contagion and disease are perhaps the most potent
example of this mobilization, as seen in the fantastical rendering of "Ebola
terrorists." In this sense, we speak here of an infected border that politicians can activate as a conduit for systemic dangers that may spread into
the Homeland, while also falsely promising to shore up the nation against
those dangers. Yet there is another sense in which the epidemiological
metaphor works for fortified borders: it corresponds to the logic of risk-
based border policing, with its focus on transmission channels, highly
affected areas, and "outbreaks" across an extensive borderland. In this
way, the infected border—like the maps of chapter 2—melds primal fears
of affliction with (pseudo-)scientific apprehensions of risks. Further, in
this symbiosis of risk and fear, "humanitarian" border controls emerge as
closely linked to their more repressive counterparts. The biohazard suits
of the Mediterranean and the rappelling Border Patrol rescue teams in the
desert are in cahoots with the wall and the violent policing that push people into danger and into the arms of rescuers.[41]

However, there is one way in which this symbiosis between risk and
fear-based border security occasionally falls short: in its encounter with
the realities of the red zones of our global map of danger. The risk of going

is high; the risk of doing nothing may be higher still. In short, given the dangers lurking beyond the lines of division—the very dangers people are fleeing from—officials cannot always easily venture across them without taking on considerable political or physical risks.

For the Americans, the risk has been principally political. Trump's calls to punish Mexico and "build that wall" risked the relationships with Mexican border enforcers, courted for years to step up controls. For the Europeans, by contrast, risks have been not only political but also physical, as seen especially in Libya following the 2011 NATO intervention. The danger of entering the country to stem migration initially petrified European politicians and officials, and none felt it more acutely than those sent to fulfill impossible mandates beyond the cordon sanitaire. To see this intersection of the border security complex and the Timbuktu syndrome at close quarters, we need to pay a visit to the hapless European border officials entering Libya's chaos in the early post-Gaddafi era, where they would soon find themselves stuck in a country that had been plunged headlong into the ungoverned global margins.

.   .   .   .   .

Antti Hartikainen did not expect this mess. A rather jovial Finnish customs chief in his fifties—as jovial as Finnish border officials come, at any rate—Hartikainen seemed to be the man for the job of helping the Libyans secure their borders. He had served in Moldova, in Ukraine, in Georgia; and now, as he saw his officers fly into Tripoli in late May 2013, he eagerly awaited a new challenge—to lead the European Border Assistance Mission to Libya, or EUBAM-Libya, an operation with a €30 million budget for its first year, set up as European leaders anxiously sought to stem more boat arrivals over the Mediterranean.

The mission had a contorted mandate to begin with—as Hartikainen put it, to train and support Libyan border agencies "in stabilizing their country and this way maybe reduce this flow of immigrants leaving Tripoli." Yet this would prove to be mission impossible. Libya's desert south—EUBAM's initial focus, as Brussels had reassured the Libyans wary of Europeans stepping onto their turf—turned out to be out of bounds because of insecurity. When the mission heads still persevered in organizing a field trip south, Brussels vetoed it on security grounds. Yet even in northern Libya, trips to train border guards were "extraordinarily difficult," Hartikainen said in his staccato English, speaking to me down the line from his Helsinki customs headquarters where he was now safely ensconced, far from Libya's battlefields.

"First of all, we prepared something that was agreed with local border management agencies, everything was agreed even with the [Libyan] ministry of foreign affairs, their protocol office, and then at the last minute they said that no, you can't go because of security reasons, or this kind of explanation. For example, once we tried to organize a mission in Ras Ajdir," on the Tunisian border. "We canceled it maybe three times, the fourth time we managed to visit. It was very time-consuming and very frustrating to work like that." Sometimes the authorities were "playing" with them, he suspected, and sometimes there were genuine security concerns—reinforced by risk-averse Brussels officials, who had imposed the onerous security protocol on the mission. Soon enough, criticism started mounting over EUBAM's inaction. EU member state officials asked Hartikainen, "Why is it so difficult to go there; why you are not able to do this and this, and why you are not ready to visit some locations, and why you are canceling this because of security? I said, come on, it's not me who has set up these rules, it's you, the member states!" He laughed. Most of the EU officials themselves never traveled outside Tripoli, he noted; as EUBAM finally managed to leave for a trip to Gadamis on the Libya-Tunisia border, they brought some ambassadors along, and for many of them it was the first time outside the capital.

Walking around with private security contractors in Tripoli was not much fun, yet this way senior people back in Europe were at least "covering their asses," as another senior official put it. Moreover, recruitment faltered, and trainers failed to show. Frontex was supposed to be sending training officers to EUBAM, but these never appeared. "Frontex never even visited during our presence in Libya, not a single time," Hartikainen said.[42] Instead he was stuck with a rather ill-suited team, including a border police chief from Munich airport, a Danish customs officer, and other relatively junior staff meant to train the Libyan top brass on national security strategy. Hartikainen pleaded with Brussels for more senior staff, but "it's so difficult to get them to join this kind of mission," he said. Most of the higher ranks, it was clear, wanted to stay well clear of Libya.

Theirs was a wise decision. Wary of ground engagements and riven by internal fractures, and with no plan for the aftermath of intervention, NATO had in 2011 bombed a path for rebels to take over the country and lynch Gaddafi when they found him hiding with his bodyguards in a drain-pipe.[43] The initial enthusiasm over this early "success" of NATO's Operation Unified Protector was by 2013 ebbing as a messy reality unfolded on the streets of Tripoli, Misrata, and Benghazi. EUBAM had been deployed at this clinch moment in Libya's post-NATO settlement, as a bewildering set of factions were vying for power. It was by then becoming quite clear that Western powers, in their haste to force regime change without the willing-ness to stick it out, had sown the seeds of this chaos—and that no border assistance mission in the world could sort out the resulting mess.

"We intervened in Libya, some of us without the backing of the African Union, which was not a good idea," a high-level French diplomat told me in summer 2015 in his breezy offices on Quai d'Orsay as he honed his political line of attack; the decision to intervene, after all, had been taken by the previous Sarkozy government, along with counterparts including Obama and the UK's Cameron. "We intervened from the air and then we say goodbye to everybody after killing [Gaddafi]."

Now, as violence flared, one of the main targets of Libya's fighting fac-tions was the country's large sub-Saharan population, long a mainstay of the country's migration-dependent economy. Years of harsh treatment under Gaddafi, as he stepped up border policing cooperation with Italy's Silvio Berlusconi, had made them fair game for security forces and crimi-nals even before the conflict. In the summer of 2009, Gaddafi had received a sumptuous welcome in Rome as he landed flanked by his numerous female bodyguards—"amazons," as the Italian media dubbed them—before pitching his Bedouin tent in a public park. A "friendship treaty" with Berlusconi had smoothed his path to Rome, involving promises of $5 billion for colonial "reparations," which had more to do with control-ling migration and opening the country to Italian business, including to defense companies selling border security equipment. Libya's bountiful supply of sub-Saharan migrants were a perfect bargaining chip, as Gaddafi had come to realize already at the time when he used the threat of migra-tion to end international sanctions and the arms embargo in 2004. Now he started using this human resource to maximum effect.[44] In this, he drew on racist idioms of uncontrolled wilderness already familiar to us. "They have no identity," he said in his rambling Rome discourse that summer. "They come out of the forest, they say, 'In the North there's money, I'll go to Libya and then to Europe.'"[45]

By 2010, the emboldened colonel went one step further as he warned that Europe would "turn black" unless the EU handed his regime some €5 billion a year. About a year later, as NATO launched its bombing raids, he tried to make good on his promise, forcibly embarking migrants on rickety boats while promising to "unleash an unprecedented wave of illegal immigration on southern Europe." The foreigners' prospects took yet another dip once Gaddafi enlisted black Africans as mercenaries in his fight with rebels and unarmed protesters. After his fall, innocent sub-Saharan migrants were targeted by militias, civilians, and security forces. Some were lynched; others were detained indefinitely, robbed at gunpoint, or attacked with guns or knives.[46] In 2016, one report found three-quarters of migrants interviewed after their escape from Libya had experienced violence there.[47] In 2017, further reports said migrants were being captured and sold to the highest bidder for lucrative detention, extortion of their families, or slavery.[48] Amid this escalating violence, the boats that Gaddafi had warned Europe about were setting off again, bringing escapees from Libya toward the very nations that had encouraged both the hounding of the migrants and the country's descent into chaos.

Rather than triggering a rethink, the latest emergency simply reinforced Europe's default security response. Italy sent drones to patrol Libya's southern borders and trained the country's security officials, adding unchecked and uncontrolled resources to what was to become Libya's dark hole of mounting conflict. In May 2015, the EU launched a naval mission, EUNAVFOR-Med, to destroy smugglers' boats on the open sea. It was to be a fiasco of an operation, succeeding only in pushing smugglers and migrants to use flimsy rubber rafts instead of fishing vessels. Meanwhile Hartikainen's team represented the softer side of the response—a liberal-sounding EU mission to put in place "integrated border management" on Libyan soil. Yet like the other attempts to deal with Libya at a distance, it was set to become an expensive failure.[49]

Amid the chaos of post-Gaddafi Libya, EUBAM gradually withdrew from public sight. Its officials moved to "one golden cage after another," as one of them wryly noted in interview. First the team had settled into the Corinthia hotel in downtown Tripoli—haunt of many a Western reporter during the revolution—while waiting for their purpose-built compound to be prepared. As mounting insecurity kept delaying their plans, Hartikainen and his team eventually retreated into the fortified gates of Palm City, an upmarket development on the outskirts of town. In this "Disneyworld," as one visiting researcher called it, the EUBAM team were supposed to train the Libyan coast guard and customs officers—often inside the enclave's walls, or else in port, escorted there by local security forces and the mission's inept private security contractors. Such training was of limited use to the Libyan officers, as they lacked vessels and equipment, let alone a functioning state to back or finance them.[50] EUBAM's mandate was strictly to train, not to provide funds or equipment, "because they are a rich country," as Hartikainen put it, critical of the EU's rosy view of Libya. "It's stupid to train something which you can't implement," he said. As they finally managed to escape Tripoli for training sessions at a couple of Libyan border-crossing points, he recalled, "the only technical equipment [they had] was the [rubber] stamp. They didn't even have screwdrivers, it was unbelievable!"

Insecurity started shaving staff off the mission, as more and more officers decamped to a new "support office," safely based on Malta. Politicians and insiders soon started whispering about EUBAM as a fiasco, and maybe it would have quietly ended there: with a glossed-up score sheet produced by Brussels technocrats, giving some nice spin to the "achievements" and "lessons learned" from the mission. But something was about to go awfully wrong.

By March 2014, as fighting was stepping up around Tripoli, EUBAM awaited a rather delicate delivery. The mission's latest private security contractor—the Canadian GardaWorld—was having weapons delivered into Tripoli airport, the site of fierce fighting. The consignment was promptly stolen, including "23 assault rifles, 70 handguns and more than 42,000 rounds of ammunition," according to a UN report detailing illicit arms flows in Libya. "Militias controlling the airport were very likely responsible," the report noted, while raising concerns over the arming of Libya's belligerents; the EU's antifraud office soon opened an investigation into the incident amid accusations that the mission's previous security contractor had lacked arms licenses. To other observers, the fracas rather raised questions about ineptitude; or as one formerly Tripoli-based official quipped, "If you can't even control your own toys. . . ."[51]

Hartikainen did not give up, however. On May 20, he and his officers exited Palm City to settle into their last holdout in Libya, the Peacock Compound, which was finally getting ready to receive them after much back-and-forth over more security measures imposed via Brussels. "In the beginning we were going to have like a wooden kind of chalets," Hartikainen recalled with his customary dry laughter, "and in the end we had bunkers."

At least their bunkering was to be mercifully brief. By July 2014, as the fighting intensified, everyone was pulling out. EUBAM stationed a vessel in port, ready for a "migrant-style shipping"—ironic, given their mission was to aid the Libyans in halting other foreigners from fleeing along pre-cisely the same route. The mission was being drastically downsized in Tripoli, as officers were discreetly flown out for early leave or, eventually, for remote work from back home. "They called this teleworking," Hartikainen said dismissively. "It was not a good measure. . . . Many of them, I think that they did almost nothing, just followed what was hap-pening [in Libya] and that's it." The mission was fraying, leaving only the thinnest presence on the Libyan ground. "We were among the last who left," Hartikainen insisted, against insinuations the mission consisted of a bunch of "scaredy-cats." Yet once the Americans and the French upped sticks, he called it a day. "Now it's time for us also to go," he told Brussels. "I didn't want to stay there any longer, I was becoming nervous, and EU members are getting angry if we don't now go." On July 31 they set out in a convoy for the Tunisian border. Once in Tunis the mission retreated into a hotel, from which the team tried to train the Libyans remotely. They organized workshops abroad, in Istanbul and Brussels, but were asked to stop in January 2015 "for political reasons, because you can never know how these guys are affiliated in Libya and that is the challenge." Indeed, Libya's "coast guard" was infested with militia leaders playing their own economic and political game alternately as war-fighters, purveyors of bru-tal "controls," and people-smuggling facilitators.[52] The result was *mission plage* (a beach mission), as one security report dubbed EUBAM in a scath-ing assessment that January: "As around €12m, at an annual rate, is to be added to the [budget] of the first year, this starts to look expensive for a mission . . . whose efficacy and activity are close to zero!"[53]

If the aftermath of the NATO bombings in Libya showed the tragic side of Western intervention, then EUBAM was intervention in its farcical guise. Quite content with bombing from on high without risking their soldiers' lives, Western powers had ousted Gaddafi but put no security in place on the ground. As chaos deepened, instead of rethinking their remote-controlled interventions, the United States withdrew and Europe changed course; now the only objective was to halt any migrants who would try to evacuate in the wake of the embassies, oil contractors, and border guards. Libya had become a no-man's-land where securing the borders was the only remaining task, yet here even border officials feared to tread. The country was being disconnected from its European neighbors across the ancient bridge of the Mediterranean. The physical evacuation of Libya hastened the evacuation of its territory as a fully social, political, and human space in European popular and media discourse. Its slate was wiped clean, its territory slathered in red, in a back-and-forth between intervention and rebellion, between geopolitics and criminality, and between the Timbuktu syndrome and the border security complex. Yet Western powers—except for a few of their loose-tongued foreign affairs officials—took no responsibility for the mapping of danger at the shores of the Mediterranean. Instead, leaders looked for scapegoats and found them in the human smugglers, portrayed as "modern slave traders" or "traffickers" who had to be "combated" via naval operations.

It was left to practitioners such as Hartikainen to see through the folly. He had a warning in store for the strategists who were launching their military campaign against smugglers in mid-2015. "It's not very realistic," he said in his down-to-earth manner. "When you are dealing with the Libyans you need to remember that if you don't have approval, if you are not able to cooperate with the Libyans in this kind of operation, then you should never do it because later on when this conflict is over, how to set up this cooperation [on borders] if you manage to get them angry now? Their behavior is like that, they will remember this kind of thing," he said with his dry laughter. For him, as for his US counterparts dealing with the fallout from Trump's attacks on Mexico, connections were key—and the hastily drawn sanitary cordons were cutting precisely those connections.

Returning to our epidemiological frame, the Libya debacle shows how risks of "contagion" may persist even when border fixation and risk-based interventions work as one. Yet the infected border remained, as in the United States, politically and symbolically functional. Positing smugglers as the transmitters of the border affliction helped draw attention away from disastrous military interventions, as well as from the main target of the militarized border response—the smugglers' desperate clients. And the "boat people," as they arrived, reinforced the resolve to secure the cordon sanitaire drawn to protect Europe against the gathering dangers.

.   .   .   .   .

Lampedusa's Centro di primo soccorso e accoglienza, or "welcoming center" for short, lies up in the island's hills, a good distance from the port with its *gelaterie* and sun decks. It offers a strange welcome, surrounded by fences and guarded by police; and like most migrant "reception" or detention facilities in Europe today, it is also rather hard to find. I bike across Lampedusa; I search for it on Google Maps; I ask around. No luck. Migrants and refugees, as they finally escape the blank spaces of the Libyan hellhole and the Sahara Desert, here find themselves in another cartographic blank. And, like a cut-price Caillié for today's cut-out geography, I persist in planting my academic flag in it. Even though the center is a closed facility, I have heard that internees escape it through a hole in the perimeter fence, gathering under the shade of a tree outside. But where is this tree?

Finally, an Italian researcher friend, Paolo, e-mails me. He has some news about the fence:

> I am attaching a Lampedusa map with a big red star.
> The star is the *centro*.
> There are three dead end streets around it.
> One is at the right (it touches on the star, and there is the official entrance).
> One is above the star.
> The other is underneath the star.
> The hole in the fence should be underneath the star.
> This means that we should start searching there.

We set off on our bicycles, intrepid explorers of the hinterland of Europe's border. Heading uphill from the port, we hit a dirt road surrounded by dry grass; dogs bark as we leave the last scattering of hamlets behind. "There it is," Paolo says. Below us, in a natural depression, sits the *centro*—a cluster of three-story-tall barracks, one of them rebuilt after earlier residents set fire to it, at the time when Berlusconi kept filling it to show his European counterparts he needed more funds to handle his self-imposed "national emergency." We descend the escarpment among stones and spiky grass. I step on rusty old barbed wire marking the edge of the military zone in which the center is located, cursing myself for walking in flip-flops. A few Africans loiter behind the fences. We wave awkwardly; they wave back. Mattresses cover the yard around them, some stacked into cave-like protections against the summer heat.

I have an eerie sense of *déjà vu;* the overcrowded center looks almost exactly like the Spanish detention and reception facilities that I know so well from my years traveling along the country's borders. If the operations at sea and in port resemble a cordon sanitaire and a first line of medical-military defense, these "reception" centers rather recall quarantine: places far away from human habitation, hosting darker-skinned foreigners behind tall fences, stuck in their own state-imposed version of the no go world.[54] On Lampedusa, a clandestine video of late 2014 showed camp workers hosing down naked residents, as if cleaning afflicted cattle, yet even watching such a video—let alone waving to those inside from the perimeter—makes us complicit in the containment. My unease of the previous night in port returns as we descend the slope; I am not for the first time playing the role of voyeur in Europe's sordid border spectacle.[55]

We continue along the camp walls. At the female section of the camp, a lone woman is clutching the fence around her dismal, tiny yard as the men saunter by outside. *Zona militare, vietato passare,* says the signs dug into the underbrush as we search for the hole in the external fence: military zone, passage prohibited. At last we find the tree and settle down on an old bus bench positioned under it, light a cigarette, and wait.

Eventually they come. Alas, not the West African passengers of the previous night, but three Somalis who have been staying for a week on Lampedusa. Ibra stretches out his hand and flashes a rather buck-toothed smile; he is a tall, skinny man looking much younger than his twenty-five years, dressed in the camp's red-blue standard-issue jogging suit. He introduces his friends, the older, stubble-cheeked Aziz and quiet twenty-something Daud, and explains that they jumped out of the window in the female quarters.[56] Police do not seem to mind, just as they do not seem to care about the seventy-two-hour limit to detention at the center stipulated in Italian law. For the *clandestini,* another set of rules applies.

As we walk, Ibra explains his ordeal in perfect English. He has come all the way from Uganda, where he was studying information technology. He left his two small children behind with his mother as he set out on the road to reunite with his wife, who arrived in Rome by air, with the help of relatives. "I knew it was dangerous, but I never thought it was this dangerous," he says. "I would never tell anyone to do this journey like me, *too danger.*" Trundling across the Sudan-Libya desert borderlands in the smugglers' pickup, he saw the bodies of migrants who had died of dehydration, scattered in the sands like human confetti. "The Sudanese smugglers were good," he says as we pick up the pace heading into town, locals and tourists glancing our way. The Sudanese brought lots of water for their clients; but in Libya, they received only one water bottle per person for two days. "And if you give your friend because he is ill, then you will die."

In Tripoli, it got worse. He was warehoused with hundreds of others in a vast hangar for six months, now with another smuggling ring. "You have to convince the smugglers that you don't have rich relatives at home," Ibra says; otherwise they will torture or beat you to extract more money from the family. Still, smugglers' warehouses were better than detention, where extortions and beatings were administered by rote. Ibra avoided being detained, and finally the time for his escape had come. Ready for swift embarcation, the smugglers "take three in each hall, so that passengers don't know each other and [organize to] kill the captain." The captain left Ibra and his fellow passengers on their boat once he said they had entered "European waters," making a satellite call to the coast guard's rescue center in Rome. Finally a Korean trawler picked them up on the coast guard's behalf, towing them into port. "We are safe here," Ibra says as we enter Lampedusa town, deserted in the afternoon heat. Even a fenced-off camp is a boon after the boat and the warehouse and the desert.

So far, our story of the infected border has treated migrants as rather passive; yet as Ibra's example shows, migrants may swiftly become experts at navigating the overlapping geographies of the no go world. His journey, moreover, should make us revisit our theme of mirroring from the

Interlude. As Ibra and thousands of other migrants headed northwards, they drew on the spatial and temporal opportunities that now opened up between green and red zones, undermining the official quest for control.

Consider time. For domestic reasons, European politicians were in 2015 making it very clear they would seal the border at the earliest opportunity—so, not for the first time, migrants from far and wide saw their momentary chance before the door slammed shut. The time of preemption, so crucial to border strategy, was in other words cut short by the migrants' time of anticipation. It was now or never, as Ibra knew, and as Syrians knew when setting off from Turkey.

Next, consider space. Ibra had lingered along the shoreline of Libya, which Hartikainen and his men were not allowed to tread, before zigzagging across the patrolling areas of the Mediterranean. As he finally headed toward "European waters," Ibra, his fellow-passengers, and his smugglers knew full well the power of our cartography of deepening borders. They actively participated in the scrambling of the world map of danger as their movements permeated its neatly drawn edges. Picked up by men in biohazard suits and quarantined in a military site, Ibra also failed to enact his officially sanctioned role on the fear-infected border. Instead, he somehow managed to map his own geography of hope onto the deadly borderlands, however tenuously.[57] In Lampedusa town, he showed me a Facebook picture of himself from Uganda, suited and smiling, giving a thumbs-up to the camera. "That's how I look!" he laughed as he pinched his camp-provided jogging suit. "My wife can't see me like this." In town he had to buy some new clothes, he insisted; his mind was already with her in Rome, unconcerned by the obstacles ahead of him.

.   .   .   .   .

It is a tough task to untangle the collective failures behind the chronic European "migration crisis." Two decades of ever-stricter border controls have principally served to displace desperate people onto riskier routes across deserts and seas; the thousand-fold drownings in the Mediterranean are not natural disasters but manmade emergencies. But the story goes deeper than this. As this chapter has suggested, the border security complex needs to be seen as part of a wider affliction besetting Western interventions in global danger zones, well outside the fortified borderlines (as well as inside them, in fevered domestic politics). Through their remote-controlled military intervention in Libya, NATO cleared a path for rebels and jihadists to emerge, and with them a zone of multiple dangers at the very edge of Europe. Seeing the violence and displacements unleashed in this zone, European leaders did not learn their lessons. Rather, they initially wavered and dithered, lingering on the Libyan margins. They cut off sea rescues, then reinstated them, then cut them off again; they launched military action against the migrant boats, while arguing that they were not targeting the boats' passengers; and they spied on terrorists from on high while leaving Libya's warring factions to fester. Eventually the Italians did partially step across the cordon, with brutal results. But whatever other short-term "successes" European authorities may claim for their hardening stance, one stands out: their symbolic victory in unspooling a long cordon sanitaire across the Mediterranean, promising to separate green from red zones, and European citizens from the threat of external contagion. Behind this line—in military zones in port, behind camp walls, outside "European waters," or gathered by masked men on the deck of a warship—the afflicted border crossers may be contained and controlled.

Yet as we have seen, from Trump's wall to Tripoli's waters, the border security complex constantly springs surprises. Fixation with the border opens spaces for counteraction. Fear of the outside may paralyze. Hands cannot stay clean à la Trump, as new barriers inevitably trigger dramatic new breaches. Moreover, the infected border remains, as we have noted, a potent symbolic resource: the fear of contagion *attracts* psychologically, financially, and politically. Italy's Berlusconi knew this when he kept Tunisian migrants forcibly stranded on Lampedusa in 2011 in front of the world's cameras while announcing a national emergency, and so did the Northern League, which, rebaptized as "the League," joined the country's new government in 2018 thanks in large part to well-channeled migration fears. In the United States, Trump's forerunners mobilized fear as a resource, setting the stage for his full-throttled fear epidemic. In high politics, the border thus works as both affliction and remedy. It *has* to be breachable; contagion must threaten the Homeland, the better for the border to shows its Janus face of a cordon sanitaire in need of virtually endless investments.

We have here approached the border as a site of both enforcement and political mythmaking, but we must also note that in the marketplace of myths no storyline ever prevails with finality. At the end of the long summer of 2015, activist networks were joining forces across Europe, tapping into migrants' own networks and preempting the police response with blankets, kind words, and a place to sleep. Traveling across the bridge linking Denmark and Sweden one day that autumn, I glimpsed—as I had on Lampedusa—a brief irruption of a "countermapping" against the geography of fear, separation, and danger. The very pathways through Europe that were treated as transmission channels for the migratory "threat" briefly turned into channels for linking the hopes of someone like Ibra with the hopes of volunteers and ordinary citizens joined in solidarity-based action. To turn to another anthropological master of the threshold, Victor Turner, in the borderlands there emerged a brief sense of togetherness—what he would have called an evanescent *communitas*.[58]

"Abandon all hope" reads the epigraph to this chapter, but maybe Dante should not have the last word. Still, while hope remains latent, optimism is today in short supply. The brief *communitas* of 2015 has long passed. The smooth train ride from Copenhagen to Malmö has been interrupted by double ID checks since Sweden closed its borders. In Germany, asylum seekers are being locked up rather than welcomed; in Italy, the League promises to deport half a million migrants; and in country after country, the nationalist Right clamors for more border security. Amid the lockdown, the border keeps infecting European politics, just as it does in the United States, where Trump keeps sending in the military while his plan for a wall is stalling in Congress. Yet bolting the door has not assuaged the fears—quite the contrary. However much they try, Western leaders cannot shake off this self-induced affliction, in which the media, border officials, and citizen-voters all remain thoroughly implicated.[59]

The notion of contagion has worked on two levels in this chapter. On the one hand, I have used it as shorthand for how risk-based border policing and fear-peddling politics in different ways draw on idioms or logics of epidemiology and infection when dealing with "unwanted migration." On the other hand, I have emphasized that fear-based renderings of migration are themselves contagious and viral. The two may come together when risk-based operations along migratory routes interlock with the transmission of political fears. But this twin-track propagation may equally be undermined, whether by activists and migrants spreading a more hopeful story or by the enemy—as seen when transmission channels for migratory "contagion" are hijacked by jihadists for their own propagation of fear. Our fundamental lesson, here as in the war on terror, is that danger is systemic and reflexive, forever at risk of appropriation and extension into new domains. As we will see next, this is the case not just at our infected borders but also in another arena seemingly disconnected from our politics of fear: international aid.

5 THE SNAKE MERCHANTS

> My theory is very simple: The reptilian always wins. I don't
> care what you're going to tell me intellectually. I don't care.
> Give me the reptilian. Why? Because the reptilian always
> wins.
>
>   Clotaire Rapaille

Thus spoke Clotaire Rapaille, advertising guru and anthropologist extraordinaire, when asked to explain his craft of marketing by fear.[1] Wild-haired, powder-caked, and with a penchant for red velvet suits, Rapaille was as good at plugging his own persona as at selling his corporate clients' wares: to the journalist Jacques Peretti, visiting the marketeer's suitably Gothic chateau in France, he looked like "a cross between Louis XIV and Michael Jackson."

Rapaille's eureka moment had come in the aftermath of 9/11, or so the story goes. One day, he had glanced at his television and seen a CNN report of booming Humvee sales that "set fireworks off in his head." As Peretti recounts it, "Ordinary Americans were buying a military vehicle designed to withstand a one-hundred-pound mortar bomb attack in order to do their weekly shop at the supermarket. What, Rapaille thought, would Freud have made of this?" In essence, Rapaille concluded that "Humvee sales were exploding because the unconscious part of the American consumer's brain was responding to the primal fear of another terrorist attack."[2] What Rapaille called the "reptilian brain" was circumventing the cortex with its tedious rationality. Consumers shelled out for the ridiculously oversized and accident-prone Humvees because they tapped into those reptilian instincts. "If you put a machine gun on top of them, you will sell them better," he quipped.[3]

Fear sells, Freud's nephew knew when he laid the groundwork for modern advertising in the early twentieth century. In the post-9/11 years, Rapaille was among the pioneers who bought into fear as its value again started increasing dramatically—though rich Western citizens had never been safer before, and though they were more likely to be killed "by their toaster than by a terrorist attack," as Peretti puts it.[4] Rapaille's quip in our epigraph posits the primacy of fear as an ahistorical human universal, but while the reptilian brain may always be on a winning streak, it was clear that the post-9/11 era presented an extraordinary host environment for the creature—an opportunity Rapaille and his fellow marketeers lost no time in exploiting. Their reptilian instincts set us up for the pages that follow, where we shall see how another market, that of aid rather than Humvees, has tapped into the dark recesses of our mind and our times, with disturbing consequences for everyday life in the shadow of intervention.

But let us first travel far from Rapaille's glitzy world, swapping a French chateau for a corrugated-steel roof baking in the Sahelian sun of May. In the Bamako of our opening chapters, thirty-nine-year-old Djibril Konté was squatting on the concrete floor of his one-room flat, next to his family bed, searching for his most treasured possessions.[5] He had fallen on hard times, and it showed, I thought when I first saw him again these days in May 2014, several years after our last encounter: his piercing, opportunity-hunting gaze, his two-day stubble, his quick gait, and his stream of monologue in which he strove to convince me—to convince anyone—that he was a man who meant business, a man who knew Bamako like the back of his hand, and so a man who could do the job. Any job. But no jobs were forthcoming.

There it was. Djibril opened his old steel cabinet and pulled out a tattered pile of papers. "My father gave them to me," he said. His father was a grand *marabout,* a Muslim sage popular in Mali's folk version of Islam, and these were his writings on how to make *gris-gris* charms. "I have never shown this to my visitors before," Djibril said as he pointed at the obscure squiggles on page after page. Here, a diagram for obtaining wealth; there, another for winning a political race; there, another for getting your wife to love you again. Red text—cursive Arabic in complicated patterns—wound its way around and across diagrams of other, darker kinds, showing how to make a colleague or superior fall ill so you could obtain their position, or how to take revenge on enemies.

"I have more of this here, in a big suitcase," Djibril said with palpable excitement. He had always wanted to walk in his father's footsteps and become a big marabout, but now times were too tough for this line of business. Mistrust was coursing through Bamako, he told me as we leaned back against the frame of his family bed. A few days earlier, a prominent local politician had come to notify him of some good news—Djibril's application for a plot of land had been approved. But this was the exception to the rule. "People are not honest anymore, these are things of the past." His father's diagrams, charts, and *gris-gris* formulas, what could they do? Who wanted them? Where was the demand? People no longer paid up front, he said, as they did not trust the marabout; they did not trust anyone. "Nowadays, if anything, people want things to do harm," the red-scrawled stuff of his secret pile. Everyone "ate" from everyone else's misfortune.

I had come to know Djibril in 2010 as president of a Malian association of "returnees" set up after his and other migrants' expulsion from the clandestine overland trails toward Spain. He had since then found on-off work on development projects through his association, yet as the 2012 conflict began, donors and Western NGOs took flight—leaving Djibril and many other workers, brokers, and helpers without an income. As we met again, I knew I was expected to bring solace of some kind: my proposition was that he could work as my research assistant. The best assistance he gave, however, was via his own bitter stories of lost opportunities and of mobilization around danger. For as the crisis hit, Djibril did not turn to his father's black magic in the drawer for sustenance—rather, he toyed with tapping into the much larger resource offered by Mali's rampant dangerization.

One example stands out. We had just interviewed a Malian woman displaced by the conflict, who like others lambasted the lack of aid and how false beneficiaries "ate all the money." As Djibril pondered her account over lunch, he tied together his own story of mistrust and menace with the new marketplace of aid in Mali. "In order to be rich, you have to threaten," he said with a flat laugh. "In our [deportee] association, we have one thousand members; we buy some arms, make a [black Islamist] flag, take a Westerner hostage, and we've solved it!" This is what the separatists and jihadists were doing in the north, Djibril said, mobilizing a menace to get money and attention. "You have to be a robber, a murderer, a traitor. Everyone is just doing that, thinking of themselves."

Djibril's offhand sarcasm was a small example of how Malian society was adapting to the danger-driven gaze of the country's postdevelopment era—or, rather, to a period in which "development" itself was being framed as a security concern in ways that presented opportunities every bit as magical as those of his father's dark diagrams.

Look around, and you may see this fear-driven aid game in town through Djibril's eyes. In Bamako, everyone seemed to be pitching to donors and decision makers the urgent need to address an underlying problem, *or else* threats would come and visit them. As you may have noted, I have myself replicated that kind of justification in this book, arguing that blowback may follow from wrong-headed interventions! This kind of compulsive reasoning opens an opportunity for well-placed inhabitants of putative danger zones, who suddenly find themselves sitting on a prized asset.

Djibril's dilemma was certainly not shared by most Malians, who went about their daily lives with no thought of tapping into the business of menace. But it was the multi-million-euro question that all those brokers big and small who tried to leverage the international aid business needed to answer: How to act when your strongest international asset was no longer your "development potential," as in better times, but rather the risk that you and your countrymen presented to others?

We will now continue with our task of breaking up the map of danger and distance by considering how fear and danger have come to serve as a privileged connective medium, linking international donors and interveners with inhabitants, organizations, and politicians in putative danger zones. We have already seen evidence of such linkages in Somalia's African deployments and in Libya's fear-ridden lands, but here our connections will by and large be of a subtler sort, in terms of the marketplace of international aid. A systemic look at this marketplace, much like our account of the infected border, reveals that fear is contagious: Put simply, people and institutions respond to how they have been framed, often undermining the interveners and their aim of quelling the dangers. Fear brings leverage, as Rapaille would agree, yet small-time brokers such as Djibril were not really those cashing in on it. Rather, his frustrated attempts to tap into the aid world point us toward a much larger market in fear that has emerged and consolidated across global danger zones and beyond, generating Rapaille-sized rewards for those best positioned to exploit it.

.   .   .   .   .

For some influential voices, the world is moving in the right direction. Sweden's Hans Rosling, a global health professor of irrepressible enthusiasm, led the way on this argument until his untimely death in 2017. Once he lined up seven huge snowballs on a wall for a BBC broadcast, each representing one of the world's seven billion people, to explain how our world is no longer set in a binary between rich and poor but has a rising middle in between the extremes. Even if Rosling added danger to that neat picture—pointing at the snowball representing the "bottom billion," he quipped, "That's from where Ebola emerged; this is where Boko Haram hides"—he recognized the positive potential even in poorer regions. In another TV appearance, the host told him that "right now the current situation consists of wars, conflicts, chaos," and Rosling responded by invoking Nigeria's successful elections; when the reporter asked about Boko Haram, Rosling lifted his foot onto the table and pointed at his shoe. "You can choose to only show my shoe, which is very ugly, but that is only a small part of me," he said: to him, the media held up this shoe and falsely called it the world.[6]

Indeed, if we follow Rosling's sane advice to embrace "factfulness" in our daily lives, we may soon spot positive indicators aplenty, including in sub-Saharan Africa.[7] Over the decade to 2016, real income per person rose by 30 percent on the continent. Extreme poverty rates remain high at 35 percent, yet are heading down year after year. In a statistic that sounds deceptively positive—given its rather generous definition—one-third of the continent is now considered middle class, according to the African Development Bank; that is, they are spending between $4 and $20 a day. "By 2060, more than a billion Africans are expected to join them," said one *Time* journalist as he related this litany of good news. As he put it, mobile money—already a reality in countries such as Kenya—"has also enabled Africans to leapfrog decades of financial development in just a few years."[8]

The enthusiasm over "Africa Rising," like other optimistic frames, may help steer aid in positive directions, though it also risks downplaying the politics of unsustainable debt and vast resource transfers out of the continent.[9] Yet whatever the case, in the "danger zones" and their environs, rosy liberal frames soon lose their relevance: here dystopians still carry the day. This is so because, from Humvee sales to African aid, fear sells. Rapaille's reptilian brain wins over cortex-fed statistics on "Africa rising" when it comes to international aid politics, especially when helped along by media outlets with a shoe fetish. Donor governments, in turn, respond to public and media perceptions. If it bleeds, it leads, journalists say; we may add that in today's aid world the donor only really cares if it scares. And in few regions is this more evident than in the Sahel.

·   ·   ·   ·   ·

The Sahel may draw a blank for most Western citizens, yet if there is one popular imaginary defining it, it is as a stage for prolonged crises, including food insecurity, recurrent droughts, climate change, high population growth, and gloomy economic prospects. "Nothing is more chronic than the Sahel," was how one resigned humanitarian chief put it to me, and many others seconded this perception. The region's manifold problems are real enough, but the most chronic ones are not, as a rule, intercontinental security problems. Still, they are increasingly addressed by big donors—if at all—as "root causes" of emerging or immediate threats *to the West.*

The United Kingdom has been a leading proponent of this shift. "The world community cannot ignore the critical role of poverty and inequality in increasing risks for us all," the UK Department for International Development argued in the Tony Blair years.[10] Migration, instability, terror, and criminal contraband all posed severe risks—and so aid instruments should address them. A few years later, the Foreign and Commonwealth Office warned that Islamic extremism in the Sahel was "an increasing threat to UK interests" and that "a failure to increase engagement would carry greater risks." Increased "engagement" meant not just traditional security, as the defense secretary at the time, Michael Fallon, made clear when discussing defense versus development spending: "The biggest problem we are facing now, in Libya, in Liberia, even in Nigeria where they have lost control of the northern province, in Sudan, in Yemen . . . is that these states are starting to fail and that's where in the end—sadly—you end up having to intervene with armed force. So these aren't opposites. [The UK development secretary's] budget and mine you should add together; they are security budgets."[11] In another intervention, amid the "refugee crisis" of 2015, Fallon argued that "we can use our overseas aid budget—and this is where it should be used—to help stabilize some of these countries and discourage this kind of mass migration from them."[12]

Keeping people sedentary and dampening extremism have become twinned drivers of not just much British but also European aid—linking, as Fallon did, long-term development goals to border security and counterterrorism. In European strategies for the Sahel and the wider "arc of instability," migration fears have spurred the aid-security machinery into overdrive following the 2015 "crisis" at the borders. At the Euro-Africa summit of November 2015 in Valletta, the EU launched an Emergency Trust Fund "to tackle root causes of irregular migration in Africa," which eventually ended up with a pledged €3.3 billion in the pot.[13] In tandem, the EU's Migration Partnership Framework, launched in 2016, promised further billions and political momentum through joined-up development aid and migration "compacts" with key countries including Mali. As the EU announced in 2018 that it was increasing its spending in Africa to some €36 billion over seven years in order to prevent migration, its foreign affairs chief, Federica Mogherini, argued: "If you want to manage migration and if you want to prevent further security threats in particular terrorism, there is one single place where you have to invest all your political, economic and diplomatic efforts and that is the belt of the Sahel and the Horn of Africa. . . . That is where all our challenges could be solved, or could deteriorate into something dangerous."[14]

Let us not buy into the buzz too readily, however. Much of the aid, for a start, was old wine in new bottles. Further, insiders accused EU member states of simply tapping into the large Trust Fund for their own pet projects, while official reports lambasted the wider EU expenditure on migration for suffering from "misdirected finances, lack of accountability and repeated breaches of basic human rights."[15] Yet rather than dwell on the problems behind the aid facade, let us focus on the *logics* of these European initiatives, which in essence amounted to exporting a punitive model of migration control to African states under the guise of addressing "root causes," "saving lives," and "stepping up investments in partner countries."

Figure 8. A soap-making business set up with Spanish development funding, Dakar, 2011. Photo by author.

Spain and France had been doing this for years in West Africa despite evidence that even if the aid were remotely successful, increased economic development would initially lead to *more* migration. This was a big if, however. In Senegal in 2010, I had seen how Spanish development money had been thrown at anything from spurious "awareness-raising" about the risks of boat migration to artisanal soap businesses supposedly empowering women in migration-affected coastal communities—with the idea that these piecemeal efforts would somehow "combat" high-risk migration of mostly unemployed young men. Still, the EU was now busy replicating these bilateral deals and sending out the message that "development" melded with border security would somehow staunch the migratory flows, while pretending that this was somehow a "new approach to better manage migration."[16]

"Security," we may say, is today's soap of choice for washing away the world's manifold dangers. In policy, everything from "climate" to "human" and "bio" is getting the word attached to it.[17] Much scholarly ink has been spent on such "securitizations," including the securitization of development, or how development has come to be framed in terms of security priorities for donor states, including on migration.[18] Given the wealth of attention paid to this "nexus" in recent years, we may easily succumb to the impression that securitized development is a new phenomenon, yet that is not the case. By some accounts it reaches back to the "Truman doctrine" of underdevelopment that helped kick-start the Cold War, or even to the colonizers' concerns with channeling and controlling African migrations before that.[19] We will return to this longer historical perspective, but for now a brief look at the largest aid and security actor today—the United States—will offer us a more detailed view on this shifting relationship to security over more recent decades.

In the introductory speeches at the 2014 US-Africa Leaders Summit, "Africa rising" seemed at first glance to be the watchword. American talk of investing in a "continent of limitless promise" (in Vice President Biden's words) was meant to contrast with China's focus on natural resources. Yet if Beijing could be accused of caring mostly about digging out the continent's minerals and energy supplies, underneath Washington's business-like gloss lurked a darker seam as well—that of security.[20] In a conference call to the summit, Ben Rhodes, deputy national security adviser for strategic communications, summed up the stakes by building a rhetorical bridge between development and security as he waxed lyrical on the "enormous opportunities" on offer "as African countries continue to develop their capabilities as security partners of the United States and as democratic partners of the United States." He went on: "What we believe is unique about the American contribution is our focus on African capacity-building and integrating Africa into the global economy and security order."

Security is now paramount in US aid programming: USAID's website says that "since 9/11, America's foreign assistance programs have been more fully integrated into the United States' National Security Strategy," with development, diplomacy, and defense constituting the "three Ds" or pillars "for promoting and protecting U.S. national security interests abroad."[21] Given such rebranding, we may expect a dividing line after the start of the war on terror in US development aid. But again, this is not quite the case. Looking back at national security strategies from the Reagan years, we see how "long term political and economic development" is recognized as being key to reduce "the underlying causes of instability of the Third World, help undermine the attractiveness of totalitarian regimes, and eventually lead to conditions favorable to U.S. and Western interests."

Yet if security has long been linked up with development, the focus of this nexus has indeed shifted in the post–Cold War years toward *transnational* threats, especially terrorism. The aim, among other things, has in the words of Obama's national security strategy of 2010 been to "use development and security sector assistance to build the capacity of at-risk nations and reduce the appeal of violent extremism."[22] In the Sahel, this shift has seen strategies evolve to "analyze and address the 'push' and 'pull' drivers of violent extremism with development tools," in the words of Nancy Lindborg, assistant administrator for democracy, conflict, and humanitarian assistance under Obama. "While the recent rise of violent extremism in West Africa cannot be directly attributed to drought, chronic food insecurity, or weak governance," she told the House of Representatives in 2013, "each of these factors can indirectly exacerbate instability in the region. Just as droughts and floods result in crisis because of the Sahel's underlying chronic vulnerabilities, structural 'push' factors can create the conditions that favor the rise of violent extremism. USAID's 2012 policy on countering violent extremism [CVE, later redefined by Trump as exclusively against "Islamic extremism"] defines push factors as high levels of social marginalization, poorly governed or ungoverned areas, government repression and human rights violations, endemic corruption and elite impunity, and cultural threat perceptions."[23]

In the age of Trump and rising nationalisms, when prominent voices call for the end of aid altogether, Lindborg's holistic take on interactions between security, governance, and development may appear as the enlightened self-interest of a bygone era. But in using security as justification for development interventions, donors have been engaging in a strategy that risks diverting attention from the urgency of perennial problems *in themselves*. Worse, it also risks distorting analysis of cause and effect between poverty and insecurity, or between climate and displacement, while seeing such issues through the red-tinted glasses of danger. This, we may add, is a tendency that if anything is set to worsen amid the rise of the nationalist Right across donor nations.

To give aid officials their due, the "security-development nexus" does not usually offer a simple linear view of social conditions generating specific threats. Rather, technocrats increasingly treat security as part of a "complex system" characterized by feedback loops and nonlinear causality, as implied in the much-cited motto of "no security without development, no development without security," or in the many invocations of "resilience," a term we will return to soon. Let us, then, take the aid professionals at their word and approach securitized aid in *systemic* fashion by doing what they themselves rarely do—turn our gaze onto the donors' role in reshaping the system in which aid brokers and recipient nations jockey for position. As we will see, the aid relationship is in the Sahel and beyond being remolded around insecurity and danger—generating feedback loops between donors, recipients, and brokers in a fear-driven marketplace.

.   .   .   .   .

One early evening in May 2014, I sat in Djibril's communal courtyard around a brewing teapot while his children came and went. As he spoke while pouring tea into our tiny glasses, his frustration was palpable. "You see, there are no jobs, what can we do? We have to leave, don't we?" Not for the first time, he told me he might want to set off again on the overland "adventure" to Europe. I nodded but also reminded him of the dangers on the road. He equivocated; perhaps he did not actually want to leave again. The sun set over the yard as Djibril kept talking; a strip light flickered to life atop his door and his children gathered on the bench underneath, schoolbooks in hand. "So this is why the youth go and join MUJAO [Movement for Oneness and Jihad in West Africa, one of Mali's jihadist groups], or go take a boat to Spain, or die in the desert," he said, continuing along the lines of his earlier argument. I shifted awkwardly on my seat. I knew what was going on: Djibril was, in a not-so-subtle way, using the risk of his own potential to migrate to make sure that I kept my word and employed him.

I might have let Djibril's half-hearted flirtation with the fear market—his migration plans and black Daesh flag—pass as mere shows of sarcasm, if it wasn't for how they chimed with what I had heard from other underemployed aid brokers in West Africa during my years of research on migration and conflict. In 2010, I had been told by members of Senegalese deportees' associations similar to Djibril's that they were the "real illegals" who were *really* "fighting migration," unlike the police or the NGOs running risk-awareness campaigns with Spanish development funding. The deportees, like Djibril, were all too aware of the stakes for the donors, and of the development aid manna that was passing them by. "If no money comes soon from Europe, we will set off again," said one leader, and "this time we'll be one hundred thousand, or thousands of twelve-year olds" who could not be deported because of their age. In the remarks of such hopeful aid brokers, we glimpse how danger may be mobilized reflexively by those seen as being both risky and "at risk": the youth of West Africa whom Robert Kaplan once described as "loose molecules in a very unstable social fluid, a fluid that was clearly on the verge of igniting."[24]

Traveling up the social scale, institutions large and small were similarly honing their fear pitch in the marketplace of aid. Senegalese NGOs had taken to trumpeting their "clandestine migration" credentials in leaflets and posters, and in next-door Mali dozens of associations had sprung up to cater to the new donor focus on managing mobility and its "risks."[25] When donor interest swung round to terrorism amid Mali's worsening plight, so did the aid brokers, as one humanitarian association in Gao exemplified to me in 2011. The association, set up to care for migrants deported from Algeria, aimed to help deportees reestablish themselves, as well as to "keep the youth in place" via local development projects. The youngsters of Gao, one of the association's leaders explained, "have nothing to do and so they risk heading off on migration, or they risk becoming drug traffickers, get involved in prostitution and all that, or what is even more serious, they risk becoming coopted by local militias or assimilated into organizations such as al Qaeda. They are ready to come into town nowadays, to take these youngsters and insert them into their structures. This is our big fear." Never mind the chronic unemployment and penury of northern Mali, which was the biggest threat to the region in its own right: to have the ear of Western donors, you had better invoke the terrorist threat—or, better, combine it with migration into a veritable reptilian feast.

It was not only small-time brokers and associations who clamored for securitized aid. During my fieldwork on migration in Mali in 2010 and 2011, national authorities had started positioning themselves in direct response to European priorities on fighting migration and terror. The Malian police, for one, used the "risk" of irregular migration through the Sahara as a way of pushing for more development money. "Europe needs to help us with projects in villages. That way, people can become sedentary," pleaded one border police chief, while also asking for more funds to patrol Mali's desert borders. Eyeing their European-provisioned police colleagues with envy, the Malian gendarmerie called for EU manna to rain down on their remote border posts, too: they needed computers, generators, vehicles, and even petrol for these vehicles! These demands were justified, again, by recourse to our familiar threat cluster of migration, criminality, and terror. To the gendarmes, Central and West African migrants stranded in Mali after expulsion from Algeria incarnated the dangers. If the gendarmerie did not get funds to set up "transit centers" for the migrants, they told me, the consequences would be dire: "They'll steal, rob, even kill, or they can be recruited by AQIM [Al Qaeda in the Islamic Maghreb]. It's a big problem."[26]

On higher political levels, the same pleas were in evidence. In April 2014, to give one example, Mali's president Ibrahim Boubacar Keita signed an agricultural accord with Morocco at a UN-sponsored conference by which Moroccan investors could exploit a large tract of fertile land around the Niger River. "The development of agriculture in sub-Saharan Africa will certainly prevent these young Africans from emigrating or joining terrorist cells operating in the wide and vast desert of northern Mali," the president said, motivating the controversial decision.[27] This was far from a one-off. In late 2017, the news magazine *Jeune Afrique* asked Keita how he would respond to those French voters who thought France's counterterror operation Barkhane was too expensive, and he responded: "That Mali is a dam and if this dam breaks, Europe will be flooded."[28] Keita did not have to spell out what kind of flood was awaiting if the operation was cut—reptilian fears of the coming dangers helpfully filled in the blanks for his target audiences.

Scholars of postcolonial Africa have long remarked on what they term "extraversion" in political life on the continent—that is, attempts by gatekeepers and state officials to leverage external dependency to their advantage.[29] The pitches by Malian brokers, associations, police, and politicians alike seem to show such extraversion at work. They indicate, we may say, a reflexive dangerization of the Self, presenting Mali and its population as a potential threat if donors do not cough up the funding. But it is incorrect to assume that this is a specifically "African" phenomenon. In fact, international agencies and aid groups—themselves both acting as donors and recipients—played the same game as their African counterparts, even if their dangerization was not of the Self but of the aid recipient Others.

Many NGO and UN officials in Dakar and Bamako acknowledged in interviews that they often ended up playing the fear card to combat donor fatigue for the Sahel, even though they recognized the problems with it. Sometimes the aid pitch was blunt, as when Trump's chosen head of the UN World Food Programme, David Beasley, told the media that Daesh commanders fleeing Syria were now targeting the Sahel, using the lack of food as a recruitment tool and as a way to push Africans into Europe. The message to donors was clear—fund WFP or face the consequences: "If you think you had a problem resulting from a nation of 20 million people like Syria because of destabilisation and conflict resulting in migration," Beasley warned in words echoing those of the EU's Mogherini, "wait until the greater Sahel region of 500 million people is further destabilised. And this is where the European community and international community has got to wake up."[30]

Usually the pitch was subtler than this, however. Take the United Nations Environment Programme, which linked its climate change planning for the Sahel to donor priorities over migration and conflict via the technical terminology of risk: "A number of adaptation policies in the region recognise the linkages between changing climatic conditions and behavioural responses such as migration and conflict, but few so far have included provisions addressing these risks. Systematically considering these issues in adaptation planning can reduce conflict and migration risk, help prioritise adaptation investments and strengthen climate change adaptation capacity."[31]

As I scrambled to find positive cartographies of the Sahel to include as an antidote to our maps of fear, I hit upon a promising specimen: the much-advertised plans for an $8 billion, four-thousand-mile "Great Green Wall" of trees to be planted against the desert across the region. The Wall might have some positive holistic thinking to commend it (though it has come in for criticism on this front, too).[32] Yet it was as tied to dangerization as the political utterances we have heard so far—evident when Monique Barbut, the UN's desertification chief, justified it in these words: "Ensuring vulnerable communities are resilient to climate change is our *first line of*

Map 11. Promotional image for the Great Green Wall. © United Nations Convention to Combat Desertification.

defence against the growing challenges of forced migration, food insecurity, civil conflict and extremism." Migration and terror, media reports of the initiative made clear, were the principal targets of the wall of trees, whose very name readily borrowed from last chapter's border barriers.[33]

In Mali and the wider Sahel, donor priorities have shifted the modus operandi of brokers in politics and aid, leading to escalating dangerization in a self-reinforcing feedback loop. More damagingly, as the stakes keep rising in the mobilization of development for security ends, traditional development brokers risk being elbowed aside. For once the aid market reworks itself around security, adept merchants of fear start cornering it. This risks sending dangerization into overdrive, as we will now see—

stepping momentarily out of the aid world proper and into the wider marketplace of fear of which it is increasingly a part.

.   .   .   .   .

So far, we have seen how specific fears and dangers have become trump cards in the aid market. Now, something very similar is happening in international intervention writ large. This was exemplified to me one day in 2014 at UN headquarters. As I interviewed a top peacekeeping chief about the perils of intervention, he lingered on a crucial part of the political picture—how to convince powerful states to participate in dangerous missions. In particular, he lamented the "lack of interest from the international community" in the violence besetting Central African Republic, as well as its lack of a functioning state. But, he thought out loud, the latter also presented an opportunity when speaking to major powers, as it allowed for presenting the country's natural resources as being at risk of falling into the hands of violent extremists such as Boko Haram. "This was one of our appeals, let's move in quickly and occupy the space before others do that because then you will have a big problem on your hands."

If the Department of Peacekeeping Operations knew how to hold Western powers' attention, so did African states, security forces, and even paramilitary groups. Besides terrorism, fear of migration was a major card up their sleeves. Consider Sudan: in 2017, the country's Rapid Support Forces, an unsavory paramilitary group counting former Janjaweed fighters among its members, kept bringing their efforts at cracking down on migrants and smugglers to international attention precisely at the time when the EU's Partnership Framework was making inroads into East Africa and the Horn.[34] Or consider Mali's neighbor, Niger. Sitting astride a prize asset—the central desert route to Libya—the regime saw its chance amid Europe's migration panic and grabbed it. "Niger needs a billion euros to fight against clandestine migration," the foreign minister said in May 2016 as his country's president, Mahamadou Issoufou, positioned himself as an indispensable strongman. The gamble paid off: in December the following year, the EU announced it would support Niger with assistance of precisely €1 billion by 2020. Meanwhile France's president, Emmanuel Macron, landed in Niamey with praise for Issofou as a paragon of democracy despite the country's disputed elections, bringing further offers of some €400 million in aid.[35] The reasons are not hard to see. Niger was in everyone's crosshairs because of the incipient G-5 Sahel counterterror force organized by five regional states with strong French support, while harsh migration controls kept escalating, with Italy sending hundreds of soldiers to crack down on supposed "human smugglers."[36]

Donor priorities regarding danger and security, in short, have not just spawned incentives for aid recipients to bolster their fear pitch but also fattened up the security sector and repressive regimes across Africa and beyond. Libya's fragile authorities and savvy militias have gained handsomely from the migratory threat; so have regimes in Morocco, Mauritania, Sudan, Niger, Mali, and more countries besides. London's Overseas Development Institute has estimated—loosely in the extreme, given the lack of transparency in such security-tied financing—that Europe spent €15 billion between December 2014 and September 2016 to convince neighboring states to crack down on migration, including trust funds and bilateral deals covering Turkey, Syria, and sub-Saharan Africa.[37] This is before we count the *political* gains, which can be substantial indeed, whether in propping up strongmen, as with Niger's Issofou; ensuring that the Europeans stay out of contentious "internal" affairs, as in Morocco's occupation of Western Sahara; or facilitating recognition of a junta, as in Mauritania after its 2005 coup d'état.[38]

To put it bluntly, in the fear market of international security interventions, the reptiles are out in force, smelling a juicy prey. It is not hard to see what gets them salivating over migration controls: the EU-Turkey deal to contain Syrian refugees. In the summer of 2015, Recep Tayyip Erdoğan had been in a tough spot owing to looming snap elections—and, rather fortuitously, soon the country's maritime borders opened, with thousands upon thousands of Syrian refugees embarking for Europe. On the back of the European scramble to stem the crisis at any cost, Erdoğan ended up benefiting politically from lavish promises of billions in aid and visa-free travel for Turkish citizens. Even if the latter has not materialized yet, the political gains have still proven substantial for an increasingly authoritarian Ankara positioning itself as a bulwark against migration. And African countries, long content with small change for their border security efforts, are quite rationally taking note.

Some "partner" regimes, including Ankara, skillfully tap into the migration and terror markets at once. Others specialize in the latter, and one day in spring 2016, I meet one of their salesmen in Addis Abbaba. Abderaman sweeps into the hotel café, white *boubou* flowing round him and mobile phone in hand. My newfound friend the Chadian military attaché sits down, orders a Sahel-style tea, and goes straight to the point: *"Nous connaissons bien la guerre,"* he starts us off while downing his tea, before calling his embassy to inquire about this ruffled academic in front of him. Clearly, as I approached his offices, they thought I was a funder or official of some sort, not a useless researcher. Nevertheless, now that he has an audience, the attaché continues with his pitch. The Chadians know their business in the danger zone, and they hope it may expand further still. Abderaman talks of Chad's soldiers in Central African Republic and of the lack of resources. "You can't go to an American and pay him eight hundred [dollars]" to go fight, he argues. But "we, the Chadians, we have killed in battle, we have collected the flesh of our dead soldiers." Their martial strength is legendary, as proven on Mali's battlefields—*"Chad est le plus fort."* They should be paid double, he suggests, "to replace the white soldiers," such as the French counterterror forces. "We can handle Mali, but they need to increase pay from 50,000 to 100,000 [CFA francs] and the fighting morale will follow, otherwise why would we fight the Tuareg?" Besides, why don't they deploy us into Somalia, he asks, replacing the AMISOM troops? "We really know war. We are not afraid to die. We'd even be ready to send forty thousand [soldiers] to Somalia, but there are no resources!"

The mobilization around danger was played with brio by the indispensable Chadian warriors, who everyone—especially the French, and their hand-picked choices for head of UN peacekeeping—knew could not be pushed around, however many stories of abuse kept surfacing. Abderaman, who in the hotel café rambled on about the falsity of rape allegations against Chadian soldiers in CAR, was keenly aware of this leverage, yet he was just a low-level sales rep. Higher up, Chad's strongman leader, Idriss Déby, was strengthening his iron-fist rule over his restive and desperately poor country thanks to the resources and diplomatic goodwill showered on him by his Western partners (a relationship temporarily imperiled, for the United States, by Trump's travel ban of autumn 2017).[39]

If the Chadians were steadfast in their service provision, the fear market also provided wilier regimes with a fretful weapon. *Stoking* fears, reptilian-style, was their duplicitous game. In Algeria, recall how Bush's war on terror had provided legitimacy and manna for the country's security state, even though Algerian security operators had allegedly themselves played a key role in stoking the threat (as seen again in 2017, when French intelligence suggested the Algerian security services were protecting a key jihadist leader, Iyad ag Ghaly). Outside Africa, consider Syria, where an even larger disaster unfolded once Bashar al-Assad's regime decided to let jihadists and violent criminals out of prison en masse, fueling an incipient "war on terror" in which the dictator could present himself to Western interveners as a necessary evil.[40]

But the master of the reptilian pitch was the West's old foe and short-lived friend Gaddafi, who used the threats of both migration and terror-ism to his advantage. A self-made fear marketeer of the Rapaille school, the Libyan leader had in an earlier incarnation happily donned the drag of danger and terror as he played into his Reagan-assigned role of "mad dog of the Middle East" for the global stage. Then, in the 2000s, he instead sought to gain leverage by using migrants as a threat against Europe, as we saw in our last chapter: first to lift sanctions, then to ask for payouts, and finally to press for an end to NATO attacks.[41]

However, let us not fall into the old trap of seeing non-Western "partner states" as sullied by danger and their Western counterparts as nothing but their unwitting helpers. European ministers, once they embraced their inner reptilians, had much to gain on the fear market themselves. In the summer of 2017, the Italian interior minister Marco Minniti embarked on horse-trad-ing with conflictive Libyan tribes and militias, stepping outside the cordon sanitaire to make them sign up for a détente of sorts. "Only when I reassured them that I was from Calabria," he told reporters, "a region where deals and alliances are sealed with blood, did they finally agree to sign." Minniti's "desert diplomacy" was accompanied by a push to equip, train, and coordi-nate with the violent Libyan coast guards. The result was dwindling refugee numbers and short-lived acclaim back home—as well as more suffering for those pushed back to what the Italian foreign ministry itself called the "hell" of Libya, in an apparent breach of international refugee law.[42]

Minniti sought to confront fear, he told reporters, describing it as "a legitimate feeling, one democracy needs to listen to and deal with." Fair point, we may say, but "listening" was not really the goal. Rather, in the negotiations over Libya, fear served as the glue connecting embattled factions and international actors in a lucrative market. "Dangerized" diplomacy is sometimes a risky prospect, and it is true that Minniti and his counterparts in Tripoli, Ankara, and elsewhere do not always gain as much as they often loudly proclaim. Yet from a systemic perspective, what is important is not the particular outcome of each and every "transaction" but the entrenchment of the fear market with its set of rules and incentives. Even if they might not always cash in on their trades, all these fear merchants knew precisely which buttons to press, however clumsily underlings such as Abderaman or rulers such as Gaddafi might at times have pressed them with fat diplomatic fingers.

Bringing Rapaille's reptilian fears to bear on the wider marketplace of international intervention, as we have done here, shows us how repressive regimes and security forces have managed to position themselves as necessary bulwarks by tapping into and even stoking fears and dangers. This duplicitous "game" was played equally well by nonstate actors, we must note.[43] Among such actors were the mercenaries. In 2017, one of their ilk, David Prince—founder of the infamous Blackwater mercenary firm—offered to solve the migration crisis in Libya by deploying his own private forces, just as he was angling for more business in Trump's Afghan battlefields.

Worse, the enemies in the fight against migration and the war on terror were themselves tapping into the fear market, as we have already seen hints of in earlier chapters. Along Libya's shores, some human smugglers said they kept business going not just for the easy money but to put pressure on Europe to send aid to their home regions.[44] In terrorism, fear is evidently at the heart of the gruesome business, and its value increases with political and media attention. Recall last chapter's brutal video on Libyan shores, and its usage of the psychology of the border: Daesh and its fellow murderers are experts in conjuring menace, updating the nineteenth-century shock techniques of "propaganda of the deed" for the world of social media and twenty-four-hour newscasts.[45] Their snuff movies of beheadings, the executioner in black, victim in Guantánamo jumpsuit, cut out just as the deed is done—ensuring that the video passes muster with the sensibilities of Western editors while the cut-off head sways on repeat in the reptilian brain of the intended spectators.

The media play their part, too. Editors keep acting as willing consumers and conduits for snuff: swaying heads, bloody bomb attacks, or the chopped-off hands and desecrated shrines that shot northern Mali's resident jihadis to fame in 2012. Fox News may have plowed a lonely furrow as it broadcast images of a Jordanian pilot burned to death in a cage by Daesh in 2015, yet even as competitors complained about the attention the murderers received, they kept buying into the reptilian pitch of the terrorizers. In the fear market, the media's turbo-charging of fear meant the stakes kept rising, generating incentives for ever more spectacular attacks. As one British newspaper commentator put it, "Overhyping terror assists just two groups of people. One is the security industry, the other is the terrorists. Journalism has become useful idiot to them both."[46]

Idiotic it may seem, but media organizations have embraced their inner reptilians for quite rational reasons. In one of the broadcast media's most lucrative segments—sports—editors have held to policies of not filming nude streakers and other attention seekers as they run onto the playing field, knowing full well that giving them the limelight will encourage others and so delay the profitable game. In terrorism, by contrast, the deed itself is what puts eyeballs on screens.[47]

The fear market, in sum, is much wider than the aid world of central concern to this chapter—it encompasses jihadists, media outlets, smugglers, security forces, and repressive and democratic regimes, all vying for different corners of the marketplace. Yet not every security actor is a reptilian red in tooth and claw. Some of those stepping up to the fear-laden marketplace play a subtler game, shedding their military skin as they pitch their ideas to its development segment. And, as it happens, one of them is familiar to us: Stanley McChrystal, on his return from the battlefields of Iraq and Afghanistan. At the risk of singling him out yet again, his thoughts on how to engage with crisis zones let us discern some of the logics shared by funders and aid entrepreneurs in the fear market. Moreover, his proposal for international aid is propped up by an intellectual framework that ties us into the story so far: that of epidemiology.

.   .   .   .   .

McChrystal's fall from his pedestal as "the world's best warrior" had been swift following his disastrous outing in *Rolling Stone:* firing, retirement, and then, as happens with so many disgraced figures from the life of business, war, and politics, an invitation to join us academics with a post at Yale. We would be forgiven for assuming that, safe in the last-chance saloon of academia, McChrystal would happily spend his days philosophically justifying the terrifying methods of his JSOC days. But no: McChrystal was onto a Big Idea, whose intellectual scaffolding may have been provided by his network experiments in war, yet whose edifice was all shiny and new.

"How to Treat Threats of Ebola and ISIS," said the headline to a piece of his for CNN. Writing with a medical expert and Yale colleague, Kristina Talbert-Slagle, McChrystal went full throttle on the epidemiological narrative that we have already traced at the rich world's borders, but with a fresh analytical twist. "The opportunism of Ebola and ISIS in many ways mirrors that of the opportunistic infections that prey upon people with AIDS, exploiting their long-weakened systems," wrote the warrior and the public health scientist. "Several lessons from the long, painful struggle of the AIDS epidemic can inform our approach to Ebola and ISIS as global health security crises."

AIDS could teach us two things in particular: first, that "the host can't be brought back to health unless the opportunistic infections are treated"—meaning "state-of-the-art, targeted therapy." This the United States had done, McChrystal assured his readers, by "deploying targeted approaches in Liberia, Iraq and Syria" that addressed "these invasive threats." Yet the second point, to him, was more important, and more neglected: "Unless the underlying immunodeficiency is treated, people with AIDS will be vulnerable to ongoing waves of infection. The same is true with Ebola and ISIS. Unless we address the underlying causes of national immunodeficiency that facilitated their emergence, more infectious disease outbreaks, other insurgencies, or to-be-determined threats will recur."

All of this may recall the linking of ISIS and Ebola threats in media depictions, as well as how these were at times bundled together with the threat of the irregular migrant coming across the US-Mexico border, reenvisioned as carrier of a deadly disease. McChrystal's intervention posited a subtler form of equivalence, however, meshing the *logics* of the two "epidemics" of Ebola and insurgency. Treating the "underlying immunodeficiency" meant, to McChrystal, fixing the derelict health system of Sierra Leone or regaining the trust of locals in war-ravaged Iraq or Afghanistan.

It might mean opening schools for Afghans, talking to their elders, help-ing their farmers get their crops to market. As McChrystal answered an audience member at one of his talks, who asked what "remedies" were available for Afghanistan comparable to medications for AIDS: "The first vaccination is education. . . . And then the next thing you do is help busi-nesses grow."[48]

In short, McChrystal was pitching for the same securitized develop-ment as everyone else, while developing a compelling epidemiological lan-guage for it that put focus squarely on how threats emerge in a failing *system*. As he and Talbert-Slagle pleaded in their CNN piece, even though politicians knew of the "vulnerable systems in Sierra Leone, Guinea, Liberia, Iraq and Syria," after 9/11 and its frustrations, "It is tempting to adopt a defensive crouch and respond only to the threats before us, allow-ing the remainder of the problem to fester. That is a mistake. And the history of the AIDS epidemic argues that ultimately, it won't work." Rebuilding national systems might not be "a popular strategy for a war-weary nation," they said, "but in a globally connected world, we may not have a choice."

On the face of it, their thinking was sound: you cannot just treat "symp-toms" and fail to deal with the etiology, or the causes of affliction. Speaking at Yale, McChrystal said: "What you're really talking about is a nation that is sick, it's infected, it's infected with an insurgency and that's a challenge to the very existence of the nation itself."[49] The nation as an organism, a complex system, which needs assistance to rebuild its defenses—this was counterinsurgency of the kind McChrystal had fought in Iraq and Afghanistan, where he had in hindsight come to see his forces as an "immune system" fighting pathogen-insurgents. To him, fighting a virus and fighting a military insurgency were similar tasks, seen through the holistic lenses of medicine and epidemiology.

As with his take on counterinsurgency, McChrystal's epidemiological twist on aid was not his innovation alone.[50] Medicine and militarism have borrowed metaphors back and forth down the ages, as Susan Sontag notes in her *Illness as Metaphor*. In the 1880s, medical discourse rendered bac-teria as "invaders," while on the military side US airpower has long been described as "surgical."[51] In the war on terror, metaphors of disease and infection have kept proliferating. The United Kingdom's Blair once stated that a "mutation" had given rise to a "fanatical strain" of Islam, making the "virus" of terrorism emerge; Richard N. Haass, a veteran of US administrations, noted the need for "prophylactic measures at home and abroad" against this "virus."[52] In Afghanistan, Lieutenant General William Caldwell urged a move away from talking about combat operations "in the language of war," instead saying his task was "curing Afghanistan" and treating it as "an ailing patient" whose aggressive infection must be eliminated. Here, scholars note, "counterinsurgency becomes chemotherapy."[53] By contrast, David Kilcullen, the anthropologist-cum-counterinsurgency expert, deployed the medical metaphor to justify "population-centric" interventions instead of air strikes. "Terrorist infection," he wrote in *The Accidental Guerilla,* was "part of the social pathology of broader societal breakdown, state weakness, and humanitarian crisis."[54]

In this stream of disease(d) metaphors, McChrystal's AIDS-based model did not just join up belligerent and population-centric approaches to distant threats: it also drew on the full symbolic charge of his disease of choice. In her dissection of American ideas of the immune system, *Flexible Bodies,* anthropologist Emily Martin has observed that the AIDS crisis came to frame the immune system as a "defended nation-state, organized around a hierarchy of gender, race, and class."[55] As Sontag notes, plagues have long been used as judgments on societies, and diseases as signs of social disorder; AIDS, for some time, came to incarnate this judgment in its putative links to race, sexuality, and territory.[56] As she put it, "The AIDS epidemic serves as an ideal projection for First World political paranoia. Not only is the so-called AIDS virus the quintessential invader from the Third World. It can stand for any mythological menace." And later: "AIDS is one of the dystopian harbingers of the global village, that future which is already here and always before us, which no one knows how to refuse."[57]

While a few years ago this might have read as hyperbole, it seems less so in the age of Trump, with his infamous rant on Haitian immigrants carrying AIDS.[58] And it was precisely this well-worn metaphor of global menace, rehearsed since the 1980s, that our Yale writers sought to deploy when rolling AIDS, Ebola, and ISIS into one. As smarter-suited versions of whimsical Rapaille, they played on reptilian fears even as they appealed to the intellect of the cortex, all the while bringing innovations in networked military thinking to bear on the civilian marketplace of development.

· · · · ·

I have dwelt on McChrystal's machinations because they reveal starkly how a complex systemic perspective on danger may feed into, rather than counteract, a crude "reptilian" pitch based on fear. His epidemiological model combined these two strands masterfully, but it was not an outlier: rather, in treating the nation as an infected patient, it dovetailed with a myriad of policy initiatives on complex systems and "resilience."

I won't bore you, dear reader, with a lengthy exposition of this most slippery of terms, which essentially refers to the capacity of a unit (individual, ecosystem, community, physical object) to "bounce back" from a moment of stress. Let us simply note that the r-word is everywhere today. It figures in aid policies, in attempts to counter violent extremism, in earthquake-preparation programs, and in climate change plans such as our Green Wall example. It appears in state-building efforts, and in educational strategies in rich and poor nations alike; even during my son's first few days at school as a four-year-old, his teacher threw in a mention of the need to "build pupils' resilience."

Like McChrystal's epidemiological model, the r-word is symptomatic of complexity thinking, or treating a problem through a systemic, "ecological" perspective in which causes are nonlinear and feedback loops abound. Like metaphors of disease and affliction, it is also framed by our current dystopian horizons. Put up with the shocks the world will throw at you, the resilience thinkers say, or else you risk deterioration and collapse. As groaning shelves of self-help and business books tell us, we should really try our very best to be more like a bendy bit of wood that pings back when you twist and pull it, rather than breaking under pressure. "The armor you need for modern life," is one British newspaper's take on the r-word—in other words, resilience may well be the Humvee of the mind.[59]

I tried to be that bendy bit of wood myself when bracing for interview after interview on resilience planning for the Sahel. And disquisitions there were aplenty. The r-word was on everyone's lips, and in everyone's strategy: the EU had its versions, UN agencies had theirs, as did national authorities and donor agencies.[60] Some aid officials liked it, some detested it. Some insisted it must be a development term; others, including the UN in its "integrated" Sahel strategy, used it as a way to interlock development, humanitarianism, and governance.[61] Some saw it as a way of getting donors' attention; others, as the last thing donors wanted to fund, even if they paid lip service to it. Some thought it put focus on the most "vulnerable," others that it excluded them. To optimists, the term was a "Trojan horse" that let interveners and locals smuggle a grassroots model of change into the citadels of top-down development programming.[62] To critics, it was Trojan in another sense—a useful device for sneaking security and "neoliberal" agendas into a faux-radical framework.

But we shouldn't make too much of all this buzz. Academics have expended plenty of effort on showing how resilience may be used as a tool to reshape and "discipline" populations, not least in the "global South." Yet often the donors do not care enough about the inhabitants of, say, Mali even to want to reshape them in the first place. As one European aid official in Mali put it to me, after reeling off a list of projects on water and sanitation, forestry, food security, and more, "It's a bit of the Emperor's new clothes" for existing projects, but "It's the politicians who decide what we do."[63]

Buzzword or something more, resilience makes McChrystal's model seem less of an oddball theory and more just an alarmist restatement of the commonsense wisdom of the day. One UNICEF official in Senegal asked me rhetorically one day why it was that Boko Haram, Mali's MUJAO jihadists, and others were "able to infiltrate local communities." To her, the answer lay not in security approaches but in development and, above all, resilience. The question donors should be asking, she said, was this: "What are the vulnerabilities that have contributed to this insecurity?"

If the emphasis differed, what everyone did seem to agree on was whose resilience was under discussion. Resilience—like the *acquired* immunodeficiency syndrome of McChrystal's epidemiological model—was the responsibility and property of the target individual, community, or nation. Instead of proposing a shared developmental narrative along the lines of the postwar modernization doctrine, resilience thinking allows for an exit strategy: develop local resilience in the Sahel, the theory goes, and international donors and agencies can eventually start pulling back.

Yet as we have seen in the rampant dangerization among Mali's aid brokers or African security forces, the donors and external interveners must be seen as *part* of the system, warts and all. To return to the McChrystal and Talbert-Slagle model, one commentator has noted how their "geographical imaginary vision" presented external intervention as part of the solution, not the problem.[64] To them, special forces and drone operations contained the "contagion" and targeted individual "pathogens," and so gradually helped break down their "network," while the larger counterinsurgency strategy of winning hearts and minds worked on getting the immune system back in order.

In Iraq, McChrystal had adapted complexity thinking to warfare; yet now that he and his Yale colleague applied this model to the presumably infected *nation,* he reverted to simplicity. Why should the metaphor of the body and its immune system end at a nation's colonial-era borders? In an Afghanistan or Iraq racked by invasions, sullied by billions of dirty dollars for warlords in office, and put under international tutelage and occupation, we may well ask *who* was ill—was it the Afghan or Iraqi nation-state, or something bigger, beyond their territories? It was clear, for one, that Daesh had risen from the ashes of the Americans' prison-dungeons of postinvasion Iraq. Here McChrystal the medic was applying a poison pill or, worse, misdiagnosing the patient as source of an infection his military operations were themselves transmitting—with some help from the reptilian forces and regimes buttressed by the occupiers.

In securitized aid more broadly, the "systems view" on security rarely encompassed such external interveners. Consider the Americans' CVE programming against extremism, cited above. On the face of it, its long list of "root causes" is quite sound, mentioning as it does state repression as a risk factor. In one comprehensive study of drivers of "extremism" in Africa by the United Nations Development Programme (whose motto, as it happens, is "Empowered lives, resilient nations"), seven out of ten respondents saw "some form of government action" as the "tipping point" that triggered their decision to join an extremist group. The UN secretary-general, commenting on the report, noted how "93 percent of all terrorist attacks between 1989 and 2014 occurred in countries with high levels of extrajudicial deaths, torture and imprisonment without trial."[65] Now, state repression and impunity, we should note, have frequently been *facilitated* by the US export of the war on terror—yet on this "root cause," the CVE list was conspicuously silent.[66]

The complex systems view, in other words, was as a rule rather myopic. McChrystal, for one, recognized this once he slipped back into his military skin. Looking back on the Soviet-era proxy war in Afghanistan, he said, "On the surface it looks as though for a relatively small investment, and no Americans killed, we beat the Soviet Union. We gave the Soviets their Vietnam. In so doing though, we changed Afghanistan. We created these warlord groups that fought a civil war that then allowed the rise of the Taliban. We created problems that we are now facing."[67] Some years earlier, before 9/11 and his rise to stardom, he had summed up precisely this line of thinking in these words: "We must ensure that the cure we offer through intervention is not worse than the disease."[68] Yet his Yale-era metaphors of disease, epidemiology, and pathogens stopped short of such broader complexity analyses: instead, they defined the infected patient as Other, set beyond a neat analytical *cordon sanitaire*. To take us back to Rapaille and his marketing of fear, in projecting danger away from the self, McChrystal acted somewhat like a suburban Humvee driver who assumes the threat is "out there," beyond the massive bumpers, not realizing he may himself be the most dangerous thing on the road.

The seemingly holistic language of resilience and systems thinking, in other words, has served to delimit the affliction and so to frame the remedy—allowing powerful interveners to excise themselves from the picture while justifying their operations via sophisticated jargon. Indeed, whatever the short-term merits of more enlightened resilience projects in helping locals cope with their environment, it was becoming quite clear in my endless encounters with the r-word that resilience thinking was first of all bolstering *institutional* resilience across the board. It gave donors, aid agencies, NGOs, and recipient governments something to talk about, and a language through which to channel their often rather vague aims and projects. As a term that was bendy in the extreme in itself, it could tie together sectors ranging from humanitarians and development actors to security officials, even as it allowed them to act as if they all owned their own version of resilience. And it let the politicians who funded it all strengthen their own role as resilience champions for vulnerable Others far away while stemming financial, political, and security risks to the Homeland. In other words, a systemic term served to prop up a system of aid intervention that increasingly took its cue from the security sector and its concern with the containment of propagating dangers.

.   .   .   .   .

In this chapter, we have taken aid and security professionals at their word in approaching aid as a system—and, more specifically, as a marketplace. The marketplace of aid is increasingly tied into a wider market of fear, which generates feedback loops through the incessant pitches and "solutions" proposed by brokers and donors alike. In conclusion, we must put this story of recent shifts in aid back in the historical frame of our map of danger: that of colonialism and its long aftermath.

Let us first return to colonial West Africa. There, as we have already noted in passing, colonizers were concerned with managing subject *populations,* including their purportedly threatening migrations. Even as the French depended on forced and unforced labor for their coastal plantations, they fretted about their newly urbanized African subjects as they sought to channel and control these subjects' movements. In the early Cold War days, this colonial vision of population management was to some extent superseded by the state-centric Truman doctrine: the worldwide fight against poverty now became tied to the battle for domination between the West and the Soviet Union. Yet one eminent security and development scholar, Mark Duffield, has noted how in the later postwar period, shifts in global capitalism—accompanied by the eventual demise of the Soviet foe—were leading to a growing exclusion of large parts of the poor from "development" as conceived on the nation-state checkerboard. In this shift, he argues, the postwar "world of nations" was being replaced with a "world of peoples" in which populations again emerged as a key target of funders and interveners in their potentially threatening guise. In this, Duffield suggests, our world has come to resemble the colonial era, resurrecting its concerns with population control.[69]

However sharply we wish to draw this historical shift, Duffield's epochal story does help direct our gaze toward the systems of population management in place during the heyday of empire. These systems, we should note, concerned not only apprehensions about migration, or risks of insurgent politics, but also other dangers that tied into the models and metaphors considered so far—infection and infestation.

There is a rather well-known story from colonial times, in part probably apocryphal, that goes like this: in nineteenth-century British India, the colonizers feared the threat of venomous snakes, so they instituted a bounty for locals who killed them. Soon dead snakes started piling up in their thousands, yet the problem was nowhere near solved: more always seemed to appear. The British suspected some natives were breeding snakes in order to kill them and cash in on the reward and thus ended the policy. In response the breeders released their snakes, magnifying the threat. The "Cobra effect" is how economists have labeled this phenomenon—trying to fix a problem in a wrong-headed way that exacerbates it.[70]

A similar tale concerning the French colonies, backed up by the historical record, has made the rounds. In Vietnam, the colonizers thought to build Hanoi into a Paris of the east, and so they set about creating a cocoon for the white masters with streets, villas, and a modern sewage system, all set apart from the natives. Yet a menace lurked on the margins of this world, in the sewers built exclusively for the whites—rats. The colonizers were afraid that bubonic plague would take hold in the natives' quarters and spread across the cordon sanitaire, so they paid Vietnamese ratcatchers to descend into the drains and capture the creatures. As the problem persisted, they put a bounty on the tails of the rodents. The more tails native town-dwellers brought in, the more they would be rewarded. Yet however many tails the colonial bureaucrats received, the pests kept proliferating. After some time, the French discovered that locals had taken to cutting off the rats' tails, leaving them to run away, and presumably to breed again—producing yet more rats, and so more tails.

When bubonic plague did strike Hanoi in 1903, its cause was not the native quarter that the French had feared would bring pestilence upon them. Rather, it was the International Colonial Exposition, which had ferried goods and people into Hanoi in a show of imperial grandeur, rodents being the roadshow's joyriders. Through their monetization of the rodent menace, the colonizers had created an economy that reinforced the problem, while the danger they had feared all along was realized through the channels of empire, not through any native plague affliction.[71]

Such colonial-era stories, anecdotal as they are, point to our key concern in this chapter—the systems effects of outsiders' priorities that, when framed around combating assorted dangers, often end up reinforcing them. The marketplace of aid, just like Rapaille's marketplace of advertising, is not an ahistorical one: the reptilian does not always win, in all places and at all times. Rather, by putting fears of transnational threats at the heart of much development work (and by reframing migration as one such threat), donors are yet again securitizing the relationship between the world's rich and poor, generating large incentives for reflexive dangerization among brokers large and small.

Incentives for stoking threats, we may add, have been well noted in the scholarship on war. In his *Useful Enemies,* the conflict scholar David Keen shows that wars are not always meant to be won. Rather, enemies and threats serve important functions for those who stand to gain from continued violence, and as a result collusion tends to abound in warfare—as it does in security interventions of other kinds, including border controls, as we have seen. When the fight against terror or migration is backed by multibillion deals offered up by the richest powers on the planet, the "asset" of fear surges in value, skewing not just security markets but also the aid market, in which organizations try to stay attuned with, or ahead of, funders' needs by adapting tones of menace in their messaging.[72]

"In order to be rich, you have to threaten," Djibril had scathingly told me in Bamako, and he was right (though, to bring us a rare happy ending, by 2018 he had settled into his newly built home while working as a state-sanctioned traditional healer, his earlier thoughts of mobilizing menace replaced by tranquil family life). His own fling with the fear market hinted, however, that you do not usually need to threaten outright: suffice to help identify the threat, collaborate in the "solution," and by doing so make yourself indispensable—in the process opening opportunities for reinforcing the very dangers feared by the donor. The more subtly you play this game, the higher the rewards. In short, be a resilient actor in the fear market, and you shall prevail. As danger starts motivating investments in everything from sanitation projects to migrant sensitization campaigns, the biggest winners are indeed those who cast the most threatening spells. For in a "reptilian" market, it goes without saying, the real reptiles always win.

6 WHERE THE WILD THINGS ARE

> I passed through the lonely Indian town
> > Deep sunk 'twixt the walls of wheat,
> And the dogs that lived in the land came down
> > And bayed at me in the street.
> But I struck with my dog-whip o'er nose and back
> > Of the yelping, yellow crew,
> Till I cleared a pathway athwart the pack,
> > And I and my horse went through.
>
> Rudyard Kipling, "The City of the Heart"

Where the Wild Things Are, the 1960s children's story by Maurice Sendak, starts with the boy Max chasing the family dog down the stairs in his wolf pajamas. "Wild thing," his mother shouts to him; "I'll eat you up!" he responds, and is sent off to bed without food. That night a forest grows in his room. The trees become the world all round, and he is cast out to sea. Drifting among strange sea monsters, for a night, a week, and a year, he arrives at the shores of the wild things, who raise their beastly arms as he disembarks, half as greeting, half in menace: "The wild things roared their terrible roars and gnashed their terrible teeth and rolled their terrible eyes and showed their terrible claws." Yet Max is not afraid. He stares them down, looks deep into their monstrous eyes, and frightens them. Let the ruckus commence! Max becomes the king of the wild things, and dances through the night, and then sails back to his bedroom through a night, a week, and a year, where his food is waiting for him; and it is still warm.[1]

In the past chapters we have met assorted wolves and reptilians, and now it is high time to set sail for the land of monsters. "Where the wild things are," you may recall, is how self-styled Pentagon visionary Thomas

Barnett referred to the parts of the Gap where "people still go medieval on one another." It may seem daft to take Barnett's word for it and recast the war on terror as a children's fairytale, but the story resonates in its psycho-geography of danger, a term to which we will shortly return—the lure of the wild darkness, the promise of mastering it, the return to safety. As I now read *Where the Wild Things Are* to my own sons, propped up on the bedroom pillows, I recall the titillation I once felt when little Max's bedroom door closed, night descended, and a tangled forest beckoned us to a land of monsters. In the story, the space of safety and the space of wilderness are telescoped into one another—as Max travels into his dreamworld, time is compressed, an hour becomes a year, and the wilderness is already in his room. Without going all Freudian on poor little Max, we may quite easily see how the wild things are a projection of the child's emotions into the imagined Other, and into an elsewhere. He is their king. He stares them down and returns the fright. He goes wild in his own dreamscape before returning and removing, in that final scene, his wolf suit to become a hungry boy yet again.

Max and his monsters lead us into a different cartography from those of earlier chapters: the map in our minds, and its interaction with the nooks and crannies of the danger zone. But let us move stepwise to that intimate map of twenty-first-century intervention by a detour from the lands of wild things to those of empire, where another wolf-suited man-boy was once running free.

This the colonial era tells us: that attempts to shield off the "native" world from the workings of imperial power constituted make-believe of a kind that almost puts Max's adventures to shame. The French realized this the hard way in Hanoi, when their meticulously constructed sewage system for white folks turned out to be the perfect vehicle for a rodent infiltration, and native ratcatchers ascended from the sewers clutching bundles of slain rats. And the young Rudyard Kipling, soon to be yarn-spinner-in-chief to the British Empire, faced this realization, too. As he came down from the cool hideaway of Dalhousie in imperial India to the hot bustle of Lahore as an eighteen-year-old, disease was assailing the "Civil Lines," the colonial compounds set apart from the natives at a presumably safe distance.[2] Kipling was deadly afraid of cholera, that "breath of the Devil," yet the fear of disease would not keep him tamed. He rode into the night in his poem, his "dog-whip of work and fact" aloft, replacing the tale of separation with one of bravery and rational domination. As a reporter he headed down the alleyways, befriending tea drinkers and opium smokers, before sneaking back across the Civil Lines at night.[3] The colonial world he construed for himself was a wild frontier on the edges of which teetered "White Town," the manicured lawns and manservants of a slice of Britain in India, to which he could always return. Like Max, Kipling may have briefly fancied himself the master of both.

.   .   .   .   .

On today's world map of danger, the Civil Lines have returned as the fortified bastions of risk-averse interventions. The US military, for one, contrasts the worlds outside and inside "the wire," or the perimeter around their green zones, headquarters, and forward operating bases. Inside the wire dwell soldiers, paper pushers, and paper-pushing soldiers cuddled up in a golden prison. Outside lurks the black and red zones, where only the chosen few are allowed to tread. Yet those inside still dream of the wild world beyond, its promises and perils: prohibition fuels passion about the realms outside the wire.

In this chapter, we will consider this interaction between the mental map of visitors and the terrains of the danger zone itself. The threats and risks of the latter are not perfectly mappable: rather, they take shape in close interaction with the individual and collective projection of danger into specific places, times, people, and encounters. Certain road junctions, bars, compound gates, neighborhoods, and times of day *feel* more dangerous, as we saw already in Bamako's protests in chapter 1. This "ambiance" is itself tied up with the manner in which security is organized: its blind spots, its risk priorities, its politics. Some workers cower inside bunker walls, while others seek to break free of the strictures; their employers often respond to rebelliousness by reinforcing the prohibitions and slamming the gate shut. The enemy, in turn, interacts with official tactics and structures, inscribing its version of danger upon the landscape. A bunker wall shifts targeting to vehicles; armored SUVs spur more potent IEDs; and as one organization fortifies its headquarters, it helps transform others into soft targets, skewing the marketplace of violence. Through this beastly dance, a peculiar, wild forest grows outside the bolted gates of the new Civil Lines—a space where prohibition stamps desire and fear on the everyday map of markets, teahouses, hotels, and homes.

Our task is to map the psychogeography of danger of this world. Psychogeography is an obscure folk art of sorts, concerned with "the manner in which the contemporary world warps the relationship between psyche and place."[4] The original avant-garde psychogeographers saw "drifting" as an urban art form—in the words of Will Self, one of its enthusiastic literary adherents, they were "rollicking Situationists who tottered, soused, across the stage set of 1960s Paris, thereby hoping to tear down the scenery of the Society of the Spectacle with their devilish *dérive*." Yet instead of drunkenly ambling up the streets of Marais, we will here weave our way through a darker geography of claustrophobic compounds, of roads leading into no go zones, and of savagery relegated to the blank spots. Visitors to the danger zone, like the modern Parisian flâneur resurrected by the psychogeographers, help *make* it as they move through it, or as they linger on its margins. Danger is incarnated in the shuffle of hesitant feet, in the grind of the wheels of an SUV, in the clang of closing compound gates, in the rhythms of daylight and witching hour. In other words, we will inquire into the human dimensions of the time, space, and psychology of danger—moving from bunkers to the wild world outside the wire, and drifting as we do so across some of the most dangerous places of today's world: from Kabul and Afghanistan's hinterland to war-ravaged Syria and beyond. Among researchers, aid officials, reporters, and combatants, we will see how the psychogeography of danger may be at times claustrophobic and paranoid, and at times beset by a feverish desire to go outside, don the wolf suit and even become one with the dangers.

This intimate dimension of the danger zone also allows us to discern more clearly some of the political stakes in the walling and bunkering on world margins. The philosopher of militarism Paul Virilio once sketched this story in his own psychogeographic wanderings through the open-air war museum that is the French Atlantic coastline. Barricades and ramparts may seem to indicate military muscle, he observed, yet they also betray fragility. Amid the dunes lay a scattering of German concrete bunkers that to Virilio symbolized the last gasp of two-dimensional war. The Nazis' concrete monstrosities, he mused, "were in fact the final throw-offs of the history of frontiers, from the Roman limes to the Great Wall of China; the bunkers, as ultimate military surface architecture, had shipwrecked at lands' limits, at the precise moment of the sky's arrival in war." The sea-facing bunkers were vain bulwarks against the dangers of the sky and the void of the sea, which taunted Hitler and his commanders—"this moving and pernicious expanse, alive with menacing presences."[5]

In the psychogeography of the danger zone, then, we face a double resurrection: of colonial-era ramparts, and of bunkers of wars past. Amid these zombie structures, nightmares meld with facts, which means we will at times—like Virilio in his day—need a dose of poetic license on our journey. Set aside Max and his fairytale: it is often in fictional recollections of war that we most clearly see the intimate, psychological side to the bunkered encounter. In one novel set in a Forward Operating Base (FOB) in occupied Iraq, *Fobbit*, we hear how American soldiers "cowered like rabbits in their cubicles, busied themselves with PowerPoint briefings to avoid the hazard of Baghdad's bombs, and steadfastly clung whiteknuckled to their desks." The book's author was once himself a "Fobbit," as the FOB dwellers are known in military parlance. "If the FOB was a mother's skirt," the narrative voice deadpans, "then these soldiers were pressed hard against the pleats, too scared to venture beyond her grasp." The soldiers active outside the wire came and went in the canteen, leading the protagonist, a fighter-turned-Fobbit called Abe Shrinkle, to miss his war and its raw masculinity with an almost childish longing: "They smelled of sweat, unwashed uniforms, and, if one strained hard enough, the undermusk of blood that always reminded Abe of sniffing warm pennies."[6]

In today's world of advanced risk matrices and crudely divided geographies, the interveners may seem to have it all under control, yet dangers assail the new Civil Lines from above and below. In the past two chapters we have already seen some pernicious side effects of the fear market and of the infected border, but a further problem for interveners lurks in the difference between calculable risks and unknowable, even uncanny dangers. Only some parts of what goes on in distant danger zones—visible on the Control Risks map with which this book began, in the spurious leveraging of risk and resilience in the aid marketplace, and in the bunker architecture protecting precious internationals—can be captured and managed by the architects of risk. Other parts of it elude them. An excess, a bit unaccounted for, always remains, torn off the accounting sheet and tossed onto the fire.

Fobbit's hero, Abe Shrinkle, eventually has to face up to the uncontrolled presence of danger as he hears the swoosh of a mortar leaping through the dazzling Iraqi sky while he is sipping a beer by the pool. One moment he lazes on an inflatable mattress, and the next the insurgent attack has left his mortal remains splattered onto the laps of the poolside women.[7] Shrinkle's mortar-severed arm, snug in a horrified sunbather's lap, seems an apt metaphor for the visceral side of global danger that today's intervening organizations, civilian and military, keep doing their very best to ward off. Yet their prohibitions also work psychologically on their charges—they set visceral fears and dangers prowling on the mental maps of risk managers, soldiers, aid officials, and visitors, and it is into these terrains of fantasy and horror that we must now tread.

.   .   .   .   .

If *No Go World* had been a gutsier book, I would now be strapping on my walking boots (or donning the wolf suit) to stomp up and down the streets of danger. To tread in Kipling's footsteps! Alas, in deference to the risk strictures of academia, I will not. Instead, I must find other ways of exploring the everyday psychogeography of danger from the outside in. And what better way to start than with my own hesitations at the margins of Mali's danger zone, and with the claustrophobic risk systems I encountered there.

The obstacles in heading to the relative safety of Bamako loomed over me in springtime 2014. My employer had risk protocols, travel safety, and ethics forms aplenty—all of which conspired to make a trip anywhere north of the capital an impossible prospect. There was a reason for this: duty of care and insurance rules are getting more demanding each year, and employers more risk averse and control-obsessed. Now, the more I immersed myself in this world of risk before and after my trip, the less in control I felt. One day, the university's security company explained how their security app for my phone would "geolocate" me throughout my time in Mali. I would have to "check in" twice a day, ensuring I was not kidnapped—and this even though no kidnappings had taken place in Bamako, a city far removed from the front lines and too risky for jihadists to negotiate with a hostage in tow. I attended security workshops, where I learned how to cower in the case of a complex attack on a hotel and how to distinguish the sound of machine guns. The university's security manager taught me how to detect an "attack cycle," with the aim of eventually turning me into my own security expert engaged in "tradecraft" of a kind more familiar from spy novels and *Homeland* episodes—all with the idea of regaining some control and satisfying those stringent insurance requirements.

In other words, already before I left for Bamako, the risk meetings, the form filling, the training, and the app tracking were coloring my perceptions of Mali. In my pocket, a swipe on my smartphone now revealed an app that had a distinctly military look: Who would any kidnappers think I was? The potential risks lurking around each corner were taking on a reality of their own in my mind, and the app served as a reminder that all was not well, that I was treading into an area from which we researchers were expected to stay well clear.

My example from Mali, small as it is, allows us to expand our view of hard security away from just blast walls and bollards. Apps, training, code words, tradecraft: the *ritual* of breaching the invisible line into danger zones sets them apart well before one steps into a bunkered compound. For this reason, and drawing on psychogeographers' fling with urban architecture, I will talk of an *architecture of risk* that encompasses bunkering as much as it does technology, risk protocols, and temporal regulations for daily movement. Like the sidewalks of 1960s Paris, this architecture generates an uneven emotional landscape through which the traveler treads at her own peril, potentially seeing danger round every corner.

If the psychogeography of Bamako was already making me rather paranoid before I left the United Kingdom, my stay in the city was to be a cakewalk compared with what visitors to other danger zones face today. To better grasp the psychogeography of danger, we will now follow vicariously in their footsteps. Our first destination will be the ground zero of global danger and a missing piece on our map: Kabul A researcher colleague of mine, "Jonathan," will as our alter ego take us to the stage set of one of the world's most dangerous cities before we drift further into the land beyond, into its spectacle and its silences.

· · · · ·

The cartography of no go lands and safety is but a bird's-eye view of global danger that dissipates as soon as your plane descends and an armored SUV greets you at the tarmac of Kabul airport. As you are weaving into central Kabul, as Jonathan did on a regular basis, an everyday psychogeography starts replacing the abstract map of security risk with its red and green zones. Guy Debord, *grand-père* of the psychogeographers, once remarked on how the ambiance of the streetscape infiltrated into the mind of the drifting Parisian flâneur.[8] Likewise, Kabul's Brutalist bunkers and road-blocks draw a treacherous mental map in the visitor's mind, assailed by threats known and unknown. Borders between safety and danger are set along specific streets, delineated by the armored exteriors of vehicles, estab-lished by the gates of compounds, and marked in time by the tick-ticking clock of terror. In the fortified "Kabubble," as the expat world of the capital is known, the daily rhythm is defined by official restrictions on movement that stretch from "green city"—traveling between safe destinations allowed— to "white city," or lockdown. And lockdown is increasingly what life is about for civilian expats, while US officers roar past in helicopters shuttling them from airbase to headquarters, rattling the windows of the aid workers, embassy officials, soldiers, and locals ensconced in their separate worlds.

Jonathan, like Kipling in his time, had no patience with this cloistered Kabubble. He had embarked on fieldwork for his PhD in 2014, and his research on Afghan politics would soon take him to far-flung parts that few foreigners dared visit. He had been quite surprised to see his research approved: before leaving, a university administrator had just told him to "please stay in touch with your embassy and good luck!" Yet as violence escalated, the academic powers back home were getting jittery. One day, he recalled, "they e-mailed me and said, 'We heard you're in Afghanistan.' Yes, that's true, I responded. 'We need to do a proper risk assessment now,' they continued." Jonathan followed the low-profile "acceptance-based" strategy long used by aid workers: staying with other foreigners in an unguarded compound in Kabul, he had built trust with locals while avoiding the capital's international limelight. Yet this would not do. And now, as he kept moving through the Afghan hinterland in a bat-tered Toyota Corolla, talking to villagers and grizzled warlords, the health and safety managers were finally on his trail. Fearing he would be forced to leave, Jonathan ended up calling the university's security contractor while back in Kabul, as they had demanded. He then realized that the contractor—let's call it Hammer, Inc.—was a militarized outfit made infamous in the occupation. Moreover, it had itself been targeted in a recent attack, leaving two of its employees dead. "Afghan media portrayed it as an attack against a CIA compound," Jonathan told me in dismay. "It's not looking good if the organization that is doing my risk assessment is getting attacked itself."

Having armed contractors turn up in wraparound sunglasses and armored cars was not going to happen, however, because of a second problem: hard men as they were, Hammer, Inc. deemed it too dangerous to assess Jonathan's house themselves. Instead they subcontracted a multinational security conglomerate to visit his sleepy middle-class neighborhood, and they in turn sent a local worker who "asked ridiculous questions such as 'Do you have a fire extinguisher in your house, where is the closest first aid kit,' and so on," Jonathan recalled with a laugh.

Eventually the contractor's report was sent to the university, and, rather predictably, it played up the dangers. The risk of assault was increased for Westerners who followed a "low-profile approach" and "live amongst the local community," it said. The university had to consider its "duty of care and responsibility" as well as "the ramifications of Jonathan being abducted, killed, or injured in either a direct or indirect attack and the subsequent investigation to determine what measures had been undertaken to mitigate this effectively." Hammer, Inc. told the university it had two options. It could reinforce Jonathan's security by moving him into a fortified complex with armed guards and even close protection teams, or, failing that, "It is our recommendation that he not be allowed to return to Kabul now or in the near future under your authority."

"They recommended to pull me out immediately because of risk to my university and my own life," Jonathan said, "but what annoyed me most about the report was that they didn't really do a risk assessment but an assessment of *me*." They simply "copy-pasted media reports on what happens in Afghanistan, showing it's an area of threats" where "everything is dangerous."

Jonathan eventually broke free from Hammer, Inc.'s steely embrace once the university management realized that the contractor had a conflict of interest as both definer of the problem and purveyor of the solution.

Figure 9. Navy "Seabees" assemble a blast-protection HESCO barrier at Camp Bastion, Helmand Province, Afghanistan, 2009. © US Navy.

Yet his brush with the security world illustrates the obstacles travelers face as they seek to tread beyond the wire. A vast risk architecture has been put in place to shield visitors from venturing into the wild, involving physical bunkers as much as private security providers and strict rules on movement—and Kabul is today the busiest bazaar for this slice of the global fear market. "Security contractor" is a common job description for foreigners in the Afghan capital, with salaries among those with enough expertise—including many ex-military men targeted on veteran websites—in the US$100,000–250,000 bracket per year, tax free.[9] Kabul has been transformed into an intricate landscape of checkpoints, concrete barriers, and fortified compounds, where any stray foreign freelance journalists or researchers of Jonathan's kind risk being photographed, questioned, and warned by local security "contractors" whenever they are not escorted around by an expensive bodyguard.[10] And behind locked doors, the remaining international interveners now find themselves ensconced, like castaways waiting for rescue.

In 2016, I set out to understand this expensive risk architecture from the interveners' perspective, as I and a colleague surveyed a selection of international aid workers at a time of escalating attacks and accelerated withdrawal. Anger, desire, and fear seeped out of those bunker walls, as we will see—revealing a conflictive bunker politics and a tense psychogeography rumbling away under the hard surface of intervention.

.   .   .   .   .

Afghanistan was not in a good spot in July 2016, as Obama announced he was slowing the pace of his long-planned military drawdown. Aware of the domestic weariness caused by this slow-grinding war, he also realized Afghan forces were not ready to take charge and that the Taliban were making gains and staging attacks.[11] Our survey, conducted a few months earlier with sixty-four international staff in Kabul, revealed the strains on expatriate life amid increasing restrictions on their daily lives.[12] Two emotions permeated aid workers' responses to our questions: anger toward bosses and security providers, and anxiety about the consequences of the bunkering these had put in place.

The scathing adjectives came thick and fast: security measures were "irrational and inappropriate," arbitrary, inconsistent, "doing more harm than good," "unhealthy," "knee-jerk" and "amateur." As one international aid agency worker said, hard security was "a largely useless approach, fueled by Field Safety staff consisting largely of ex-military personnel." Another respondent, a consultant, said: "Honestly, it's rubbish. They don't have a specific person in charge, just one of the other researchers/managers who is suddenly made a 'security adviser.' A guy who has never been in a similar context, has no experience in that regard, and who loves to dress like an American contractor. Doesn't really make me feel much safer that he's deciding where I can and cannot go." Yet another offered: "They're mostly just trying to be able to prove they did everything they could so that if something happens nobody can sue."

After the 2001 invasion, the Kabubble had been a rather different place, with compound parties and wild nights galore. At this high tide of occupation, hard security had been a political asset: a cortege of armored cars screamed "VIP" and ensured the visitors would be let into secured parts of town. While this symbolism persisted, by 2016 security was no longer just a sign of political importance but also a daily chore, an obstacle to access, and a prison of daily life. In the words of Sune Engel Rasmussen, the *Guardian* newspaper's Kabul-based reporter and one of the few European journalists left in Afghanistan in 2017, Kabul "used to be like *Boogie Nights*—now it's more like *Panic Room*."[13]

Our survey took the pulse of the panic room at a time of escalating fears. One large European development agency had seen a worker kidnapped in Kabul in August 2015, and as a consequence its workers were taken out of the country. Those who eventually returned had been forced to move into a secure compound, where one worker summed up their new life: "Reduced movement and no go policy; obligation to stay in the compound; working and living in one building; no contacts with nationals; no shopping facilities or possibilities." In our survey, we had asked whether workers moved by foot or car from home to office; we had forgotten that most of them no longer left their compound at all. As one UN official pointed out, "I walk to my office, 'cause it is in the same building. My organization would never allow me to walk, though I would feel relatively safe doing so."

Some workers bent the rules, at times in collusion with superiors who reported back to HQ that all procedures had been followed. As one development contractor said, "If you follow all the advice, you'll go crazy simply because you won't be able to leave your residence." Others, however, did not have that choice. As one aid researcher told us, "We used to not follow [the advice] very much, but then they locked us up in a compound and there's literally no choice whether to break the rules or not anymore. . . . Locking your kids up is easier than looking out for them."

No longer free-roaming VIPs, international workers were increasingly treated as precious goods bolted into a warehouse. Yet the bunkered existence failed to instill a sense of safety for many of our respondents, whose criticism echoed academic findings on the perils of hard security.[14] "The security measures create an attractive veneer of security but would do little if we were directly targeted," said one UN agency worker. "If anything, it makes us more conspicuous and less effective," as funds are diverted and locals distanced from the visitors. One frustrated UN official said hard security "only serves to isolate us and makes us more vulnerable," while another offered: "The harder the security, the more attention it draws, thus the less secure it can make you feel. The more people are in one place, again, the more likely the target is perceived as 'juicy.'" One aid worker expressed similar alarm after being moved from a private house to a "secure" compound in a high-profile neighborhood: "Before, I felt safer because no one would carry out a complex attack to get five foreigners. But now there are many of us and it might just be worth it."

Some suggested that the security provision could have worked if it *had* been completely "hard," but noted that there were weak links aplenty—and the weakest of all was the Afghan guards at the gates.[15] The guards "make me nervous," confessed one respondent. Another agreed: "Local male guards prevent me from feeling at home in our building, and they would be useless in an emergency." One UN agency worker suspected the Afghan National Police stationed at a checkpoint outside their door "would conveniently be missing at the time of a raid." With good reason, we may add—this was what had happened when the Intercontinental Hotel was attacked by gunmen in January 2018.[16]

Amid this suspicion, let us briefly consider the shifting risk architecture of Kabul and the Afghans' place in it. The worldwide private security business has many quirks, including accusations of connivance between friend and foe—"Every warlord has his security company," one Afghanistan-based contractor once quipped, and similar rumors made the rounds in other countries of brisk business.[17] Less spectacular, though no less disturbing, is the peculiar *distribution* of risks, echoing what we have seen in earlier chapters. As the security sector sought to repair its image after Iraq's bloodied Blackwater scandals, and as it subsequently expanded worldwide, it needed manpower. With the expansion, a hierarchy of security jobs consolidated.[18] In Kabul as elsewhere, expensive Western security contractors increasingly took on "advisory" roles or worked in close protection teams, while local staff were hired to guard the outer perimeters of compounds, along with employees from poorer nations such as Nepal. Drawing relatively low salaries, these workers were the first to get killed in the case of an attack, much as was the case with the frontline African peacekeepers in Mali. At military installations in Kabul, one development agency respondent noted how NATO compounds seemed layered in concentric circles, with Western soldiers at the core, Asian forces in the next "layer," and at the gates scantily protected Afghan guards. Those stuck outside these concentric circles—civilians—faced the largest risk of all, as seen on bloody display next to the fortified German embassy in May 2017, when a massive bomb hidden in a sewage tanker took more than eighty lives.[19] Local Afghans also faced *economic* risks as entry points kept being choked off to the city, blocking their trades and commutes. In this, the bunkered-up Kabul streets were but a taster of worse to come, as the Trump administration drew up plans for an extended "green zone" enclosing much of central Kabul behind the wire.[20]

Many of our respondents empathized with the plight of Afghan citizens and bemoaned the growing separation. One senior UN manager said: "Our interaction with locals is limited to work hours with national colleagues. But we are not allowed to visit them in their homes or have them over for dinner at ours for what is described as security reasons. We can't go shopping or eat in a restaurant. We live in a fear-driven bubble." A UN political officer said security management "scares employees," as some who had not worked in the country before ended up "terrified of the country and its people."

The disconnect inhibited workers' ability to build the close relationships needed to provide aid, to put together policies, and to help the Afghan administration with its innumerable "state-building" tasks. "There's no real working with Afghan ministries anymore," one international official said. "We cannot go out and we cannot invite them into the compound either. A lot of our staff are now working from outside Afghanistan, which makes things more complicated, too." One UN agency worker complained that hard security was making contact with humanitarian beneficiaries impossible, while an NGO staffer lambasted the "us/them mentality" that "is almost built into the system."

Frustration gnawed away at the bunkered internationals. Many *wanted* to reach "outside the wire," yet now they were being reduced to onlookers and rubber-stampers. One respondent summarized their predicament as "no freedom; constant discussion of insecurity, including with local staff and patients who are far more affected." An international NGO consultant vented about not being able to meet Afghan friends inside her compound "because there are only internationals allowed, which feels like an insult," or outside it "due to security restrictions on where I am allowed to go." To her, the separations resembled a "segregated apartheid system."

The sense of being "locked up," being treated like "kids," and not having any choice was diminishing workers' sense of control over their lives. Insecurity affected mental well-being for all but one of our respondents, and half of respondents said it did so "quite a lot" or "a lot." While the risk of becoming a target was a major worry, the security measures added a large dose of cabin fever. As one respondent said: "I requested a transfer to Ukraine, because Afghanistan and South Sudan left me burned out, constantly on the edge of a fight or tears, drinking too much, etc. It's not the insecurity itself, it's the crushing measures put in place as a reaction to insecurity." Lockup brought "constant underlying stress" and punishing work schedules, others noted, as well as ensuing "emotional breakdowns." Cohabiting in close quarters with one's bosses fed the unease, as did having one's every move controlled by them. Indeed, many remarked on the constant monitoring as the most difficult aspect of their daily lives. One international NGO worker found it "patronizing" and "an extreme intrusion on my privacy that my security manager (and often also the other expats) knows exactly where I am, who I am with, and what I am doing. . . . I hate every little part of your life being monitored."

In the "golden prison," as another worker called it, a sense of purposelessness sometimes set in. As one official with an international organization lamented, "There is no more free time. We are barely allowed to go out and barely allowed to have friends over. So we spend most of our free time working or with colleagues, waiting to leave the country again."

Hard security may seem technocratic, but the workers in our survey reacted viscerally, emotionally, and politically to it, while noting its beneficiaries: the security companies and bosses with their backs covered. For the international officials bunkered into their battlements, there was no deliverance in sight, only transfer somewhere else, or a rest and recuperation stint abroad. They were fed up with the impositions from on high that hemmed them in, locked them up, and disregarded their skills, their views, and even their well-being. To them, the psychogeography of Kabul was becoming claustrophobic, even carceral. Why, we may then ask, were they there at all?

There were good individual reasons to stay put beyond genuine "peacebuilding" motives. The pay was high, and young workers could easily jump up the career ladder through a posting in the Kabubble. Their employers also had good reasons to keep going. Some organizations were tied directly to the political goals of home ministries, as official or semiofficial development agencies, while all of them depended financially on the generous aid funding spent in Afghanistan. For donor governments, finally, politics advocated against leaving. To them, "locking up the kids" in a "golden prison" where they were left to "count the days before leaving" served a clear purpose. As one respondent noted, it indicated a semblance of "normality," and it safeguarded governments against accusations that the lives of aid workers and soldiers had been lost unnecessarily since the 2001 invasion. As aid money kept flowing, as the EU sought mass deportation deals with Kabul, and as the United States escalated its military forays into the Afghan hinterland, keeping a clutch of internationals bunkered up in Kabul ensured some civilian continuity for Western donors, even if this continuity was being reduced to window dressing. Remaining in Afghanistan at a remove also allowed political leaders to skirt questions around their clouded rationales for intervening—not to mention questions over where their promised $15 billion in development funding until 2020 would end up.[21] Reduced to token signs of an international presence, the workers of the Kabubble faced a simple choice, made starker by the eventual move of ever more aid agencies into a self-contained "green zone" complex. Grin and bear it, and you will save money for a house back home and build a lucrative future career; or leave altogether.

As we drift through the Kabubble, we may discern how an all-pervasive risk architecture conspires to define the daily life and psychological horizons of bunkered interveners. But we must remember that there are always those, like my friend Jonathan, who slip through the gates to boldly go where no risk manager has gone before. This is what we will do next, by setting out on a brief escapade into the Afghan hinterland before stepping further outside the wire into the land where the wild things are.

.   .   .   .   .

Right after the Afghan invasion, in the harsh winter of 2002, a latter-day descendant of the Kiplings and Cailliés of the colonial era decided to walk from Herat to Kabul, across high mountain passes and Pashtun lands. This man was the Briton Rory Stewart, an intrepid and well-read fellow eventually destined to wind up as latter-day viceroy of UK-occupied Iraq. The best-selling book based on his journey, *The Places in Between,* starts with a quote from the fourteenth-century traveler John Mandeville: "The country is quite covered by darkness, so that people outside it cannot see anything in it; and no one dares go in for fear of darkness." But like Kipling escaping the confines of the Civil Lines, Stewart did go in. He bought himself a well-wrought walking stick in the bazaar and left behind the press pack of Herat, sheltered in their spy-infested cocoon of a hotel sipping Turkmen champagne.

Walking in the footsteps of the Moghul emperor Babur on his journey from Central Asia to India, Stewart escaped inept bandits, ate stale *naan* bread and gritty rice in the houses of warlords and commoners, and bantered in Dari with illiterate descendants of Genghis Khan and former Taliban fighters. He was accused of espionage and of being an infidel. His Afghan *shalwar kemis*, baggy trousers, and Chitrali cap got ever more soiled and tramp-like, while his adopted dog, Babur, struggled along with him through the snow. Yet he was taken in wherever he went, knocking on the doors of derelict fortresses in the Afghan highlands. "Whatever I experienced when walking would never approach the hardness of daily life in a village," he reflected as he eventually neared occupied Kabul after a final, generous welcome the previous night. He had faced hostility and suspicion when pushing through the snow-covered highlands. But as he swerved onto the home stretch, "I had felt I no longer needed to explain myself to my hosts—that I was at last entitled to sit alongside them and share their food—and I loved the night and those men for it."

On Stewart's first day of walking out of Herat, a jeep drove up behind him. A reporter and a photographer for the *Los Angeles Times* wanted to cover his story. As they shot, the photographer asked: "Have you read *Into the Wild* . . . that book about the wealthy young American who headed off into the Alaskan wilderness to find himself and then died on his own in the snow?"[22] Stewart paid the photographer little attention: to the Herat press pack, he was descending into a dark wild world where they could not go, yet all he wanted was solitude and the long road, whatever it might bring.

Stewart sought out ordinary Afghan life at a time of invasion, and he received his deserved accolades for it. But many of those civilians who voluntarily enter the danger zones have on their mind something more—or less—than this pedestrian psychogeography: a confrontation with danger itself. Among them are assorted writers, war tourists, explorers, and not least reporters.[23] From Afghanistan to Syria and Libya, a peculiar breed of journalists have left their imprint on the hinterland as they tread into the wild, leaving press pack, hotels, and bunkers behind.[24] On our next leg we will trace the psychogeography wrought by their movements, drifting as we do so from one wretched landmark to another on our global map of danger.

.   .   .   .   .

"The rush of battle is often a potent and lethal addiction, for war is a drug," begins *The Hurt Locker,* one of the many half-formed Hollywood attempts to cover the Iraq invasion. As the text dissolves on screen and gives way to the camera-flickering, rubbish-strewn roads of Baghdad, the effect is already kicking in: soon dust rises from an IED explosion, consuming an American soldier in its fire.

The Hurt Locker pulses with the adrenaline of warfare, yet its opening quote is in fact from a war correspondent, not a combatant. Soldiers, after all, have little choice over where they are sent. Yet what makes reporters and other assorted travelers follow in their footsteps?

Michael Hastings, who had conducted the McChrystal interview for *Rolling Stone* that led to the general's ouster, recognized the addictive style of *Hurt Locker* as a war-addled reporter. Author of *I Lost My Love in Baghdad,* Hastings had lost his girlfriend in Iraq in 2007, killed during a kidnapping by al Qaeda. Yet despite this, he kept going back for more. Before his first trip, he had read up on all the classic chroniclers of wars past—Capra, Herr, Loyd, and Hedges. "Not all war correspondents are junkies," he wrote. "But for many, dark, intoxicating forces keep pulling them back to new conflicts. . . . We're not going to get shot or face court martial if we refuse an assignment. We can tell ourselves that it is our duty to democracy to cover these conflicts, our duty to tell the victims' stories. But we do what we do by choice: each patrol, each mission, each trip to a scene of a suicide bomb, is optional." He concludes in joyful gloom: "Addictions destroy, junkies usually die, and the war always wins."[25]

Among the masters of danger journalism today are the folks over at VICE News, an outfit that is bucking the media trend. Unlike staid media groups of old, VICE has pulled in young wild things with its punk brand and daredevil journalism, and key to its macho appeal is exposure to danger. Yet as I visit their offices on the edge of the City of London—exposed brick, hipster coffee shop, long bike racks—it becomes clear the VICE punks have a distinctly complicated relationship with security.

Robert is a photojournalist and VICE veteran whose boyish looks belie his stints in Kabul, Mogadishu, Aleppo, and Kurdistan.[26] Yet reflecting on his escapades as we meet, he seems just as frustrated as our bunkered aid workers. In Kabul, he was locked inside. "We were going mental. . . . I was just longing to be let out of our compound, but was never allowed without this one Western security guard." One time, he convinced his local helper "to take just me without the ex-SAS [UK special forces] heavy, to a swimming pool." Another time, they escaped to have coffee at another compound, which turned out to be the "exact same as ours." In Mogadishu, Robert's next destination, "we never left the base" at the airport, despite there being "one of the most beautiful beaches you've seen" just next to it, and despite the fighting that needed covering in town. In Aleppo, Robert was among the last Western journalists to visit, and there he did get to escape the straitjacket. The risk management was "all bullshit, all just for insurance purposes." The security minder stayed behind on the Turkish border for safety, so Robert entered without escort, texting his locations back to the security official. Robert's anger mounted as the minder forced him out for security reasons—"The most dangerous thing is going in and out. What makes a danger zone a danger zone is the lack of ability to withdraw from it."

Like an amateur psychogeographer, Robert recalled the emotional effect of crossing into danger zones, a "devilish *dérive*" if ever there was one. "It's mental rather than actual danger," he said. "You feel so much more at risk, vulnerable, on edge. . . . You're in an area you shouldn't be in." He felt he was unprotected and "naked" should anything go wrong—as it did in conflict-hit parts of Ukraine, where he was briefly kidnapped. At the time, he was in the gray area between freelance and staff and knew he had to take such risks to make a name for himself. "It's more dangerous for freelancers, they go further than staff want to go, to make their shit worth buying. Otherwise we just send our guys."

The political visibility of danger zones opened an opportunity for plucky young journalists such as Robert: Afghanistan, Somalia, and Syria were their Klondike, where a name could be made. But there was something more to it, as Hastings had recalled when watching *The Hurt Locker*—the lure of danger. As VICE's macho image hints none too subtly, and as the gender makeup of the war reporters indicates, the danger zone is a testosterone-perfumed area of digging and perseverance, and of prestige and thrill gained through confrontation with the world outside the wire.

To drift even further away from our Kabubble, I saw this myself on Bamako's media scene in 2014, where freewheeling freelancers and stringers gathered on hotel terraces each night. Their scene was a hotbed of gossip about risky escapades into northern Mali, Niger, Central African Republic, and beyond, and it was clear that status stemmed as much from having been there as from having bagged the best story. One story stuck with me, and this time the protagonist was female for a change: a Swedish reporter relating her visit to CAR during intense fighting. She told me of visiting the morgue in Bangui, of inspecting blades burrowed into bodies, and of observing massacred civilians dumped by hapless African peacekeepers in front of journalists. What struck me as she recounted all this was not just her own insouciance but rather that she did not write any story on it. It was all the same, more misery, and editors had heard it all, she said, and if they wanted something they could always use news agency copy.

The lure of danger lingered in my mind as I spoke to another war journalist, Karlos Zurutuza. Karlos had left his job as a Basque schoolteacher to start a new life as a roving reporter and had moved from insurgency to insurgency ever since: Kurds in Turkey, Baluchs in Afghanistan and Pakistan, Amazigh in Libya, Polisario in Western Sahara. Traveling into high-risk zones on assignment was an "immense privilege," he insisted. "Nobody forced me to go to Afghanistan and Libya." His biggest problem, rather, was competition from freelancer newbies, who as he saw it sought cheap kicks from proximity to danger.

A "new Facebook generation" of citizen-freelancers cut into journalists' margins, he said; their presence justified the meager pickings editors paid to bona fide reporters as cheap stories kept coming from Benghazi, Aleppo, Kabul. In Libya's 2011 revolution, Karlos had seen young Western men turn up in the cities, caught up in the swirl of Gaddafi's downfall.

They were not making a living off journalism, he said. "These were young guys who were just war tourists who arrived from Egypt or Tunisia, posting on Facebook and Twitter." To them, "It's easy, it's fun, it's super cheap. . . . They are just there for the fun and the ego, to inflate their ego." Amid the competition, Spanish newspapers now paid fifty euros per story; soon they might well ask to get it for free.

Danger was the draw for the "Facebook generation," up to a point. For next the Syrian uprising happened, and many of the Libya citizen-reporters traveled on to what they thought was just another part of the "Arab Spring." They were wrong. "Aleppo had nothing in common with Benghazi and Tripoli." As Karlos noted, in Libya the internationals were useful—NATO intervention was forthcoming. For the rebels of Syria there was no such hope for intervention, and so no use for the visitors, who did not help matters as they failed to file proper stories or build trust. The "local fixers expect a story, not a tweet." Karlos was on neither Twitter nor Facebook. Like his Swedish counterpart in Central African Republic, he could go weeks without filing a story; he took an "anthropological" approach, he said. And like Stewart in his way, he used subterfuge. He grew a beard in Afghanistan to look like a Tajik; he wandered Baghdad's streets dressed in a cheap castaway jacket from the markets, blending in ("I could be an Arab"), and he traversed Libya's hinterland in the company of people he had known for years, while the international reporters and hangers-on clustered in Tripoli, Benghazi, and Misrata. "Journalists go where there are journalists, which is something I never understood." But despite himself, he too was becoming addicted to danger, as he realized when entering Syria in 2013 without a local fixer. One day, he perceived someone shooting from a distance; as he realized it was not a sniper, he started laughing. "This has to stop—I can't laugh when somebody is shooting at me!" Karlos had come to think of himself, he said, as "indestructible."

As with our bunkered aid workers, let us linger a little on the risk architecture of war journalism. One Spanish photojournalist, Andoni Lubaki, had a simple phrase for journalists' plight in danger zones—they are a "sack of money with legs." To the insurgents, they were a source of ransom and a propaganda tool, as he knew after being taken hostage by jihadists in Aleppo. Media back home, he told me, had failed to adhere to an embargo on his story, and so put his liberation in peril. Yet these were the very same media groups that depended on freewheelers such as Andoni and Karlos to bring in the pictures and stories, as they kept pulling out core staff and cutting their exposure to risk. From the media organizations' perspective, this was rational enough, much as for Kabul's interveners when they withdrew behind the barricades. They could still get the stories and pictures—but now the risk was off their books. If something happened, there were few if any legal obligations to occasional contributors who wrote cheaply about the most dangerous corners of the planet.[27]

True, more responsible media organizations are gradually wising up to the dangers and have started refusing freelance stories from Syria, or demanding risk training for those filing from Afghanistan.[28] However, we must note that those worst off in the journalistic risk architecture are not the international freelancers but local journalists and "fixers." "Many people think they can cover a war from their hotel room and occasionally hire local journalists for the dangerous tasks," said one notorious VICE freewheeler, Paul Refsdal, while mentioning the "disposable Chechens" who during the region's brutal conflict "were given a camera and $50. If they returned alive, they were given another $50 to continue rolling."[29]

One comprehensive recent study noted that "greater reliance on fixers in conflict zones," along with their eroding status, had "created a scenario in which fixers are in ever greater danger."[30] Not all of them were "local," and many were indeed well-trained journalists in their own right. One of their kind, a young fixer-reporter from Iraq, told me of ending up in a Turkish prison after stints at the Kurdish front lines of Syria with a range of Western media organizations. Unlike his Western colleagues, he had no recourse to diplomatic support and little by way of legal assistance. The "ethics of it" was wrong, he said. "We are very beneficial to them, yet if we are arrested, we are not [treated as] an employee."

Yet despite the blatant inequality of the media's architecture of risk, fixers and freelancers keep lumbering up to its steps. It is perhaps easy to see why. The higher the obstacles for sending ordinary staff into dangerous fields, the bigger the market slice for outsiders. What is more, danger confirms status in the journalistic pecking order, as seen in Bamako. It may become an end in itself, darkly titillating as visiting freelancers or Facebook-fueled wannabes get to peer into the "heart of darkness," sometimes for little or no pay. Karlos, like his fellow Spanish war correspond-

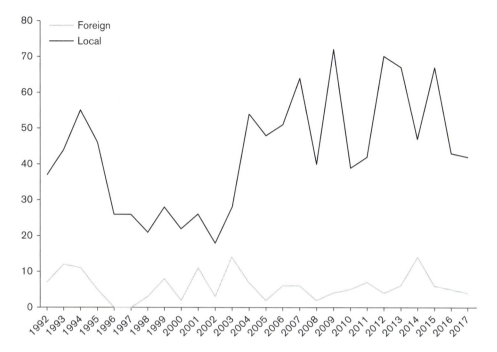

Figure 10. Killings of journalists worldwide, 1992–2017, local versus foreign. Source: Committee to Protect Journalists, www.cpj.org/killed/.

ents, recalled how his trips had sometimes cost him more than what newspapers paid him—for war zones are not just dangerous but also terrifyingly expensive.

As we now veer back toward our psychogeography of danger, let us also revisit Afghanistan. By 2017, the *Guardian*'s Rasmussen noted in interview how media organizations and freelancers alike had downshifted amid the West's political equivocation and the escalating attacks, including against aid groups.[31] As Trump unleashed the "Mother of All Bombs" on the remote district of Achin, Sune headed there in a battered Corolla to hear from villagers and soldiers what had really happened. However, most of the press stayed away; the civilian interveners remained stuck in their bunkers; and so did many of their military counterparts. Asked about the controversy over the number of dead, a US military spokesman said: "We have not been able to go in and do that assessment" of casualty numbers, "and we're probably not going to." It was "too dangerous," he said, and the military had "better things to do with our time."[32] As the war heats up, the conditions are no longer there for the kind of international scrutiny that did eventually follow the 2001 invasion: press packs, blanket coverage, and roaming or embedded reporters backed by news organizations that, for all their faults, could at least reveal glimpses of what was happening in the hinterland. Next, it is into these black zones that we will move, donning our wolf suit to roam among the wild things of warfare.

·   ·   ·   ·   ·

> Now this is the Law of the Jungle—as old and as true as
>   the sky;
> And the Wolf that shall keep it may prosper, but the Wolf
>   that shall break it must die.
>
> Rudyard Kipling, "The Law of the Jungle"

For all their daring, war reporters often encountered insurmountable barriers to entering the black zones of violence. Paco Torres, the Spanish correspondent of our opening pages, had in 2013 found his and colleagues' way into northern Mali temporarily blocked "for their own safety," while the French military ended up filming its own war for television.[33] War's first casualty is the truth, goes the saying, and military forces have long sought to distance viewers back home from the horrors of conflict, the gore and the grief.[34] Marking their territory in the reds and blacks of danger, as we noted in the Interlude, is a supremely useful way of enforcing this distance. As we again take up our earlier attempt to peek behind the barricades, what we *can* discern, at least, is that the horror of the black zone is not uncontrolled but bound by certain rules and drivers that tie us back into the architectures of risk and into the psychology of danger.

As Obama wound down official wars, the unofficial ones kept expanding, out of sight and out of mind, in a trend continued by Trump. Joint Special Operations Command had been left to "run wild," as an insider put it, and its wild men roamed through the world's danger zones, free and unencumbered. In Somalia, ruthless warlords in US pay praised their JSOC colleagues as the muckraker Jeremy Scahill followed them around on their patrols: "They are teachers, great teachers." As the insider put it, "The world is a battlefield and we are at war."

Only it was a shadow war, in which killing could surpass boundaries of the permissible. Recall Barnett's exhortation to use all means in places where people still go medieval on one another, Kagan's to go slay the monsters, and JSOC's industrial-scale answer to both. The ethos was perhaps best captured by Robert Cooper, a diplomat-turned-adviser to Britain's Blair, when he wrote that "among ourselves" in the West "we keep the law but when we are operating in the jungle, we must also use the laws of the jungle."[35]

But these "laws" were not just about the strong eating the weak. I cite Kipling above because his poem chimes with the modus operandi of the JSOC beasts prowling the night. As it continues, "For the strength of the Pack is the Wolf, and the strength of the Wolf is the Pack" while "the word of your Head Wolf is Law." McChrystal, who as onetime head of JSOC we now wheel out for one final time, enforced an iron command that in turn enjoyed a direct line to Washington. Through this arrangement, JSOC could unleash its feral force on the hinterland, no questions asked, while allegedly circumventing traditional military command structures.[36]

Michael Hastings, reflecting on the Vietnam syndrome, noted that its main lesson was not really to avoid another version of Vietnam: rather, "It was to *seal off the horror:* to ensure that only a small group felt and saw it."[37] McChrystal certainly recognized the dark space he had been put into when he identified with the colonial-era Lawrence of Arabia, seeing "his JSOC troops as modern-day tribal forces: dependent upon one another for kinship and survival."[38] Penning these lines, the journalist Dana Priest recalled that when she first spotted JSOC warriors at a Qatar airbase, she could not place these men within the military structures she knew: their uniforms were "not quite right" and they had "unkempt beards and dirt on their hands."[39] Afghan villagers had a term for them: "We call them the American Taliban," they said as they peered insecurely into Scahill's camera in *Dirty Wars,* remembering how bushy-bearded soldiers had visited destruction upon their homes in the dead of night. In brief, theirs was tribal, savage warfare *by design.* The shaggy beards and ill-fitting clothes recall the ostentatious drag of wars past, frequently used to strike fear into civilians and enemy alike. Consider the gunmen who roamed Liberia's roads in the late

1990s, bedecked in blond wigs, wedding costumes, and Halloween masks in a ghoulish display of bloodlust and supposed invincibility.[40] Hastings compared McChrystal to Kurtz in Conrad's *Heart of Darkness,* a figure resurrected in the Vietnam movie *Apocalypse Now:* a loose cannon, a fighter left to rage in the wild, his men out of control.[41] Yet JSOC's esprit de corps was as well tuned as their savagery was minutely calibrated: the "laws of the jungle" would expect nothing less of the wolf pack.

If JSOC's forces were wild by design, so were their foes. We must now briefly visit those among the enemy who are as much "war tourists" as the civilians we have so far considered—the coddled Western youngsters going into the hellhole of war. From Syria to Iraq, Daesh acolytes turn up, fresh from the suburbs of London, Brussels, and Gothenburg (or, as is less reported, from their equivalents in Casablanca and Tunis). Some get their moment of attention in the inverted world of violent jihad, their horrific atrocities transformed into warped signs of heroism or, if nothing else, fifteen minutes of fame in media thirsty for stories of distant danger. Volunteers have joined the anti-Daesh forces, too, yet for all the reporting of their adventures, around them a peculiar silence reigns. In July 2017, as the United Kingdom saw its fourth citizen die fighting on the front lines against Daesh, the Foreign Office refused to comment on his fate. Instead, it produced its standard response, based on our familiar map of risk: "Anyone who does travel to Syria, for whatever reason, is putting themselves in considerable danger."[42] As for those joining the dark side, there were starker warnings in store. Rory Stewart, by now airdropped into Westminster, was among the Conservative ministers who made clear that, for British citizens venturing to Daesh in Syria, "Unfortunately the only way of dealing with them will be, in almost every case, to kill them."[43]

Let us leave to the side the legal implications of assassinating your own citizens, or the simple get-out clause of the red-painted map of bureaucrats. Instead, we return to psychogeography. Of course volunteer fighters of whichever side put themselves in danger, we may retort: for war is a drug, and danger is one of the very things that makes foreigners trickle into Syria. As anthropologist Scott Atran, a keen scholar of the psychology of militarism, provocatively asks, "When did 'moderate' anything have wide appeal for youth yearning for adventure, glory, and significance?" The black zones and no go signs do not just keep people out but also keep drawing youngsters in—promising confrontation with danger and, in that confrontation, some degree of glory, belonging, and even "cool."[44]

The mirroring is disturbing as one kind of monster finds another in the jungle. For the insurgents as for the special forces, this jungle follows its own laws. In the foundational tract of Daesh, *The Management of Savagery*, its author Abu Bakr Naji writes that "while fools preach 'moderation' [*wasatiyyah*], security and avoidance of risk," true fighters should draw on the "rebelliousness of youth" to stage indiscriminate attacks, sowing fear among citizens while triggering further counterattacks.[45] Savagery or *tawahhuš* —alternately translated as chaos, barbarism, or beastliness—is about spreading confusion through arbitrary attacks, setting the scene for the emergence of a "caliphate." Danger and savagery were Daesh's aims, and indiscriminate drone attacks and "black ops" helped clear the slate while recruiting more youthful rebels to the cause. Danger, here, emerges as a psychological and strategic resource for fighters on all sides, luring volunteers—alongside reporters—into the land where the wild things are.

.   .   .   .   .

Drifting through the danger zone, our psychogeographic journey has touched upon motivations for a brush with danger among travelers, reporters, soldiers, and insurgents. Catching our breath, let us now take stock of the wider historical picture, without which we are at risk of not seeing the jungle for the trees. Returning to Afghanistan, we must draw out some of the psychopolitical dimensions of the architecture of risk, and of the visitors roaming beyond its perimeter.

Afghanistan's long history of foreign invasions holds up a mirror to the interveners of today, as many observers note. Indeed, the fourth "Anglo-Afghan war," beginning in 2001, had marched in the ignominious footsteps of its colonial predecessors in 1839–42, 1878–80, and 1919. Yet the interveners and invaders of the twenty-first century had not learned many lessons. Most important, they failed to *listen* and understand the war-torn society that they entered, and that they visited with yet more violence and destruction.

Britain's first disastrous incursion into Afghanistan in the nineteenth century was long blamed on cowardly political officers and faulty military

tactics. Yet this was the wrong conclusion, according to our Afghan cice-
rone, Rory Stewart. Military authors, taking stock in the nineteenth century, "suggest that the situation could have been saved with a clear strategy, good leadership, sufficient resources, and enough troops," he writes.
"And they foster the idea—as the Soviet military did in 1988—not only
that they were not defeated, but that they could have won outright if they
had not been let down by bad planning, logistics, and tactics, and then
been withdrawn by cowards." However, Stewart rather asks why policy
makers chose to invade Afghanistan in the first place. "Senseless" theories
held that replacing the Russia-friendly ruler of Afghanistan with the
India-exiled former Afghan king Shah Shuja would appease the unruly
leaders of the Punjab while creating safe space between Russia and British
India. Yet Britain's imperial grandees ignored Afghan resistance to the
king and to invasion. Stewart cites Mountstuart Elphinstone, the leading
Afghan expert of the day, saying that some "27,000 men" could take
Kandahar and Kabul, "but for maintaining [the new king] in poor, cold,
strong, and remote country, among a turbulent people like the Afghans,
. . . it seems to me to be hopeless." The Afghans, hitherto neutral, would
"be disaffected and glad to join any invader to drive you out."

"The uncomfortable truth," Stewart writes, "is that experienced, ener-
getic, knowledgeable men launched a war on the most flimsy of theories."
As for the lessons for the fourth Anglo-Afghan war starting in 2001,
Stewart notes how accounts of the first Anglo-Afghan war, the second
British humiliation in 1879, and the humiliation of the Soviet Union in
1979 have "tempted readers to echo British Prime Minister Harold
Macmillan's favorite line: 'Rule number one in politics is: never invade
Afghanistan.'" Yet, he retorts, "There is in fact little in common between
the Afghanistan of Shah Shuja and the Afghanistan of Hamid Karzai. If
the first Anglo-Afghan war tells us anything it is not about Afghanistan,
but about ourselves. It is a parable less of 'an unchanging East' than of an
unchanging West."[46]

Western forms of intervention may carry echoes from wars past, but
they are hardly unchanging. Consider the form intervention takes. To
Stewart himself, it was clear that those who attach the label "neocolonial"
to today's international administrators in countries such as Afghanistan
risked drawing false equivalences. "Colonial administrations may have

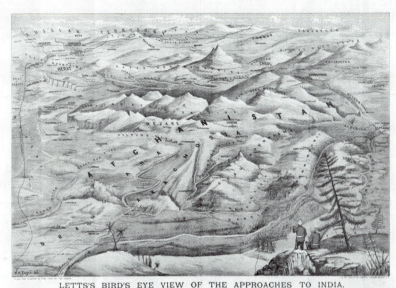

LETTS'S BIRD'S EYE VIEW OF THE APPROACHES TO INDIA.

Map 12. "Letts's Bird's Eye View of the Approaches to India," by W. H. Payne of Letts, Son & Co. in London, early twentieth century. The map visualizes the "Great Game," with a menacing Russia on the horizon and the dream of colonial dominance over Afghanistan. The left corner states "Flags for sticking in this view, 6d. per packet." Courtesy Library of Congress, Geography and Map Division.

been racist and exploitative, but they did at least work seriously at the business of understanding the people they were governing," he noted in *The Places in Between.* "They recruited people prepared to spend their entire careers in dangerous provinces of a single alien nation." Today's interveners, by contrast, "have got the prestige without the effort or stigma of imperialism." And as their policies fail, no one notices, in a "charming illusion of action"—as illustrated by the window dressing on Kabul's international scene.[47]

As we have seen, there are "rational reasons" for remote intervention: the risk architecture transfers risks away from precious internationals while perpetuating the useful political illusion of action and presence. Yet this risk architecture encounters its ruin, Virilio-style, once it clashes with the *strategic* reasons for intervention. The nineteenth-century Great

Game in Central Asia was meant to open markets and create imperial buffers between Russia and British-held India—in that sense, it was about establishing a geopolitical risk architecture writ large, a point that we will shortly retake in our Conclusion. The stoking of mujahideen fighters during the Soviet occupation served, in similar fashion, to fight the Cold War by proxy. Afghanistan may be as strategically positioned as ever today, yet now other aims jostle with those of yesteryear's geopolitics. If in Anglo-Afghan wars past the threat was Russia by way of Kabul, since 2001 the threat is proclaimed to be Afghans themselves. As we have seen in other danger zones, the threat cluster of migration, drug flows, terrorism, and generalized regional instability constitutes at least the public rationale for intervention. Yet the internationals' modus operandi is terribly out of sync with the quest to target such "population-centric" phenomena: retreating behind the ramparts, they soon falter owing to a shallow understanding of local society. The bastions of intervention may seem solid and impenetrable, yet they belie a much larger insecurity. They presage, we may even say, the ends of empire, rather than a new version of it.

·   ·   ·   ·   ·

If Stewart's startling quip of an unchanging West needs some historical nuance, his point rings true in a deeper sense. *If the first Anglo-Afghan war tells us anything it is not about Afghanistan, but about ourselves.* Going to the "ends of the world," the Western "we" does not find an unchanging Other to be fought, befriended, or subdued. Instead, "we" find ourselves looking into a distorted mirror, inherited from history.[48]

Nearing our destination, let us dwell on this psychology of Self and Other under the sign of danger. In Afghanistan, we have seen the intervening Self staring out through the panes of the Kabubble; we have followed "him" via reporters peering into the darkness outside; and we have seen him roam free in the wild, projecting his own darkness onto the blank spaces on the map. But we began this chapter with Kipling and the colonial period, and it is into history that we must look yet again, while peeling back the masks worn through time by the intervening Self.

War and violence have always stirred deep human fears and desires, and the fighters, explorers, and reporters in today's danger zones are but the latest in a long line of visitors to distant conflict, human moths drawn to the flame of danger. In colonial times, serving empire overseas was a way of breaking free from shackles back home and of affirming one's manliness, as Kipling knew. In the words of one scholar of this period, heroic masculinity became central to British imperial identity—linking together "the new imperialist patriotism, the virtues of manhood, and war as its ultimate test and opportunity."[49] In tandem with the high tide of empire, consider the martial fervor of fin-de-siècle Europe, when war and sacrifice for the national idea were seen as a manly reassertion of will against the supposedly emasculating, rational capitalism of the day.[50] As imperial wars came home to roost in the First World War, some combatants joyfully embraced the war's promise. Among them was a certain Winston Churchill, who in 1916 wrote to a friend from the front lines in France: "I think a curse should rest on me—because I love this war. I know it's smashing and shattering the lives of thousands every moment—and yet—I can't help it—I enjoy every second of it."[51]

In an echo of the late nineteenth-century crises in capitalism and empire, today emotional forces are trumping reason for many young men (and some women) seeking a larger purpose and a bigger thrill. But our historical context offers new takes on an old martial theme precisely through the very uneven mapping of global danger that we have traced in this book. The conjuring up of red and black zones, combined with the desire by risk-averse powers to bunker up, draw borders and retreat, offers a tantalizing opportunity once the door slams shut. Our danger zones serve simultaneously as sites of exploration, with their echoes from precolonial times, and of inglorious, exhilarating war, not only for wayward Westerners but for youth from elsewhere too. In a world of globalizing danger, the wilderness outside the wire—the night world of monsters—presents a potent chance for an encounter with something larger than the fragile self.

In this chapter we have approached the subjective side to the danger zone by means of psychogeography, which itself is admittedly a risky move, given the tongue-in-cheek approach even of its putative founder, Guy Debord. But let us embrace our poetic license by returning to the yarn of our opening lines as we search for clues to one remaining puzzle—how psychology interacts with strategy in the danger zone.

Little Max, we noted, projected the "wild things" of his mind into distant lands, setting the stage for their monstrous protagonism. In psychoanalysis, *projection* is the term used to refer to the psychological operation whereby feelings that a subject refuses to recognize, or rejects, are "expelled from the self and located in another person or thing."[52] In other words, it is a psychological defense mechanism, at work especially in paranoia. Drawing on this, we can identify one kind of paranoid psychogeography at work inside the wire in Kabul, where distance—besides generating resistance—sometimes fueled fear and suspicion of the world outside the compound walls. Among the warriors outside the wire, we can rather discern how the projection of danger melds paranoia with paramilitarism, justified by recourse to the law of the jungle. This space for spiraling violence has been made possible thanks to a specific spatial, political, and legal order of intervention: in a word, through a risk architecture that slams the door shut and does not want anyone to hear what happens outside. As Mum closes the door to Max's bedroom, we may say, she already anticipates his wild escape.

But let us not put too much emphasis on the instigators of violence on either side: they have benefited from too much attention already, and their brutality is at any rate shielded from full view. Rather, this chapter has focused on the civilians who linger on the margins or tread into the wild, and on how a desire to cross the line keeps haunting aid officials, researchers, and reporters. Yet here is the irony: those who do go tend to end up reinforcing the projection of danger to distant lands through their bravery and the tales they bring back. They, and their fighting counterparts, present to us the inverse of the risk-averse world of late modern societies through their defiance and embrace of danger. Through them, the danger zone takes on an uncanny human dimension, wolf-suited if need be, for audiences back home. Returning to Max's tale, we may fancy them as creatures of the dark forest of night to our world of daylight and safety. Yet even as we shield ourselves from this world and suppress it, the forest keeps growing in our mind's room, where it infiltrates our waking hours with its monstrous smells, sights, and premonitions.

CONCLUSION

DANGER UNMAPPED

We think of the key, each in his prison
Thinking of the key, each confirms a prison

T. S. Eliot, *The Waste Land*

T. S. Eliot, the Missouri-born poet with a soft spot for the armchair anthropology of his day, intones his *Waste Land* in a peculiar British-accented voice on the recording: "What are the roots that clutch, what branches grow / Out of this stony rubbish?" Eliot's time of a century ago was haunted by crumbling towers and dead lands, a world in disorder and disarray. Fear haunted the ruins:

> There is shadow under this red rock
> (come in under the shadow of this red rock),
> And I will show you something different from either
> Your shadow at morning striding behind you
> Or your shadow at evening striding to meet you;
> I will show you fear in a handful of dust.

We have not been through a world war just yet, only a financial crash and almost two decades of the "war on terror," yet similar dystopian visions haunt our new world disorder a century after the publication of Eliot's *Waste Land*. They also haunt these pages, as I am all too aware. In some ways, this is jarring. As I now add some final lines to the story of the map, I sit in an Oxford library in front of an iMac screen: outside are immaculate lawns and punting boats lolling on the River Cherwell. Like the armchair anthropologist who once inspired Eliot—James Frazer of *Golden Bough* fame—I can draw my maps and sketches of far-off worlds, yet danger and ruins are nowhere to be seen round these spots.

And yet, in the years since I first began this project in 2014, the world has changed. Borders are becoming chronically infected in Western democracies, and the Far Right is in ascendance. This is so, not least, because danger and fear have crept into the green zones of our maps in a way and at a speed that I did not envisage in my incipient study. As I travel into London with my family, I choose which Tube carriage to enter on the basis of my awareness of the tactics of terror. Every time I look at the news, I know we may receive yet another installment of the sinister serial of multifarious atrocities. Trump risks nuclear Armageddon by Twitter, and his widely broadcasted words stir anger, fear, and further danger. The political world seems flustered, temperamental, and ready to ignite, in echoes of the years preceding the First World War.

The "geopathology" of danger traced in the past chapters has become endemic. Yet there is still hope. "A map of the world that does not include Utopia is not worth even glancing at, for it leaves out the one country at which Humanity is always landing," is one of Oscar Wilde's well-known quips, and the sentiment was not far from Eliot's mind either, as his *Waste Land* brought us stepwise from the "stony rubbish" toward a Christian-inspired redemption. I had badly wanted to envision Utopia as well, ending with an arrival at the Shangri-La of our map of danger. This is how my sea chart for this journey might have unfolded.

We must *reconnect*. Just go, grab your pickax, and work away at those walls! We should remind ourselves that what happens in Syria, Somalia, Afghanistan, and Libya, like the problems racking the sub-Saharan Sahel, is our shared challenge, and so, too, are the people displaced by war, despair, and insecurity. Many practical steps can be taken to reconnect and reclaim a global public good, even if the door may not be swung open all at once. Instead of remote-controlled interventions focused on elusive dangers, we must bolster genuine peace missions under the United Nations. Among the conflict-hit countries visited in this book—from Libya to Afghanistan—it is striking that only one today has a peacekeeping operation: Mali, which is moreover the UN's deadliest in the past years. As we positively reconnect, we must moreover undo some of the dangerous connections we have created over the years. This means rethinking the rationales for intervention; steering resources toward nationals and their capacity to resolve conflict; and halting Western military escapades and arms sales, which add to the dangers, as we now see in the horrors befalling Yemen. As concerns migration, including the displacements caused by wars of choice, leaders must realize that border security generates destructive blowback, and so shift attention from reinforcement toward positive cooperation on mobility with poorer countries. At home, the fears and anxieties of citizens need to be addressed, too, via genuine efforts toward social protection and equality, not expensive theaters of "security."

My manifesto could go on like this, even turning the map of danger upside down—reframe human movement as opportunity, conflict zones as laboratories for a cosmopolitan politics of solidarity, and poorer nations as frontiers for shared investment. Yet at each turn of this utopian road map, dark presences loom over us, impossible to avoid. Alongside us are the jagged rocks and deep ravines of hatred and fear. Ahead looms the abyss of nationalism. And behind, a large massif casts its long political shadow: the colonial past. I may wish for it to be otherwise, but the "we" of my draft reconnection manifesto would not just come across as hopelessly naive to policy makers and unpalatably cosmopolitan to anxious citizens and nationalists; it also carries paternalistic echoes from Kipling's colonial times. Perhaps, I wonder as I pace up and down the river paths of Oxford, this colonial history may itself hold a key to the prison of our present?

.   .   .   .   .

Throughout this book, we have sought out resonances between the danger zones of today and those of the colonial era. In this spirit, let us return to one of the colonizers' geopolitical strategies, itself inherited from empires past—that of buffering away the dangers.

As the Great Game in Central Asia geared up in the early nineteenth century, the British were hoping to turn Afghanistan into a buffer state governed by a compliant ruler, as we saw in the last chapter. At this time, a "threefold frontier" came into play in the colonial imagination, of a kind that the arch-imperialist Lord Curzon was later to articulate. In

Afghanistan, the British wanted a "frontier of separation" rather than a "frontier of contact" with the dangers lurking round the edges of the territories they controlled. As the legal scholar Tayyab Mahmud puts it, "The first frontier, at the edge of directly controlled territory, enabled the colonial regime to exercise full authority and impose its legal and political order. The second frontier, just beyond the first, was a zone of indirect rule where colonial domination proceeded through existing institutions of social control. The third frontier was a string of buffer states which, while maintaining formal political autonomy and trappings of statehood, aligned foreign relations with the interests of the British." To defend this layered frontier, the British "deployed a racist recruiting doctrine" known as martial race theory. The idea was to raise a new Indian Army, bolstered by the presumably fierce Punjabis, to serve as the "Empire's fire brigade" or "the iron fist in the velvet glove."

It is not hard to spot parallels to this colonial era in how, wittingly or unwittingly, peacekeepers, Western militaries, border agencies, and other actors map out and conduct their interventions around the danger zones of today. From the battlefields of Mali to Somalia, and from Libya's borders to Kabul's bunkers, we have seen how powerful Western governments and the international organizations they help fund have put in place various forms of remote controls to keep global danger at bay and how outsourced fighting forces and even whole countries are transformed into useful buffers.

In forging an illusory mode of control over global margins, such remote interventions tend to generate as many problems as they purportedly solve: to return to our reptilians, the quest to kill the cobra of danger seems to lead to the breeding of more snakes. It would be easy to say, in a word, that remote interventions in distant danger zones are counterproductive, and leave it at that. However, the Afghan colonial example hints that something more complicated may be afoot. Curzon's mapping of a threefold frontier reveals how global powers have long put a great deal of thought into how they may shield themselves from, *and* how to mobilize to their strategic and even economic advantage, the dangers gathering outside the "Civil Lines." Besides a vicious cycle of endangerment, we see here the *strategic* importance of buffers and danger zones. As powerful interveners protect themselves and extend their reach through buffering, they also push most of the consequences of their actions further down the

chain. Those suffering the consequences may eventually include even citizen-voters at home, as Grégoire Chamayou suggests in his *Drone Theory*
when comparing the colonial usage of martial races with Predator and
Reaper assassinations. "Once warfare became ghostly and teleguided," he
concludes in a darkly futuristic voice, "citizens, who no longer risked their
lives, would no longer even have a say in it," even as they might be left to
face the dangerous consequences through blowback at home.[1]

But again, in the neat buffering seen in today's security interventions,
the interveners' hold may be more tenuous than it seems. Before we
denounce the "imperialism" of our times, recall how we began our story of
the map, not with Curzon's era of high colonialism, but with the early colonial encounter and its attempts to gain a fragile foothold in unknown,
sometimes hostile lands. All is not well in the palace if the emperors live
in fear of their citizens treading the farthest reaches of the earth, and if
their writ does not extend there. Their maps are worth little if they turn
out to be crude Borgesian approximations of a shifting territory they do
not know and control. Worse, if the projection of danger into distant lands
generates incentives to fuel it, the problem will keep rebounding.
Meanwhile the countermappings of the enemy ensure that danger keeps
haunting the Homeland. The more efforts the powerful put into walling
off the dangers, the nearer those dangers seem to draw.

The time has come to produce our own map of global danger, in order
to better understand the pathologies of dangerized intervention. To do so,
we must split it into two superimposed layers—disassembling danger, as
we did in our opening pages, into its calculable and emotional elements,
risk and fear.

·   ·   ·   ·   ·

For the *map of risk,* let us shift to the most mundane of examples away
from danger zones and colonial buffers—the sedate lull of an Oxford college next to the River Cherwell. Yes, this is my home, a terraced house
owned by a college. Yes, the example is ridiculously far away from everything else in this book. But hear me out. Being college owned, the house is
subject to bizarre rules, common on British shores, around fire safety.
There are sensors blinking red in every room, every hallway. Their

function? To capture the slightest whiff of risk. The result? A ferocious alarm starts blaring across the whole terraced row of houses pretty much as soon as someone starts frying a steak. It also starts off on its beastly roar for no reason at all: a bit of condensation in the attic will do; a draft from a window; a spider crawling in for cover; a handful of dust. On many a cold winter's night, we have found ourselves fumbling in the dark, fetching the kids, slumping downstairs to stand in the doorway until someone comes to turn off the blare, as loud—or so it feels—as an air raid in wartime Dresden.

Now, you may wonder: Why would anyone put in place such a system? It wakes everyone for no good reason. It scares the kids. It is, quite clearly, absurd overkill. Yet, from the viewpoint of the college, it makes sense. One day I speak to the premises manager, who says that if it did not have this system, the college (and those in charge) would be liable in any lawsuit by residents hurt or damaged by a real fire. It would also risk losing insurance payouts. The system cuts financial and legal risk, in other words, while keeping insurance premiums within bounds. I argue against this, my patience ebbing: but the system generates larger risks! Have the managers never read the tale of the boy who cried wolf? If the fire risk system keeps setting off spurious alarms, residents get inured to real danger. In addition, I plead, think of the costs to our working lives, as we go sleepless and stand in the cold. Think of our visitors, wrenched out of bed; think of our children's well-being; think, not least, of our lack of well-seared steak! But it is to little avail. The thinking has already been thunk. The problems I raise do not enter into the official calculus: they are invisible on the college's balance sheet of risk. Instead, the manager suggests the fire company will come in, for the umpteenth time, with fancy new sensors and scurrilous tweaks to the settings. All will be well—until the next air raid commences.

For the manager, the risk calculus is beneficial *in the short run, for a select group*. It keeps the biggest risks at bay for the "core" college powers, even as it generates trouble for us residents—and potentially larger trouble for the college in the long run, should a real fire start. This risk calculus, in turn, is tied up with a range of vested interests: the insurance provider can keep customers on their toes and payouts to a minimum; the fire safety company makes big money off the proliferating sensors and servicing; the college middle managers have their backs covered, and so forth.

Now consider the economies of risk in border security. Here the powers that be (let's call them the College) have put in place the highest-grade sensor system the market has to offer. The blinking sensor lights and the big red alarm buttons reassure; they limit any short-term political fallout and liability; but they also blow any trouble at the borders out of all proportion. To deal with this additional risk, the College keeps coming back to the fire company (that is, to border agencies, defense contractors, and pliant neighboring states) for more servicing, more advanced sensors, and better "solutions" that the company and its subcontractors are all too willing to provide. The outsourcing, quite beautifully, also transfers risks and responsibilities onto these contractors, who will be in the line of fire if something goes wrong (but who may also transfer responsibilities elsewhere, preferably to their own subcontractors). While profits rise for these outfits, and the College insulates itself from any larger liabilities, those without a stake in the system are left to deal with the everyday costs of intervention—among them, the "residents" (border communities) and the "visitors" (refugees and migrants). The risks and costs *to them* are off balance sheet.

Or consider the previous chapter's "architecture" of risk in remote-controlled intervention, now in its economic dimension. Hiding staff behind bunker walls is expedient, as it shields risk managers, bosses, and political paymasters from political, legal, and financial risk should an attack take place. It also generates gains for companies providing security at the cost of assuming some risk, while those on the front line face steeper risks and smaller gains from their dangerous travails. We have also seen how bunkered intervention adds to the dangers as oversight ebbs and hostile forces stir in the hinterland—pushing the largest problems into the lap of ordinary citizens with no stake in the system, while blowback eventually comes back to haunt the cloistered internationals, reinforcing the security model still further.

The "risk map" is trite and everyday—it seems to be a model applicable to everything! Yet this is precisely why it is rather useful. The economies of risk at work in dangerized interventions are shared across large swaths of society in late capitalism. In these economies, something or other gets politically defined as a "risk," and interests are then generated around the management of this risk. For a pedestrian example, consider the wider fire risk regime in the United Kingdom, in which Big Tobacco managed to lobby the government in the 1980s to see furniture as the risk factor in house fires, rather than indoor smoking—thereby transferring regulatory costs from cigarette peddlers onto sofa makers, and in turn generating vested interests for fire-retardant companies, and so on in a cycle of investments.[2] Or let us consider hotter political topics. The privatized US prison-industrial complex needs prisoners, so it helps produce them and pockets the gains while generating costs for others. In the financial crisis as in the sweeping privatization of public services, big banks and outsourcing firms knew they could privatize profits and "socialize" risk, as their failures would eventually wind up on the balance sheet of taxpayers. The "war on drugs" wreaks havoc in countries such as Mexico but keeps US drug enforcement agencies and their partners sweet. Big Oil generates gains for itself and "negative externalities" for ecosystems and ordinary citizens.[3] I could go on with other examples of such great heists today, but let us instead return to Curzon and see his vision as a risk map too, in its way—dull as this may sound. The threefold colonial frontier of risk, danger, and relative power can be depicted as concentric circles, with arrows between them.

The arrows heading away from the colonial core denote bundles of risk transferred to the next layer outwards. Risk entails both opportunity and threat: that is, there are gains (upside risk) to be had for those willing to shoulder the downside risk. Each of the layers takes on a differently weighed risk bundle, but as you travel outwards through them—moving further down the hierarchy—the costs start to weigh more heavily than the gains. Colonial forces closer to the metropole have their risk bundle skewed toward benefits, while the "martial races" have theirs skewed toward costs. Once we arrive outside the perimeter, pure costs are dumped onto those with no stake in the system. In other words, costs keep being pushed outwards, beyond the gates of the citadel, whose risk calculus is concerned with risks only to its core, not to outlying areas.

This map of risk transfers, we should note, corresponds to the smaller scale of concentric circles we saw in last chapter's risk architecture of Kabul compounds: Western soldiers or officials ensconced in the bunkered core, with layers of risk-facing protectors around them. The Kabubble and Curzon models illustrate some fundamental gains for powerful interveners. Even if they stoke or at least fail to decrease the risk of insecurity, dis-

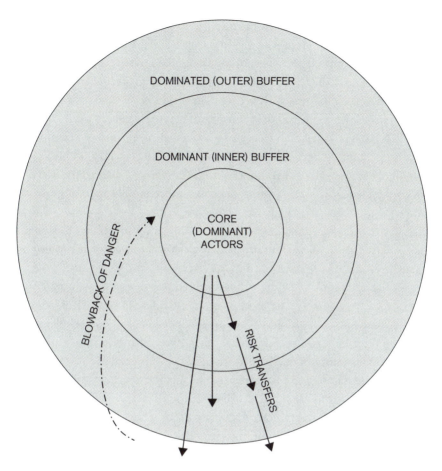

Figure 11. A "risk map" of the threefold frontier.

placement, or violence in the aggregate, they may well succeed in exporting it and insulating the core from its harmful effects through a system of buffers. In other words, much of the blowback can be recycled back down through the risk economy, and so the cycle begins again, with more fortifications and divisions. This means that there are few political incentives to steer a different course, as long as the risk calculus as seen from the core is beneficial to the Curzons and Colleges in charge.

One day I try out some potential solutions on risk with our domestic manager at the college. I know he must cover backs, so telling him to remove the protective shield against liability—those damn fire sensors and blaring alarms—is not going to work. So instead I say to him: We must find a compromise whereby you can convince the insurance company that you are doing your bit, while allowing us to live our lives without risk of an air-raid moment. How do we do that? Let me train as a fire warden, at my cost in time and risk, in terms of future responsibility. If I do so, I say, the college must in turn assume some risk, and shift its calculus, in a quid pro quo. It may desensitize the sensors, lower alarm volumes, or look more holistically at fire safety across the housing estate, and so convince the insurer it is addressing risks in a more embedded way. To convince the manager to take on some costs and risks, I also raise the political risk to the college of business as usual: I will get all neighbors to sign an angry letter and will take matters to the college president if nothing is done! We must *share* the risks, I insist: give some and take some.

Similar trade-offs and compromises on risks are happening every day in the crisis and conflict scenarios of previous chapters. In university security offices, risk managers think of ways to convince insurers that scholars can manage their own risk responsibly while still ensuring that the employer adheres to its "duty of care." In fortified aid headquarters, managers let staff exit the gates to get the work done, skirting protocols, while some media organizations now train freelancers on security and share the risks should anything happen. More daring aid groups, such as MSF, are devising ways of staying put and finding a new trade-off with risks in the field.[4] For all the good efforts, however, a more equal sharing of risk is often missing from the picture. As we have seen, peacekeepers and UN civilian workers such as Monica in Mali shoulder costs and responsibilities as they try to break out of their imposed, risk-averse bubble, and if something goes wrong, they have only themselves to blame. The same goes for many NGO workers, embassy staff, and others, including us academics.[5] Something similar occurs in displacement crises on a bigger scale, where countries and communities that "go it alone" in assisting people on the move often find themselves shouldering huge risks and costs. Consider, for instance, the ordinary Malians—including Djibril of chapter 5—who opened their doors to the internally displaced, leaving courtyards in Bamako brimming with families asleep on mattresses under the open skies. The risks of doing something did not stop ordinary Malians with precious few resources to step up, time and again, as was also in evidence when northern communities pooled their meager funds to open schools while the state administration and international organizations stayed away.[6] Yet such local "humanitarians" are as a rule left alone, shouldering the risks themselves, rather than seeing any quid pro quo for their efforts. Instead, shared risk taking and responsibility can be systematized and rewarded across the board. The advice is common sense enough: in peacekeeping, start by providing African forces with the resources and training they require, thereby reducing the cost of implementing an "African solution"; but at the same time, make sure richer countries also step up and show they are ready to shoulder some of the downside risk, and through these two measures create a genuinely shared mission. Encourage aid workers, diplomats, and peacekeepers to take sensible risks beyond the compounds that house them—for their first task is to connect with, and understand, their host society and ordinary people's ways of dealing with the "crisis" that has befallen them.

In peacekeeping, at least, those responsible have started to push for collective international efforts to address the problems, including via calls for more equitable deployments into dangerous missions.[7] For all the resistance among powerful states, there is still hope. Now, can we imagine similar steps toward trade-offs on borders and migration? The politics is tortuous, and politicians and ordinary voters alike have a stake in the status quo. In global deliberations diplomats may at least start broaching the principle that those who shoulder bigger risks should be rewarded, while making efforts to share these risks as far as politically possible. Pushing this further, imagine if those who are now most affected by the "downside risk" from European border security—including border communities in southern Europe, neighboring countries, cities facing an influx, and migrants and refugees themselves—made common cause and assumed certain risks in exchange for a new deal based on shared responsibility. Something of this sort has already happened, we should note, in the war on drugs and on climate change, where broad coalitions are pushing for a "de-risking" approach that takes account of the full costs and "externalities" to all those people and places affected by business as usual. The blaring alarms and angry sensors of the borders may be removed if another system is put in place that satisfies the basic requirement of protection. Legal routes, more investments in conflict resolution, and a new deal with neighboring countries may all be part of the package—as may an agenda of reinforced protections for citizen and noncitizen alike in destination countries, acting as a control mechanism for labor migration and a safeguard for ordinary people.

We may perhaps start to see how, via the risk map, we can kill three birds with one stone. First, we may undo the tyranny of geography so beloved by the doom peddlers of this world; second, we may come to grips with the systemic nature of global danger; and third, we may thus begin to de-exoticize it. On the risk map, the danger zone, rather than being a place marked by red-painted road signs, is something more akin to how food safety experts use the term—the risky temperature range in which bacteria flourish. The danger zone is the circuit of arrows on the map above; it is the circular dangerization that keeps raising the political temperature to the point where the alarms yet again start blaring their tiresome noise. In other words, the danger zone is not out there: it is already with us, and there is nothing stopping us from working on dismantling its circular logics.

To avoid this "overheating," as anthropologists have termed the runaway processes of conflictive globalization, those affected by the system may wrest some control and assume some longer-term risks in exchange for longer-term gain.[8] Yet as we thus return to our coordinates of Utopia with a new road map in hand, problems still loom ahead. Why should the powerful accept a new arrangement, if the first one, like Curzon's, serves them jolly well? As we have seen, the gains are plentiful on many levels, whether we look at counterterror warriors or border chiefs, remote interveners or security bureaucrats—not to mention governments and citizens seeing distinct gains from a not-in-my-backyard approach. This question, of course, is political, and it cannot be answered in full on these pages. But it can be linked up with our second map, that of fear.

.   .   .   .   .

To get at some of the crude logics of dangerized intervention, our risk map has flattened analysis to the plane of risk economies and vested interests. Our map of fear is reductive in another sense: through it, geography takes its revenge, to paraphrase Kaplan.[9] The risk map is not exclusive to that slippery historical entity we keep referring to as "the West"; rather it is shared throughout late capitalism, if unevenly, as we suggested in chapter 2. The map of fear, however, is largely—if not exclusively—about the historical West's emergence in relation to its more or less distant Others. We need a basic schema, a simple metaphor, to capture what this map is about, and for this we need look no further than our medieval *mappae mundi*.

At the center of the Herefords and the Psalters stands Jerusalem; on the margins lurk the monsters. The center-margin model is overlaid with another dichotomy: the Christian world as *light in a world of darkness.* This "founding metaphor" may be too starkly drawn, but this starkness is precisely what long made it so effective for the historical surge of the West, from the time when Europe moved from the *mappa mundi*'s margins to its center in the age of discovery and onwards, to Enlightenment and empires with a civilizing mission. We see this luminous metaphor at work in the writings of the Kaplans and Barnetts of today as they draw battle lines between emotion and reason, between fear and control, between barbarism and an enlightened liberal order. The West is the beacon, the bringer of civilization; it is the "city upon a hill" or "the light of the world"—dividing light from dark, up from down, core from margin, culture from nature.[10] Some pundits may get the dichotomies mixed up (Barnett, I'm looking at you), which only serves to reinforce these metaphorical alignments even further.

In colonial and slaving times, these metaphors inevitably took on the hue of racism, as Kenyan author Ngũgĩ wa Thiong'o once showed by recourse to architecture. On the old Gold Coast, he wrote, there stood a trading fort where the light-flooded upper floor was set aside as the palatial dwellings for the white governor, while the dark ground level was packed with enslaved Africans waiting for shipment across the seas. The "wild" others, tamed and shackled, were a resource in more ways than one in such examples from our violent past—they served not just to bolster the nascent capitalist world economy and fill the coffers of the human traffickers but also to set the Western Self on a pedestal, all the more erect, wa Thiong'o suggests, owing to the basement world on which it depended.[11]

One side needs the other: light feeds on darkness, and it knows itself only via its Other. But this schema is also haunted by fear of the Other and of the dark outside—recall the fourteenth-century Mandeville quote in the previous chapter. In British India, the colonial plans to destroy venomous snakes were a response to widespread fear among white settlers of these savage infiltrators into their cloistered dwellings. Fears of rebellion, needless to say, abounded too. In medicine, the strange condition of "tropical neurasthenia," a nervous diagnosis besetting white males, proved a useful tool for managing the anxiety-ridden divide between Self and Other while excusing all sorts of ill behavior. In the slave trader's dark basement dwells a human resource of boundless promise but also a danger of affliction, should the line be crossed.

As we have seen, this fear of crossing over is accompanied by a *desire* to do so, either to spread light or to become one with the darkness. In Conrad's *Heart of Darkness,* the depths of the Congo lure in the outsiders, only for them to eventually discover that the darkness is their own. Recall Kristol and Kagan in chapter 2, as they urged their fellow conservatives not to sit complacently in the American "city upon a hill" but rather get out there and slay the monsters, acting as the world's Leviathan; Barnett's exhortation to go into the Gap; or Cooper's to heed the law of the jungle.

Now, in a world where the beacon is dimming and towers are falling, to paraphrase Eliot, such armchair generals face a problem. The Rest are catching up and clearing the jungle. Yet the map of fear need not be affected by our rewrought geopolitics; it does not obey the simple calculus of the risk map. For what is a balance sheet next to pride, honor, and heroism? Instead, the urge to reinforce the old divide grows stronger. The Other must be projected outwards even more fiercely: the darkness, the Gap, the remote, and the wild must be firmly set apart. The light may shine once more on our pedestal, making the Self great again.

Here my analogy with the risk bureaucrats of an Oxford college falters, for no such "mythical" schemas are attached to our fire procedures in college! The map of fear sets emotion against the risk map's instrumental rationality; it substitutes relationships for the latter's mere transactions. It also purveys a *narrative* like the old *mappae mundi*, not simply a navigational chart like the medieval sea cartographies. These dimensions of the map of fear indicate why a reasoned debate around evidence may quite easily be ignored by those who resort to emotion for their momentum, as we saw in the Brexit and Trump campaigns. Saying that most migrants in the United States are law abiding and contribute to society and the economy cannot remove the Trump-produced image of a criminal rapist from its affective slot—and the same goes for the small statistical risk of falling victim to terror among Western voters, or evidence that "tough" border security or counterterror generates more problems down the line. At the same time, insurgents and enemies reinforce the divide by inverting the picture. The city upon a hill becomes, in bin Laden's old countermapping, "the House of War," set against the lands of victimized believers. Drawing on this bifurcation, Daesh in 2015 set a clear objective for their atrocities— to "bring division to the world and destroy the grey zone" for Muslims, turning them toward the "caliphate."[12]

As we bring the maps of risk and fear together, we see the two sides of the story traced in this book: on the one hand, the "scientific" risk map, with its calculated economies and interests; on the other, a fantastical, psychosocial map of desire and fear. Superimposing these, we may discern the complex relationships that are being built around danger from the counterterror and peace enforcement fronts of Mali and Somalia to the bunkers of Kabul and the barriers of the borders. We need to start, here, by accounting for both the rational and the emotional, and both the strategic and the symbolic, dimensions of dangerization. In the "Timbuktu syndrome" and the border security complex, the map of fear spurs politicians and interveners to stake their claims around putative danger zones; yet the risk map mitigates against full-frontal involvement, keeping gains and costs in check. Through these superimposed maps, we may also discern who the big winners are: those who embrace dangers and risks in a quest to reinforce the embattled Self. Here are the descendants of Conrad's Kurtz: Italy's interior minister fearlessly bartering with Libya's militias; the McChrystals and Flynns; and tricksters like Gaddafi. Such figures are the entrepreneurs in the fear market of today. They do not cry wolf—they go to the wolf, or become the wolf, sometimes at the risk of losing it all. Even the fearful Trump is a winner as he disregards the map of risk with its dreary flow charts, instead throwing himself headlong into the fire and the fury. Through these wolves of our politics, rather than light spreading into the danger zones, we see the descent of darkness all round.

We began this book with an investigation into the "geopathology" of intervention, and to this notion we must now return. Part of our analysis has centered on the rational functions of seemingly pathological ways of mapping and intervening upon the world, as we just saw in the last paragraph. But we must widen our view to perceive the madness lurking behind the method. Risk and fear may both be functional in their limited ways, but they also betray a deeper anxiety and a wider retreat. The map of risk, for one, is symptomatic of a *politics of irresponsibility* and is widely perceived as such, not just by the aid workers and others cited in this book, but also by wide sections of the citizenry in crisis-hit nations and beyond. Consider the Malians' protests against what they saw as French attempts to dispose of their dirt in the former colonial backyard, or similar suspicions marring European and American militarism in next-door Burkina Faso and Niger.[13] The irresponsibility is compounded when risks are not just offloaded to those less powerful but also transferred from one "risk map" to another. Witness the chain of events that contributed to Mali's chaos and the 2015 "refugee crisis," both of which to a large extent lead back to the West's door, whether through remote bombardment of Libya, dithering in Syria, or drawdown in Afghanistan irrespective of the local economic consequences.

The map of fear reveals a similar degree of irresponsibility, as we see not least in that onetime epicenter of our dangerized world, Iraq, both in its invasion and in the spurious call to arms that preceded it. But this "map" also reveals a pathology all its own—a growing political paranoia, fed by fears projected into distant lands. As the West is busy treating countries such as Afghanistan and Mali as security objectives, it leaves the door ajar for other actors such as China to court national leaders with a view to tapping into resources and opportunities. Here, the "geopathological" danger zone, as opposed to the real systemic one, is indicative of a deeper historical shift—a harbinger, we may surmise, of the gradual fall of "the West" from its historical pedestal.

I began this conclusion with Eliot's *The Waste Land* for its dystopian resonance with our fractious present. The geopathological paranoia of today mirrors that of the lead-up to the First World War of Eliot's poem: the time when Curzon and his fellow colonial officials drew up plans for the buffered frontier may have been a high point of empire, yet the old order was by then already in retreat, and the war was fought in part to shore up the imperial fragments against the ruins.[14] As the age of North Atlantic dominance slowly draws to a juddering close, are we again hearing cruel calls for war in the distance?

Around us, dreams lie squandered, the dead tree gives no shelter, and meanwhile the climate clock tick-tocks in the background. *"Hurry up please it's time"* whispers Eliot's poem as carbuncular clerks fiddle about in a world bereft of hope. *Hurry up.* Yet as we noted at the outset, in *The Waste Land* there is also the stirring of thunder—the thirst for redemption. In our own danger-laden world, we may yet see hopeful political narratives emerge, uniting around the common good. Instead of a politics of irresponsibility and paranoid division, we may well hear growing calls for shared responsibility and protection of citizens and newcomers alike.

By contrast, Eliot, in his conservatism and religiosity, sent a poetic missive with *The Waste Land* not unlike Kristol and Kagan's call in the 1990s United States to go forth and slay the monsters. As thunder breaks, these are the words reverberating amid the ruins:

> *Datta:* What have we given?
> My friend, blood shaking my heart
> The awful daring of a moment's surrender
> Which an age of prudence can never retract
> By this, and this only, have we existed
> Which is not to be found in our obituaries
> Or in memories draped by the beneficent spider
> Or under seals broken by the lean solicitor
> In our empty rooms

Whose thunder, whose daring, will define the political path ahead? Powerful forces from the White House down are converting fear into righteous, effective anger, breeding lilacs out of the dead land. Their heroism and sacrifice in the face of danger make sense on the map of fear; but they may also be justified and calculated on the map of risk by the "lean solicitors" of the apparatus of government and intervention. On these superimposed maps of risks and danger, the war is lost. Opponents of the fear peddlers cannot win, or reach their Shangri-La. Perhaps fear may be mobilized in other ways, attaching to what really matters—rampant global warming, for a start.[15] But this is not enough. Looking beyond the politics of fear, opponents above all need another *story*, and a positive road map charting a path across the obstacles ahead. Whatever map and whatever tropes we choose for our story—whether of protection, of equality, of global solidarity and responsibility, or all of these—we may learn some lessons from seeing how the dominant maps of risk and fear work, as well as from tallying their escalating political, financial, and human costs. The prison of danger has been thought for us, yet its walls are flimsy; we do not need a key to break free. The monsters in the dark may be dispelled as soon as enough people start seeing clearly how powerful forces are conjuring them for their own monstrous ends. Meanwhile, those who stake their claims to our world of danger need no new map, but rather a mirror through which to see the signs of their own affliction.

ACKNOWLEDGMENTS

It's the usual story: too many people to thank, too little space, and a problem of not breaking ethnographic anonymity to boot. So I will simply thank a few people and institutions by name while leaving out many of those who generously have given their time, insight, and friendship in Mali and elsewhere over the years.

Huge thanks to Mary Kaldor at the London School of Economics for believing in this project from the start, when I arrived in 2014, and for welcoming me so warmly into her research unit. My colleagues there—among them Sam Vincent, Dominika Spyratou, Anouk Rigterink, Sabine Selchow, Iavor Rangelov, Ali Ali, and Florian Weigand—have been a great inspiration. Ali and Florian have kept ideas flowing, and I have learned much from their expertise on the Middle East and Afghanistan respectively. At LSE, I also remain as grateful as ever to Deborah James and Mathijs Pelkmans for their great support and friendship.

At University of California Press, my thanks to Naomi Schneider, Benjy Malings, Chris Sosa Loomis, Alex Dahne, Dore Brown, and colleagues for their brilliant work. A special thanks to Lia Tjandra for her cover design, to Elisabeth Magnus for her careful copyediting, and to Samantha Clark for her thorough indexing. At Oxford, my institutional home since 2016, I am very grateful for the input and inspiration provided by great colleagues—Dace Dzenovska, Tom Scott-Smith, Nicholas Van Hear, Xiang Biao, and many more. My students in the master's program in migration studies and the DPhil program in international development are fantastically inspiring too—you show us there's still hope in our trying times.

At Stockholm University, special thanks to Shahram Khosravi, Johan Lindquist, Hege Høyer Levestad, and Ulf Hannerz, who have inspired and exchanged ideas over the years. At the School of Oriental and African Studies, my first great teachers in anthropology kept me going, including to Mali: Trevor Marchand, Nancy Lindisfarne, Nayanika Mookherjee, Parvati Rahman, and many more. Elsewhere, Martin Saxer helped me think through remoteness: chapter 2 is indebted to him, and to our colleagues working on a collective project in this vein. Pierluigi Musarò helped with chapter 4; Pam DeLargy shared inspiring ideas and findings on borders; and Bruce Whitehouse provided encouragement and feedback on Mali. Commenters on my article in *Current Anthropology* (Andersson 2016) helped move the project forward: Bruce, again, as well as Gabriella Körling, Jeff Sluka, Nicholas Farrelly, and Mark Maguire. Thanks, too, to University of Chicago Press for allowing the reuse of material from this article. I'm of course also extremely grateful to the book's anonymous peer reviewers, who helped improve it no end: the usual mea culpa applies when it comes to errors of omission and commission.

Two readers in particular have made a huge difference. Hans Lucht provided generously abundant and perceptive comments on my manuscript at review stage, and then read parts of it again—his contribution has been fundamental. David Keen has been my most important source of feedback, sparring, and scholarly inspiration for the project as a whole, and his repeated readings of chapters and discussing of ideas have proven the best support imaginable—huge thanks!

Institutionally, I wish to thank AXA Research Fund, which financed the core research part of the project. I have also benefited from support via the European Research Council (as part of Mary Kaldor's Security in Transition project), from my earlier PhD financed by the UK Economic and Social Research Council, and from Oxford's Oppenheimer Fund. Views expressed in this book are mine and not those of the funders.

My parents, Sara and Vincent, have inspired and supported me throughout, including by sharing books, news reports, and ideas. Inspiration aplenty has also come from my little ones, Eirik and Aaron, who asks when I will be ready with the "book of dragons." Finally, this book is dedicated to Cristina, who made the project come about and heroically put up with me through it all; without her, it would certainly not have been completed.

POWER OF NARRATION, NARRATION OF POWER

AN ANTHROPOLOGICAL APPENDIX

This book is the story of a political world gone wild. As it builds its narrative of global danger, the red zones inevitably taint it by association. We may seek to dispel the power of our politics of fear, yet at each turn we risk reinforcing it. At the same time, the closer we look into the black hole of the Gap, the more likely it is to confound and disorient us with its dark glow. As we have fanned out across the world, from Bamako to Kabul and back again, we have ended up with a hall of mirrors and with fragmentary glimpses. In this resides the challenge in taking anthropology's favored way of working—intimately, understanding the social world inside out—into a global sphere of power by the means I will reflect on in this brief academic appendix: through narration.

Like maps, stories are treacherous. They may lead us down dead ends, and they may confuse as much as clarify; and woe betide the social scientist turned storyteller! Here, then, is a brief defense of narration from the ramparts of academia—a few road signs, if nothing else, for other attempts to narrate power in our "dark times."[1]

To be human is to tell stories: *Homo sapiens* is also a *Homo narrans*. Narration yokes together emotion, knowledge, and power—over the self, over our understanding of the world, and over others. Telling tales about our lives, we build a Self out of fragments. Telling tales on the public stage, the powerful control the grand political narratives of our time. Their stories engage in battle: witness how narrators of a wounded nationalism today style themselves as heroes fighting back dark threats or outwitting "globalists." The metastory of winning the narrative war itself forms part of the story told by the new fear peddlers in power.

Looking out onto this battlefield from our studies, scholars struggle to make sense of the storytelling and its powerful emotional swirl of anxiety, fear, and anger. How can we speak back against political narratives depicting a migrant invasion, an existential threat of terror, a fundamental insecurity that stirs wrath against Others and promises safety through hard sovereign power?

The relative public silence of academics when faced with the political stories of our times does not just affect the harder social sciences, enamored with lining up fact against affect. Anthropologists and humanists, too, have long had a rather troubled relationship with emotions.[2] In a hard-hitting critique, the political scientist Ian Shapiro has gone as far as to lambaste academia for divorcing itself from social reality and retreating into abstract formulas, obscure jargon, and petty pedantry.[3] We may not wish to join his critique all the way, but our political turmoil does throw up a massive challenge to students of society: How do we write about power and politically mobilized emotions when our principal tools are rational analysis and careful empiricism—often, moreover, relayed in a language divorced from the reality around us?

The stakes are high, not just for scholars, but for public life. We may decry the denigration of "expert voices" all we like, but a more fundamental problem is the division of labor through which expertise is rendered irrelevant in the first place. Planting their flag on the "rational" turf—the left-hand side of the brain, if you will—academics and technocratic politicians have abandoned the emotional right-hand side, which is swiftly being colonized by others peddling emotional messages of immense power.[4] This we saw in the Brexit vote, with Trump, in Italy, and we will see it again: a divide every bit as deep as that between the near and the far traced in this book.

However, the borderline between rationality and affect is itself illusory. The political appeal of emotional messages is itself buttressed by rational interests and genuine grievances, while on the "left-hand" side, numbers themselves tell a story all their own, as liberal voices know when building their own emotive stories of the world. In other words, the divide is already being bridged through the stories we tell, and in how these link reason and emotion. The challenge is to tell them better.

All this is a long-winded way of saying that, in *No Go World*, I have experimented with the narrative form. It is an "essay" in the sense of attempt, with all the risks this involves, including guilt by association. But at least this puts it in good company. Experiment has redefined ethnography since the 1980s, when an onslaught of criticism of anthropology initially led to some degree of intellectual paralysis, followed by bouts of creative reworkings of the genre. Anthropologists started crafting different modes of ethnography—cut-up collages, literary-infused analyses, and more, much more. There were those who put the voices of their participants center stage—among these Lila Abu-Lughod in her *Writing Women's Worlds,* whose stories of Bedouin women displaced the anthropologist's old monologue and gaze. There were studies that "cut across" large slices of public life, from Emily Martin's *Flexible Bodies* to Anna Tsing's *Friction.* Yet with some exceptions, anthropologists all too rarely experimented with authorial narration as a tool both for the anthropological project and for conveying our thoughts beyond the usual academic publics.

This is odd, given anthropology's history of public engagement through the literary forays of the likes of Claude Lévi-Strauss and Margaret Mead. It is odd, moreover, since many insiders would agree that anthropologists and storytellers are close cousins. The British anthropologist Edmund Leach once quipped that anthropologists are failed novelists—a charge I for one am happy to live with. From the other side, some novelists argue, rather, that their kin are anthropologists in disguise. Kurt Vonnegut, who dropped out of his anthropology studies at Chicago, called it "a science that was mostly poetry," influencing his fiction. More recently, Tom McCarthy wrote, "As a novelist, I am fascinated by the figure of the anthropologist. What he or she embodies for me is a version of the writer minus all the bullshit, all the camouflage or obfuscation—embodies, that is, the function of the writer stripped down to its bare structural essentials. You look at the world and you report on it. That's it." He continues imagining the anthropologist's rarefied world in the Lévi-Straussian wilderness, a world in which right of passage into others' worlds is assured for the masculine hero—the very inheritance Abu-Lughod had sought to tear apart with her Bedouin stories:

> You spend time with a tribe, observe the way they fish and hunt, discern the contours of their rituals, beliefs and superstitions, tune into their unspokens and taboos. Then, after a year or so of this, you lug your note-packed trunk down to a dilapidated jetty from which a series of small rubber-trading boats and giant ocean liners carry you back to your study, where, khakis swapped for cotton shirt and tie, saliva liquor for the Twinings or iced scotch your housekeeper purveys you on a tray, you write the Book on them: the Great Report that maps the world you have been observing at its deepest and most intimate level, sums the tribe up, speaks its secret name.[5]

McCarthy notes that Bronisław Malinowski, the father of modern social anthropology, "understood the discipline that he was forging as essentially a literary one."

But if old-school anthropology was literary in its inception, the stories it told echoed with—or at least played off—the stories that Western powers sought to tell about the world and their rightful place in it. It is not hard to see, in other words, how anthropologists in the era of colonial and, later, US dominance found willing audiences for their Great Reports.[6]

Today's anthropologists face a tougher sell for their treatises. The narrative nexus between novelist and anthropologist has been lost, except perhaps in the memoirs of scholars looking back on their days in the mythical field—yet even those recollections fail to revive the lost allure of Lévi-Strauss and his *Tristes tropiques*.[7] Indeed, today's academic anthropologists are largely (though not wholly) bereft of a public voice, writing for specialist readers alone. "Anthropology should have changed the world, yet the subject is almost invisible in the public sphere outside the academy," complained one of the major proponents of a "public" anthropology, Thomas Hylland Eriksen, over a decade ago.[8]

There is, we may say, no particular reason why a peculiar discipline borne of the colonial encounter "should" have access to wider publics. Moreover, our trade is certainly not the only one stuck on the academic hamster wheel, too busy trip-trapping over one "metric" after another to be able to tell stories that resonate. Still, I do find the absence of a discipline whose strength has been to reconfigure social analysis from the "ground up" particularly jarring as the calls for such a vision grow ever louder—consider the financial crisis, the populist surge, or indeed the walled-up borders and intractable conflicts at the heart of this book.[9]

Anthropologists may have survived our discipline's crisis of representation of the 1980s, but we still face a crisis of relevance. Still, consider the names of influential "anthropological visionaries" scattered throughout *No Go World*, from David Kilcullen the counterinsurgency master to Clotaire Rapaille the advertising guru, or even Ashraf Ghani, the Columbia-trained president of Afghanistan who makes a footnoted appearance. They all have stories to tell: of why insurgency emerges, of how marketing works, of how to fix failed states (the title of Ghani's book).

We cannot simply roll our eyes at how such intellectual entrepreneurs capture public and political attention while our own Great Reports go by unnoticed. Instead, we may learn from them to tell our *own* stories, however rough around the edges they may be. We must do so, since otherwise—as Anthonius Robben argued in his book *Iraq at a Distance*—other entrepreneurs and pundits will simply find it easier to "sell" their attractive tales, chiming as they usually do with the narratives of those in positions of power.[10]

We may also learn from the yarn-spinning skills of historians. Eriksen puts this point in a fictive historian's mouth:

> The historian and the anthropologist discuss the relative merits of their subjects. The anthropologist says, in a smug voice: "Well, if you historians intend to study a river, you have to wait until it has dried out. You then enter the dry riverbed with your magnifying glasses and whatnot. We anthropologists, on the other hand, wade straight into the messy wetness of the river and stay there until we have been able to make sense of it as it flows by." The historian lights his pipe, looks out of the window and answers slowly: "Yes, I suppose you are right. Yet, you anthropologists seem to dry out the living river, while we historians endeavor to bring water to the dry riverbed."[11]

Part of the problem may well be the institutional game of specialization, which has involved, for anthropology, attempts to defend our turf by turning ethnography into a reputable scientific method—as Malinowski himself strategically did. Tim Ingold, who has criticized the notion that ethnography is the core of the discipline, put it well when saying that anthropology today "remains compliant with the protocols of normal science. These protocols enforce a division between the real world, from which we are expected to gather 'data,' and the world of theory, in which these data are to be interpreted and fashioned into authorized knowledge. . . . This procedure fatally compromises the core mission of anthropology, which is to demonstrate—by precept and example—how to do our thinking in and with the world we inhabit: in response to its summons, rather than after the fact."[12]

This may sound a tad pretentious, and—like the critique of mere "research" occasionally voiced by others[13]—it grates, for one, against my own joy in the *work* of "fieldwork" (which may well be inherited from my working-class roots as much as from doctoral training). But Ingold's critique at least gets at the analytical problem identified at the start—how our scholarly voice and analyses fail to capture social reality by dividing up and separating out here and there, research and writing, learning and knowing, reason and emotion.

Yet I believe there is leeway in ethnography still, in more ways than one. In the project that became *No Go World*, my attempt to get my hands dirty in fieldwork came up short. Instead of bridging the divide to enter the risky "field" on the other side, I ended up taking that divide itself as my object of inquiry. In doing so, I took as my starting point the anthropological frontier zone where our traditional methods reach their point of near impossibility. Participant-observation here may not just be a fundamental part of anthropology's educational ethos, as Ingold suggests, but may also function as a tool for "testing the waters."[14] How far does it reach, and what does this limit tell us?

My story, then, is not an "ethnography" in the strict sense. I was not following in the footsteps of McCarthy's old anthropological hero. This itself, I sensed, was significant, and spoke of broader shifts on our geopolitical map. Some years ago, one perceptive member of our trade pointed out how the "stability in the ethnographic field" once guaranteed by colonial power no longer holds.[15] Very few social "tribes" are compelled to welcome us no matter what, and there is no iced scotch and public fame awaiting us on the way back to the jetty. Protection is no longer guaranteed, the way it was in the colonial and even Cold War days: indeed, anthropologists' time-worn quest for knowledge of the insecure Other is becoming intimately tied up with the insecurity of the anthropological Self.

In this sense, *No Go World* became a metastory of sorts as I narrated the mapping of danger and the story it tells about our present. In its fragments, problems of writing and research ensued, and it is worth dwelling briefly on these, too, as they should ring familiar to anyone studying the workings of power. My story was not centrally about individuals—not even individual presidents and world leaders—but about *systems* of intervention, from peacekeeping and aid to border security and counterterror, and their interlinkages. To grasp what goes on in such systems ethnographically, "from the inside," I would need full access to the interveners, yet these were nowhere near as accessible as the villagers of old-school anthropology. Moreover, even if I *did* get access to key personae, by writing (*grapho*) the "people" (*ethnos*) I was likely to lose sight of the systemic nature of the world of intervention. What to do?

My imperfect solution was to take the narratives, artifacts, and ideas circulated by powerful interveners as my object of inquiry. As concerns research, my fieldwork in Bamako expanded into a series of shorter visits and some two hundred interviews across disparate sites, from UN headquarters in New York to the port of Lampedusa, besides long spells in well-stocked Oxford and London libraries. As concerns the writing, I wanted to map the political power of narration through the narrative form itself, in an attempt to see the world of mappers and interveners from the inside. Making the strange familiar and the familiar strange is anthropology's sometime motto, and I hope it shines through on these pages: our world of encroaching dangers, rendered in newly strange light.

It bears repeating that anthropological narration needs to be approached—and taught—as a craft. Yet this craft, I found, was rendered more difficult as I sought to narrate an analytical understanding of a system as opposed to a way of life, a community's struggles, or the fate of an "informant." Consider the treacherous behavior of protagonists. As any novelist will tell you, they never do what you tell them to: they colonize space, shout "Me! Me!", and altogether ignore your pleadings for them to stand in line. Nonfiction writers have learned to measure precisely how much analytical and historical weight these protagonists can carry on their backs before they collapse. In this book, I faced the same conundrum. Take General McChrystal, who makes impromptu appearances in *No Go World* as the seeming villain of the piece. "I'm not sure there's this evil hand running the machinery," said one clear-eyed reviewer of my draft—and indeed there isn't. I had let him take over. This is what some journalists do in their storytelling—that is, not simply using the narrative device of the protagonist for pegging an analysis to a human story, but rather turning the protagonist into the centerpiece and even the *cause* of the problem under scrutiny. In our anthropological attempts to understand the systemic workings of power, we cannot let this happen. I may have done so with my McChrystals and Rapailles, or I may have erred in the other direction, reducing them to mere fragments, not bearers of stories. Yet when one is telling a story of a system, the main protagonist must on some deep level be the system itself, in all its fragmentation.

We may query, of course, whether there is a "system" there at all. Are we not rather facing a mishmash of interventions large and small, of conflictive actors staking their claims without much coordination? Do we not risk giving these actors too much power by narrating them in a systemic frame? This problem, of course, reaches wider than narrative approaches, also affecting studies of power of a more overtly analytical bent.[16] However, here again I believe that mimicking the political deployment of narration by "narrating back" allows us to approach power obliquely, the better to chip away at its claims to dominance. "What the map cuts up, the story cuts across," was one of Michel de Certeau's aphorisms.[17] In that spirit, here's hoping that other, more complete essays than mine may in times to come cut across the road map of doom in novel ways, setting signposts for a different map and a different narrative.

NOTES

1. Many names in this book, including this one, are pseudonyms, either at the express request of interviewees or simply to safeguard anonymity in standard ethnographic fashion.

2. For a cartographic perspective on the "dragons," see Van Duzer (2013).

3. Of course, monsters of one kind or another have always been with us; see chapter 2 for a brief reflection on the Cold War. What I am hinting at here is the overlap between certain historical depictions (and placements) of fantastical dangers and the monstrous, and the representation and mapping of today's non-state dangers—in ways, I should add, that differ from the times of the Cold War and the Second World War.

4. On suicide attacks, see Overton (2016). Numbers have gone down since 2015; see Control Risks (2017).

5. In UN peacekeeping, increasing fatalities have accompanied a sharp rise in the number of soldiers on mission—and so the *ratio* of deaths, if anything, is falling. See statistical analysis by Henke (2016) (which, we must note, does not include the extremely deadly AU mission in Somalia). Concerning terror attacks, one report based on the Global Terrorism Database has said of the pattern in western Europe, "Terrorist attacks were frequently non-lethal, took place primarily in the 1970s and 1980s and have declined since the early 1990s" (START 2016, 1).

6. Lemieux (2017) notes that only 3 percent of worldwide deaths in terror attacks occurred in Western countries between 2000 and 2014.

7. Action on Armed Violence (2018).

8. According to Humanitarian Outcomes data for 2017, 158 major incidents of violence against humanitarian operations occurred in twenty-two countries, affecting 313 aid workers, of which 285 were national staff (Stoddard, Harmer, and Czwarno 2018). As their briefing states, "Because these attacks took place mostly in contexts of severely constrained access for international aid organisations, 2017 also saw a steep rise in the number of victims belonging to national and local NGOs, reflecting the near universal reliance on national staff and organisations to take on the riskiest of operational roles in the most insecure areas." For fatality ratios, see the Aid Worker Security Database, https://aidworkersecurity.org/incidents, which lists 10 international staff fatalities versus 129 national staff fatalities for 2017.

9. The figures for the AU mission to Somalia, AMISOM, are disputed; the AU has given a much lower figure. See van der Lijn and Dundon (2014) for a discussion, as well as chapter 3.

10. As scholars and journalists note, both these markets have proven very hard to quantify, not least owing to the secrecy involved both in military outsourcing and in the drone and automation business; see Risen and Rosenberg (2015).

11. The term is from Mark Duffield (2001), whose work is an important inspiration for this book as a whole. See also Duffield (2005, 2007). On the "stay and deliver" agenda and its "paradoxes of presence" in aid, see Collinson and Duffield (2013, 3).

12. On the perils of fieldwork, see Nordstrom and Robben (1996); Sluka (1990); Kovats-Bernat (2002); also Andersson (2016b).

13. Campbell and Conrad (2014).

14. Public Radio International (Campbell and Conrad 2014) has crunched these numbers.

15. Lemieux (2016).

16. With some hesitation, I will use first-person plural at times to refer to Western governments and their electorates, largely for stylistic reasons and in order to place myself in the text. Yet there is an analytical ambiguity to this "we" that may usefully be exploited in looking for alternative approaches built on proximity and engagement rather than global distance and fear. See also Conclusion.

17. On the Silk Roads and a strong intellectual case for focusing on connectivity and pathways, see Frankopan (2015). On the popular globalization literature, see chapter 2.

18. Beck (1999), expanding on his earlier work on risk society.

19. Arjun Appadurai (2011), in his work on finance, distinguishes between risk (management) and uncertainty in the financialization of capitalism in

recent decades, drawing on Weber, Knight, and Mauss. In short, while accepting his distinction, I use *risk taking* here as colloquial shorthand for this embrace of and play with uncertainty in finance, which, as Appadurai also notes, links back to "risk proper." As he writes, "The primary feature of the ethos of financial players in the past few decades, those who have both played and shaped the financial game, is to be found in a working (though not consciously theorized or articulated) disposition toward exploiting uncertainty as a legitimate principle for managing risk" (2011, 525).

20. See Sassen (1991) on global cities and Sassen (2014, 18) on "expulsions" in contemporary capitalism.

21. Compare Sassen (2014). The geographical specializations traced here are not always exclusive but rather overlapping. Mineral or oil deposits drive intervention in many remote regions, in turn fueling the production of danger. The ISIS/Daesh rampage through Syria and Iraq, for instance, was long on the political and media backburner in the West—until it neared the oil fields of Kurdistan *and* until it started with its spectacular killings of American hostages, upon which followed US air bombardment. The hunger for sub-Saharan Africa's resources (Burgis 2015) frequently dovetails with interventions in the danger zone. In the Sahel, France wishes to protect its strategically important uranium plant in Niger against attacks while eyeing up resources in the Malian north, which it once saw as part of its projected Sahel/Sahara area of influence even after its former colonies' independence, upon the discovery of Algerian oil in 1956. Compare notes 8 and 9 to chapter 1 and the concluding section to chapter 2.

22. For an analysis of the discourse of a "new normal" in EU migration governance, see Geddes and Hadj-Abdou (2017).

23. On the politics of fear and the borders of the West, see Chebel d'Appollonia (2012). On psychopolitics, see Han (2017).

24. See, for instance, this *Financial Times* story on the Hungarian leaflet: "Hungary Says London Is a 'No-Go' Zone Due to Immigration," *Financial Times*, September 21, 2016, https://www.ft.com/content/a29fbf40–8000–11e6–8e50–8ec15fb462f4.

25. Vernon (2014, 43).

26. Among the texts referred to here are Huntington (2009) and N. Ferguson (2004); see chapter 2 for a longer discussion of such intellectual scenario builders. On benevolent "postmodern" empire, see also R. Cooper (2002).

27. Mishra (2017).

28. Anthropological studies of proliferating security apparatuses and discourses, of kinds only partly covered in this book (see especially chapter 5), include Goldstein (2010); Maguire, Frois, and Zurawski (2014); Masco (2014).

29. On this positive story via hard evidence, see Rosling (2018) and chapter 5.

30. Of course, we may query the usefulness of the "Western" label, as I will go on to do at certain points in this book. Certainly, this historical construct can

readily be questioned as an increasingly inaccurate gloss on a jumble of fractious polities. However, as we will see in the Conclusion and in the colonial examples throughout, there are reasons why a somewhat simplified "Western" focus is still warranted as a tool for considering the historical emergence of the interventionist patterns of the present, including those in UN and NATO guise.

31. For a theoretical take on mapping as processual rather than representational, see Kitchin and Dodge (2007).

32. In relation to note 30 above, another danger concerns the Western-centrism of the argument, which is to some extent addressed in chapter 2. The reason for putting Western interveners center stage is their continued key role in crisis zones, yet, as will be seen, this central role is becoming fragile indeed.

33. Yet another line of criticism would be that a focus on "narrative power" and security intervention sidelines a discussion of the grievances and economic injustices that underlie conflict and fear-based politics. I will allude to this perspective in all chapters, especially chapter 2 and the Conclusion: however, I am also aware that this economic dimension would need a book all its own. On how security strategies and apparatuses overlap with "neoliberal" politics, see especially Goldstein (2010). On economic exploitation and marginalization in sub-Saharan Africa, the literature is vast: see, for instance, J. Ferguson (2006).

34. On dangerous yet "rational" delusions in political life, see Keen (forthcoming).

35. This security-dominated approach contrasts starkly with that of China, not least on the African continent. While the latter's "peaceful rise" is itself a source of contention and is often based on exploitative relationships with poor yet resource-rich countries, it has nevertheless generated rather different and in many ways less harmful dynamics than the West's reframed relations with these countries. See also Conclusion.

1. THE TIMBUKTU SYNDROME

1. Chambers (1835, 342).

2. Boahen (1964, 29).

3. For more on Laing's exploits, and those of other explorers, see the website of the Princeton University project *To the Mountains of the Moon*, http://libweb5 .princeton.edu/visual_materials/maps/websites/africa/contents.html, from which the quote here is taken; see also Caillié ([1830] 1992). For a popularized account, see English (2017).

4. Lederer (2015).

5. The debate on shifts in UN peacekeeping is too vast to delve into here, but briefly: on the African "laboratory," see Tardy and Wyss (2014); on links between

imperial legacies and peacekeeping, especially in Francophone Africa, Charbon-neau (2014); for a critical take on "robust" peace operations and the use of force, Berdal and Ucko (2015). See also the 2015 UN report of the High-Level Panel on UN Peace Operations (UN 2015).

6. These border control priorities are outlined in my previous book (Andersson 2014). See also chapter 4.

7. For nuance, we must note that there is mixed evidence of arms used in the conflict; some may be traced to Libya, while other weapons were stolen from Malian government arsenals. See Conflict Armament Research (2013) for details.

8. Mali's conflict has generated a wealth of analysis, much of it in French (e.g., Galy 2013). In brief, some commentators have highlighted the complex and shift-ing groups competing for power, influence, and resources, trying to move the debate away from the binaries between friend and enemy, jihadist and separatist, northern and southerner (e.g., Boisvert 2012). Others have perceptively cautioned about the risks of a rushed peacekeeping involvement (Utas 2013), including in the form of remote-controlled war (Rogers 2013), or have nuanced the critique of French military intervention by contesting elements of the resource-grab and "neoimperialist" critiques (Whitehouse 2017). Malian and foreign voices alike have highlighted the fragility of democratic and economic gains in Mali in the pre-coup years, when aid kept pouring in even as the state and its services were under severe strain and corruption was rampant—all of which fueled the discon-tent contributing to Mali's descent into chaos (Whitehouse 2017; Konaté 2013; Bergamaschi 2014). Further, in the north, patronage relations served to control illicit cross-border flows, with large gains back in Bamako, adding fuel to the fire (Guichaoua 2013). Digging deeper, anthropological and historical accounts have highlighted the fraught social dynamics in northern Mali, inherited from colonial times, among Tuareg "nomads" and black African "settlers"—itself a highly fluc-tuating divide—and how these are being reshaped through migration, water scar-city, and economic shifts (Whitehouse 2013; Lecocq 2010). Whitehouse (2017, n.p.), summarizing existing explanations of what went wrong in Mali, argues that the country's "destabilization must be recognized as a co-production of inside and outside forces—a composite assemblage of self-serving Malian elites, donor gov-ernments oblivious to their actions' harmful consequences, and foreign actors pursuing their own ends," with echoes back into the colonial period.

9. For a critique of neocolonialism by Malian and Senegalese intellectuals, see Traoré and Diop (2014); but see Whitehouse (2017) above. The work of Keenan (2009, 2013) is also emblematic of the strong argument around outside involve-ment. His assertions center on how Algerian security services, abetted by the US war on terror, largely created and "exported" the jihadist groups based in north-ern Mali. His argument has however met with criticism, including concerns about its evidence base (e.g., Soares 2012). See also chapter 2.

10. See notes 8 and 9 above.

11. As for the United States, a top official at the State Department told me in 2014 that they did not seek to establish a large and visible footprint in Mali. "The Tuareg threat," he said, "is more [of a threat] to Europe." Besides, US diplomatic relationships might be hurt by military ventures. "The more we are [seen with] the French," he said, "the more [we] may undermine our own influence." The United Kingdom largely shared this assessment (UK FAC 2014).

12. E.g., Solomon (2013).

13. This was not just my own preference: as Soares (2012) has noted, academics working on Mali—not least anthropologists—had long concentrated on the country's plentiful cultural riches in their research, leaving the political problems rumbling below the surface much less examined. This has now shifted dramatically, as Mali-bound researchers are increasingly affiliated with security-focused research institutes close to Western donor governments, as was the case with the European researcher cited later in this chapter.

14. Autesserre (2014) and further references above. The ground-level view of how intervention works in practice, pursued in this chapter, owes much to the approach taken by her and other authors writing in a similar vein, including Smirl (2015).

15. The name has been changed. The quotes from Monica are based on field notes written as soon as possible after our discussions, in standard ethnographic fashion.

16. Kaldor (1999).

17. The term *archipelago of intervention* is Duffield's (2010). For academic perspectives on aid fortification, see Duffield (2010); Fast (2014); and Collinson and Duffield (2013).

18. Chandrasekaran (2006).

19. See Dyrberg (2014) for a report from Danish media on soldiers in a "luxury hotel."

20. Civilian officials including Westerners were eventually deployed up to Timbuktu for office work, while UN agencies (UNHCR, WFP UNICEF) gradually started deploying into rural areas in the Timbuktu region, using (well-trained) local staff: that is, some complexity to this geographical division of labor was eventually introduced, albeit with big caveats. The policy on using nonwhite staff in the north was rarely formalized explicitly but was common to all the UN agencies and NGOs I interviewed; sometimes it included deploying black Western staff up north as well, as some officers confided. National staff would of course also include Tuareg northerners, not only "black" Africans, as in the case of "Moussa," my friend cited later in this chapter.

21. On remote humanitarian management in Syria, see Fradejas-García (forthcoming). See also chapter 6.

22. The name has been changed.

23. See Lianos and Douglas (2000, 110–11). Thanks to an anonymous peer reviewer of Andersson (2016b) for making the link to their work.

24. The name has been changed.

25. See DIIS (2017) on the gap between the real and the advertised equipment that political leaders in troop-contributing countries provided for their soldiers.

26. Sweden is not part of NATO, but its military forces have become very closely aligned with it.

27. Other researchers and practitioners have noted how the usual UN troop contributors from South Asia, long seen as ill-prepared and ill-equipped by Western countries, were suddenly the cream of the crop in Mali relative to the soldiers brought in from West African nations.

28. Sexual abuse and prostitution have long been rife in peacekeeping missions, and evidence suggests this continues to be the case despite official zero-tolerance policies (on this, see especially Clarke's 2015 article on a leaked internal UN report). Further steps are being taken at the UN at the time of writing to remedy this situation. In Mali, to give an example from 2014, one aid worker told me how, in Gao, poor young women had been coming to do AIDS tests. They were not the typical profile for these tests, so the doctor asked them why—and was told it was because the soldiers demanded paperwork before sleeping with them.

29. In Mali, this essentially meant the Europeans deployed only to areas covered by medical evacuation. In Afghanistan, such caveats had previously earned Europeans deployed in NATO's International Security Assistance Force (ISAF) the nicknames "I Saw Americans Fight" or "I Suck at Fighting" among US soldiers; Hastings (2012, 26).

30. DIIS (2017, 35).

31. The name has been changed.

32. The UN chief also noted that while security risk had initially been the primary reason for the division of labor up north, now the main rationale was cost; yet insecurity kept being put forward as the explanation for depending on national and "regional" staff.

33. Since Mali's period as "aid darling," Western donors often turned a blind eye to much of these losses, not least with regard to nonearmarked "budget support" (Bergamaschi 2014). In the north, as Malian aid workers pointed out to me, the problem of humanitarian supplies ending up in the wrong hands goes back even further, to the 1970s droughts; as is often the case, a massive influx of funds and resources into a crisis-hit area by an unregulated humanitarian "industry" can have pernicious side effects. The free-for-all marketplace of the "humanitarian international" (De Waal 1997) had however been given an even more destructive twist in Mali by 2014, thanks to the lack of transparency via insecurity-based subcontracting in the danger zone.

34. See Fast (2014) on how a concern with "external threats" has driven humanitarian risk management strategies, with too little attention paid to what she calls their "internal vulnerabilities," including the very risk-based reorganization of their work described here.

35. Similar observations were made by other interviewees in the aid world. The head of one leading NGO's regional emergency operations, for instance, noted that "the amount of time [you spend] in kidnap negotiations" is perhaps more important than the actual ransom payment; it was a "twenty-five-hours-a-day job" in his words. As he asked, "Why take that when [you can] get somebody with the correct profile?" This meant African workers—a much smaller pool of potential staff. The temptation, the official admitted, was to say, "Let's just get a warm body and put them behind the desk."

36. UN Operations and Crisis Centre (2018).

37. Guichaoua and Lebovich (2017); on the nineteenth-century jihads, Hanson (1996).

38. Chatwin cited in Hannerz (2004, 243); also English (2017).

39. On risk-transfer war and the "Vietnam syndrome" (including debates over the term's applicability), see M. Shaw (2005).

40. Kalb (2013).

41. Trouillot (2003).

42. There is no space here to go into the shifting dynamics of violence, jihadism and militia groups, and the historical and ethnic grievances that play into these dynamics; for a regional-focused summary, see Guichaoua and Lebovich (2017).

2. REMOTENESS REMAPPED

1. Niva (2013, 190). See Scahill (2014, 3–7) on the selective usage of assassinations following the 1976 ban, and its expansion post-9/11.

2. This paragraph, including quotations, is based on the analysis by Epstein (2001).

3. Quoted in Gusterson (2016, 119–20).

4. See Scahill (2014) on this neoconservative backstory.

5. Suskind (2004, n.p.).

6. Khanna (2016, xvi).

7. See Khanna's own Connectivity Atlas at https://atlas.developmentseed .org/.

8. Friedman (2006, 7–10).

9. See the Thomas Friedman Op/Ed Generator (Mayer 2017).

10. See Project Loon's website at https://x.company/loon/journey/.

11. See especially Goldin and Mariathasan, who in their *The Butterfly Defect* (2015) drew attention to such systemic risks on a global scale.

12. As Khanna (2016, xviii) writes, "Even as connectivity makes the world more complex and unpredictable, it also offers the essential pathways to achieve collective resilience." Chapter 5 returns to resilience.

13. Kristol and Kagan (1996, 31). These sentences summarize an argument made by Stuart Elden, whose *Terror and Territory* (2009, 11 and passim) is fundamental reading for the themes covered here.

14. Kaplan (1994, n.p.).

15. As Elden (2009, 10) notes, "Clinton apparently had a copy of Kaplan's 1994 article faxed to U.S. embassies across the world."

16. Elden (2009, 14).

17. For a critique of the notions of failed and fragile states, see Nay (2013); for an example, cowritten by Afghanistan's current president, Ashraf Ghani, see Ghani and Lockhart (2008).

18. Gregory and Pred (2006, 1).

19. Robin (2004a, 2–4).

20. Gregory and Pred (2006, 2). Similar points regarding the interrelation between "marginal"/wild and "central"/safe spaces have been made more broadly in the anthropology of the state; see Das and Poole (2004).

21. See Holmes (2017).

22. Piper (2002, 6).

23. Khanna (2016, xx).

24. Robert Louis Stevenson, quoted in Cep (2014, n.p.).

25. Said (2003).

26. Trouillot (2003).

27. Edwin Ardener ([1987] 2012, 522), in his theoretical take on remoteness, says (with a hint of essentialism reproduced in my own account), "In the West, we are 'space specialists': we easily realize our conceptual spaces as physical spaces— for that is, in many respects, the European theme."

28. On the Hereford, Alexander is rather busy keeping the Sons of Cain at bay. See Mappa Mundi, Hereford Cathedral website at https://www.themappamundi .co.uk/mappa-mundi/.

29. Van Duzer and Dines (2016, 227). On the Hereford map, the anthropophagi are hidden behind a wall.

30. An odd fact on Tolkien: it was a mapmaker trained by the British Ministry of Defence, Pauline Baynes, who drew the mountain ranges of Middle Earth. See Cep (2014).

31. On this awe-inspiring aspect, see Barber and Harper (2010, 19).

32. Quoted in Harley (2001, 52), whose critical geography has inspired large parts of this chapter.

33. See Mary Louise Pratt (1992) on the monarch-of-all-I-survey genre; also Piper (2002, 7). See Burnett (2000, 5–6) on how an earlier generation of studies of British imperialism had relied on a narrow geographical definition of empire—

the areas painted red—whereas later generations shifted focus to economic rela-tionships, and so considered "informal empire" including debtor nations and dependents "in the red." A third generation (including Harley 1988), inspired not least by Edward Said, explored how the "red areas" facilitated knowledge about and enabled intervention on the colonized "Other," inspiring these lines.

34. Mahmud (2011).

35. Anne McClintock quoted in Piper (2002, 6).

36. Yet amid this celebration of empire, witness also signs of subversion: Atlas, holding the globe of the world, bears a sash across his chest saying "Human Labour." See Harley (1988), Biltcliffe (2005), and the "Collector's Notes" on Cor-nell's digital collections site: https://digital.library.cornell.edu/catalog/ss:3293793. For an account of British-Russian rivalry at this supposed high point of British colonialism, see Frankopan (2015).

37. Borges's short story (1998) picked up a thread from Lewis Carroll's *Sylvie and Bruno Concluded;* see Cep (2014).

38. Harley (2001, 57).

39. Said (2003, xxvi).

40. Piper (2002, 12). On the survey, see Edney (1997).

41. Piper (2002, 12–13).

42. On cartographic anxiety—a term coined by Derek Gregory in the sense used here—see, e.g., Painter (2008) and Saxer (2016).

43. Piper (2002).

44. Quotations in this paragraph and life detail in the next are from Asher (2008, chap. 2).

45. T. Roberts (2015).

46. A. McDougall (2007, 17).

47. English (2017, 30). On the Catalan Atlas, the Malian emperor is named as "lord of the negroes of Guinea."

48. Boahen (1964, 16).

49. Gregory (2004).

50. Boahen (1964, 24).

51. Park quoted in A. McDougall (2007, 20). See also English (2017).

52. Quotations from A. McDougall (2007, 17–23). McDougall argues that the Sahara worked as a mirror to the Orient for the Western colonizing powers and as an inverse to the slavery abolition movement. In these and other ways, we may say, the *projection* of fears and dangers into the desert came to play an important role in European political debates.

53. Brachet and Scheele (2019, 7–16).

54. Frankopan (2015). On intra-Saharan connections, see J. McDougall and Scheele (2012).

55. See Gardini (forthcoming) and Penfield (forthcoming) on Madagascar and Amazonia respectively. The notion of "Zomia," developed by Willem van

Schendel (2002) and James C. Scott (2010), is updated to "Zomia 2.0" by Rippa (forthcoming). On the Golden Triangle, see also Rippa and Saxer (2016).

56. The debate on "insider" versus "outsider" perspectives will not be lingered on here, as our main concern is external interveners' viewpoints. Martin Saxer and I are in the process of putting together a special issue on remoteness—including versions of the above-cited works by Brachet and Scheele, Fradejas-García, Gardini, Penfield, and Rippa—that will reflect on these ethnographic intricacies.

57. On Saharan connectivity, Bensaad (2005); Brachet (2009); McDougall and Scheele (2012); Scheele (2012).

58. Powell (2004); also Keenan (2013) and Scheele (2012).

59. Ellis (2004, 460).

60. A. McDougall (2007). The paraphrase on the blank space of the Sahara is from Scheele (2012, 235). Elsewhere, she writes with James McDougall about the need to appreciate the region's deep connections, contrasting these with Western portrayals of the Sahara as "a deserted place, where the permanent struggle of humanity against nature has deprived people of one of their most human characteristics, namely, the ability to change and to creatively influence the course of events" (J. McDougall and Scheele 2012, 9). For this, they say, long-term research is needed; sadly, precisely the kind of fieldwork now largely foreclosed by danger and risk.

61. On nonplaces, see Augé (1995). On the notion of "havens" in the war on terror, see Elden (2009, 25).

62. General Jones quoted in Keenan (2013, 16).

63. Ellis (2004, 462–63); also Keenan (2009, 2013). As noted, some critics have urged caution in accepting all of Keenan's conclusions, but the wider point about the strong gains by "partner states" playing a double game in the "war on terror" are persuasive; see Keen and Andersson (2018) for a related analysis. See also chapter 5.

64. Guichaoua (2013).

65. On an earlier "arc of crisis" across the Middle East, see Bialasiewicz et al. (2007).

66. Quotations in this paragraph are from Depardieu (2017b, n.p.).

67. On the attack, see Depardieu (2017a). Malagardis (2017) reflects on a previous interview with Depardieu and on the attack.

68. See the UK's column "Foreign Travel Advice: South Africa," at https://www.gov.uk/foreign-travel-advice/south-africa/terrorism (advice current as of September, 19, 2018).

69. See Rodríguez (2017).

70. See, e.g., Gettleman (2015) on Kenya and Grierson and Mason (2015) on Tunisia.

71. Anthropologist Scott Atran has noted that the foundational text of ISIS or Daesh, *The Management of Savagery*, exhorts adherents to hit "tourist resort

that the crusaders patronise" as well as other targets outside and within the Muslim world to sow maximum confusion, sap political will, and disperse military deployments. See Atran (2015, n.p.).

72. UK FAC (2014, 38), my italics.

73. "France to 'deploy troops' to fight Sahara militants," BBC report, May 8, 2014, www.bbc.co.uk/news/world-africa-27327759.

74. A brief semantic note: I use the term *threats* here because we are here dealing with specific issues—terrorism, narcotics, irregular migration—that are incorporated into risk analyses of various official kinds in a rather technical fashion. By contrast I use the term *danger* when referring to the wider imaginaries through which such threats are made socially, politically, and psychologically meaningful and urgent. The two terms clearly overlap, however, so I sometimes use them somewhat interchangeably.

75. James Ferguson, as he traces the uneven capitalist exploitation of Africa under "neoliberalism," critically adapts French colonial lingo to contrast "usable" and "unusable" Africa. Yet what I suggest here is that *Afrique inutile* may itself be extremely *useful*—especially when its resource is the negative one of danger. See J. Ferguson (2005, 2006); see also chapter 5.

76. Mahmud (2011, 8–9).

77. Goldin and Mariathasan (2015).

78. Hirsch quoted in Gusterson (2016, 117).

79. See, e.g., I. Shaw (2013) on "Predator Empire."

3. THE TYRANNY OF DISTANCE

1. On the US intervention in 1993, see De Waal (1998).

2. For the Henry quotes in this opening section, see AFRICOM conference transcript, "U.S. Can Offer 'Continental' Approach to African Security, Pentagon Official Says," September 23, 2007: www.africom.mil/media-room/transcript/6061/us-can-offer-continental-approach-to-african-secur. On AFRICOM's co-optation of human security discourse, see Branch (2011, chap. 7). On AFRICOM containment strategies, see McNeill (2017).

3. See Elden (2009, 14) on PNAC's 2000 report *Rebuilding America's Defenses*.

4. On the structure of AFRICOM, see Branch (2011).

5. McNeill (2017).

6. "Volumetric" power is proving analytically productive for interactions among anthropologists and political geographers; see Billé (2017), inspiring these lines, and his edited series for *Cultural Anthropology*, Speaking Volumes, https://culanth.org/fieldsights/1247-speaking-volumes.

7. Elden (2009) draws on Peter Sloterdijk's (2009) notions of *Luftbeben,* or air tremors, and "atmoterrorism" to explore these dimensions; see also Elden (2013). Besides Weizman (2007), discussed later, see Virilio (1986, 2008), whose account

of the intersection of three-dimensional battle space and military speed will be revisited in the Interlude.

8. See Landler (2016a).

9. See, for instance, *Washington Post* columnist Charles Krauthammer's (2011) attack on Obama's foreign policy.

10. Quoted in Branch (2011, 216).

11. Barnett's writings sparked plenty of critical commentary in his day; see Bialasiewicz et al. (2007) for a summary, as well as Elden (2009); Keen (2012); S. Roberts, Secor, and Sparke (2003).

12. An additional important factor in the reluctance to enter Rwanda was the highly planned and extremely brutal killings of Belgian troops on the eve of the genocide. As Annan noted in his memoirs, "A senior Rwandan official later said of the plan to kill the Belgian peacekeepers that 'we watch CNN too, you know.'" Actively playing on the fears of casualties among interveners was, not for the last time, to be part of the strategy of the aggressor. See Annan and Mousavizadeh (2012).

13. For other advocates of "liberal empire" around the time of the Iraq invasion, see, e.g., N. Ferguson (2004) and R. Cooper (2002): see also Introduction.

14. Barnett (2004, 153).

15. Barnett (2004, 154).

16. For these developments, and the quote, see Ploch (2011).

17. Barnett ([2003] 2016, n.p.); italics in original.

18. See Keen (2012, 188) for the "medieval" example.

19. See Masco (2014, 187) on Barnett and counterterrorism; see Gregory (2011a) on the "everywhere war."

20. Barnett (2004, 49).

21. For an interesting anthropological discussion of global scenario thinkers, and the self-fulfilling nature of some of their interventions, see Hannerz (2015 and 2016).

22. See Roberts, Secor, and Sparke (2003) for the original argument around "neoliberal geopolitics."

23. On the shift from containment to "integration" under George W. Bush, see Elden (2009). On hybrid strategies incorporating elements of containment and integration under Obama, see Dueck (2015, 23).

24. Kaplan (1994, n.p.), also quoted in Elden (2009, 10).

25. AFRICOM's growing reach has for instance been criticized by air force insiders; see Branch (2011, 222).

26. See Burton (1856) for the full account.

27. Citations respectively from Dowden (2008, 90) and Fergusson (2013, 4).

28. Dowden (2008, 108). The hotel example he mentions is from the 1990s.

29. At the airport headquarters, the official noted, meetings with visitors involved a peculiar choreography of blatantly unequal security. If the visitor did not get clearance for entry to the camp, the UN official would sit inside an armored car parked beyond the compound gates while the visitor stood outside on the tarmac, speaking through the bullet-proof pane.

30. See comment piece by MSF's Unni Karunakara (2013).

31. Menkhaus (2010, 332).

32. Menkhaus (2010).

33. This included, among many other attacks, the helicopter assault force deployed to kill Saleh Ali Saleh Nabhan, who was involved in the 1998 US embassy attack in Kenya (Priest and Arkin 2012, 252).

34. For the full report, cited throughout this section, see Turse (2015).

35. Penney et al. (2018).

36. See a second *Intercept* report, Currier and Maass (2015).

37. On US involvement with warlords, see, e.g., Branch (2011, 220) on CIA support in the mid-2000s; as he notes, it is worth recalling the contested nature of US interventions, as the State Department protested this initiative. See also journalist Jeremy Scahill's documentary *Dirty Wars* (2013, dir. Richard Rowley).

38. The name has been changed.

39. Obama had envisioned equipping the CTPF with up to $5 billion "to train, build capacity and facilitate partner countries on the front lines." The CTPF in fiscal year 2015 included US$220 million for East Africa, principally related to training and support for AMISOM and Somalia's forces in the fight against al Shabaab; see US DoD (2015, 14).

40. See Bruton and Williams (2014, 3) for a brief discussion of the contested fatality counts.

41. Statements from interviews carried out in Addis Ababa with AU security and political officials in 2016.

42. Bruton and Williams (2014, 86).

43. See Journalists for Justice (2015) on the Kenya Defence Forces' alleged criminal trade in sugar and charcoal, and collusion via this trade with al Shabaab. The KDF has, unsurprisingly, denied the report; see Allison (2015). Subsequent UN reports found evidence of collusion via the charcoal trade; see Buchanan (2016).

44. For a discussion of *xeer*, see Issa-Salwe (1994); on pastoral democracy, see Lewis (1961).

45. De Waal (2015).

46. As De Waal (2017) notes, "Most of the [possibly 260,000] deaths could have been prevented if the Obama Administration had been more alert to a disaster caused by its decision to leave the Patriot Act untouched." For the broader argument on famine crimes, see De Waal (2008b).

47. See Weizman (2007, 11).

48. Mishra (2017, 248); Lindqvist (2001).

49. Quotations from Gregory (2011b, n.p.).

50. Mahmud (2011); see also Conclusion.

51. Menkhaus (2013, 71); Elden (2009, 103).

52. Mishra (2017, 248).

53. Whitehouse (2012, n.p.), citing Stephen Ellis.

54. See Burke (2017).

55. For a summary of recent positive and negative trends in Somalia, see the UN envoy Michael Keating's assessment as of September 2018 (Keating 2018).

56. Barnett (2004, 179).

57. Barnett (2004, 160).

INTERLUDE

1. Gusterson (2016, 41).

2. See Mutter (2015a) for the critique. On antidrone systems, see White's (2017) report from the London arms fair.

3. On UNHCR's surveillance UAVs, see UNHCR (2016). The UN insists on the term UUAV (unarmed UAV) because of how UAV has come to be associated with killing campaigns.

4. The term *militarized policing* was used in interview by a UN Department of Peacekeeping Operations official to describe the innovations of the Force Intervention Brigade in the Congo; see also Berdal and Ucko (2015).

5. Europa Press (2017).

6. On such terminology, see Hastings (2012b); also Power (2013).

7. Priest and Arkin (2012, 222).

8. Of course, the term *no go zone* has until quite recently tended to indicate an area set off by the military or public authorities, rather than an area supposedly dominated by insurgents or criminals.

9. Priest and Arkin (2012).

10. Gusterson (2016, 148–49).

11. Gusterson (2016, 130). Note, however, that US presidents have sought to launch military attacks without congressional approval well before drone strikes became commonplace. See C. Savage (2011) for an overview.

12. Chamayou (2015, 57).

13. Virilio (2008, 19).

14. Priest and Arkin (2012, 210).

15. Quoted in Gregory (2011b).

16. Gregory (2011b, 194); Virilio (1989).

17. Kaplan (2006, n.p.).

18. See Mutter (2015b), drawing on G. Shaw's (2010) notion of "playing war." Attempts to introduce bravery medals for drone operators have encountered stiff air force resistance; see Gusterson (2016).

19. Quotes from Gregory (2011b, 200 and 206).

20. Hastings (2012a, 15–16) lists the epithets.

21. Hastings (2010b).

22. Priest and Arkin (2012, 225, 227).

23. Priest and Arkin (2012, 236). As Niva (2013, 191) puts it: "The EXORD listed 15 nations and the types of operations (kill, capture or provide assistance) permitted under various scenarios, and it gave the pre-approvals required for JSOC to carry them out. Unlike the CIA, whose *covert* operations under Title 50 of the U.S. Code required congressional notification, JSOC's *clandestine* operations were governed by Title 10 of the U.S. Code governing traditional military activity, which relaxed this standard. In other words, JSOC was given the rare authority to select individuals for its kill list and then to kill or capture them without notification, which amounted to considerable executive authority."

24. Priest and Arkin (2012, 236).

25. McChrystal (2015, 24–25).

26. McChrystal (2015, 25).

27. McChrystal (2015, 251).

28. On the "Law," see N. Ferguson (2016). McChrystal borrowed readily from the strategist John Arquilla, whose writings include the influential *Networks and Netwars* (Arquilla and Ronfeldt 2001).

29. McChrystal (2015, 214 and 2018). Emphases in original.

30. Hersh quoted in Niva (2013, 191).

31. Scahill (2011).

32. JSOC was rumored to be at two bases inside the country, in Kismayo and Baledogle. See Turse (2015).

33. Hastings (2012a, 15).

34. For more on JSOC's operations, see Naylor (2015).

35. Hastings (2012a, 15–16); Scahill (2014).

36. Maguire (2015).

37. Chamayou (2015, 62); Gregory (2011b, 192).

38. In itself, this is nothing new, as we have already seen in the early colonial air wars. Today's laboratory for shadow drone warfare is the same "AfPak" borderland that the British used for advanced bombing campaigns in the interwar years. One colonial-era captain, a Sir John Bagot Glubb, thought aerial bombing of "semi-civilized" and "primitive races" held a "tremendous moral effect . . . largely due to the demoralization engendered in the tribesman by his feeling of helplessness and his inability to reply effectively to the attack." See Chamayou (2015, 62).

39. Chamayou (2015, 62; 77, quoting Gibson 2009).

40. Taussig (1993).

41. See AP (2017).

42. Scahill (2014, 104–5).

43. Flynn, Juergens, and Cantrell (2008, 58).

44. On the drone campaigns in Pakistan, see Kilcullen and Exum (2009). On blowback from counterterror, see Kilcullen (2009).

45. Scahill (2014, 107 and 175).

46. Hastings (2012a, 110).

47. On the business background of SCL and CA, see Doward and Gibbs (2017). In 2015, an article by a retired British commander praised the virtues of target audience analysis (TAA), which was being rolled out for NATO Strategic Communications (StratCom). TAA, he explained, would be "delivered by the UK company SCL, who have spent over $40 million and 25 years, developing this group behaviour prediction tool." See Tatham (2015, 51).

48. Doward and Gibbs (2017); Albright (2016a).

49. Albright (2016b, n.p.). Besides PsyOps, Cambridge Analytica built on trial runs in non-Western electioneering, including in Nigeria and the Caribbean, using, not for the first time, formerly colonized nations as a laboratory for bigger business in the homeland. See Cadwalladr (2018a).

50. Albright (2016a, n.p.).

51. On surveillance capitalism, see Zuboff (2017).

52. See George Monbiot's (2017) article on the shadow world of financing, with links to *Observer* and *Guardian* reports.

53. The exact link between Cambridge Analytica and the Canada-based AggregateIQ, involved in Nigeria as well as in the Brexit vote, is unconfirmed at time of writing; on the Nigeria campaign, see Cadwalladr (2018b).

54. See Channel 4's undercover investigations, "Exposed: Undercover Secrets of Trump's Data Firm," March 20, 2018, https://www.channel4.com/news /exposed-undercover-secrets-of-donald-trump-data-firm-cambridge-analytica.

55. Masco (2014) argues for a continuity between the "national security affect" stirred by especially the US government in times of Cold War nuclear fears, and the war on terror today. For the journalist's quote, see Moore (2017).

56. Sheckley (1953). For an intriguing analysis of *Watchbird* and security, see Maguire (2015).

57. "Hated in the Nation," *Black Mirror*, episode 6, Netflix, scripted by Charlie Brooker.

4. WOLVES AT THE DOOR

1. Cuttitta (2014).

2. The biopolitics of disease, othering, and migration is by now rather well documented; see, for instance, Fassin (2001) and Ticktin (2011).

3. A growing academic literature considers the conflict between border security, presented as a "silver bullet," and the structural factors influencing migration patterns, as well as the counterproductive effects of border enforcement itself. See, e.g., Massey, Pren, and Durand (2016); De Haas (2007); Cornelius et al. (2004); Andersson (2016a).

4. "Bridge" simplifies the different ways in which Braudel (1975) and Horden and Purcell (2000) highlighted historical human connectivity across what the latter authors called (in a timely link to our present) the "corrupting sea."

5. See Rutkowski et al. (2014) and Lemberg-Pedersen (2015).

6. See especially Vallet (2014). The *Washington Post* and the *Financial Times* give slightly different figures for the presence of walls worldwide; see Granados et al. (2016) and Greaves and Faunce (2017) respectively.

7. W. Brown (2010).

8. See, e.g., Jones (2016); Pallister-Wilkins (2015); Walters (2011); Vaughan-Williams (2015); Andersson (2014).

9. In other words, I am concerned here with the politics of fear on national and supranational scales, rather than on the local scale of Lampedusa, where migration has long been a regular feature of daily life. On the political fears, see media reports, e.g., L. Brown, Pickles, and Wyke (2015).

10. See Malkki (1995) on refugees in the "national order of things."

11. For more on border controls and otherness, see, e.g., Andersson (2014) and Musarò (2013).

12. On the "diseased heart of Africa" and biomedicine under colonialism, see Comaroff (1993, 305–6).

13. On Nazi Germany and wider usages of disease metaphors in genocide, see R. Savage (2007); also Bauman (1989).

14. Bashford (2006).

15. Yew (1980, 489). For a powerful cinematic rendering of this process of arrival, see Emanuele Crialese's *Nuovomondo* (2006).

16. The state's "monopolization of the legitimate means of movement" grew significantly from the time of the First World War onwards (Torpey 2000).

17. For a short and perceptive summary of this point—widely acknowledged in the academic literature on border controls and smuggling—see Bradol (2018), building on Médecins sans Frontières' long experience in border regions.

18. On the use of words such as *marauding* to describe migrants, see Shariat-madari (2015).

19. On the Canary Islands, see Mujica (2014). On Czech blogs about migration, see Koudelkova (2018). On the Hungarian prime minister's intervention, see Feher (2015).

20. If we include EU and returning migrants in the EU migration figure, the total is 4.7 million for 2015, the most recent year available; see Eurostat, Statistics Explained, "Migration and Migrant Population Statistics," http://ec.europa.eu/eurostat/statistics-explained/index.php/Migration_and_migrant_population_statistics.

21. For a review of evidence on terrorism, see Crisp (2017), paraphrased here. See Andersson (2016a) for other data on overall migration figures referenced here. See De Waal (2008a, 345) for citation on borders and health control, as

well as Bashford (2006). Ebola is a particularly apt example of the misalignment of disease vectors and migration, given that its rapid onset does not accord with the long-running trajectories of overland migrants.

22. On the budget, see Stone (2018); on the border guard increase, see "Juncker: EU Will Send Additional 10,000 Guards to Borders," BBC News, September 12, 2018, https://www.bbc.co.uk/news/world-europe-45492746.

23. De Genova (2002); Heyman (1995).

24. See DHS budget in brief at US DHS (2018). The percentages listed in the document correspond to the total budget authority of $77 billion, rather than to the adjusted net discretionary budget authority of $44 billion.

25. Massey, Pren, and Durand (2016).

26. Chebel d'Appollonia (2012).

27. CNN clip, "Update on CNN Cameraman with Ebola," October 6, 2014, uploaded to YouTube October 6, 2014, https://www.youtube.com/watch?v=aOMgenA56Ao.

28. See USDHS website, August 24, 2009, www.dhs.gov/alexander-garza.

29. Fox News clip, "Sen. Rob Schaaf Fears ISIS Will Infect Themselves with Ebola, Cross the Mexican Border into the U.S.," October 23, 2014, uploaded to YouTube October 24, 2014, https://www.youtube.com/watch?v=1BbggqYBFag.

30. See Santana (2014).

31. Killough (2014). On Trump's claims in the 2018 mid-term campaign, see Vazquez (2018).

32. Quotes and paraphrasings are from Douglas (2002, chap. 6, "Powers and Dangers"). The classic theorist of thresholds and rites of passage is Van Gennep (1909).

33. On the fakery argument, see news reports such as Herman (2015). On the tactics of ISIS, see Atran (2015), who writes: "The greater the reaction against Muslims in Europe and the deeper the west becomes involved in military action in the Middle East, the happier Isis leaders will be. Because this is about the organisation's key strategy: finding, creating and managing chaos." See also Bolt (2012) on terrorist tactics.

34. Though widely discussed, this accusation has so far been rather hard to back up via solid evidence—difficult, we may add, in part because of the remote interventions in the "danger zones" of Syria. See "Migrant Crisis: Russia and Syria 'weaponising' migration," BBC News, March 2, 2016, https://www.bbc.co.uk/news/world-europe-35706238.

35. W. Brown (2010, 109).

36. Schwartz (2018). Hans Lucht's insights into Trump's psychology, conveyed during the manuscript review, have proven very helpful for this passage. The germ example, also mentioned to me by Lucht, has been reported, e.g., by *Newsweek* (Sinclair 2017). See Guarino's (2017) report in the *Washington Post* report for the elevator example.

37. This paragraph is based on interviews with high border officials in both the United States and Europe between 2010 and 2016. On epidemiological models in criminology, see Rose (2007) and Andersson (2018); on preemptive controls of disease in relation to border security, see Bashford (2006). On Frontex risk analysis, see Andersson (2014).

38. On different kinds of bordering—risk-based versus sealing off, to put it crudely—see especially the comprehensive work of Bigo (2014) on different "universes" of border control. While he argues that different kinds of border professionals perceive the border respectively as "solid," "liquid" and "gaseous," militarized risk-based policing of the kind described here in the US case clearly straddles these categories.

39. See De León (2015) on the "land of open graves"; Williams (2016) on the Border Patrol's monopolization of rescues; and the report by Coalición de Derechos Humanos and No More Deaths (2016) on the Border Patrol's documented practice of destroying water tanks put out in the desert by activists.

40. Quantitative analyses of deterrence policies carried out internally by the Department of Homeland Security show that "border enforcement build-up did not have a big impact" on the drop in Mexican irregular migration into the United States, as one analyst summarized it in a meeting I attended in 2015.

41. On the humanitarian-security nexus, see Andersson (2017); Pallister-Wilkins (2015); Williams (2016).

42. The problem with the Frontex trainers was said to stem from "administrative problems," yet as officials noted, if the agency had wanted a ground presence it could still have sent officers for visits.

43. On the tensions within NATO and a sober "insider" assessment of the mission's problems, see Engelbrekt, Mohlin, and Wagnsson (2014); for a reporter's view, see Hilsum (2013).

44. See Greenhill (2011) on "weapons of mass migration."

45. Donadio (2009).

46. For more on mercenaries and lynchings, see Engelbrekt, Mohlin, and Wagnsson (2014) and Hilsum (2013).

47. Crawley et al. (2016, 8).

48. "IOM Learns of 'Slave Market' Conditions Endangering Migrants in North Africa," International Organization for Migration press release, April 11, 2017, https://www.iom.int/news/iom-learns-slave-market-conditions-endangering-migrants-north-africa. IOM's reports from the region often need to be treated with caution, however, given its long-standing role as "service provider" for Western donor governments; see Brachet (2015) for a critical academic assessment of their Libya operations. For reports highlighting the inhuman conditions in Libyan detention, see, e.g., HRW (2017) and Amnesty International (2015). For in-depth ethnographic studies, see Achtnich (2017) and Lucht (2012).

49. On Italian surveillance and security resources in Libya after Gaddafi, see Antonio Mazzeo's blog, http://antoniomazzeoblog.blogspot.it/. On the failures—widely predicted beforehand—of EUNAVFOR-Med, see, e.g., House of Lords (2017).

50. For instance, one Libyan navy officer, interviewed by my colleague, had hardly heard of the EU mission, describing its effects as "intangible."

51. UNSC (2015, 35). For more on the accusations against the security contractor, see, e.g., Intelligence Online; "Argus in Conflict with Former Libyan Advisor," May 27, 2015, https://www.intelligenceonline.com/corporate-intelligence_the-red-line/2015/05/27/argus-in-conflict-with-former-libyan-advisor,108075208-ART, and the Stop Wapenhandel website at http://stopwapenhandel.org /node/1736.

52. See, for instance, Obert (2017) as well as Wintour (2018) on the UN asset freeze against "a former militia leader, Abd Al Rahman al-Milad, who is the head of the EU-funded regional unit of the Libyan coastguard in Zawiyah." Beyond the coast guards, Libya's notorious migrant detention centers may have been notionally under the control of Libya's Department for Combating Illegal Migration but were in practice run with heavy militia involvement. See Refugees International (2017).

53. See Gros-Verheyde (2015).

54. In the Spanish reception centers of Ceuta and Melilla, to give one example, residents could not leave until their TB tests—inked on their upper arms—had been given the all-clear. Claims about diseased migrants were however readily disproven by the center's doctor, who correctly pointed out that the young men and women arriving in the enclave after long trans-Saharan journeys were more fit and healthy on average than the local population. See Andersson (2014).

55. On the border as spectacle, see especially De Genova (2002); also Andreas (2000) and Andersson (2014).

56. The names have been changed.

57. See Kleist and Thorsen (2016) on migratory geographies of hope; also Lawson (2007).

58. On *communitas,* see Turner (1974); compare Andersson (2014) for another such case among Ceuta's migrants.

59. One reception center worker called Germany's new detention facilities "black boxes." "The local population isn't allowed to go inside," he told the *Guardian,* "so they project all their greatest fear into what is going on inside them. . . . Now there is only fear of refugees" (Oltermann 2018).

5. THE SNAKE MERCHANTS

1. Rapaille (2004) in an interview for *Frontline,* included in the PBS documentary *The Persuaders* (2004).

2. Quotations here are from Peretti (2017).

3. Quoted in an Alternet report (Holloway 2015).

4. Peretti (2017).

5. The name has been changed.

6. "Hans Rosling on Global Income Disparity (and Snowballs)," BBC News-night, January 22, 2015, YouTube, https://www.youtube.com/watch?v=DoSTNRhoceY; on Danish TV, "Hans Rosling: Don't Use News Media to Understand the World," DR Nyheder, September 4, 2015, YouTube, https://www.youtube.com/watch?v=xYnpJGaMiXo. The term *bottom billion* was coined by economist Paul Collier; see Introduction.

7. Rosling (2018).

8. Bremmer (2016).

9. On debt distress, see Kpodo (2018). On how resource transfers *out of* Africa are outpacing inflows (including of aid and investment), see Hickel (2017).

10. UK DfID (2005, 8).

11. Forsyth (2014).

12. BBC report, "UK Aid Can Help Deter Mediterranean Migrants, Says Fallon," June 21, 2015, www.bbc.co.uk/news/uk-33215266.

13. European Commission, "President Juncker Launches the EU Emergency Trust Fund to Tackle Root Causes of Irregular Migration in Africa," press release, November 12, 2015, http://europa.eu/rapid/press-release_IP-15-6055_en.htm.

14. Wintour (2018).

15. Searing critique of member state direction was voiced to me directly by a UK Foreign Office official in 2018 but was also well noted elsewhere. For the quote, paraphrasing reports from the EU and British Members of the European Parliament, see Wintour (2018).

16. For more on the Partnership Framework, see EC (2016); on the Trust Fund, see European Commission, "Emergency Trust Fund for Africa," https://ec.europa.eu/trustfundforafrica/. On why economic development may increase migration, see De Haas (2007). On development funds for border security, see Andersson (2014) and Frowd (2014).

17. On the proliferation of security (as discourse and as "apparatus"), see Maguire, Frois, and Zurawski (2014); Masco (2014).

18. Some scholars have now reversed the term to instead talk about the "developmentization of security," which seems to indicate that this literature has come of age. See Pugh, Gabay, and Williams (2013).

19. See Goldstein (2010) on security discourse and its links to neoliberalism, going beyond 9/11; see Gupta (2015) on poverty as threat in the postwar era; compare Escobar (1995) for a classic critique of Truman-era development (itself criticized as in need of nuance by, e.g., Mosse 2004).

20. For more on the US framing of African "problems," including the Biden quotation, see McGreal (2014).

21. USAID, "Branding," www.usaid.gov/branding. The final quotation here is from the draft "3D Planning Guide" (USAID 2012).

22. For this example and that of the previous paragraph, see US National Security Strategies of 1987 and 2010 respectively (Reagan 1987; Obama 2010).

23. The transcript is now unavailable on the USAID website. On Trump's rebrand, see Ainsley, Volz, and Cooke (2017).

24. Kaplan (1994, n.p.). On the fluid lines between being "risky" and "at risk," see Aradau (2004).

25. In Mali, the creation of a European migration management center was a catalyst for this explosion; see Andersson (2014).

26. These examples are relayed in more detail in Andersson (2014).

27. See Benmehdi (2014).

28. Soudan (2017).

29. Bayart and Ellis (2000).

30. Boffey (2018).

31. UNEP (2011, 65).

32. On the Wall project's problematic assumptions around desertification and how to "fight" it, see Laestadius (2017).

33. Quotation (my italics) from "World Leaders Renew Commitment to Strengthen Climate Resilience through Africa's Great Green Wall," UNCCD News, February 12, 2015, www2.unccd.int/news-events/world-leaders-renew-commitment-strengthen-climate-resilience-through-africas-great. See also Filipovic (2017).

34. On the RSF, see, e.g., the report "Sudan's RSF Arrests 64 Illegal Migrants Near Libyan Border," *Sudan Tribune*, January 25, 2017, www.sudantribune.com/spip.php?article61475.

35. On the original Niger bid, see Fick (2016). On the EU aid announcement, see "EU Will Support Niger with Assistance of €1 Billion by 2020," European Commission press release, December 13, 2017, https://ec.europa.eu/europeaid/news-and-events/eu-will-support-niger-assistance-eu1-billion-2020_en. On Macron's visit, see Fagan (2017).

36. On the Italians, see Kington (2017).

37. ODI (2016, 11).

38. See Andersson (2014) for a discussion of Morocco and Mauritania.

39. H. Cooper, Shear, and Searcey (2017).

40. See Keen (2017) for an authoritative report on how Western states' war-on-terror framework has "played into the hands" of al-Assad and jihadists alike.

41. On Gaddafi's active collusion in the Reagan-era branding of him, see Adam Curtis's documentary *Hypernormalisation* (2016).

42. The UN human rights chief called Libyan detention an "outrage to humanity" in November 2017; see "Libya's Detention of Migrants 'Is an Outrage to Humanity,' Says UN Human Rights Chief Zeid," UN News, November 14, 2017,

https://news.un.org/en/story/2017/11/636022-libyas-detention-migrants-outrage-humanity-says-un-human-rights-chief-zeid. In May 2018, migrants from Niger sued Italy over coordination with the Libyans; see Scherer (2018), mentioning the "hell" reference. The legal discussions on Europe's culpability under international law, as funder and supporter of the Libyans taking people back to their shores against *non-refoulement* principles, are ongoing; see Frei (2018).

43. See Keen and Andersson (2018) for an analysis of these dynamics using the "games" metaphor (rather than the market lens deployed here).

44. Kingsley (2015).

45. For a comparative historical perspective on propaganda of the deed in nineteenth-century Europe and in jihadist violence today, see Bolt (2012).

46. Jenkins (2016).

47. On sports and streakers, see Osgood (2016).

48. Shelton (2013).

49. On "holistic" approaches to war, see Shelton (2013). For the CNN comment piece cited throughout this section, see McChrystal and Talbert-Slagle (2014).

50. As Hastings (2012a, 71) notes, McChrystal took his cue from Petraeus's cultivation of the media in presenting his strategy after 2009 as new when in fact "every general for the past five years has claimed to be doing a counterinsurgency strategy."

51. Sontag (1991, 67).

52. Elden (2009, 17–18).

53. See Gregory (2011c, 204–5), quoting Caldwell and Hagerott (2010), on how this "biopolitics" justified the taking of civilian lives.

54. Kilcullen (2009, 35).

55. Martin (1994, 52–53). Already in the 1960s, a militarized vision of the immune system was present in an arterial submarine sent to rescue a Soviet defector, as Martin notes, yet the panic around AIDS enabled a wealth of depictions specifically of the "body at war."

56. Sontag (1991, 140).

57. Sontag (1991, 148, 178).

58. See, e.g., Politi (2017).

59. Rainey (2014), referencing "emotional resilience."

60. On the UN resilience-building approach in the Sahel, see "Common UN Approach on Resilience Building in the Sahel, September 2012," UN update, October 19, https://reliefweb.int/report/mali/common-un-approach-resilience-building-sahel-september-2012.

61. In USAID in Washington, I was told aid staff stayed away from using the term *resilience* in relation to security and countering violent extremism, only to hear *resiliency* pop out of the mouth of one of the CVE officers as soon as we started talking.

62. De Weijer (2013), who also makes the point in the following sentence.

63. For a critique of any "disciplining" function of resilience in creating supposed "neoliberal subjects," see Chandler (2014). Compare McNeill (2017) on the limited "biopolitical" objectives of US operations in Africa.

64. Haslan (2016, 155–56).

65. UNDP (2017) and Wintour (2017).

66. On impunity in the war on terror, see, e.g., Keen (2012).

67. McChrystal (2016).

68. Quoted in Scahill (2014, 104).

69. Duffield (2001, 4–5). In other words, Duffield argues that the "strategic complexes" of global liberal governance have fomented a "subordinating social relationship" rather than a complete closing of the door.

70. See L. Price (2017); as he notes, the British strategy eventually shifted away from a "headhunt" to an epidemiological and sanitation-based model, a conclusion of relevance to our previous sections on epidemiological thinking. On the "Cobra effect," see Siebert (2001).

71. The rat story summarized here is based on Vann (2003). Thanks to David Keen for mentioning the Cobra and Rat effects to me.

72. Keen (2012).

6. WHERE THE WILD THINGS ARE

1. Sendak (1963).

2. Allen (2007). For a postcolonial and psychological analysis of Kipling in India, see Nandy (1995).

3. As reported in the BBC documentary *Kipling's Indian Adventure* (2016, dir. Christopher Walker), www.bbc.co.uk/programmes/b071xz0p.

4. Quote from the prologue to Self (2013).

5. Virilio (2008, 12, 30).

6. Abrams (2014, 281).

7. Abrams (2014, 316).

8. Debord ([1955] 2006).

9. Brassfield (2016).

10. Rasmussen (2016).

11. See Landler (2016b).

12. This section draws on a longer paper in progress (Weigand and Andersson forthcoming). The online survey was qualitative and nonrandomized, complementing field research and interviews in February-March 2016.

13. Rasmussen (2016).

14. See, e.g., Fast (2014); Collinson and Duffield (2013); Avant (2007); Andersson and Weigand (2015).

15. Many workers criticized the dangerous lack of holistic thinking. As one respondent said: "While [the security measures] are based on a hard security

approach they often do not interlink at all with other efforts at 'securing' a location, including considerations about the location of the compound, soft security-type engagement with locals and the neighborhood, etc." Meanwhile, some respondents found themselves without holistic approaches in another sense, as their "acceptance-based" NGOs failed to provide any security arrangements at all—the other side of the coin to the bunkering in focus here.

16. See Safi (2018b).

17. Reports of collusion between local security providers and warlords were rife: Roston (2009), cited here, estimated that at least 10 percent of the Pentagon's logistical contracts in Afghanistan were used for paying insurgents. Elsewhere, UK-based security companies shared rumors with me of how less scrupulous competitors were accused of stoking threats to stay in business, for instance in the piracy-hit "high-risk" area off Somalia's coastline.

18. One chief executive, interviewed in London in 2016, noted how far the sector had come since the dark days of the early Iraq invasion, when he himself as a British force commander in Basra would not have contemplated going anywhere near the Blackwater-type outfits that wreaked havoc among Iraqi civilians.

19. See analysis in Graham-Harrison (2017).

20. Nordland (2017).

21. Nordland (2017).

22. Stewart (2004, 26), whose book is also the source of earlier citations in this section.

23. On tourism in danger zones, see Lisle (2016).

24. Hastings (2010a).

25. Hastings (2010a, n.p.).

26. The name has been changed.

27. As one initiative noted, "Few news organizations provide comprehensive safety support to the freelancers and stringers from which they commission stories." See Cantenys (2018).

28. On the refusal of freelance stories from Syria, see Goulding (2013). In an interview, Sune Engel Rasmussen told me about editors' increasing demands that reporters filing from Afghanistan undergo risk training.

29. See Refsdal (2011).

30. Report by Global Investigative Journalism Network (Klein and Plaut 2017).

31. Safi (2018a).

32. Rasmussen (2017).

33. See *Serval: Quand l'armée filme la guerre* (2016, dir. Martin Blanchard), YouTube, https://www.youtube.com/watch?v=Ky--yxARl6A.

34. The First Gulf War "did not take place," as French philosopher Jean Baudrillard memorably put it. See M. Shaw (2005) for a historical discussion.

35. R. Cooper (2002, n.p.). While Cooper distinguished "postmodern," "modern," and "pre-modern" (failed) states in his analysis, his "jungle" exhortation has

been taken up by authors seeing it as exemplary of the war on terror in particular; see Elden (2009) and Keen (2012).

36. See Scahill (2011).

37. Hastings (2012a).

38. Priest and Arkin (2012, 228).

39. Priest and Arkin (2012, 223–24).

40. On the rationales for violence in Liberia, see Ellis (1999).

41. Priest and Arkin (2012, 240); Hastings (2012a, 76).

42. Blake (2017).

43. McCann (2017).

44. Atran (2015a, n.p.) and his speech at the UN (2015b).

45. Atran (2015a, n.p.).

46. Quotations here are from Stewart (2012). See also Frankopan (2015) on the British-Russian "Great Game."

47. Stewart (2004, 247–48).

48. Thanks to Hans Lucht for making this perceptive point.

49. Dawson (1994, 1).

50. Mishra (2017).

51. Quoted in Biedler (2016, 3).

52. Laplanche and Pontalis (2004, 349).

CONCLUSION

1. In 1902, the British economist John A. Hobson explained how to resolve the dilemmas of militarism at little cost—by using "lower races" instead of working-class Britons in imperial wars. Yet he also warned that this form of "outsourcing" (to use today's term) "enhances the risks of wars, which become more frequent and more barbarous in proportion as they involve to a less degree the lives of Englishmen." See Chamayou (2015, 187–88). Quotes on the "threefold frontier" earlier in this section are from Mahmud (2011).

2. BBC *Panorama* investigation, December 2017, summarized in Cook and Kemp (2017).

3. I discuss some of these examples (climate and drugs) and their shared logics with migration controls in Andersson (2016a), and jointly with David Keen in Keen and Andersson (2018); on privatization, see, e.g., Monbiot (2018).

4. On innovations at MSF, see Neuman and Weissman (2016).

5. Another example of academic risk transfer concerns the onerous "ethics" protocols being instituted at universities, whose main purpose is mitigating institutional risk exposure and liability.

6. See Sahelien.com, "Mali: À Razelma, l'école a repris grâce au soutien communautaire," video reportage, posted on YouTube March 28, 2018, https://www.youtube.com/watch?v=55SqqU3XESQ.

7. For a summary of recent developments, see UN Department of Peacekeeping Operations, "Strengthening Peacekeeping Requires Collective Action, UN Official Tells Security Council," press release, September 12, 2018, https://peacekeeping.un.org/en/un-news/strengthening-peacekeeping-requires-collective-action-un-official-tells-security-council.

8. Eriksen (2016).

9. Kaplan (2012).

10. See, for instance, Ronald Reagan's Election Eve discourse of 1980 (Reagan 1980). Compare Kristol and Kagan (1996).

11. Wa Thiong'o (2016, 91–92).

12. Atran (2015, n.p.).

13. In Niger, locals complained to reporters about the self-serving economic and strategic interests of the Americans. See Penney (2018).

14. See Frankopan (2015).

15. On how fear has been invoked as a productive force in opposed strands of political life—from liberalism and conservatism to the post-Holocaust writings of Hannah Arendt—see Robin (2004a, 2004b). Compare chapter 2, as well as Nussbaum's (2018) more recent take on fear across the political spectrum. Largely in agreement with such authors, I for one have doubts about the usefulness of fear for a more positive political project, rather putting emphasis in this brief conclusion on the need for new narratives building on other emotions and frames (besides the obvious need for more fundamental structural and policy changes). See also Appendix.

AN ANTHROPOLOGICAL APPENDIX

1. Fassin (2011).

2. On anthropology and emotions, see Beatty (2014). Emotions are of increasing interest across the social sciences, though my focus here is on outreach rather than on emotions as an empirical topic. We should also note that I talk about "emotions" rather loosely here for the sake of a fluent read, rather than following Han (2017) in distinguishing emotion, feeling, and affect.

3. Shapiro (2005).

4. This idea is David Keen's, whom as always I remain hugely indebted to.

5. McCarthy (2015).

6. The political "relevance" of anthropology continued in this sense into the Cold War era; see D. Price (2016).

7. E.g., Rabinow (1977). Recently, interest in narration is clearly growing; see, e.g., Beatty (2009). However, while Beatty posits a distinction between narrative and systemic approaches, *No Go World* seeks to conjoin the two, as noted in this appendix.

8. Eriksen (2006, 1).

9. There are many exceptions, from migration to high finance and beyond, too numerous to mention here, but see Gusterson (2013) for reflections on anthropology's public role and Besteman and Gusterson (2005) for an example of it.

10. Robben (2010).

11. Eriksen (2006, 21).

12. Ingold (2016).

13. Forte (2011).

14. Ingold (2014).

15. Kovats-Bernat (2002, 211).

16. For a compelling critique of systemic perspectives in Foucauldian studies of power, see Walters (2012).

17. De Certeau (1984).

WORKS CITED

Abrams, David. 2014. *Fobbit*. London: Vintage.

Achtnich, Marthe. 2017. Mobility in crisis: Sub-Saharan migrants' journeys through Libya and Malta. PhD diss., University of Oxford.

Action on Armed Violence. 2018. The burden of harm: Monitoring explosive violence in 2017. Report. https://aoav.org.uk/wp-content/uploads/2018/04/Explosive-Violence-Monitor-2017-v6.pdf.

Ainsley, Julia Edwards, Dustin Volz, and Kristina Cooke. 2017. Exclusive: Trump to focus counter-extremism program solely on Islam. Reuters, February 1. www.reuters.com/article/us-usa-trump-extremists-program-exclusiv/exclusive-trump-to-focus-counter-extremism-program-solely-on-islam-sources-idUSKBN15G5VO.

Albright, Jonathan. 2016a. #Election2016: Propaganda-lytics & weaponized shadow tracking. Medium.com, November 22. https://medium.com/@d1gi/election2016-propaganda-lytics-weaponized-shadow-trackers-a6c9281f5ef9.

———. 2016b. What's missing from the Trump election equation? Let's start with military-grade psyops. Medium.com, November 11. https://medium.com/@d1gi/whats-missing-from-the-trump-election-equation-let-s-start-with-military-grade-psyops-fa22090c8c17.

Allen, Charles. 2007. *Kipling Sahib: India and the Making of Rudyard Kipling, 1865–1900*. London: Abacus.

Allison, Simon. 2015. Think again: Who profits from Kenya's war in Somalia? Institute for Security Studies, December 7. https://issafrica.org/iss-today /think-again-who-profits-from-kenyas-war-in-somalia.

Amnesty International. 2015. "Libya is full of cruelty": Stories of abduction, sexual violence and abuse from migrants and refugees. Amnesty International, May. https://www.amnesty.org/download/Documents/MDE1915782015ENGLISH .pdf.

Andersson, Ruben. 2014. *Illegality, Inc.: Clandestine Migration and the Business of Bordering Europe*. Oakland: University of California Press.

———. 2016a. Europe's failed "fight" against irregular migration: Ethnographic notes on a counterproductive industry. *Journal of Ethnic and Migration Studies* 42 (7): 1055–75.

———. 2016b. Here be dragons: Mapping an ethnography of global danger. *Current Anthropology* 57 (6): 707–31.

———. 2017. Rescued and caught: The humanitarian-security nexus at Europe's frontiers. In *The Borders of "Europe": Autonomy of Migration, Tactics of Bordering,* edited by Nicholas De Genova, 64–94. Durham, NC: Duke University Press.

———. 2018. Profits and predation in the human bioeconomy. *Public Culture* 30 (3): 413–39.

Andersson, Ruben, and Florian Weigand. 2015. Intervention at risk: The vicious cycle of distance and danger in Mali and Afghanistan. *Journal of Intervention and Statebuilding* 9 (4): 519–41.

Andreas, Peter. 2000. *Border Games: Policing the US-Mexico Divide*. Ithaca, NY: Cornell University Press.

Annan, Kofi A., and Nader Mousavizadeh. 2012. *Interventions: A Life in War and Peace*. New York: Penguin Press.

AP (Associated Press). 2017. Michael Flynn to disclose advisory role linked to Cambridge Analytica. *Guardian,* August 4. www.theguardian.com /us-news/2017/aug/04/michael-flynn-cambridge-analytica-disclosure.

Appadurai, Arjun. 2011. The ghost in the financial machine. *Public Culture* 23 (3): 517–39.

Aradau, Claudia. 2004. The perverse politics of four-letter words: Risk and pity in the securitisation of human trafficking. *Millennium* 33 (2): 251–77.

Ardener, Edwin. [1987] 2012. "Remote areas": Some theoretical considerations. *HAU: Journal of Ethnographic Theory* 2 (1): 519–33.

Arquilla, John, and David F. Ronfeldt. 2001. *Networks and Netwars: The Future of Terror, Crime, and Militancy*. Santa Monica, CA: Rand.

Asher, Michael. 2008. *Sands of Death: An Epic Tale of Massacre and Survival in the Sahara*. London: Phoenix.

Atran, Scott. 2015a. Mindless terrorists? The truth about Isis is much worse. *Guardian,* November 15. www.theguardian.com/commentisfree/2015/nov/15 /terrorists-isis

———. 2015b. Scott Atran on youth, violent extremism and promoting peace. Speech to the UN Security Council, April 23. *Neuroanthropology* (blog), April 25. http://blogs.plos.org/neuroanthropology/2015/04/25/scott-atran-on-youth-violent-extremism-and-promoting-peace/.

Augé, Marc. 1995. *Non-places: Introduction to an Anthropology of Supermodernity.* London: Verso.

Autesserre, Séverine. 2014. *Peaceland: Conflict Resolution and the Everyday Politics of International Intervention.* Cambridge: Cambridge University Press.

Avant, Deborah. 2007. NGOs, corporations and security transformation in Africa. *International Relations* 21 (2): 143–61.

Barber, Peter, and Tom Harper. 2010. *Magnificent Maps: Power, Propaganda and Art.* London: British Library.

Barnett, Thomas P. M. [2003] 2016. Why the Pentagon changes its maps. *Esquire,* September. www.esquire.com/news-politics/a1546/thomas-barnett-iraq-war-primer/.

———. 2004. *The Pentagon's New Map: War and Peace in the Twenty-First Century.* New York: G. P. Putnam's Sons.

Bashford, Alison, ed. 2006. *Medicine at the Border: Disease, Globalization, and Security, 1850 to the Present.* Basingstoke: Palgrave Macmillan.

Bauman, Zygmunt. 1989. *Modernity and the Holocaust.* Ithaca, NY: Cornell University Press.

Bayart, Jean-François, and Stephen Ellis. 2000. Africa in the world: A history of extraversion. *African Affairs* 99 (395): 217–67.

Beatty, Andrew. 2009. *A Shadow Falls: In the Heart of Java.* London: Faber and Faber.

———. 2014. Anthropology and emotion. *Journal of the Royal Anthropological Institute* 20 (3): 545–63.

Beck, Ulrich. 1999. *World Risk Society.* Cambridge: Polity Press.

Benmehdi, Hassan. 2014. Mali: Morocco, Mali to boost agricultural collaboration. *Magharebia,* April 25. Republished by AllAfrica. http://allafrica.com/stories/201404282480.html.

Bensaad, Ali. 2005. Le Sahara, vecteur de mondialisation. *Maghreb-Machrek* 185:7–12.

Berdal, Mats, and David H. Ucko. 2015. The use of force in UN peacekeeping operations: Problems and prospects. *RUSI Journal* 160 (1): 6–12.

Bergamaschi, Isaline. 2014. The fall of a donor darling: The role of aid in Mali's crisis. *Journal of Modern African Studies* 52 (3): 347–78.

Besteman, Catherine Lowe, and Hugh Gusterson. 2005. *Why America's Top Pundits Are Wrong: Anthropologists Talk Back.* Berkeley: University of California Press.

Bialasiewicz, Luiza, David Campbell, Stuart Elden, Stephen Graham, Alex Jeffrey, and Alison J. Williams. 2007. Performing security: The imaginative geographies of current US strategy. *Political Geography* 26:405–22.

Biedler, Philip D. 2016. *Beautiful War: Studies in a Dreadful Fascination.* Tuscaloosa: University of Alabama Press.

Bigo, Didier. 2014. The (in)securitization practices of the three universes of EU border control: Military/navy—border guards/police—database analysts. *Security Dialogue* 45 (3): 209–25.

Billé, Frank. 2017. Introduction: Speaking Volumes. *Cultural Anthropology* website, October 24. https://culanth.org /fieldsights/1241-introduction-speaking-volumes.

Biltcliffe, Pippa. 2005. Walter Crane and the Imperial Federation Map showing the extent of the British Empire (1886). *Imago Mundi* 57:63–69.

Blake, Matt. 2017. British man and two Americans killed fighting Isis in Syria. *Guardian*, July 11. https://www.theguardian.com/uk-news/2017/jul/11 /british-man-luke-rutter-killed-fighting-isis-in-syria.

Boahen, A. Adu. 1964. *Britain, the Sahara, and the Western Sudan, 1788–1861.* Oxford: Clarendon Press.

Boffey, Daniel. 2018. Isis trying to foment a wave of migration to Europe, says UN official. *Guardian*, April 26. www.theguardian.com/world/2018/apr /26/isis-trying-to-foment-a-wave-of-migration-to-europe-says-un-official.

Boisvert, Marc-André. 2012. Mali: The unexpected crisis, a year later. . . . Mats Utas blog, December 12. https://matsutas.wordpress.com/2012/12/31 /mali-the-unexpected-crisis-a-year-later-guest-post-by-marc-andre-boisvert/.

Bolt, Neville. 2012. *The Violent Image: Insurgent Propaganda and the New Revolutionaries.* London: Hurst.

Borges, Jorge Luis. 1998. *Collected Fictions.* Translated by Andrew Hurley. Harmondsworth: Allen Lane.

Brachet, Julien. 2009. *Migrations transsahariennes: Vers un désert cosmopolite et morcelé (Niger).* Paris: Croquant.

———. 2015. Beyond war and peace: The IOM and international migration control in Libya. Working Paper 124, International Migration Institute, University of Oxford. https://www.imi-n.org/publications/beyond-war-and-peace-the-iom-and-international-migration-control-in-libya.

Brachet, Julien, and Judith Scheele. 2019. *The Value of Disorder: Autonomy, Prosperity, and Plunder in the Chadian Sahara.* Cambridge: Cambridge University Press.

Bradol, Jean-Hervé. 2018. The state: From sieve to smuggler. Médecins sans Frontières, September 10. www.msf-crash.org/en/node/5516. Originally published as "Les passeurs sont le plus souvent des fonctionnaires et non de mystérieux criminels," *Le Monde*, September 10.

Branch, Adam. 2011. *Displacing Human Rights: War and Intervention in Northern Uganda.* Oxford: Oxford University Press.

Brassfield, Melanie. 2016. $100k security contracting jobs for veterans. *G.I. Jobs.* www.gijobs.com/contracting-jobs-for-veterans-overseas/.

Braudel, Fernand. 1975. *The Mediterranean and the Mediterranean World in the Age of Philip II.* London: Fontana.

Bremmer, Ian. 2016. These 5 facts explain the good news about Africa. *Time,* March 3. http://time.com/4246821/these-5-facts-explain-the-good-news-about-africa/.

Brown, Larisa, Kate Pickles, and Tom Wyke. 2015. Northern Italian towns are ordered to stop accepting migrants because the situation "is like a bomb ready to go off," as 6,000 refugees are rescued in one weekend desperately trying to reach Europe. *Daily Mail,* updated June 9. www.dailymail.co.uk /news/article-3115235/Northern-Italian-towns-ordered-stop-accepting-migrants-situation-like-bomb-ready-6–000-refugees-rescued-one-weekend-desperately-trying-reach-Europe.html.

Brown, Wendy. 2010. *Walled States, Waning Sovereignty.* New York: Zone Books.

Bruton, Bronwyn E., and Paul D. Williams. 2014. *Counterinsurgency in Somalia: Lessons Learned from the African Union Mission in Somalia, 2007–2013.* MacDill, FL: Joint Special Operations University Press.

Buchanan, Elsa. 2016. UN report finds Kenya still funding al-Shabaab terror group through illegal sugar and charcoal trade. *International Business Times,* updated November 8. www.ibtimes.co.uk/un-report-finds-kenya-still-funding-al-shabaab-terror-group-through-illegal-sugar-charcoal-trade-1590462.

Burgis, Tom. 2015. *The Looting Machine: Warlords, Tycoons, Smugglers, and the Systematic Theft of Africa's Wealth.* London: William Collins.

Burke, Jason. 2017. Somalia bombing may have been revenge for botched US-led operation. *Guardian,* October 17. www.theguardian.com/world /2017/oct/17/somalia-bomber-was-ex-solider-whose-town-was-raided-by-us-forces.

Burnett, D. Graham. 2000. *Masters of All They Surveyed: Exploration, Geography, and a British El Dorado.* Chicago: University of Chicago Press.

Burton, Richard Francis. 1856. *First Footsteps in East Africa; or, an Exploration of Harar.* London: Longman.

Cadwalladr, Carole. 2018a. Cambridge Analytica's ruthless bid to sway the vote in Nigeria. *Guardian,* March 21. https://www.theguardian.com/uk-news /2018/mar/21/cambridge-analyticas-ruthless-bid-to-sway-the-vote-in-nigeria.

———. 2018b. Revealed: Graphic video used by Cambridge Analytica to influence Nigerian election. *Guardian,* April 4. https://www.theguardian .com/uk-news/2018/apr/04/

cambridge-analytica-used-violent-video-to-try-to-influence-nigerian-election.

Caillié, Réné. [1830] 1992. *Travels through Central Africa to Timbuctoo; and across the Great Desert to Morocco; Performed in the Years 1824–1828.* London: Darf.

Caldwell, W., and M. Hagerott. 2010. Curing Afghanistan. *Foreign Policy,* April 7. www.foreignpolicy.com/articles/2010/04/07/curing_afghanistan.

Campbell, Bradley, and David Conrad, prod. 2014. If you follow US travel warnings, "Out of Africa" is more a strategy than a summer read. Public Radio International, July 8. https://www.pri.org/stories/2014–07–07/us-travel-warnings-out-africa-more-strategy-summer-read.

Cantenys, Maria. 2018. Journalism needs freelancers, and freelancers need protection. Open Society Foundations, February 23. https://www.open societyfoundations.org/voices/journalism-needs-freelancers-and-freelancers-need-protection.

Cep, Casey N. 2014. The allure of the map. *New Yorker,* January 22.

Chamayou, Grégoire. 2015. *Drone Theory.* London: Penguin.

Chambers, Robert. 1835. *A Biographical Dictionary of Eminent Scotsmen.* Vol. 3. Glasgow: Blackie and Son.

Chandler, David. 2014. *Resilience: The Governance of Complexity.* London: Routledge.

Chandrasekaran, Rajiv. 2006. *Imperial Life in the Emerald City: Inside Baghdad's Green Zone.* London: Bloomsbury.

Charbonneau, Bruno. 2014. The imperial legacy of international peacebuilding: The case of francophone Africa. *Review of International Studies* 40 (3): 607–30.

Chebel d'Appollonia, Ariane. 2012. *Frontiers of Fear: Immigration and Insecurity in the United States and Europe.* Ithaca, NY: Cornell University Press.

Clarke, Joe Sandler. 2015. Sex abuse poses "significant risk" to UN peacekeeping, says leaked report. *Guardian,* March 24. https://www.theguardian.com /global-development-professionals-network/2015/mar/24/sex-abuse-un-peacekeeping-leaked-report.

Coalición de Derechos Humanos and No More Deaths. 2016. Disappeared, part 2: Interference with humanitarian aid. www.thedisappearedreport.org /uploads/8/3/5/1/83515082/disappeared_report_part_2.pdf.

Collinson, Sarah, and Mark Duffield. 2013. Paradoxes of Presence: Risk Management and Aid Culture in Challenging Environments. With Carol Berger, Diana Felix da Costa, and Karl Sandstrom. Report, March. London: Humanitarian Policy Group. https://www.odi.org/sites/odi.org.uk/files /odi-assets/publications-opinion-files/8428.pdf.

Comaroff, Jean. 1993. The diseased heart of Africa: Medicine, colonialism, and the black body. In *Knowledge, Power, and Practice: The Anthropology of*

Medicine and Everyday Life, edited by S. Lindenbaum and M. M. Lock. Berkeley: University of California Press.

Conflict Armament Research. 2013. Rebel Forces in Northern Mali: Documented Weapons, Ammunition, and Related Materiel, April 2012–March 2013. Report, April. London: Conflict Armament Research/Small Arms Survey. www.smallarmssurvey.org/fileadmin/docs/E-Co-Publications/SAS-SANA-Conflict-Armament-Research-Rebel-Forces-in-Northern-Mali.pdf.

Control Risks. 2017. Terrorism and new ideologies. Report, December 18. https://www.controlrisks.com/riskmap-2018/articles/terrorism-and-new-ideologies.

Cook, Chris, and Phil Kemp. 2017. How fire-safe is British furniture? BBC News, December 13. https://www.bbc.co.uk/news/uk-42343237.

Cooper, Helene, Michael D. Shear, and Dionne Searcey. 2017. Chad's inclusion in travel ban could jeopardize American interests, officials say. *New York Times,* September 26. https://www.nytimes.com/2017/09/26/world/africa/chad-travel-ban-american-interests.html.

Cooper, Robert. 2002. The new liberal imperialism. *Observer,* April 7. www.theguardian.com/world/2002/apr/07/1

Cornelius, W. A., Takeyuke Tsuda, Philip L. Martin, and James F. Hollifield, eds. 2004. *Controlling Immigration: A Global Perspective.* Stanford, CA: Stanford University Press.

Crawley, Heaven, Franck Düvell, Katharine Jones, Simon McMahon, and Nando Sigona. 2016. Destination Europe? Understanding the dynamics and drivers of Mediterranean migration in 2015. MEDMIG final report, November. https://www.compas.ox.ac.uk/wp-content/uploads/PR-2016-MEDMIG_Destination_Europe.pdf.

Crisp, Jeff. 2017. Refugees: The Trojan horse of terrorism? openDemocracy, June 5. https://www.opendemocracy.net/can-europe-make-it/jeff-crisp/refugees-trojan-horse-of-terrorism.

Currier, Cora, and Peter Maass. 2015. Firing blind: Flawed intelligence and the limits of drone technology. *Intercept,* October 15. https://theintercept.com/drone-papers/firing-blind/.

Cuttitta, Paolo. 2014. "Borderizing" the island: Setting and narratives of the Lampedusa "border play." *CME: An International E-Journal for Critical Geographies* 13 (2): 196–219.

Das, Veena, and Deborah Poole, eds. 2004. *Anthropology in the Margins of the State.* Santa Fe, NM: School of American Research Press.

Dawson, Graham. 1994. *Soldier Heroes: British Adventure, Empire and the Imagining of Masculinities.* Abingdon: Routledge.

Debord, Guy. [1955] 2006. Introduction to a critique of urban geography. Republished in translation in *Situationist International Anthology,* edited by Ken Knabb, 8–11. Berkeley: Bureau of Public Secrets.

De Certeau, Michel. 1984. *The Practice of Everyday Life.* Berkeley: University of California Press.

De Genova, Nicholas. 2002. Migrant illegality and deportability in everyday life. *Annual Review of Anthropology* 31: 419–47.

De Haas, Hein. 2007. Turning the tide? Why development will not stop migration. *Development and Change* 38 (5): 819–41.

De León, Jason. 2015. *The Land of Open Graves: Living and Dying on the Migrant Trail.* Oakland: University of California Press.

Depardieu, Hervé. 2017a. Mali: L'appel à l'aide du propriétaire du Campement, l'hôtel visé par une attaque terroriste. *Le Monde,* June 30. www.lemonde.fr /afrique/article/2017/06/30/l-appel-a-l-aide-du-campement-de-bamako-l-hotel-vise-par-une-attaque-terroriste-il-y-a-quelques-jours_5153846_3212.html.

———. 2017b. La vie à Bamako, au rythme des SMS d'alerte et des "conseils aux voyageurs." *Le Monde,* January 12.

De Waal, Alexander. 1997. *Famine Crimes: Politics and the Disaster Relief Industry in Africa.* Oxford: James Currey.

———. 1998. US war crimes in Somalia. *New Left Review* 1 (230): 131–44.

———. 2008a. Medicine at the border: Disease, globalization, and security, 1850 to the present. *Global Public Health* 3 (3): 343–46.

———. 2008b. On famine crimes and tragedies. *Lancet* 372 (9649): 1538–39.

———. 2015. *The Real Politics of the Horn of Africa: Money, War and the Business of Power.* Cambridge: Polity Press.

———. 2017. The Nazis used it, we use it: Alex de Waal on the return of famine as a weapon of war. *London Review of Books* 39 (12): 9–12.

De Weijer, Frauke. 2013. Resilience: A Trojan horse for a new way of thinking? ECDPM Discussion Paper No. 139, January. European Centre for Development Policy Management. http://ecdpm.org/wp-content/uploads/2013/10 /DP-139-Resilience-Trojan-Horse-New-Way-of-Thinking-2013.pdf.

DIIS (Danish Institute of International Studies). 2017. African Peacekeepers in Mali. Copenhagen: DIIS. http://pure.diis.dk/ws/files/762381/DIIS_RP_2017_2_WEB.pdf.

Donadio, Rachel. 2009. Qaddafi pays a business call on Berlusconi. *New York Times,* June 10. www.nytimes.com/2009/06/11/world/europe/11italy.html.

Douglas, Mary. 2002. *Purity and Danger: An Analysis of the Concepts of Pollution and Taboo.* London: Routledge.

Doward, Jamie, and Alice Gibbs. 2017. Did Cambridge Analytica influence the Brexit vote and the US election? *Observer,* March 4. https://www .theguardian.com/politics/2017/mar/04/nigel-oakes-cambridge-analytica-what-role-brexit-trump.

Dowden, Richard. 2008. *Africa: Altered States, Ordinary Miracles.* London: Portobello.

Dueck, Colin. 2015. *The Obama Doctrine: American Grand Strategy Today.* New York: Oxford University Press.

Duffield, Mark. 2001. *Global Governance and the New Wars: The Merging of Development and Security.* New York: Zed Books.

———. 2005. Getting savages to fight barbarians: Development, security and the colonial present. *Conflict, Security and Development* 5 (2): 141–59.

———. 2007. *Development, Security and Unending War: Governing the World of Peoples.* Cambridge: Polity Press.

———. 2010. Risk-management and the fortified aid compound: Everyday life in post-interventionary society. *Journal of Intervention and Statebuilding* 4 (4): 453–74.

Dyrberg, Rikke. 2014. Danmark siger nej til FN: Fly og soldater hjem fra Mali. *Avisen DK*, June 26. www.avisen.dk/danmark-trodser-fn-fly-og-soldater-hjem-fra-mali_273856.aspx.

EC (European Commission). 2016. Migration partnership framework: A new approach to better manage migration. Fact sheet. https://eeas.europa.eu/sites/eeas/files/factsheet_ec_format_migration_partnership_framework_update_2.pdf.

Edney, Matthew H. 1997. *Mapping an Empire: The Geographical Construction of British India, 1765–1843.* Chicago: University of Chicago Press.

Elden, Stuart. 2009. *Terror and Territory: The Spatial Extent of Sovereignty.* Minneapolis: University of Minnesota Press.

———. 2013. Secure the volume: Vertical geopolitics and the depth of power. *Political Geography* 34: 45–51.

Eliot, T. S. *The Waste Land and Other Poems.* 1999. London: Faber and Faber.

Ellis, Stephen. 1999. *The Mask of Anarchy: The Destruction of Liberia and the Religious Dimension of an African Civil War.* New York: New York University Press.

———. 2004. Briefing: The Pan-Sahel Initiative. *African Affairs* 103 (412): 459–64.

Engelbrekt, Kjell, Marcus Mohlin, and Charlotte Wagnsson, eds. 2014. *The NATO Intervention in Libya: Lessons Learned from the Campaign.* London: Routledge.

English, Charlie. 2017. *The Book Smugglers of Timbuktu: The Quest for This Storied City and the Race to Save Its Treasures.* London: HarperCollins.

Epstein, Edward J. 2001. Fictoid #3: The lair of bin Laden. Edward Jay Epstein blog. www.edwardjayepstein.com/nether_fictoid3.htm.

Eriksen, Thomas Hylland. 2006. *Engaging Anthropology: The Case for a Public Presence.* Oxford: Berg.

———. 2016. *Overheating: An Anthropology of Accelerated Change.* London: Pluto Press.

Escobar, Arturo. 1995. *Encountering Development: The Making and Unmaking of the Third World.* Princeton, NJ: Princeton University Press.

Europa Press 2017. Localizan en tierra a otros cinco inmigrantes tras la llegada de una patera vacía a Benidorm. News report, August 27. www.europapress .es/comunitat-valenciana/noticia-localizan-tierra-otros-cinco-inmigrantes-llegada-patera-vacia-benidorm-20170827193514.html.

Fagan, Laureen. 2017. Macron's Sahel trip spotlights security, migration investments. *Africa Times,* December 24. http://africatimes.com/2017/12/24 /macrons-sahel-trip-spotlights-security-migration-investments/.

Fassin, Didier. 2001. The biopolitics of otherness: Undocumented foreigners and racial discrimination in French public debate. *Anthropology Today* 17 (1): 3–7.

———. 2011. Policing borders, producing boundaries: The governmentality of immigration in dark times. *Annual Review of Anthropology* 40:213–26.

Fast, Larissa. 2014. *Aid in Danger: The Perils and Promise of Humanitarianism.* Philadelphia: University of Pennsylvania Press.

Feher, Margit. 2015. Europe's existence threatened by influx of migrants, says Hungary's Orban. *Wall Street Journal,* updated July 26. www.wsj.com /articles/europes-existence-threatened-by-influx-of-migrants-says-hungarys-orban-1437827281.

Ferguson, James. 2005. Seeing like an oil company: Space, security, and global capital in neoliberal Africa. *American Anthropologist* 107 (3): 377–82.

———. 2006. *Global Shadows: Africa in the Neoliberal World Order.* Durham, NC: Duke University Press.

Ferguson, Niall. 2004. *Colossus: The Rise and Fall of the American Empire.* London: Allen Lane.

———. 2016. It takes a network to defeat a network. *Boston Globe,* March 28. https://www.bostonglobe.com/opinion/2016/03/28/takes-network-defeat-network/yeGQH2UTxyp1bxmie1tEkL/story.html.

Fergusson, James. 2013. *The World's Most Dangerous Place: Inside the Outlaw State of Somalia.* London: Black Swan.

Fick, Maggie. 2016. Niger asks EU for €1bn to stem migrant flow. *Financial Times,* May 4. https://www.ft.com/content/fd2c92e2–11d0–11e6–91da-096d89bd2173.

Filipovic, Jill. 2017. Will Africa's Great Green Wall discourage migration to Europe? *Guardian,* July 19. https://www.theguardian.com/global-development-professionals-network/2017/jul/19/will-africas-great-green-wall-discourage-migration-to-europe.

Flynn, Michael T., Rich Juergens, and Thomas L. Cantrell. 2008. Employing ISR: SOF best practices. *Joint Force Quarterly* 50: 56–61.

Forsyth, James. 2014. Michael Fallon: Parliament needs the "courage" to vote for war. *Spectator,* September 27. www.spectator.co.uk/2014/09/we-shouldnt-be-ambiguous/

Forte, Maximilian C. 2011. Beyond public anthropology: Approaching zero. Keynote address to the 8th Annual Public Anthropology Conference, American University, Washington, DC. http://open-anthropology.org /pacfortekeynote2.pdf.

Fradejas-García, Ignacio. Forthcoming. Humanitarian remoteness: Aid work practices from "Little Aleppo." Unpublished manuscript.

Frankopan, Peter. 2015. *The Silk Roads: A New History of the World.* London: Bloomsbury.

Frei, Nula. 2018. Circumventing non-refoulement or fighting "illegal migration"? *EU Migration Law Blog,* March 23. http://eumigrationlawblog.eu /circumventing-non-refoulement-or-fighting-illegal-migration/.

Friedman, Thomas L. 2006. *The World Is Flat: A Brief History of the Twenty-First Century.* New York: Farrar, Strauss and Giroux.

Frowd, Philippe M. 2014. The field of border control in Mauritania. *Security Dialogue* 45 (3): 226–41.

Galy, Michel. 2013. *La guerre au Mali.* Paris: La Découverte.

Gardini, Marco. Forthcoming. Malagasy "red zones": Bandits, insecurity, and the economic centrality of "remote" areas. Unpublished manuscript.

Geddes, Andrew, and Leila Hadj-Abdou. 2017. Changing the path? EU migration governance after the "Arab spring." *Mediterranean Politics* 23 (1): 142–60.

Gettleman, Jeffrey. 2015. A catch-22 in Kenya: Western terrorism alerts may fuel terrorism. *New York Times,* February 23. www.nytimes.com/2015/02/24 /world/africa/as-tourism-sags-on-kenyan-coast-terrorists-could-lure-the-unemployed.html.

Ghani, Ashraf, and Clare Lockhart. 2008. *Fixing Failed States: A Framework for Rebuilding a Fractured World.* Oxford: Oxford University Press.

Gibson, Trent A. 2009. Hell-bent on force protection: Confusing troop welfare with mission accomplishment in counterinsurgency. Master's thesis, Marine Corps University, Quantico, VA. https://apps.dtic.mil/dtic/tr/fulltext/u2/ a508083.pdf

Goldin, Ian, and Mike Mariathasan. 2015. *The Butterfly Defect: How Globalization Creates Systemic Risks, and What to Do about It.* Princeton, NJ: Princeton University Press.

Graham-Harrison, Emma. 2017. Why deadly Kabul bombing is crisis for all of Afghanistan. *Guardian,* May 31. https://www.theguardian.com/world/2017 /jun/01/kabul-bombing-crisis-afghanistan-civilian-society-government-.

Granados, Samuel, Zoeann Murphy, Kevin Schaul, and Anthony Faiola. 2016. Raising barriers: A new age of walls. *Washington Post,* October 12. https:// www.washingtonpost.com/graphics/world/border-barriers/global-illegal-immigration-prevention/.

Goldstein, Daniel M. 2010. Toward a critical anthropology of security. *Current Anthropology* 51 (4): 487–517.

Goulding, Tom. 2013. The risks are huge, but freelance war correspondents shouldn't be shunned for having the courage to take them. *Independent,* February 25. https://www.independent.co.uk/voices/comment/the-risks-are-huge-but-freelance-war-correspondents-shouldnt-be-shunned-for-having-the-courage-to-8509988.html.

Greaves, Simon, and Liz Faunce. 2017. Rise of the border wall shows there is more that divides us. *Financial Times,* March 26. www.ft.com/content/9d4d10cc-0e28-11e7-b030-768954394623

Greenhill, Kelly. 2011. *Weapons of Mass Migration: Forced Displacement, Coercion, and Foreign Policy.* Ithaca, NY: Cornell University Press.

Gregory, Derek. 2004. *The Colonial Present: Afghanistan, Palestine, and Iraq.* Malden, MA: Blackwell.

———. 2011a. The everywhere war. *Geographical Journal* 177 (3): 238–50.

———. 2011b. From a view to a kill: Drones and late modern war. *Theory, Culture and Society* 28 (7–8): 188–215.

———. 2011c. Lines of descent. openDemocracy, November 8. https://www.opendemocracy.net/derek-gregory/lines-of-descent.

Gregory, Derek, and Allan Pred. 2006. *Violent Geographies: Fear, Terror, and Political Violence.* New York: Routledge.

Grierson, Jamie, and Rowena Mason. 2015. Tunisia and Britain in diplomatic row as UK tourists fly home. *Guardian,* July 10. www.theguardian.com/world/2015/jul/10/uk-tourists-fly-home-tunisia-criticises-travel-advice-sousse.

Gros-Verheyde, Nicolas. 2015. Mission plage pour EUBAM Libya. Bruxelles2, January 19. www.bruxelles2.eu/2015/01/19/mission-plage-pour-eubam-libya/.

Guarino, Ben. 2017. Shaking hands is "barbaric": Donald Trump, the germaphobe in chief. *Washington Post,* January 12. www.washingtonpost.com/news/morning-mix/wp/2017/01/12/shaking-hands-is-barbaric-donald-trump-the-germaphobe-in-chief/.

Guichaoua, Yvan. 2013. Mali: The fallacy of ungoverned spaces. *Mediapart* (blog), February 12. https://blogs.mediapart.fr/yvan-guichaoua/blog/120213/mali-fallacy-ungoverned-spaces.

Guichaoua, Yvan, and Andres Lebovich. 2017. America's options in Niger: Join forces to reduce tensions, or fan the flames. *Conversation,* November 2. https://theconversation.com/americas-options-in-niger-join-forces-to-reduce-tensions-or-fan-the-flames-86655.

Gupta, Akhil. 2015. Is poverty a global security threat? In *Territories of Poverty: Rethinking North and South,* edited by Ananya Roy and Emma Shaw Crane, 84–102. Athens: University of Georgia Press.

Gusterson, Hugh. 2013. Anthropology in the news? *Anthropology Today* 29: 11–13.

———. 2016. *Drone: Remote Control Warfare.* Cambridge, MA: MIT Press.

Han, Byung-chul. 2017. *Psychopolitics: Neoliberalism and New Technologies of Power.* London: Verso.

Hannerz, Ulf. 2004. *Foreign News: Exploring the World of Foreign Correspondents.* Chicago: University of Chicago Press.

———. 2015. Writing futures: An anthropologist's view of global scenarios. *Current Anthropology* 56 (6): 797–818.

———. 2016. *Writing Future Worlds: An Anthropologist Explores Global Scenarios.* Basingstoke: Palgrave Macmillan.

Hanson, J. H. 1996. *Migration, Jihad, and Muslim Authority in West Africa.* Bloomington: Indiana University Press.

Harley, J. B. 1988. Maps, knowledge, and power. In 1988. *The Iconography of Landscape: Essays on the Symbolic Representation, Design and Use of Past Environments,* edited by Denis Cosgrove and Stephen Daniels, 277–312. Cambridge: Cambridge University Press.

———. 2001. *The New Nature of Maps: Essays in the History of Cartography.* With Paul Laxton. Baltimore: Johns Hopkins University Press.

Haslan, Marouf A., Jr. 2016. *Representing Ebola: Culture, Law, and Public Discourse about the 2013–2015 West African Ebola Outbreak.* Madison, WI: Fairleigh Dickinson University Press.

Hastings, Michael. 2010a. *The Hurt Locker,* and what it means to be addicted to war. *Huffington Post,* May 4. www.huffingtonpost.com/michael-hastings /emthe-hurt-lockerem-and-w_b_486463.html.

———. 2010b. The runaway general: The profile that brought down McChrystal. *Rolling Stone,* June 22. https://www.rollingstone.com/politics/politics-news/the-runaway-general-the-profile-that-brought-down-mcchrystal-192609/.

———. 2012a. *The Operators: The Wild and Terrifying Inside Story of America's War in Afghanistan.* London: Orion.

———. 2012b. The rise of the killer drones: How America goes to war in secret. *Rolling Stone,* April 26. www.rollingstone.com/politics/news/the-rise-of-the-killer-drones-how-america-goes-to-war-in-secret-20120416.

Henke, Marina E. 2016. *Has UN Peacekeeping Become More Deadly? Analyzing Trends in UN Fatalities.* Report, December. New York: International Peace Institute. https://www.ipinst.org/wp-content/uploads/2016/11/1612_ Peacekeeping-Fatalities.pdf.

Herman, Barbara. 2015. Is ISIS beheading video of 21 Egyptian Christians fake? Film experts argue "yes." *International Business Times,* February 22. www.ibtimes.com/isis-beheading-video-21-egyptian-christians-fake-film-experts-argue-yes-1824034.

Heyman, Josiah. 1995. Putting power in the anthropology of bureaucracy: The Immigration and Naturalization Service at the Mexico-United States border. *Current Anthropology* 36 (2): 261–87.

Hickel, Jason. 2017. Aid in reverse: How poor countries develop rich countries. *Guardian*, January 14. https://www.theguardian.com/global-development-professionals-network/2017/jan/14/aid-in-reverse-how-poor-countries-develop-rich-countries.

Hilsum, Lindsey. 2013. *Sandstorm: Libya from Gaddafi to Revolution*. London: Faber and Faber.

Holloway, Kali. 2015. Fear sells, and we're all buying: How marketers channel dark forces to rake in billions. *Alternet*, March 17. www.alternet.org/media/fear-sells-and-were-all-buying-how-marketers-channel-dark-forces-rake-billions.

Holmes, Jack. 2017. Fox News went full Team America with the bomb coverage. *Esquire*, April 14. https://www.esquire.com/news-politics/videos/a54514/fox-news-mother-of-all-bombs/.

Horden, Peregrine, and Nicholas Purcell. 2000. *The Corrupting Sea: A Study of Mediterranean History*. Oxford: Blackwell.

House of Lords. 2017. Operation Sophia: A failed mission. House of Lords, European Union Committee, 2nd Report of Session 2017–19, July. https://publications.parliament.uk/pa/ld201719/ldselect/ldeucom/5/5.pdf.

HRW (Human Rights Watch). 2017. World Report 2017. https://www.hrw.org/world-report/2017.

Huntington, Samuel. 2009. The Hispanic challenge. *Foreign Policy*, October 28.

Ingold, Tim. 2014. That's enough about ethnography! *HAU: Journal of Ethnographic Theory* 4 (1): 383–95.

———. 2016. Enough about ethnography: An interview with Tim Ingold. Interview by Susan MacDougall for *Cultural Anthropology*, April 5. https://culanth.org/fieldsights/841-enough-about-ethnography-an-interview-with-tim-ingold.

Issa-Salwe, Abdisalam M. 1994. *The Collapse of the Somali State: The Impact of the Colonial Legacy*. London: A. M. Issa-Salwe in association with HAAN Associates.

Jenkins, Simon. 2016. The question terrorists love: "Can you guarantee safety at Euro 2016?" *Guardian*, June 10. www.theguardian.com/commentisfree/2016/jun/10/question-terrorists-love-guarantee-safety-euro-2016-france.

Jones, Reece. 2016. *Violent Borders: Refugees and the Right to Move*. London: Verso.

Journalists for Justice. 2015. *Black and White: Kenya's Criminal Racket in Somalia*. Report, November. Nairobi: Journalists for Justice. www.jfjustice.net/downloads/1457660562.pdf

Kalb, Martin. 2013. It's called the Vietnam syndrome, and it's back. Brookings Institution, January 22. https://www.brookings.edu/blog/up-front/2013/01/22/its-called-the-vietnam-syndrome-and-its-back/.

Kaldor, Mary. 1999. *New and Old Wars: Organized Violence in a Global Era.* Cambridge: Polity Press.

Kaplan, Robert D. 1994. The coming anarchy. *Atlantic Monthly*, February. www .theatlantic.com/magazine/archive/1994/02/the-coming-anarchy/304670/

———. 2006. Hunting the Taliban in Las Vegas. *Atlantic Monthly*, September, www.theatlantic.com/magazine/archive/2006/09/hunting-the-taliban-in-las-vegas/305116/.

———. 2012. *The Revenge of Geography: What the Map Tells Us about Coming Conflicts and the Battle against Fate.* New York: Random House.

Karunakara, Unni. 2013. MSF president: Why MSF decided to leave Somalia. Médecins sans Frontières, September 26. https://www.msf.org.uk/article /msf-president-why-msf-decided-leave-somalia.

Keating, Michael. 2018. UN envoy Keating briefs the Security Council on the situation of Somalia on 13 September 2018. Report from the UN Assistance Mission in Somalia, September 13. https://reliefweb.int/report/somalia /un-envoy-keating-briefs-security-council-situation-somalia-13-september-2018.

Keen, David. 2012. *Useful Enemies: When Waging Wars Is More Important Than Winning Them.* New Haven, CT: Yale University Press.

———. 2017. *Syria: Playing into Their Hands.* Saferworld report, October. www.saferworld.org.uk/resources/publications/1141-syria-playing-into-their-hands.

———. Forthcoming. *Shame.* Princeton, NJ: Princeton University Press.

Keen, David, and Ruben Andersson. 2018. Double games: Success, failure and the relocation of risk in fighting terror, drugs and migration. *Political Geography* 67: 100–110.

Keenan, Jeremy. 2009. *The Dark Sahara: America's War on Terror in Africa.* London: Pluto Press.

———. 2013. *The Dying Sahara: US Imperialism and Terror in Africa.* London: Pluto Press.

Khanna, Parag. 2016. *Connectography: Mapping the Future of Global Civilization.* London: Weidenfeld and Nicolson.

Kilcullen, David. 2009. *The Accidental Guerilla: Fighting Small Wars in the Midst of a Big One.* Oxford: Oxford University Press.

Kilcullen, David, and Andrew McDonald Exum. 2009. Death from above, outrage down below. *New York Times*, May 16. https://www.nytimes.com /2009/05/17/opinion/17exum.html.

Killough, Ashley. 2014. Joe Biden explains how Ebola is like ISIS. CNN, October 3. http://edition.cnn.com/2014/10/03/politics/biden-ebola-isis/.

Kingsley, Patrick. 2015. Libyan people smuggler derides EU plan for military action. *Guardian*, April 21. https://www.theguardian.com/world/2015/apr/21 /libyan-people-smuggler-tells-eu-to-destroy-ships-and-help-coastguard.

Kington, Tom. 2017. Italy sends 500 troops to Niger to tackle traffickers and jihadists. *Times*, December 28. https://www.thetimes.co.uk/article/italy-sends-500-troops-to-niger-to-tackle-traffickers-and-jihadists-kmxx9kzbr.

Kitchin, Rob, and Martin Dodge. 2007. Rethinking maps. *Progress in Human Geography* 31 (3): 331–44.

Klein, Peter W., and Shayna Plaut. 2017. Fixing the journalist-fixer relationship. Global Investigative Journalism Network, November 16. https://gijn.org /2017/11/16/fixer/.

Kleist, Nauja, and Dorte Thorsen, eds. 2016. *Hope and Uncertainty in Contemporary African Migration*. Abingdon: Routledge.

Konaté, Doulaye, ed. 2013. *Le Mali entre doutes et espoirs: Réflexions sur la nation à l'épreuve de la crise du Nord*. Bamako: Editions Tombouctou.

Koudelkova, Marketa. 2018. Hating thy (imagined) neighbour: The role of morality and values in response to the "migration crisis" in the Czech Republic. Unpublished MSc diss., University of Oxford.

Kovats-Bernat, J. Christopher. 2002. Negotiating dangerous fields: Pragmatic strategies for fieldwork amid violence and terror. *American Anthropologist* 104 (1): 208–22.

Kpodo, Kwasi. 2018. IMF warns of rising African debt despite faster economic growth. Reuters, May 8. www.reuters.com/article/us-africa-imf/imf-warns-of-rising-african-debt-despite-faster-economic-growth-idUSKB-N1I9114.

Krauthammer, Charles. 2011. The Obama doctrine: Leading from behind. *Washington Post*, April 28. https://www.washingtonpost.com/opinions /the-obama-doctrine-leading-from-behind/2011/04/28/AFBCy18E_story .html.

Kristol, William, and Robert Kagan. 1996. Toward a neo-Reaganite foreign policy. *Foreign Affairs* 75 (4): 18–32.

Laestadius, Lars. 2017. Africa's got plans for a Great Green Wall: Why the idea needs a rethink. *Conversation*, June 18. https://theconversation.com/ africas-got-plans-for-a-great-green-wall-why-the-idea-needs-a-rethink-78627.

Landler, Mark. 2016a. For Obama, an unexpected legacy of two full terms at war. *New York Times*, May 14. https://www.nytimes.com/2016/05/15/us /politics/obama-as-wartime-president-has-wrestled-with-protecting-nation-and-troops.html.

———. 2016b. Obama says he will keep more troops in Afghanistan than planned. *New York Times*, July 6. https://www.nytimes.com/2016/07/07 /world/asia/obama-afghanistan-troops.html.

Laplanche, Jean, and Jean-Bertrand Pontalis. 2004. *The Language of Psychoanalysis*. London: Karnac Books.

Lawson, Victoria. 2007. Introduction: Geographies of fear and hope. *Annals of the Association of American Geographers* 97 (2): 335–37.

Lecocq, Baz. 2010. *Disputed Desert: Decolonisation, Competing Nationalisms and Tuareg Rebellions in Northern Mali*. Leiden: Brill.

Lederer, Edith M. 2015. Mali appeals for international intervention in Libya. Associated Press, January 7. https://apnews.com/e26fad9f-c2344e2e85314775c402365a/mali-appeals-international-intervention-libya.

Lemberg-Pedersen, Martin. 2015. Unravelling the drivers behind EU border militarization. University of Oxford, Faculty of Law, *Border Criminologies Themed Blog Series on the Industry of Illegality*, October 28. https://www.law.ox.ac.uk/research-subject-groups/centre-criminology/centreborder-criminologies/blog/2015/10/unravelling.

Lemieux, Frederic. 2016. What is terrorism, and is it getting worse? *Conversation*, September 20.

———. 2017. What is terrorism? What do terrorists want? *Conversation*, May 23.

Lewis, Ioan M. 1961. *A Pastoral Democracy: A Study of Pastoralism and Politics among the Northern Somali of the Horn of Africa*. London: Oxford University Press.

Lianos, Michalis, and Mary Douglas. 2000. Dangerization and the end of deviance. In *Criminology and Social Theory*, edited by David Garland and Richard Sparks, 103–26. Oxford: Oxford University Press.

Lindqvist, Sven. 2001. *A History of Bombing*. London: Granta.

Lisle, Debbie. 2016. *Holidays in the Danger Zone: Entanglements of War and Tourism*. Minneapolis: University of Minnesota Press.

Lucht, Hans. 2012. *Darkness before Daybreak: African Migrants Living on the Margins in Southern Italy Today*. Berkeley: University of California Press.

Maguire, Mark. 2015. Questioned by machines: A cultural perspective on counter-terrorism and lie detection in security zones. In *Resisting Biopolitics: Philosophy, Politics and Performance*, edited by S. E. Wilmer and Audronė Žukauskaitė, 159–72. London: Routledge.

Maguire, Mark, Catarina Frois, and Nils Zurawski, eds. 2014. *The Anthropology of Security: Perspectives from the Frontline of Policing, Counter-terrorism and Border Control*. London: Pluto Press.

Mahmud, Tayyab. 2011. Colonial cartographies, postcolonial borders, and enduring failures of international law: The unending wars along the Afghanistan-Pakistan frontier. *Brooklyn Journal of International Law* 36 (1): 1–74.

Malagardis, Maria. 2017. L'attaque du "petit paradis" de Kangaba renforce les inquiétudes sur l'avenir du Mali. *Libération*, June 19. www.liberation.fr/planete/2017/06/19/l-attaque-du-petit-paradis-de-kangaba-renforce-les-inquietudes-sur-l-avenir-du-mali_1577898.

Malkki, Liisa H. 1995. *Purity and Exile: Violence, Memory and National Cosmology among Hutu Refugees in Tanzania*. Chicago: University of Chicago Press.

Martin, Emily. 1994. *Flexible Bodies: Tracking Immunity in American Culture from the Days of Polio to the Age of AIDS*. Boston: Beacon Press.

Masco, Joseph. 2014. *The Theater of Operations: National Security Affect from the Cold War to the War on Terror*. Durham, NC: Duke University Press.

Massey, Douglas S., Karen A. Pren, and Jorge Durand. 2016. Why border enforcement backfired. *American Journal of Sociology* 121 (5): 1557–1600.

Mayer, Brian. 2017. The full Uruguay experience. *Thomas Friedman Op/Ed Generator*, August 4. http://thomasfriedmanopedgenerator.com/The+Full+Uruguay+Experience+ab62a9.

McCann, Kate. 2017. "The only way" of dealing with British Islamic State fighters is to kill them in almost every case, minister says. *Daily Telegraph*, October 22. www.telegraph.co.uk/news/2017/10/22/way-dealing-british-islamic-state-fighters-kill-almost-every/.

McCarthy, Tom. 2015. The death of writing—if James Joyce were alive today he'd be working for Google. *Guardian,* March 7. www.theguardian.com/books/2015/mar/07/tom-mccarthy-death-writing-james-joyce-working-google.

McChrystal, Stanley A. 2015. *Team of Teams: The Power of Small Groups in a Fragmented World*. London: Portfolio.

———. 2016. An interview with Stanley McChrystal. Interview by Michael Miklaucik. *Prism* 6 (3). http://cco.ndu.edu/PRISM-6-3/Article/1020271/an-interview-with-stanley-mcchrystal/.

McChrystal, Stanley A., and Kristina Talbert-Slagle. 2014. How to treat threats of Ebola and ISIS. CNN, October 1. http://edition.cnn.com/2014/10/01/opinion/mcchrystal-talbert-slagle-ebola-isis/.

McDougall, Ann. 2007. Constructing emptiness: Islam, violence and terror in the historical making of the Sahara. *Journal of Contemporary African Studies* 25 (1): 17–30.

McDougall, James, and Judith Scheele. 2012. *Saharan Frontiers: Space and Mobility in Northwest Africa*. Bloomington: Indiana University Press.

McGreal, Chris. 2014. Obama suggests US is better partner than China to African leaders. *Guardian*, August 5. https://www.theguardian.com/world/2014/aug/05/obama-africa-leaders-us-china-investment-summit.

McNeill, Casey. 2017. "Playing the away game": AFRICOM in the Sahara-Sahel. *Political Geography* 58: 46–55.

Menkhaus, Ken. 2010. Stabilisation and humanitarian access in a collapsed state: The Somali case. *Disasters* 34 (S3): S320–S341.

———. 2013. *Somalia: State Collapse and the Threat of Terrorism*. Abingdon: Routledge.

Mishra, Pankaj. 2017. *Age of Anger: A History of the Present*. London: Allen Lane.

Monbiot, George. 2017. How corporate dark money is taking power on both sides of the Atlantic. *Guardian,* February 2. https://www.theguardian.com

/commentisfree/2017/feb/02/corporate-dark-money-power-atlantic-lobbyists-brexit.

———. 2018. The PFI bosses fleeced us all. Now watch them walk away. *Guardian*, January 16. https://www.theguardian.com/commentisfree/2018/jan/16/pfi-bosses-carillion-money-george-monbiot.

Moore, Suzanne. 2017. Trump's "fire and fury" has revived my nuclear nightmares. *Guardian*, August 9. https://www.theguardian.com/commentisfree/2017/aug/09/trump-fire-and-fury-has-revived-my-nuclear-nightmares.

Mosse, David. 2004. *Cultivating Development: An Ethnography of Aid Policy and Practice*. London: Pluto.

Mujica, José. 2014. Siete horas "aislados" en la playa por temor al ébola tras llegar a Maspalomas en patera. *El Mundo*, May 11. www.elmundo.es/espana/2014/11/05/545a2964ca474156118b458c.html.

Musarò, Pierluigi. 2013. "Africans" vs. "Europeans": Humanitarian narratives and the moral geography of the world. *Sociologia della Comunicazione* 45: 37–59.

Mutter, Sam. 2015a. The doublespeak of drones. openDemocracy, March 17. https://www.opendemocracy.net/sam-mutter/doublespeak-of-drones.

———. 2015b. Perception, deception, and drone warfare: Clear discursive fantasy and the messy space of "play." *Geopolitical Philosophy of Drones* (blog), January 26. https://thedronephilosophical.wordpress.com/tag/virilio/.

Nandy, Ashis. 1995. *The Savage Freud and Other Essays on Possible and Retrievable Selves*. Delhi: Oxford University Press.

Nay, Olivier. 2013. Fragile and failed states: Critical perspectives on conceptual hybrids. *International Political Science Review* 34 (3): 326–41.

Naylor, Sean. 2015. *Relentless Strike: The Secret History of Joint Special Operations Command*. New York: St. Martin's Press.

Neuman, Michaël, and Fabrice Weissman. 2016. *Saving Lives and Staying Alive: Humanitarian Security in the Age of Risk Management*. London: Hurst.

Niva, Steve. 2013. Disappearing violence: JSOC and the Pentagon's new cartography of networked warfare. *Security Dialogue* 44 (3): 185–202.

Nordland, Rod. 2017. U.S. expands Kabul security zone, digging in for next decade. *New York Times*, September 16. https://www.nytimes.com/2017/09/16/world/asia/kabul-green-zone-afghanistan.html.

Nordstrom, Carolyn, and A. C. G. M. Robben, eds. 1996. *Fieldwork under Fire: Contemporary Studies of Violence and Survival*. Berkeley: University of California Press.

Nussbaum, Martha C. 2018. *The Monarchy of Fear: A Philosopher Looks at our Political Crisis*. New York: Simon & Schuster.

Obama, Barack. 2010. National security strategy of the United States. Available via the National Security Strategy Archive: http://nssarchive.us/national-security-strategy-2010/.

Obert, Michael. 2017. Can a Libyan warlord help Europe solve the migrant crisis? *Worldcrunch*, June 27. https://www.worldcrunch.com/migrant-lives-1/can-a-libyan-warlord-help-europe-solve-the-migrant-crisis. Originally published in German as "Die Menschenfänger," *Suddeutsche Zeitung,* June 8.

ODI (Overseas Development Institute). 2016. Europe's Refugees and Migrants: Hidden Flows, Tightened Borders and Spiralling Costs. Report, September. London: Overseas Development Institute. https://www.odi.org/sites/odi.org.uk/files/resource-documents/10887.pdf.

Oltermann, Philip. 2018. Germany to roll out mass holding centres for asylum seekers. *Guardian,* May 21. www.theguardian.com/world/2018/may/21/germany-to-roll-out-mass-holding-centres-for-asylum-seekers.

Osgood, Matt. 2016. Idiots on the field are the forbidden fruit of sports TV. *Slate,* September 22. www.slate.com/articles/sports/sports_nut/2016/09/why_don_t_tv_networks_show_idiots_on_the_field.html.

Overton, Iain. 2016. 2015 saw record number of countries hit by suicide bombers. Action on Armed Violence, January 22. https://aoav.org.uk/2016/2015-saw-an-unprecedented-number-of-countries-hit-by-suicide-bombers/.

Painter, Joe. 2008. Cartographic anxiety and the search for regionality. *Environment and Planning A* 40 (2): 342–61.

Pallister-Wilkins, Polly. 2015. The humanitarian politics of European border policing: Frontex and border police in Evros. *International Political Sociology* 9 (1): 53–69.

Penfield, Amy. Forthcoming. The wild inside out: Rethinking remoteness and infrastructure in an Amazonian mining region. Unpublished manuscript.

Penney, Joe. 2018. Drones in the Sahara. *Intercept,* February 18. https://theintercept.com/2018/02/18/niger-air-base-201-africom-drones/.

Penney, Joe, Eric Schmitt, Rukmini Callimachi, and Christoph Koettl. 2018. C.I.A. drone mission, curtailed by Obama, is expanded in Africa under Trump. *New York Times,* September 9. https://www.nytimes.com/2018/09/09/world/africa/cia-drones-africa-military.html.

Peretti, Jacques. 2017. *Done! The Secret Deals That Are Changing Our World.* London: Hodder and Stoughton.

Piper, Karen Lynnea. 2002. *Cartographic Fictions: Maps, Race, and Identity.* New Brunswick, NJ: Rutgers University Press.

Ploch, Lauren. 2011. Africa Command: U.S. strategic interests and the role of the U.S. military in Africa. Congressional Research Service, Report for Congress 7-5700, July. https://fas.org/sgp/crs/natsec/RL34003.pdf.

Politi, Daniel. 2017. An angry Trump reportedly said Haitian immigrants "all have AIDS," Nigerians live in "huts." *Slate,* December 23. https://slate.com/news-and-politics/2017/12/an-angry-trump-reportedly-said-haitian-immigrants-all-have-aids-nigerians-live-in-huts.html.

Powell, Stewart M. 2004. Swamp of terror in the Sahara. *Air Force Magazine,* November. www.airforcemag.com/MagazineArchive/Pages/2004/November%202004/1104sahara.aspx

Power, Matthew. 2013. Confessions of a drone warrior. *GQ Magazine*, October 22. www.gq.com/story/drone-uav-pilot-assassination

Pratt, Mary Louise. 1992. *Imperial Eyes: Travel Writing and Transculturation.* London: Routledge.

Price, David H. 2016. *Cold War Anthropology: The CIA, the Pentagon, and the Growth of Dual Use Anthropology.* Durham, NC: Duke University Press.

Price, Lloyd. 2017. Animals, governance and ecology: Managing the menace of venomous snakes in colonial India. *Cultural and Social History* 14 (2): 201–17.

Priest, Dana, and William M. Arkin. 2012. *Top Secret America: The Rise of the New American Security State.* New York: Back Bay Books.

Pugh, Jonathan, Clive Gabay, and Alison J. Williams. 2013. Beyond the securitisation of development: The limits of intervention, developmentisation of security and repositioning of purpose in the UK Coalition Government's policy agenda. *Geoforum* 44: 193–201.

Rabinow, Paul. 1977. *Reflections on Fieldwork in Morocco.* Berkeley: University of California Press.

Rainey, Sarah. 2014. Emotional resilience: It's the armour you need for modern life. *Daily Telegraph*, February 25. www.telegraph.co.uk/lifestyle/wellbeing/10660556/Emotional-resilience-its-the-armour-you-need-for-modern-life.html.

Rapaille, Clotaire. 2004. Interview with PBS *Frontline*, transcript posted November 9. https://www.pbs.org/wgbh/pages/frontline/shows/persuaders/interviews/rapaille.html.

Rasmussen, Sune Engel. 2016. Kabul's expat bubble used to be like Boogie Nights—now it's more like Panic Room. *Guardian*, July 18. www.theguardian.com/world/2016/jul/18/kabul-expat-bubble-boogie-nights-panic-room-afghanistan-war

———. 2017. Questions for US military after doubt cast on efficiency of Afghan bombing. *Guardian*, May 5. https://www.theguardian.com/world/2017/may/05/us-military-afghanistan-bomb-moab.

Reagan, Ronald. 1980. Election Eve address, "A vision for America." November 3. Available via the American Presidency Project: www.presidency.ucsb.edu/ws/?pid=85199.

———. 1987. National security strategy of the United States. Available via the National Security Strategy Archive: http://nssarchive.us/national-security-strategy-1987/.

Refsdal, Paul. 2011. Interview by VICE staff. VICE News, January 24. www.vice.com/read/paul-refsdal.

Refugees International. 2017. Hell on earth: Abuses against migrants and refugees trying to reach Europe from Libya. Field report, June.

Rippa, Alessandro. Forthcoming. Zomia 2.0: Branding remoteness and neoliberal connectivity in the Golden Triangle Special Economic Zone, Laos. Unpublished manuscript.

Rippa, Alessandro, and Martin Saxer. 2016. Mong La: Business as usual in the China-Myanmar borderlands. *Cross-Currents: East Asian History and Culture Review* 19: 240–52.

Risen, James, and Matthew Rosenberg. 2015. Blackwater's legacy goes beyond public view. *New York Times,* April 14. www.nytimes.com/2015/04/15/world/middleeast/blackwaters-legacy-goes-beyond-public-view.html.

Robben, Antonius C. G. M. 2010. *Iraq at a Distance: What Anthropologists can Teach Us about the War.* Philadelphia: University of Pennsylvania Press.

Roberts, Susan, Anna Secor, and Matthew Sparke. 2003. Neoliberal geopolitics. *Antipode* 35 (5): 886–97.

Roberts, T. W. 2015. The Trans-Saharan Railway and the politics of imperial expansion, 1890–1900. *Journal of Imperial and Commonwealth History* 43 (3): 438–62.

Robin, Corey. 2004a. *Fear: The History of a Political Idea.* Oxford: Oxford University Press.

———. 2004b. Liberalism at bay, conservatism at play: Fear in the contemporary imagination. *Social Research* 71 (4): 927–62.

Rodríguez, María. 2017. En la ciudad que nadie visita: Tombuctú, la Perla del Desierto, se derrumba sin turistas. *El Confidencial,* October 16. www.elconfidencial.com/mundo/2017-10-16/viaje-a-la-ciudad-prohibida-de-tombuctu-la-perla-del-sahara-se-derrumba-sin-turistas_1452210/

Rogers, Paul. 2013. Mali, and remote-control war. openDemocracy, February 28. www.opendemocracy.net/paul-rogers/mali-and-remote-control-war.

Rose, Nikolas S. 2007. *The Politics of Life Itself: Biomedicine, Power and Subjectivity in the Twenty-First Century.* Princeton, NJ: Princeton University Press.

Rosling, Hans. 2018. *Factfulness: Ten Reasons We're Wrong about the World—and Why Things Are Better Than You Think.* London: Sceptre.

Roston, Aram. 2009. How the US army protects its trucks—by paying the Taliban. *Guardian,* November 13. www.theguardian.com/world/2009/nov/13/us-trucks-security-taliban

Rutkowski, Krzysztof, et al. 2014. Global border and maritime security market assessment. Frost and Sullivan Report M965–16.

Safi, Michael. 2018a. Isis claims attack on Save the Children office in Afghanistan. *Guardian*, January 24. www.theguardian.com/world/2018/jan/24
/explosion-attack-save-the-children-office-jalalabad-afghanistan.

———. 2018b. Kabul hotel attack: Guests "sprayed with bullets as they ran."
Guardian, January 22. https://www.theguardian.com/world/2018/jan/21
/kabul-hotel-attack-guests-sprayed-bullets-terror-afghanistan.

Said, Edward W. 2003. *Orientalism*. London: Penguin.

Santana, Maria. 2014. Ebola fears spark backlash against Latino immigrants.
CNN, October 12. http://edition.cnn.com/2014/10/10/politics/ebola-fears-
spark-backlash-latinos/.

Sassen, Saskia. 1991. *The Global City: New York, London, Tokyo*. Princeton, NJ:
Princeton University Press.

———. 2014. *Expulsions: Brutality and Complexity in the Global Economy*.
Cambridge, MA: Belknap Press/Harvard University Press.

Savage, Charlie. 2011. Attack renews debate over congressional consent. *New
York Times*, March 22. www.nytimes.com/2011/03/22/world/africa/22powers
.html.

Savage, Rowan. 2007. Disease incarnate: Biopolitical discourse and genocidal
dehumanisation in the age of modernity. *Journal of Historical Sociology* 20
(3): 404–40.

Saxer, Martin. 2016. A spectacle of maps: Cartographic hopes and anxieties in
the Pamirs. *Cross-Currents: East Asian History and Culture Review* 21:
111–36.

Scahill, Jeremy. 2011. JSOC: The black ops force that took down bin Laden.
Nation, May 2. https://www.thenation.com/article/jsoc-black-ops-force-took-
down-bin-laden/.

———. 2014. *Dirty Wars: The World Is a Battlefield*. London: Serpent's Tail.

Scheele, Judith. 2012. *Smugglers and Saints of the Sahara: Regional Connectivity in the Twentieth Century*. Cambridge: Cambridge University Press.

Scherer, Steve. 2018. Nigerian migrants sue Italy for aiding Libyan coast
guard. Reuters, May 8. https://uk.reuters.com/article/uk-europe-migrants-
italy/nigerian-migrants-sue-italy-for-aiding-libyan-coast-guard-
idUKKBN1I93BK.

Schwartz, Tony. 2018. I wrote *The Art of the Deal* with Trump. He's still a scared
child. *Guardian*, January 18. www.theguardian.com/global/commentisfree
/2018/jan/18/fear-donald-trump-us-president-art-of-the-deal.

Scott, James C. 2010. *The Art of Not Being Governed: An Anarchist History of
Upland Southeast Asia*. New Haven, CT: Yale University Press.

Self, Will. 2013. *Psychogeography*. London: Bloomsbury.

Sendak, Maurice. 1963. *Where the Wild Things Are*. New York: Harper and Row.

Shapiro, Ian. 2005. *The Flight from Reality in the Human Sciences*. Princeton,
NJ: Princeton University Press.

Shariatmadari, David. 2015. Swarms, floods and marauders: The toxic metaphors of the migration debate. *Guardian,* August 10. www.theguardian.com/commentisfree/2015/aug/10/migration-debate-metaphors-swarms-floods-marauders-migrants.

Shaw, Ian G. R. 2010. Playing war. *Social and Cultural Geography* 11 (8): 789–803.

———. 2013. Predator Empire: The geopolitics of US drone warfare. *Geopolitics* 18 (3): 536–59.

Shaw, Martin. 2005. *The New Western Way of War: Risk-Transfer War and Its Crisis in Iraq.* Cambridge: Polity Press.

Sheckley, Robert. 1953. *Watchbird.* Published online by Project Gutenberg. www.gutenberg.org/ebooks/29579.

Shelton, Jim. 2013. Former army gen. Stanley McChrystal promotes holistic approach to war during Yale event. *New Haven Register,* March 5. www.nhregister.com/connecticut/article/Former-Army-Gen-Stanley-McChrystal-promotes-11412675.php.

Siebert, Horst. 2001. *Der Kobra-Effekt: Wie man Irrwege der Wirtschaftspolitik vermeidet.* Munich: Deutsche Verlags-Anstalt.

Sinclair, Harriet. 2017. Trump says he is scared of germs and needs to drink from a straw to avoid contamination. *Newsweek,* September 26. www.newsweek.com/trump-scared-germs-needs-drink-straw-avoid-contamination-671730.

Sloterdijk, Peter. 2009. *Terror from the Air.* Los Angeles: Semiotext(e).

Sluka, Jeffrey A. 1990. Participant-observation in violent social contexts: Managing danger in fieldwork. *Human Organization* 49 (2): 114–26.

Smirl, Lisa. 2015. *Spaces of Aid: How Cars, Compounds and Hotels Shape Humanitarianism.* London: Zed Books.

Soares, Benjamin F. 2012. On the recent mess in Mali. *Anthropology Today* 28 (5): 1–2.

Solomon, Hussein. 2013. Mali: West Africa's Afghanistan. *RUSI Journal* 158 (1): 12–19.

Sontag, Susan. 1991. *Illness as Metaphor and AIDS and Its Metaphors.* London: Penguin.

Soudan, François. 2017. Ibrahim Boubacar Keïta: "Le Mali est une digue. Si elle rompt, l'Europe sera submergée." *Jeune Afrique,* December 15. www.jeuneafrique.com/mag/498791/politique/ibrahim-boubacar-keita-le-mali-est-une-digue-si-elle-rompt-leurope-sera-submergee/.

START (National Consortium for the Study of Terrorism and Responses to Terrorism). 2016. Terrorism in Belgium and western Europe. Report, March. www.start.umd.edu/pubs/START_BelgiumTransportationCoordinatedAttacks_BackgroundReport_March2016.pdf.

Stewart, Rory. 2004. *The Places in Between.* New York: Harcourt.

———. 2012. Lessons from Afghanistan. *New York Review of Books,* August 16. Republished at www.rorystewart.co.uk/lessons-from-afghanistan/.

Stoddard, Abby, Adele Harmer, and Monica Czwarno. 2018. Aid worker security report: Figures at a glance. Humanitarian Outcomes Factsheet, August. https://aidworkersecurity.org/sites/default/files/AWSR%20Figures%202018.pdf.

Stone, Jon. 2018. EU plans to triple spending on border control in response to refugee crisis. *Independent,* June 13. www.independent.co.uk/news/world/europe/eu-border-control-spending-refugee-crisis-austria-coast-guard-mediterranean-a8397176.html.

Suskind, Ron. 2004. Faith, certainty and the presidency of George W. Bush. *New York Times,* October 17. www.nytimes.com/2004/10/17/magazine/faith-certainty-and-the-presidency-of-george-w-bush.html

Tardy, Thierry, and Marco Wyss. 2014. *Peacekeeping in Africa: The Evolving Security Architecture.* London: Routledge.

Tatham, Steve. 2015. Target audience analysis. *Three Swords Magazine* 28: 50–53.

Taussig, Michael. 1993. *Mimesis and Alterity: A Particular History of the Senses.* Abingdon: Routledge.

Ticktin, Miriam. 2011. *Casualties of Care: Immigration and the Politics of Humanitarianism in France.* Berkeley: University of California Press.

Torpey, John C. 2000. *The Invention of the Passport: Surveillance, Citizenship and the State.* Cambridge: Cambridge University Press.

Traoré, Aminata, and Boubacar Boris Diop. 2014. *La gloire des imposteurs: Lettres sur le Mali et L'Afrique.* Paris: Philippe Rey.

Trouillot, Michel-Rolph. 2003. *Global Transformations: Anthropology and the Modern World.* New York: Palgrave Macmillan.

Turner, Victor. 1974. Passages, margins, and poverty: Religious symbols of communitas. In *Dramas, Fields, and Metaphors: Symbolic Action in Human Society,* edited by Victor Turner, 231–71. Ithaca, NY: Cornell University Press.

Turse, Nick. 2015. Target Africa: The U.S. military's expanding footprint in East Africa and the Arabian Peninsula. *Intercept,* October 15. https://theintercept.com/drone-papers/target-africa/.

UK DfID (UK Department for International Development). 2005. Fighting poverty to build a safer world: A strategy for security and development. March. http://webarchive.nationalarchives.gov.uk/+/http:/www.dfid.gov.uk/pubs/files/securityforall.pdf.

UK FAC (Foreign Affairs Committee). 2014. The UK's response to extremism and instability in North and West Africa: Seventh report of session 2013–14. House of Commons. https://publications.parliament.uk/pa/cm201314/cmselect/cmfaff/86/86ii.pdf.

UN (United Nations). 2015. Report of the High-Level Independent Panel on Peace Operations. June. S/2015/446. www.un.org/en/ga/search/view_doc .asp?symbol=S/2015/446.

UNDP (United Nations Development Programme). 2017. Journey to Extremism in Africa: Drivers, Incentives and the Tipping Point for Recruitment. Report. New York: UNDP. https://journey-to-extremism.undp.org/content/downloads /UNDP-JourneyToExtremism-report-2017-english.pdf

UNEP (United Nations Environment Programme). 2011. Livelihood Security: Climate Change, Migration and Conflict in the Sahel. Geneva: UNEP. https://postconflict.unep.ch/publications/UNEP_Sahel_EN.pdf

UNHCR. 2016. UNHCR uses drones to help displaced populations in Africa. UNHCR News, November 21. www.unhcr.org/uk/news/latest/2016/11 /582dc6d24/unhcr-uses-drones-help-displaced-populations-africa.html.

UN Operations and Crisis Centre. 2018. UN peacekeeping: Fatalities by nation and mission. April 30. https://peacekeeping.un.org/sites/default/files /statsbynationalitymission_2_10.pdf.

UNSC (United Nations Security Council). 2015. Final report of the Panel of Experts established pursuant to resolution 1973 (2011). February.

USAID. 2012. 3D planning guide: Diplomacy, development, defense. Predecisional working draft, July 31. https://www.usaid.gov/sites/default/files /documents/1866/3D%20Planning%20Guide_Update_FINAL%20 %2831%20Jul%2012%29.pdf.

US DHS (US Department of Homeland Security). 2018. FY 2018 budget in brief. https://www.dhs.gov/sites/default/files/publications/DHS%20 FY18%20BIB%20Final.pdf.

US DoD (Department of Defense). 2015. Budget fiscal year (FY) 2016. Office of the Under Secretary of Defense (Comptroller), March. http://comptroller.defense. gov/Portals/45/Documents/defbudget/fy2016/FY2016_CTPF_J-Book.pdf.

Utas, Mats. 2013. The best recipe for protracted warfare in Mali is aerial bombing and rushed deployment of peacekeeping forces. Mats Utas blog, January 14. http://matsutas.wordpress.com/2013/01/14/the-best-recipe- for-protracted-warfare-in-mali-is-aerial-bombing-and-rushed-deployment- of-peacekeeping-forces/.

Vallet, Elizabeth, ed. 2014. Borders, Fences and Walls: State of Insecurity? Farnham: Ashgate.

Van der Lijn, Jaïr, and Jane Dundon. 2014. Peacekeepers at risk: The lethality of peace operations. SIPRI Policy Brief, February. www.sipri.org/publications /2014/sipri-fact-sheets/peacekeepers-risk-lethality-peace-operations.

Van Duzer, Chet. 2013. Hic sunt dracones: The geography and cartography of monsters. In The Ashgate Research Companion to Monsters and the Monstrous, edited by Asa Simon Mittman and Peter J. Dendle, 387–436. Farnham: Ashgate.

Van Duzer, Chet, and Ilya Dines. 2016. *Apocalyptic Cartography: Thematic Maps and the End of the World in a Fifteenth-Century Manuscript*. Leiden: Brill/Hes & De Graaf.

Van Gennep, Arnold. 1909. *Les rites de passage*. Paris: Picard.

Vann, Michael G. 2003. Of rats, rice, and race: The great Hanoi rat massacre, an episode in French colonial history. *French Colonial History* 4: 191–204.

Van Schendel, Willem. 2002. Geographies of knowing, geographies of ignorance: Jumping scale in Southeast Asia. *Environment and Planning D: Society and Space* 20: 647–68.

Vaughan-Williams, Nick. 2015. *Europe's Border Crisis: Biopolitical Security and Beyond*. Oxford: Oxford University Press.

Vazquez, Megan. 2018. Trump admits "there's no proof" of his "unknown Middle Easterners" caravan claim. CNN, October 23. https://edition.cnn.com/2018/10/23/politics/donald-trump-proof-unknown-middle-easterners-migrant-caravan/index.html

Vernon, James. 2014. *Distant Strangers: How Britain Became Modern*. Berkeley: University of California Press.

Virilio, Paul. 1986. *Speed and Politics: An Essay on Dromology*. New York: Columbia University Press.

———. 1989. *War and Cinema: The Logistics of Perception*. London: Verso.

———. 2008. *Bunker Archeology*. Princeton, NJ: Princeton Architectural Press.

Walters, William. 2011. Foucault and frontiers: Notes on the birth of the humanitarian border. In *Governmentality: Current Issues and Future Challenges*, edited by U. Bröckling, S. Krasmann, and T. Lemke, 138–164. New York: Routledge.

———. 2012. *Governmentality: Critical Encounters*. Abingdon: Routledge.

Wa Thiong'o, Ngũgĩ. 2016. *Se Afrika*. Stockholm: Volante.

Weigand, Florian, and Ruben Andersson. Forthcoming. Institutionalised intervention: The "bunker politics" of international aid in Afghanistan. Unpublished manuscript.

Weizman, Eyal. 2007. *Hollow Land: Israel's Architecture of Occupation*. London: Verso.

White, Andrew. 2017. DSEI 2017: T-REX makes an entrance into C-UAS. Shephard Media, September 13. https://www.shephardmedia.com/news/landwarfareintl/dsei-2017-t-rex-makes-entrance-c-uas/.

Whitehouse, Bruce. 2012. What went wrong in Mali? *London Review of Books* 34 (16): 17–18.

———. 2013. Understanding Mali's "Tuareg problem." *Bridges from Bamako* (blog), February 25. http://bridgesfrombamako.com/2013/02/25/understanding-malis-tuareg-problem/.

———. 2017. How did Mali get here? *Bridges from Bamako* (blog), May 23. https://bridgesfrombamako.com/2017/05/23/how-did-mali-get-here-part-5-institutional-explanations/.

Williams, Jill M. 2016. The safety/security nexus and the humanitarianisation of border enforcement. *Geographical Journal* 182 (1): 27–37.

Wintour, Patrick. 2017. Respect for human rights can prevent "vicious cycle" of terrorism, says UN chief. *Guardian*, November 16. www.theguardian.com /world/2017/nov/16/secretary-general-puts-countering-terrorism-at-heart- of-un-agenda.

———. 2018. EU rebuked for €36bn refugee pushback gambit. *Guardian*, June 20. https://www.theguardian.com/world/2018/jun/20/eu-increases-africa- spending-as-studies-criticise-anti-migration-efforts.

Wood, Dennis. 1992. How maps work. *Cartographica* 29 (3–4): 66–74.

Yew, Elizabeth. 1980. Medical inspection of immigrants at Ellis Island, 1891– 1924. *Bulletin of the New York Academy of Medicine* 56 (5): 488–510.

Zuboff, Shoshana. 2017. *The Age of Surveillance Capitalism: The Fight for a Human Future at the New Frontier of Power*. New York: PublicAffairs.

INDEX

Abu-Lughod, Lila, 259

The Accidental Guerrilla (Kilcullen), 197

Achin (Afghanistan), 227

Adams, John Quincy, 62

Addis Ababa (Ethiopia), 100, 106, 108, 110, 191; Kenyan embassy in, 108

Aden (Yemen), 99

Afghanistan: as ailing patient, 197, 200; Ashraf Ghani, 260, 273n; architecture of risk in, 211, 214–15, 217, 220, 225–26, 228, 231–32, 234, 236, 243–44; and bin Laden, 57–58; and British Empire, 239–40; at core of globalization, 118; deaths from terrorism in, 4; drones in, 57; European Union, 220; fear of, 3; ISAF, 271n; invasion of, 59; and journalists, 221–22, 225; and JSOC, 126; and "Kabubble," 212–14, 215–20; and McChrystal, 124, 194, 195–96, 201; military officers arriving from, 35; Navy "Seabees" in, 214 *fig;* NGOs in, 218–19; Obama and, 215; and Otherness, 234; private forces in, 193; psychogeography of, 227–28; and SCL Group, 130; security providers in, 214–15, 290n; and Trump, 64–65, 218, 227–28; uneven risks in, 36, 205–36; and US, 57–58, 197, 201, 207, 212, 214 *fig,* 220, 227–28; and Vietnam syndrome, 52; in "war on terror," 55, 59; weaponized mapping of, 64–65

Afghan National Police, 217

AFISMA, 29, 42

"AfPak" borderlands, 120, 280n

Africa: cartography of, 60–61; and "extraversion" in political life, 186; peacekeeping in, 25; and security, 268n; World Threat Map, 8m, 9m

Africa (Dowden), 100

African Development Bank, 178

"Africanization," 49, 89–90

"African solutions to African problems," 92, 109–10

African Union (AU): and AMISOM, 106, 108–112, 116, 266n; and jihadists, 100; and Libya, 162; peacekeepers from, 4–5; and "peace operations," 99; Peace Support Operations Division, 111

"Africa Rising," 178–79, 182

AFRICOM (US Africa Command), 88–92, 97–99, 102–3, 104, 105, 125; in Somalia, 90–91

Agadez (Niger), 80, 104

AIDS, 148, 195–96, 197, 271n, 288n

Air Force Magazine, 76